THE GLORY OF CHRIST IN THE OLD TESTAMENT
VOLUME 1 / **GENESIS TO ESTHER**

"As far as I am concerned this book has two very major strengths. First, it avoids getting bogged down in details, and therefore presents a very accessible summary of the main themes of each Old Testament book. Second, it is thoroughly Christ-centred, as all exposition of the Old Testament ought to be according to Christ himself."

JONATHAN BAYES (UK), professor, pastor, author

"What a welcome survey and overview of the Old Testament! Written to encourage reading of an often overlooked part of Scripture, it provides an orderly, systematic, clear view of each book, using tables, figures and maps to guide the reader. *The Glory of Christ in the Old Testament* should prove helpful to lay readers as well as to church leaders in their preparation for teaching and preaching. May it receive wide circulation around the world."

PAUL ENGLE (USA), professor, pastor, author

"Gareth Crossley's *The Glory of Christ in the Old Testament* is an insightful overview, with particular emphasis on how every book, and many specific elements in each book, point forward to Jesus Christ. Jesus is the fulfillment of every prophecy, every foreshadowing, every 'type,' every plan and intention of God to redeem a people unto himself."

PAUL HUDSON (Canada), professor, vice-president Canada, Carey International Pastoral Training

"This book is impressive in various ways, but I will simply point out the one thing I most appreciated: The readers can put this work to practical use in reading and studying the Old Testament and in proclaiming the glory of Christ by teaching and preaching from the Old Testament."

MIARA RABENJA (Madagascar), professor, pastor

"This work is marked by its clear presentation of the structure, content, and themes of the books of the Old Testament. It is also self-consciously Christ-centred, showing ways in which the Old Testament Scriptures point forward to Christ."

STEVEN D. WEST (Canada), professor, pastor, author

THE GLORY OF CHRIST IN THE OLD TESTAMENT

VOLUME 1 / **GENESIS TO ESTHER**

Gareth Crossley

GENERAL EDITOR: BOB PENHEAROW

CAREY
PRINTING PRESS

Published by
Carey International University of Theology Inc., The Villages, Florida, USA
www.careyuniversity.org

About us
Carey Printing Press is the publishing arm of Carey International University of Theology, an international Christian organization that provides theological training to spiritual leaders to shape the church and influence the nations.
General editor: Bob Penhearow

First published in 2002 as *The Old Testament Explained and Applied*.
This revised edition published in 2020 by Carey Printing Press.

© 2020 Gareth Crossley. All rights reserved. This Carey edition may not be reproduced, in whole or in part, without written permission from the publishers.

Cover and book design: Janice Van Eck

Unless otherwise indicated, all Scripture quotations are from the New King James Version® (NKJV). Copyright © 1982 by Thomas Nelson. Used by permission. All rights reserved.

The Glory of Christ in the Old Testament
Volume 1 / Genesis to Esther
Author: Gareth Crossley

ISBN **978-0-9876841-5-8** (paperback)
ISBN **978-0-9876841-6-5** (hardcover)

*Dedicated to the pastors and church leaders in
Belarus, Egypt, India, Indonesia, Kenya, Lebanon, Madagascar,
Romania, Sri Lanka, Sudan, The Philippines and the Far East
who warmly welcomed me and are faithfully serving
the Lord Jesus Christ*

Contents

Foreword	xi
List of maps, tables and figures	xiii
Introduction	1
The inspiration of Scripture	9
The central theme of Old Testament Scripture	23
Genesis	39
Exodus	69
Leviticus	97
Numbers	123
Deuteronomy	147
Joshua	171
Judges	197
Ruth	223
1 Samuel	243
2 Samuel	269
1 Kings	305
2 Kings	339
1 Chronicles	369
2 Chronicles	387
Ezra	411
Nehemiah	427
Esther	441
Select bibliography	459
Appendix: A study guide	465
Application index	513
General index	515

Foreword

The Glory of Christ in the Old Testament / Volume 1 is the first of a two-part survey of the Old Testament. This first volume focuses on the historical development of the Old Testament: Creation to Esther, while volume two, *The Glory of Christ in the Old Testament / Volume 2* focuses on Old Testament poetry and prophetic dynamics within the Old Testament: Job to Malachi.

I vividly recall the joy of meeting Dr. Crossley while in the UK a few years ago. On the train travelling back from Leeds to Paddington Station, London, I started to read Gareth's "Introduction." I had never come across a Bible survey book like this before. I clearly recall, that as the train pulled into Paddington Station, I bowed my head and was filled with worship and praise to my beautiful, glorious Saviour—and that was based on the introduction!

Gareth's skills in writing and research clearly demonstrate a man devoted to Scripture; one who not only loves the truth of the Word but seeks to live out the truth contained within the sacred Word. His pastoral heart, honed over many decades, comes to life as the reader is not only intellectually informed but heart-warmed by the wonderful truths contained within this book.

There are numerous Bible survey books on the market today, but the methodology Dr. Crossley employs in *The Glory of Christ in the Old Testament*, I believe, has exciting and valuable distinctives. Have you ever wondered about the chronology of the Bible, where each book fits in? Are you confused as to how each book is structured, the theological theme of each book? Do you know where and why the Old Testament is filled with Christology? Have you asked yourself after reading an Old Testament book: "So what?" I believe Dr. Crossley's book has the answers. In fact, each of the Old Testament books is viewed in a four-fold approach that makes this book exciting and rather unique.

First, like most Bible survey books, the historical data is presented in a clear, logical, sequential manner. Dates are clearly set forth, together with various charts. Second, Dr. Crossley draws out the primary theological themes within each Bible book and shows their significance for us today. Third, the Christology of each book is carefully and wonderfully developed. Here, the reader is confronted with the preincarnate Saviour marching through every sacred Old Testament chapter, guiding and directing the course of history in preparation for his ultimate incarnation. Finally, each of the Old Testament books has a practical and heart-searching pastoral application. The combination of all four dynamics makes this book alive, exciting and distinct.

This volume will enrich lives; it confronts the reader with the glory of Christ in the Old Testament, and it is suitable for both the young Christian and the seasoned pastor.

An Appendix by Rev. Paul Hudson is added for those who would like to use this book as the primary text to earn formal credits with Carey International University of Theology.

BOB PENHEAROW
General Editor
www.careyuniversity.org

List of maps, tables and figures

MAPS

Map 1. The journeys of Abraham	51
Map 2. Israel's journey from Egypt to Mount Sinai	79
Map 3. Israel's journey from Mount Sinai to the plains of Moab	131
Map 4. Conquest of the promised land	183
Map 5. Division of the promised land	185
Map 6. Israel's oppressors in the days of the Judges	209
Map 7. The extent of Solomon's kingdom	315
Map 8. The divided kingdoms of Israel and Judah	319
Map 9. International superpowers after the division of the united kingdom of Israel and Judah	321

TABLES

Table 1. The Hebrew Old Testament is divided into three major sections	8
Table 2. The English Old Testament is arranged under four headings	8
Table 3. The contrast between the earthly and heavenly priesthoods	114
Table 4. The feasts of the Israelites (Leviticus 23)	117
Table 5. Timeline of the completion of the tabernacle and its dismantling	127
Table 6. David's wives and sons	276
Table 7. David as a type of Christ	289
Table 8. David and Mephibosheth as a type of Christ and sinners	292
Table 9. Promises to Abraham and to David	295
Table 10. The source material for the author of Chronicles	373

FIGURES

Figure 1. Chronology of the Old Testament	36
Figure 2. The line of descent from Adam to Noah	47
Figure 3. The dimensions of Noah's ark	47
Figure 4. The line of descent from Shem to Abraham	49
Figure 5. Plan of the tabernacle to scale	83
Figure 6. The tabernacle in the wilderness	85
Figure 7. The elaborate and symbolic garments of the high priest	89
Figure 8. Military strategy in taking the city of Ai	181
Figure 9. Harmony of Samuel, Kings, Chronicles, Ezra and Nehemiah	248
Figure 10. Structure of worship in the temple	378
Figure 11. Judah and its prophets and kings: before, during and after the exile	416

Introduction

Many Christians find the reading of the Old Testament difficult. The self-discipline imposed by a commitment to read through the whole Bible in three years, or in some cases in twelve months, may indicate the reluctance with which some believers approach the Old Testament Scriptures. Like the man who continually beat his head against the wall because he felt so good when he stopped, the enforced reading of the Old Testament may produce only a similar benefit—the sense of achievement at completion.

There may be a number of reasons for reticence in turning to the Old Testament with enthusiasm. It may reside in the fact that the Old Testament is often read like irrelevant history. Does the average Christian see his or her own history in its pages? What are the possible applications for today of the particulars of the law in Deuteronomy, or the details of the sacrifices in Leviticus, or the histories of the kings or the philosophies of Ecclesiastes?

A second reason for reticence may be that so many of those who preach from the Old Testament seem to spiritualize every text and often betray more of a vivid imagination than clear principles of biblical interpretation. Lacking such imaginative skills, the average Christian avoids these thirty-nine books except for the occasional dip into well-worn passages in the Psalms, or Isaiah or a favourite story in Genesis.

A third explanation may be in the fact that few Christians see the thread or understand the flow of the Old Testament. They are not gripped by the unfolding historical drama, not thrilled by the evidences of the providence and purpose of God or enthralled by the developing picture of the promised Messiah, the Christ.

The major incentive for Christians to read and seek to understand the Old Testament is given by the Lord Jesus himself on many occasions. He points out that the prophecies of the Old Testament are essential to our understanding of his life and work and, most crucially, they authenticate the person of Christ. Jesus predicted that many would come claiming they are the Christ or prophets of God: "For false christs and false prophets will rise and show great signs and wonders to deceive" (Matthew 24:24).

For this reason, the Lord Jesus did not expect anyone to take his word alone that he is the promised Messiah. He based the recognition of his sonship on the fulfilment of the Old Testament Scriptures. In fact he said, "If I bear witness of Myself, My witness is not true" (John 5:31). Of course, this declaration has to be taken in context. Jesus is in effect saying, "If there is no other witness to who I am then there is no reason for anyone to believe me. Anyone could make such a claim." The Lord then follows his words by presenting other witnesses to his sonship: John the Baptist's testimony, the miracles he performed, the Scriptures he fulfilled and God the Father's witness (see John 5:31–47). Who told John the Baptist? Who worked the miracles through Jesus? Who gave the Scriptures? The answer in each case is God the Father and God the Holy Spirit (John 1:31–34; Acts 2:22; Hebrews 2:4; 2 Timothy 3:16; 2 Peter 1:21). Who else, but the heavenly Father and the Holy Spirit, could testify to the true Sonship of the Saviour?

John the Baptist is no longer with us. The miracles of Jesus are no longer performed before us. Yet we have abiding proof to authenticate the true Christ. The Scriptures of the Old Testament are the proof that Jesus of Nazareth is the Christ of God.

Furthermore, on the day of our Lord's resurrection from the dead, he made a notable appearance to two of his disciples on the road to Emmaus (Luke 24:13–27). These two address Jesus as if he were a stranger (v.16). They disclose their great sadness at recent events in Jerusalem. They tell of the visit of women to the tomb and their seeing a vision of angels who reported that Jesus was alive.

Jesus gently rebukes them, but not for their failure to believe the testimony of the women, nor their unwillingness to accept the word of the angels. He is critical because they have not believed the Old Testament Scriptures!

> "O foolish ones, and slow of heart to believe in all that the prophets have spoken! Ought not the Christ to have suffered these things and to enter into His glory?" And beginning at Moses and all the Prophets, He expounded to them in all the Scriptures the things concerning Himself (Luke 24:25–27).

Later that same day, the Lord appears to ten of the apostles in the upper room. Again, he challenges them regarding their lack of confidence in the Old Testament:

> "These are the words which I spoke to you while I was still with you, that all things must be fulfilled which were written in the Law of Moses and the Prophets and the Psalms concerning Me." And He opened their understanding, that they might comprehend the Scriptures (Luke 24:44–45).

The Old Testament Scriptures are the abiding proof that Jesus of Nazareth is the Christ, the Son of the living God. "The chief object of prophecy was to prepare the way for Christ, that, when He should come, He might be identified by a comparison of the prediction with its fulfilment."[1]

---

[1] Ernest W. Hengstenberg, *Christology of the Old Testament and a Commentary on the Messianic Predictions* (1847; Grand Rapids: Kregel, 1970), 10.

All may know the true identity of Jesus from the prophecies given by God spanning more than 4,000 years. Even in the beginning, when disaster fell and the first humans disobeyed the one simple commandment of God, a promise was given. Addressing the serpent, the Lord said,

> And I will put enmity
> Between you and the woman,
> And between your seed and her Seed;
> He shall bruise your head,
> And you shall bruise His heel (Genesis 3:15).

The Lord is addressing Satan who is using the serpent. In the great Revelation, the Evil One is described as "that serpent of old, called the Devil and Satan, who deceives the whole world" (Revelation 12:9; cf. 20:2).

Note the development of the text in Genesis 3:15: the Lord establishes enmity between Satan and the woman, followed by enmity between the seed of Satan and the seed of the woman. It goes on to refer to the seed of the woman as "he" or "it." Here it is made clear that one Person will struggle with another person. The one Seed of Eve will suffer but succeed! Satan will be destroyed!

Through 4,000 years of prophecies, promises and predictions, the living and true God revealed details about this one unique and glorious Seed of Eve. Gradually, the full picture emerges.

The family line of that special Seed of Eve (Genesis 3:15) is carefully mapped out. He will be of the Seed of Abraham (Genesis 26:4; cf. Galatians 3:16); of the Seed of Jacob (Genesis 28:14); of the Seed of David (2 Samuel 7:12). By the time of his appearance, the promised Seed of Eve would be revealed as no other than the Son of God. "But when the fullness of the time had come, God sent forth His Son, born of a woman" (Galatians 4:4)

Numerous details about this conquering Seed of Eve had been revealed before his eventual birth. Details of his tribe, his unique conception, his birthplace, his ministry, his miracles, his betrayal, his arrest, trial and sentence to death, his crucifixion, his grave, his resurrection and ascension, and details of his character, power and glory.

There are many threads of prophecy throughout the Old Testament. Here are some suggestions for your personal study:

1. Prophecy: The suffering successful Saviour
    a. The *message* of the Saviour's suffering
       and success Genesis 3:15
    b. The *manner* of the Saviour's suffering
       and success Psalm 22
    c. The *meaning* of the Saviour's suffering
       and success Isaiah 53
    d. The *moment* of the Saviour's suffering
       and success Daniel 9:24

2. Prophecy: The all-conquering King
    a. The Lion of Judah Genesis 49:10
    b. The Star of Jacob Numbers 24:17
    c. The Son of David 2 Samuel 7:12
    d. Birthplace, Bethlehem Micah 5:2
    e. The Son of God Psalm 45:6–7; cf. Hebrews 1:8–9

3. Prophecy: The great High Priest
    a. Abraham and Melchizedek Genesis 14:18–20
    b. Messiah and Melchizedek Psalm 110:4
    c. Jesus and Melchizedek Hebrews 7:1–9

4. Prophecy: The Spirit-filled Messiah
    a. The Rod of Jesse Isaiah 11:1–2
    b. The beloved Servant of God Isaiah 42:1–4
    c. John the Baptist's testimony Matthew 3:11–17
    d. The Lord's testimony Luke 4:18–19; cf. Isaiah 61:1–2
    e. The miracles of Jesus Matthew 11:4–5; cf. Isaiah 35:5–6

5. Prophecy: The spotless Lamb
    a. Abel and a lamb Genesis 4:3–7
    b. Abraham and a lamb Genesis 22:8
    c. Moses and a lamb Exodus 12:3
    d. Isaiah and a lamb Isaiah 53:7
    e. John the Baptist and the Lamb John 1:29, 36
    f. Peter and the Lamb 1 Peter 1:19
    g. New creation and the Lamb Revelation 5:6
    h. The church and the Lamb Revelation 19:6–9

The importance of the Old Testament for present-day Christians cannot be overstated. From the earliest days of the Christian era, these thirty-nine books have held a vital place. The new Christian converts on the Day of Pentecost, once baptized, committed themselves with great enthusiasm to the apostles' doctrine, fellowship with other believers, the breaking of bread and united prayer (Acts 2:42).

"The apostles' doctrine" was composed of a number of elements: the teaching they received directly from the Lord Jesus Christ, the things concerning the Lord which they had seen and heard for themselves and interpreting and applying the Old Testament Scriptures with specific reference to the Lord Jesus Christ. The apostles were at great pains, whether among unbelieving Jews or believing Christians, to relate everything that Jesus said and did to the thirty-nine books of the Old Testament (Acts 2:22–36; 4:9–12,24–28; 13:29–41). The Scriptures, as composed at that time, were the firm foundation for understanding and explaining the ministry, life, suffering, death, resurrection, ascension and glorification of the Lord Jesus Christ. This was the basis of the doctrine, or teaching, of the apostles.

From the beginning, the apostles' doctrine was a vital ingredient of Christian worship. There is abundant evidence throughout the book of Acts that this teaching played an important part in church life (e.g. Acts 2:42; 6:2,4). The Old Testament was to be read and carefully and faithfully explained to the church (1 Timothy 4:13; 2 Timothy 2:15).

Knowledge and understanding of the Scriptures was not, however, to be restricted to that which was gained through meetings for worship and teaching. The private study of God's Word was invaluable. How else could believers maintain a Berean mentality and investigate what the preacher said? (Acts 17:11). Without personal study of the Scriptures, believers would be vulnerable, all too easily "tossed to and fro and carried about with every wind of doctrine" (Ephesians 4:14).

Today, however, the central feature of apostolic doctrine, the relating of the person and work of the Lord Jesus Christ to the Old Testament Scriptures, seems largely to have been eliminated from preaching and teaching. With many distractions, the Bible has been sidelined and marginalized. In many quarters, enthusiasm for the New Testament is waning, and appreciation of the Old Testament is almost gone.

This book has a clear goal in mind—*to encourage the people of God in their private reading and study of the Old Testament Scriptures.*

The approach

This is an *overview* of the thirty-nine books of the Old Testament. It is not intended to be an *exhaustive* study. The objective for this book is to present a glimpse of the contents of each Old Testament book so that the overall plan and purpose of God might be clearly perceived.

The Old and New Testaments are treated as the inspired Word of God and therefore to be regarded as without error and without lack as originally given; therefore a chapter is included on the nature of inspiration. (It is usual in all definitions of inspiration to distinguish between the original Scriptures in Hebrew and Greek and any subsequent translations into Latin, English, etc. Translations are not believed to be inspired in the same sense as the original writings.)

Beneficial study of God's Word requires clear perspective—seeing each book in relation to its neighbours. See Tables 1 and 2.

The overall theme of God's revelation needs to be kept in mind. The controlling thought for the whole of the Old Testament is *preparation for the coming of the Messiah*, the Son of God. For those of a more academic bent, there is a chapter presenting the reasoned argument for this central theme. For others this chapter may be passed over without loss of benefit.

Throughout this overview, there are many biblical references cited. Consulting these references at the first reading will interrupt the flow and cause discontinuity of perspective. It will also take hours. Copious references are provided for the benefit of the preacher, the student or anyone unconvinced about any particular point being made.

Each chapter will follow an outline like this:

Introduction
Author
Historical setting
Outline
Christ and his church
Conclusion
Application and reflection

So as to ensure the historical integrity of each book, the Christological content and the present-day applications will be kept separate.

Table 1. The Hebrew Old Testament is divided into three major sections

Law	Prophets		Writings
(Torah)	*Former Prophets*	*Latter Prophets*	*(a) Poetical books*
Genesis	Joshua	Isaiah	Psalm
Exodus	Judges	Jeremiah	Proverbs
Leviticus	Samuel	Ezekiel	Job
Numbers	Kings	Hosea	
Deuteronomy		Joel	*(b) Five Rolls (Megilloth)*
			Song of Songs
		Amos	Ruth
		Obadiah	Lamentations
		Jonah	Ecclesiastes
		Micah	Esther
		Nahum	
		Habakkuk	
		Zephaniah	*(c) Historical books*
		Haggai	Daniel
		Zechariah	Ezra / Nehemiah
		Malachi	Chronicles

Table 2. The English Old Testament is arranged under four headings

Law	History	Poetry	Prophecy	
			Major	*Minor*
Genesis	Joshua	Job	Isaiah	Hosea
Exodus	Judges	Psalms	Jeremiah	Joel
Leviticus	Ruth	Proverbs	Lamentations	Amos
Numbers	1 Samuel	Ecclesiastes	Ezekiel	Obadiah
Deuteronomy	2 Samuel	Song of Solomon	Daniel	Jonah
	1 Kings			Micah
	2 Kings			Nahum
	1 Chronicles			Habakkuk
	2 Chronicles			Zephaniah
	Ezra			Haggai
	Nehemiah			Zechariah
	Esther			Malachi

The inspiration of Scripture

For twenty centuries, Christians recognized the vital importance of the Scriptures. Over recent years that conviction and confidence has been seriously eroded. The question might well be asked: "If the foundations are destroyed, what can the righteous do?" (Psalm 11:3). Take away the Scriptures as the authoritative and utterly reliable Word from God, and chaos will soon ensue. So many believers seem to be "tossed to and fro and carried about with every wind of doctrine" (Ephesians 4:14). In teaching and in practice—in the home, in the church and in society—human ideas and the counsel of the ungodly are prevalent (Colossians 2:8; Psalm 1:1). A return to confidence in the Scriptures as the Word of God is urgently needed.

Because of the confusion which is permeating the Christian church, it is important to crystallize the view of the Bible which is taken throughout this present book. Quoting 2 Timothy 3:16–17, which states, "All Scripture is given by inspiration of God, and is profitable for doctrine, for reproof, for correction, for instruction in righteousness, that the man of God may be complete, thoroughly equipped for every good work," seems insufficient for some of God's people today. It is necessary, therefore, to be more specific about the actual stance taken on Scripture throughout these pages.

The understanding of inspiration basic to this book is that the written Scriptures are the Word which God spoke and still speaks to his church. This is the final and sufficient source and authority for Christian faith and Christian living. Here in Scripture, the Lord has provided "all things that pertain to life and godliness" (2 Peter 1:3). To know God's Word is to know God's revealed will. And we can trust that Word. It is infallible (without error, entirely dependable) because an infallible God has spoken an infallible Word. He is sovereign Lord over all things. "Whatever the LORD pleases He does, in heaven and in earth" (Psalm 135:6). There is nothing incongruous, therefore, about God's producing a book which, while arising out of the experience of his children, is also, through his sovereign ordering, his precise Word to them.[1] If God is not sovereign in his revelation of himself to human beings, then he is not sovereign in anything.

It is nonsense to believe in an all-powerful God if he is incapable of communicating accurately and infallibly to his human creatures.

The relationship between the Word of God and the words of men in the writing of the Bible may be expressed like this:

> The Holy Spirit moved men to write. He allowed them to use their own style, culture, gifts and character, to use the results of their own study and research, to write of their own experiences and to express what was in their mind. At the same time, the Holy Spirit did not allow sin to influence their writings; he overruled in the expression of thought and in the choice of words. Thus they recorded accurately all that God wanted them to say and exactly how he wanted them to say it, in their own character, style and language.[2]

---

[1] Bruce Milne, *Know the Truth: A Handbook of Christian Belief* (Leicester: Inter-Varsity Press, 1982), 39.
[2] Brian H. Edwards, *Nothing but the Truth* (Welwyn: Evangelical Press, 1978), 38.

God inspired the Bible word for word (this is known as "verbal inspiration"). The Bible throughout exhibits a God who speaks. He uses words. He communicates predominantly, though not exclusively, through words. Throughout the Scriptures, there is clear evidence that these things were spoken by the Lord and were spoken in *words*. The living God spoke them.[3]

> What Scripture says, God says. The Bible is inspired in the sense of being word-for-word God-given…. The Bible, therefore, does not need to be supplemented and interpreted by tradition, or revised and corrected by reason. Instead, it demands to sit in judgement on the dictates of both; for the words of men must be tried by the Word of God.[4]

The men who recorded Scripture knew full well what they were doing. They were not in a trance. They were not "taken over" by a spirit personality. They were fully conscious, fully rational. They did not, however, always understand the *meaning* and *significance* of what they said or wrote. The prophets were "curious," in the best sense of that word, to comprehend God's purposes and timing, and went to considerable effort to discover answers (1 Peter 1:10–12).

God inspired the whole Bible, from Genesis to Revelation. All sixty-six books are infallible and inerrant. They are entirely without error as originally given. As Francis Schaeffer declares, "the Bible is without error not only when it speaks of values, the meaning system and religious things, but it is also without error when it speaks of history and the cosmos."[5]

One Author: many authors!

There are at least thirty different authors of the books of the Bible, the first writer living more than 1,500 years before the last. God used Amos the farm labourer as well as Ezekiel the priest. God used uneducated

---

[3] R.C.H. Lenski, *Commentary on Colossians, Thessalonians, Timothy, Titus and Philemon* (Minnesota: Augsburg, 1964), 845.

[4] J.I. Packer, *"Fundamentalism" and the Word of God: Some Evangelical Principles* (Leicester: Inter-Varsity Press, 1958), 47–48.

[5] Francis A. Schaeffer, *The Great Evangelical Disaster* (Westchester: Crossway, 1984), 57.

working-class men, like the apostles Peter and John (Acts 4:13), together with middle-class intellectuals like the apostle Paul (Acts 22:3; Galatians 1:14) and Dr. Luke, author of the third Gospel and the Acts of the Apostles. God used diverse men and welded their work together into one great and glorious composition—the Scriptures, the Word of God. These human agents appear to have been "of every kind of temperament, of every degree of endowment, of every time of life, of every grade of attainment, of every condition in the social scale."[6] The personality of each writer shines through the pages of his writings. The letters of Peter are distinct from those of John. The epistle of James contrasts with those of Paul.

God loves variety. This is obvious in *natural revelation*, in creation, where there is such an assortment of colours, sizes, shapes, sounds, textures, tastes and smells. It is also evident in *special revelation*, in the Scriptures, where God's "chosen vessels" are of such differing backgrounds, experiences and abilities. Not only are the human authors different, but the *kinds* of written composition are equally varied. There are historic records, biographies, extracts from civic documents, moral laws, civil and ceremonial rules and regulations, laws of hygiene, sermons, theological discourses, official decrees, personal letters, visions, dreams, poems and songs. The Bible is anything but monotonous and dull.

Authors of the biblical books retained their own temperaments, their unique experiences, their personal strengths and their personal weaknesses. Their biblical writings were infallible—the men themselves were not. In their personal lives, they were capable of making mistakes—sometimes serious mistakes, such as when Peter behaved inconsistently to New Covenant principles (Galatians 2:11–21). One author, David, was responsible for sins in relation to Bathsheba and Uriah when lust led to adultery and murder (2 Samuel 11). In spite of their sins and imperfections, God chose them and God used them. He made sure that what they recorded as Scripture was accurate. Firstly, the impulse to write was given from God. Secondly, their understanding was enlightened by the Holy Spirit so that their writings were

---

[6] Benjamin B. Warfield, *Revelation and Inspiration* in *The Works of Benjamin B. Warfield*, 10 vol. (1927; Grand Rapids: Baker Book House, 1981), 1:436.

preserved from all material error. Thirdly, they were divinely guided in the selection of their materials so that nothing was omitted or added against the will of God. And, fourthly, they received special divine help in order to complete their work accurately.[7]

One further point about the inspiration of Scripture needs to be made. As God used imperfect human instruments to communicate his Word, so he also chose to record the uninspired words of sinful men. While the words of sinful men found in Scripture were not inspired, the *record* of those words was inspired by God. An example of this distinction is seen in the book of Job. The Scriptures accurately record the words that Job's three friends used when they came to comfort him in his great distress. Many of those words are clearly contrary to some of the teaching of the Bible—they were not inspired words, but the record of them was inspired.[8] When the whole incident reached its climax, the Lord reprimanded Eliphaz: "My wrath is aroused against you and your two friends, for you have not spoken of Me what is right, as My servant Job has" (Job 42:7). This strikes a note of real caution in evaluating the arguments which form the bulk of the book of Job. The account is thoroughly inspired and consequently totally infallible—the arguments are neither. Assessment and analysis of the advice found there must be made by comparing it with other Scriptures where truth from God is clearly stated.

Without a clear grasp and a decided conviction concerning the nature of biblical inspiration, there can be no confident and beneficial study of its contents. "Grant [or accept] that the Bible is (in its original manuscripts) inerrant and infallible, and you reach the place where study of its contents is both practicable and profitable."[9]

The Old Testament Scriptures

"Your word is truth," says the Lord Jesus Christ in prayer to his heavenly Father (John 17:17). "What Christ has said concerning the authority of the Bible must itself always be regarded as having the utmost

---

[7] C. Sydney Carter, *The Reformers and Holy Scripture: A Historical Investigation* (London: Thynne and Jarvis, 1928), 17.
[8] G.J. Collier, "Notes on Inspiration," *Gospel Tidings*, Vol. 9, No. 5 (1984): 200.
[9] Arthur W. Pink, *The Divine Inspiration of the Bible* (Grand Rapids: Guardian Press, 1976), 5.

authority."¹⁰ The Lord Jesus clearly indicates that the Spirit of God was the author of the Old Testament Scriptures (e.g. Matthew 19:3–5; 22:41–44; cf. Psalm 110:1). He refers to twenty Old Testament characters. He quotes from nineteen different books. From *Genesis* he refers to the creation of man, the institution of marriage, the history of Noah, Abraham and Lot and to the overthrow of Sodom and Gomorrah; from *Exodus*, to the appearing of God to Moses in the bush, the manna, the Ten Commandments and the tribute money. He refers to the ceremonial law for the purification of lepers and the great moral law, "You shall love your neighbour as yourself," both contained in *Leviticus*, the bronze serpent and the law regarding vows in *Numbers*. At our Lord's temptation, we have three quotations from *Deuteronomy*. He refers to David's flight to Abiathar the priest at Nob, the glory of Solomon and the visit of the Queen of Sheba, Elijah's stay with the widow of Zarephath, the healing of Naaman and the killing of Zechariah—from various *historical books*. The ground of Christ's constant appeal is: "Have you not read?" or "It is written…." His constant assertion is: "The Scripture cannot be broken," "the Scriptures testify of me" and "the Scripture must be fulfilled."¹¹

The writers of the New Testament consistently shared this view of the Old Testament Scriptures. There is an undisputed acceptance of their full inspiration and absolute authority. It is not sufficient that the Lord should inspire the Scriptures; he must also lead the church to recognize those Scriptures. Accuracy in the formation of the canon, the finished collection of Scripture, is as vital as its original inspiration. Christians must be confident that what is placed in their hands is the full, unabridged and entire Word of God.

> It was not enough that God inspired the writing of each book of the Bible. He also gave to His people, in a collective sense, the spiritual perception to *recognize* in each of those books the genuine marks of divine inspiration and authority. With the Holy Spirit's guidance, they knew what spurious writings to

---

¹⁰ Edward J. Young, *Thy Word Is Truth* (Edinburgh: Banner of Truth Trust, 1963), 47.

¹¹ A.M. Hodgkin, *Christ in All the Scriptures* (London: Pickering and Inglis, 1907), 3.

reject, as well as what genuine writings to accept. Thus, over the centuries as the Old Testament books were being written, the Old Testament canon (list or group of inspired books) kept growing until it reached its completed form.[12]

Fifty-six times the New Testament writers refer to God as the author of the Old Testament. And even where the human writer is known, the divine authorship is often stated instead.[13] In Hebrews 1:5–13, for example, quotations are taken from 2 Samuel 7:14; Psalm 2:7; 104:4; 45:6–7; 102:25–27 and 110:1. The human writers are ignored and five times the apostle introduces a quotation with the phrase: "He [i.e. God] says…." The four Gospel historians refer to Old Testament writings and declare them to be words which were "spoken by the Lord through the prophet" (Matthew 1:22–23) or words of Scripture which must be fulfilled (John 19:24; cf. 19:36–37). The early church praised God for his prophetic words recorded in the book of Psalms (Acts 4:24–26; cf. Psalm 2:1–2). Then, some years later, the apostle Paul refers to God's Word in Psalm 2:7, Isaiah 55:3 and Psalm 16:10 (Acts 13:33–35).

The attitude of the Lord Jesus Christ to the Old Testament Scriptures and the attitude of the New Testament writers to the Old Testament Scriptures lead us to understand that everything from Genesis 1:1 through to Malachi 4:6 should be received, "not as the word of men, but as it is in truth, the word of God" (1 Thessalonians 2:13).

In spite of the multifarious human authors, there is only *one* divine author. The prophets of the Old Testament knew they were speaking under the influence of the living God (e.g. Isaiah 28:16; Jeremiah 7:20; Ezekiel 3:11; Amos 3:11). The consistent view of the New Testament writers is that God was speaking in and through those prophets. They were convinced that what was recorded in the Old Testament Scriptures was and is the actual Word of God (2 Timothy 3:16–17; Hebrews 1:1–2; 2 Peter 1:20–21).

---

[12] Irving L. Jensen, *Jensen's Survey of the Old Testament: Search and Discover* (Chicago: Moody, 1978), 21.
[13] Edwards, *Nothing but the Truth*, 50.

The New Testament Scriptures

In arguing for the inspiration of the *Old Testament* Scriptures, that they are God-breathed and hence without error, the authority of the Lord Jesus Christ, his apostles and the other writers of the New Testament has been presented as conclusive proof. This, however, begs the question of the inspiration and reliability of the *New Testament* Scriptures. What is the ground upon which Christians may place their entire confidence in the twenty-seven books and letters of the New Testament?

The New Testament has two overlapping and interwoven parts. The first is an infallible (error-free as originally given) record of the life, ministry, suffering, death and resurrection of the Lord Jesus Christ, the Son of God. The second is an infallible record of the teaching of God through the apostles of the Lord Jesus Christ.

Confidence that the New Testament provides an infallible record concerning the person and work of the Saviour and the teaching of God through the apostles is based upon a number of considerations.

The Spirit of truth

Before his departure back to the Father, the Lord Jesus Christ promised the assistance and supernatural help of the Holy Spirit:

> These things I have spoken to you while being present with you. But the Helper, the Holy Spirit, whom the Father will send in My name, He will teach you all things, and bring to your remembrance all things that I said to you (John 14:25–26).

The Lord did not need to choose special men with outstanding memories. Nor did the apostles need to worry about forgetting vital information entrusted to them by the Lord. The Son of God promised the Spirit of God, especially under his name as "the Spirit of truth."

The work of the Spirit of God was not, however, restricted to the ability to recall information already received. Jesus had not communicated everything during his earthly lifetime (John 16:12). The Holy Spirit would eventually supply additional information:

> However, when He, the Spirit of truth, has come, He will guide you into all truth; for He will not speak on His own authority, but

whatever He hears He will speak; and *He will tell you things to come.* He will glorify Me, for He will take of what is Mine and declare it to you (John 16:13–14, emphasis added).

The last book of the New Testament is one of many testimonies to this promise. In "the Revelation of Jesus Christ, which God gave Him to show His servants—things which must shortly take place" (Revelation 1:1), the Saviour communicates with the apostle John. Later we learn that the risen Christ used the services of the Holy Spirit as his agent. At the end of each of the letters to the seven churches in Asia Minor are the words: "He who has an ear, let him hear what the Spirit says to the churches" (Revelation 2:7,11,17,29; 3:6,13,22).

Three facts are implied by the Lord's promise of the Holy Spirit to assist the apostles:

1. That which depended upon their memory was kept free from error.
2. That which was recorded of their own observations was kept free from error.
3. God also gave them "truths imparted…directly by the Spirit of God, which they could never have arrived at by the unaided exercise of their own minds."[14]

The internal testimony

The Lord Jesus promised the Holy Spirit to his twelve apostles. Consequently the record of the life and teaching of the Lord Jesus Christ as found in Matthew and John (both apostles of Christ) is accepted as bearing the marks of that promise. But what about the writings of Luke and Mark? They were not apostles. There is no record to show that they were included in the promise concerning the Spirit.

It is evident that Luke was a respected member of the early Christian church. He accompanied the apostle Paul on many of his travels. Paul refers to Luke as "the beloved physician" present with him as he writes the letter to the Colossians (Colossians 4:14). Paul also mentions the presence of Luke when he writes his second letter to Timothy: "Only

---

[14] Albert Barnes, *Notes on the New Testament—Explanatory and Practical: Thessalonians, Timothy, Titus, and Philemon* (London: Blackie and Son, 1900), vol. 8, 241.

Luke is with me" (2 Timothy 4:11). A further reference is found in Paul's letter to his good friend Philemon. At the conclusion Paul writes, "Epaphras, my fellow prisoner in Christ Jesus, greets you, as do Mark, Aristarchus, Demas, Luke, my fellow labourers" (Philemon 23–24).

Luke accompanied Paul on his missionary journeys. He met other apostles and was ideally suited to draw together a mass of information and detail. As he states at the beginning of his record of the life and teaching of the Lord Jesus Christ,

> Inasmuch as many have taken in hand to set in order a narrative of those things which have been fulfilled among us, just as those who from the beginning were eyewitnesses and ministers of the word delivered them to us, it seemed good to me also, having had perfect [i.e. a complete or full] understanding of all things from the very first, to write to you an orderly account, most excellent Theophilus, that you may know the certainty of those things in which you were instructed (Luke 1:1–4).

Luke gathered together all the available information, both oral (by word of mouth) and written. He examined the material carefully and verified it with the eyewitnesses, apostles and disciples, and then set it down in a coherent fashion. Nevertheless, his claim alone does not demonstrate the confidence of the apostles in this record of the life and teaching of the Lord Jesus Christ. True, he was a respected member of the church, a gifted and able man. He had spent many hours, weeks, months, even years, with apostles of Christ. He had researched his subject carefully and painstakingly. But what did the apostles think of the finished result? The apostle Paul supplies an answer, almost inadvertently. He evidently accepted Luke's record as Scripture, as can be seen from his first letter to Timothy: "For the Scripture says, 'You shall not muzzle an ox while it treads out the grain,' and, 'The laborer is worthy of his wages'" (1 Timothy 5:18).

The first quotation is taken from Deuteronomy 25:4 and the second from Luke 10:7. There could be no clearer association of the writings of Luke and the Old Testament Scriptures. The Bible is bearing its own testimony to the writings of Luke. The Gospel according to Luke and the Acts of the Apostles are therefore authenticated as Scripture breathed out by God. The promise of the assistance of the Holy Spirit was not given to Luke. He did not bring teaching of Christ back to memory, nor did he experience revelations of things to come. He merely recorded accurately the remembrance and revelations of the apostles and eyewitnesses. He is an accurate historian authenticated by an apostle.

The apostles' scribes

The second New Testament historian who is not an apostle is Mark, the nephew of Barnabas, sometimes called John Mark (Acts 12:12,25; 15:37). While there is no internal verification of Mark's record as inspired Scripture, it has been generally agreed in the church through the ages that the apostle Peter provided the eyewitness material. The early church fathers Papias and Tertullian, both of whom lived in the middle of the second century A.D., claimed that Mark wrote his Gospel in partnership with the apostle Peter. Papias says, "Mark, having become Peter's interpreter, wrote accurately all that he remembered." Tertullian was even more clear in his statement: "That which Mark had published may be affirmed to be Peter's whose interpreter Mark was."[15] A careful study of the Gospel of Mark will substantially support this conclusion.

Both Peter and Paul used others, on occasions, to write their letters for them (1 Peter 5:12; Romans 16:22).

The apostles' authentication

It is important to see the unique position of these apostles. They were a personally chosen and a uniquely authenticated group of men (John 15:16). Speaking of our "great salvation," the writer to the Hebrews continues, "which at the first began to be spoken by the Lord, and was confirmed to us by those who heard Him, *God also bearing witness both with signs and wonders, with various miracles, and gifts of the Holy Spirit, according to His own will*" (Hebrews 2:3–4, emphasis added). Here it is clearly stated that God authenticated the Lord Jesus Christ and his apostles by the demonstration of supernatural miracles.

Peter spoke of this endorsement of Christ when he preached to a large Jewish congregation on the Day of Pentecost: "Men of Israel, hear

---

[15] Edwards, *Nothing but the Truth*, 112–113.

these words: Jesus of Nazareth, a Man attested by God to you by miracles, wonders, and signs which God did through Him in your midst, as you yourselves also know…" (Acts 2:22).

Paul speaks of the authorization of the apostles when he wrote to the Corinthian church: "Truly the signs of an apostle were accomplished among you with all perseverance, in signs and wonders and mighty deeds" (2 Corinthians 12:12).

The Lord Jesus is attested to be the Christ of God and the Son of God through the miraculous signs he performed (John 5:36; Matthew 11:3–5; John 3:2). Miraculous signs were also given to attest the twelve disciples and Paul as apostles of Christ and consequently they were authorized to act as the Saviour's unique representatives (Acts 5:12; Hebrews 2:3–4; 2 Corinthians 12:12).

The apostles' awareness

Together with this authentication from the Holy Spirit, the apostles had also a personal awareness, a personal consciousness of authority in the church of Christ:

> We are of God. He who knows God hears us; he who is not of God does not hear us. By this we know the spirit of truth and the spirit of error (1 John 4:6).

> These things we also speak, not in words which man's wisdom teaches but which the Holy Spirit teaches (1 Corinthians 2:13).

> For I received from the Lord that which I also delivered to you (1 Corinthians 11:23).

> If anyone thinks himself to be a prophet or spiritual, let him acknowledge that the things which I write to you are the commandments of the Lord (1 Corinthians 14:37).

> Therefore he who rejects this does not reject man, but God, who has also given us His Holy Spirit (1 Thessalonians 4:8).

Consequently it is a failure to understand and believe the Scriptures' own testimony that results in the suggestion, by some, that the teaching of Paul is not *as important* as the teaching of the Lord Jesus Christ. In reality, Paul often refers to Christ as the source of his teaching (1 Corinthians 11:23; 14:37). He is conscious of receiving authority from Christ to function as an apostle (Galatians 1:1; 1 Timothy 2:7). The apostles were the servants of Christ. They would not knowingly transmit incorrect information or communicate inaccurate commandments to the church. Paul says he and his colleagues should be considered "as servants of Christ and stewards of the mysteries of God." He then adds, "Moreover it is required in stewards that one be found faithful" (1 Corinthians 4:1–2). The teaching which is found in the New Testament Scriptures is *all* the teaching of the Lord Jesus Christ.

Along with this individual consciousness of authority, the apostles also possessed a sense of *collective authority*. This is a very important aspect of the New Testament. In spite of their great differences in personality, background and experiences, the apostles had a great respect for each other as apostles. Some twenty or thirty years after Pentecost, the apostle Peter places his words, along with those of the other apostles, on the same level with, and bearing the same authority as, the Scriptures of the Old Testament:

> Beloved, I now write to you this second epistle (in both of which I stir up your pure minds by way of reminder), that you may be mindful of the words which were spoken before by the holy prophets, and of the commandment of us, the apostles of the Lord and Savior (2 Peter 3:1–2).

The New Testament was already almost entirely formed during the lifetime of the apostles. They understood their writings to be on a par with Old Testament Scripture. Hence, Peter writes of the letters of Paul that there are "some things hard to understand, which untaught and unstable people twist to their own destruction, as they do also the rest of the Scriptures" (2 Peter 3:16). Considering the public rebuke which Peter received from Paul at Antioch (Galatians 2:11–14), the reference to Paul as "our beloved brother Paul" (2 Peter 3:15), and the acknowledgement of his writings as Scripture, is all the more powerful a testimony!

Conclusion

In this brief and broad sweep, the inspiration—and therefore the reliability—of the Scriptures of the Old and New Testaments has been examined. The living God has given the necessary confirmation that the writings of the prophets and the writings of the apostles are to be regarded as breathed out by God. Holy men of God not only spoke as they were moved by the Holy Spirit (2 Peter 1:20–21), they also wrote the Old Testament, and they wrote the New Testament, as moved by the same Spirit. Thus the solid "foundation of the apostles and prophets" is laid, "Jesus Christ Himself being the chief cornerstone" (Ephesians 2:20).

The Holy Spirit was the overseer who personally ensured that the thirty-nine books of the Old Testament are the truth which God wants to reveal to his church, and nothing but the truth. The Holy Spirit ensured that the Jewish nation first, and then the Christian church later, recognized these books which had been given by inspiration of God. The same Spirit of truth guarded the recording, the communication and the selection of the New Testament Scriptures.

But the work of the Holy Spirit in relation to the Scriptures is by no means over. As the Spirit of God alone inspired the Scriptures, safeguarded the transmission of the Scriptures and gave the perception to recognize those Scriptures, so he alone *interprets* the Scriptures. The reading of the Bible in and of itself does not bring illumination and understanding. In the days of the apostle Paul, there were Jews reading the Old Testament without understanding. They lacked enlightenment from the Spirit because they had not turned in faith to Christ (2 Corinthians 3:14–18). Even those who have turned to Christ need constantly to reiterate the prayer of the psalmist: "Open my eyes, that I may see wondrous things from Your law" (Psalm 119:18).

Here is the reliable Word from God which needs faithful translation from the original languages to communicate its truth; prayerful meditation to understand its truth; careful interpretation, comparing Scripture with Scripture, to apply its truth; and living devotion to obey its truth.

The central theme of Old Testament Scripture

The central theme of the Old Testament is Christ and his church. It is a great blessing to look back from a vantage point 2,400 to 6,000 years after the events—seeing so many of the fulfilments, the extent of which could not have been envisaged by the Old Testament authors. But lest it be thought that prophecy, types and revelations can be so easily coloured in a favourable light by a backward glance, the predictions concerning Christ and his church will be seen to have been in the heart of God from eternity:

> you were not redeemed with corruptible things…but with the precious blood of Christ, as of a lamb without blemish and without spot. *He indeed was foreordained before the foundation of the world,* but was manifest in these last times for you who through Him believe in God, who raised Him from the dead and gave Him

glory, so that your faith and hope are in God (1 Peter 1:18–21, emphasis added).

Blessed be the God and Father of our Lord Jesus Christ, who has blessed us with every spiritual blessing in the heavenly places in Christ, *just as He chose us in Him before the foundation of the world* (Ephesians 1:3–4, emphasis added).

In answering the question, "Where does the story of Jesus Christ begin?" we see that Matthew points to Abraham (Matthew 1:1–16), Luke to Adam (Luke 3:23–38) and John to eternity before time and creation (John 1:1–3). The Old Testament is shown to be the unfolding of a carefully prepared plan for the coming of his Son into the world which the Master Architect slowly and painstakingly reveals.

Jesus Christ the Son of God is the grand subject, the central theme, of the Old Testament. When the Lord Jesus is challenged about his claims to unique sonship, he presents as one of a number of proofs the content of Old Testament Scripture:

You search the Scriptures, for in them you think you have eternal life; and these are they which testify of Me. But you are not willing to come to Me that you may have life.... Do not think that I shall accuse you to the Father; there is one who accuses you—Moses, in whom you trust. For if you believed Moses, you would believe Me; for he wrote about Me (John 5:39–40,45–46).

Again and again, Jesus points his disciples to the Old Testament Scriptures and their fulfilment in him.

The apostle Paul also insists on the same solid Old Testament base for the death, burial and resurrection of Christ. Not only the events, but also the theological significance of those events is declared to be "according to the Scriptures" (1 Corinthians 15:3–4). Christ was seen by Paul in the Old Testament just as vividly as we can see him in the New Testament. Paul saw Christ in the first institution of marriage (Ephesians 5:31–32); the promise to Abraham's seed (Galatians 3:16); the rock in the wilderness journey (1 Corinthians 10:4); and the words of Moses in Deuteronomy 30:12–14 (Romans 10:6–8).

We see from the way that Paul argues before the Jews that Christ is the *subject* of the Old Testament. At Achaia, "he vigorously refuted the Jews publicly, showing from the Scriptures that Jesus is the Christ" (Acts 18:28). Before King Agrippa, Paul makes a bold claim:

> Therefore, having obtained help from God, to this day I stand, witnessing both to small and great, *saying no other things than those which the prophets and Moses said would come*— that the Christ would suffer, that He would be the first to rise from the dead, and would proclaim light to the Jewish people and to the Gentiles (Acts 26:22–23, emphasis added).

The secret of the Messiah is out. That mystery is revealed which was "kept secret since the world began but now made manifest, and by the prophetic Scriptures made known to all nations, according to the commandment of the everlasting God" (Romans 16:25–26). This "mystery, which from the beginning of the ages has been hidden in God who created all things through Jesus Christ" (Ephesians 3:9). The living God has had an "eternal purpose which He accomplished in Christ Jesus our Lord" (Ephesians 3:11).

It is not that the Old Testament has a great theme to which are added occasional prophecies and predictions about the coming of the Messiah. Nor is it a random history with the occasional spiritual gem hidden here or there. Everything found in the Old Testament has relevance at some point to the incarnation, humiliation, death, resurrection, ascension, glorification, triumphant return or future kingdom of the Lord Jesus Christ, Son of the living God (cf. Luke 24:27). Without undermining the literal and historical sense of Old Testament Scripture, this principle will be applied throughout this entire book. Andrew Bonar took the same approach to the Psalms when he said:

> our principle is, that having once found the literal sense, the exact meaning of the terms, and the primary application…we are then to ask what the Holy Spirit intended to teach in all ages by this formula.[1]

---

[1] Andrew A. Bonar, *Christ and His Church in the Book of Psalms* (1861; Grand Rapids: Kregel, 1978), viii.

Bonar made no apology in seeing Christ and his church throughout the Psalms. This principle of looking for Christ will be basic to this overview of the thirty-nine books of the Old Testament.

Revelation concerning Christ occurs in three major forms in the Old Testament: theophanies, types and prophecies. The Son of God appears in a theophany after the fall of Adam and Eve. He speaks of the woman's seed, and he predicts a violent contest with a victorious outcome (Genesis 3:15).[2] Revelation by theophany, type and prophecy has begun. Frequent new revelations will keep the expectation of the people alive, and make it continually more and more definite. Consequently, the doctrine of a coming Redeemer, even when partially misunderstood by the people at the time, becomes "the soul and centre of all theocratic expectations."[3] Each subsequent revelation in history contributes to the development, progress and enlargement of the grand and glorious purpose of God in Christ.

THEOPHANIES

Theophanies are temporary appearances of God in human form. "Christ-ophanies" might be a more accurate term for them, as any manifestation of God in human form is an appearance of the second person of the Godhead, for "No one has seen God at any time. The only begotten Son, who is in the bosom of the Father, He has declared Him" (John 1:18).

Christophanies are

> those unsought, intermittent and temporary, visible and audible manifestations of God the Son in human form, by which God communicated something to certain conscious human beings on earth prior to the birth of Jesus Christ.[4]

---

[2] Franz Delitzsch, *Messianic Prophecies* (Edinburgh: T&T Clark, 1880), 27.
[3] Ernest W. Hengstenberg, *Christology of the Old Testament and a Commentary on the Messianic Predictions* (1847; Grand Rapids: Kregel, 1970), 8.
[4] James A. Borland, *Christ in the Old Testament: A Comprehensive Study of Old Testament Appearances of Christ in Human Form* (Chicago: Moody, 1978), 10.

Distinguishing Christophanies from dreams, visions, the pillar of cloud, the Shekinah glory and the incarnation of Christ, James Borland contends that the purpose of Christophanies "was not only to provide immediate revelation but also to prepare…for the incarnation of Christ."[5]

Each appearance of the Son of God in human form reveals something about the Godhead, or something about God's will. There is an implied reference to regular appearances, or Christophanies, for fellowship with Adam and Eve before the Fall (Genesis 3:8), but after the Fall, with the exception of fellowship with Enoch (Genesis 5:22,24), the appearances have specific functions, such as the giving of a warning, a promise, an instruction or a blessing. By this means, God gave warnings of judgement to the serpent and to Adam and Eve (Genesis 3:14–19), to Cain (Genesis 4:9–12), to Noah (Genesis 6:9,13–14) and in response to the sin of Sodom and Gomorrah (Genesis 18:20–21). He made promises to Hagar (Genesis 16:7–13), to Abraham (Genesis 17:1–22), to both Abraham and Sarah (Genesis 18) and to Isaac (Genesis 26:2,24). He blessed Jacob at Peniel (Genesis 32:24–30; cf. 35:1,9–13). He gave instructions to Joshua outside Jericho (Joshua 5:13–15), to Gideon in Ophrah (Judges 6:11–23) and to Manoah and his wife about their as yet unborn son Samson (Judges 13:3–6,8–23).

Borland suggests the following purposes behind the theophanies:

- God the Son anticipated his future incarnation, intimated its possibility, prefigured its human form and even prophesied its coming reality.
- God was using a form of revelation suited to his purposes in the early history of his redemptive plan.
- God connected his work in the Old and New Testaments by appearing in human form in both.
- God was able to reveal aspects of his person in this way that no other form of revelation allowed.
- God may have sought to intimate Christ's deity and the Godhead.[6]

---

[5] Borland, *Christ in the Old Testament*, 4.
[6] Borland, *Christ in the Old Testament*, 21.

TYPES

A more difficult area of revelation is that of *types*. The Old Testament gives us types that foreshadow the New Testament fulfilment. A type is a form of analogy that is distinctive to the Bible. Like all analogies, a type combines identity and difference. David is a type of Christ; David and Christ were both given kingly power and rule. "In spite of the vast differences between David's royalty and Christ's, there are points of formal identity that make the comparison meaningful."[7]

This is the area of Christology (the study of Christ) which is most susceptible to a vivid imagination rather than the application of carefully determined principles of interpretation. We must not make an Old Testament passage mean what we would like it to mean. We must not impose our ideas upon the text. But how to safeguard against such abuse is not easy to define. The typology of Scripture does not depend upon the usage or meaning of the word *type* in the Scriptures. It is grounded upon a whole series of references where an object, person or event in the Old Testament is seen to reflect in the natural realm a truth or feature in the New Testament in the spiritual realm.

A *type* may be defined as *a figure, episode, or symbolic factor resembling some future reality in such a way as to foreshadow or prefigure it*. An *antitype* is *the future reality of the symbol*. Just as little children are taught with the help of pictures and models, so the Lord graciously teaches his people with the assistance of visual aids. But these pictures and emblems are not restricted to those young in the faith. Their significance may be best discovered by those who have a thorough acquaintance with the Scriptures.

Andrew Jukes suggests that the neglect of the study of the types in Scripture may be explained in part in

> that they require more spiritual intelligence than many Christians can bring to them. To apprehend them requires a certain measure of spiritual capacity and habitual exercise in the things of God, which all do not possess, for want of abiding fellowship with Jesus.... The types are, indeed, pictures, but to understand the

---

[7] Edmund P. Clowney, *The Unfolding Mystery: Discovering Christ in the Old Testament* (Leicester: Inter-Varsity Press, 1988), 14.

picture it is necessary we should know something of the reality. ...The real secret of our difficulty is that we know so little, and, what is worse, we do not know our ignorance.[8]

As it is "by reason of use" that mature Christians "have their senses exercised to discern both good and evil" (Hebrews 5:14), so it is by that same using of truth already possessed that spiritual advancement is made and spiritual growth takes place.

By the use of types, the Lord gives detailed insight into the person and work of his Son that no mere words could ever convey:

> Though sacrifices and ceremonies can be no ground or foundation to build up—that is, though we can prove nought with them —yet, when we have once found out Christ and His mysteries, then we may borrow figures, that is to say, allegories, similitudes, and examples, to open Christ, and the secrets of God hid in Christ ...and can declare them more lively and sensibly with them than with all the words of the world. For similitudes have more virtue and power with them than bare words, and lead a man's understanding further into the pith and marrow and spiritual understanding of the thing, than all the words that can be imagined.[9]

The institution of *marriage* is shown to be a type of Christ and his church (Genesis 2:24; Ephesians 5:31–32). The *flood* is seen as the type of Christian baptism (Genesis 7:1,4,10; 1 Peter 3:21). *Melchizedek* is a type of Christ in his priesthood (Genesis 14:18–20; Psalm 110:4; Hebrews 6:20–7:28). The whole structure of the *tabernacle*, with its ministry and services, is designated "a copy and shadow of...heavenly things" (Hebrews 8:5; cf. Exodus 25:1–28:43; Leviticus 23:3–43). It gives symbolic expression to the great truths and principles of the spiritual life: truths respecting sin and salvation, the purification of the heart and the dedication of the person and the life to God; truths and principles common to both Old and New Testament times but

---

[8] Andrew Jukes, *The Law of the Offerings* (1854; Grand Rapids: Kregel, 1976), 14–15.
[9] William Tyndale cited by Andrew A. Bonar, *A Commentary on Leviticus* (1846; Edinburgh: Banner of Truth Trust, 1966), 4.

which could only find their proper development and full realization in the New Testament revelation of Christ and his church.

As well as the clear identifications of types of Christ in the New Testament, such as the *Passover* (1 Corinthians 5:7), the *water-giving rock* (1 Corinthians 10:4) and the whole *sacrificial system* (Hebrews 10:1–10), there are others by implication, such as the *manna* in the wilderness (John 6:31–33), the *ladder* in Jacob's dream (John 1:51) and the *temple* (John 2:19). These are not the results of coincidence. They are the outworking of a brilliantly conceived and carefully executed divine plan, for resemblance or coincidence alone is not sufficient:

> to constitute one thing the type of another, something more is wanted than mere resemblance. The former must not only resemble the latter, but must have been designed to resemble the latter. The type as well as the antitype must have been preordained; and they must have been preordained as constituent parts of the same general scheme of Divine Providence.[10]

Old Testament religious buildings, ceremonies and priesthood, chosen articles and objects—whether actual, or seen in dreams or visions—are types of Christ and his unique work of salvation. But are only Old Testament symbols to be seen as types of Christ? Could it not be that historic events recorded in the Old Testament are also designed and overruled to provide glorious types of Christ and his unique saving work? Is not this the principle by which the Lord Jesus points to the serpent raised up in the wilderness? (John 3:14–15). It is not simply in the coincidence of elevation into the vertical position that the connection is made.

There are features about that period in Israel's history which shed a profound light upon the crucified One: the people had sinned (Numbers 21:5,7); the Lord sent punishment (Numbers 21:6); the people repented and sought forgiveness (Numbers 21:7); and the Lord provided the means of healing which required faith and obedience (Numbers 21:8).

---

[10] Bishop Marsh cited by Patrick Fairbairn, *The Typology of Scripture: Viewed in Connection with the Whole Series of the Divine Dispensations* (1900; Grand Rapids: Baker, 1975), 46.

Now it is to be noted that the means which the Lord adopted was horrific. The serpent is the symbol of everything that is evil, from the first book of the Bible even to the last. It was the serpent in the Garden of Eden that Satan used as his agent in tempting Adam and Eve to sin. In the book of Revelation, the devil is referred to as "that serpent of old" (Revelation 12:9). The associations could not be more unpalatable. Nevertheless, the Lord's self-identification with the serpent in the wilderness cannot be passed over lightly. He identified himself with the solution to the problem of sin. That solution was itself related to the curse of God (the poisonous serpents). Christ is seen therefore as identified, at great personal cost, with the sin (2 Corinthians 5:21), with the curse (Galatians 3:13) and with the cure (John 3:14–16; cf. Numbers 21:9). "There is life for a look at the crucified One!"[11]

Christians may derive great benefit from these divinely inspired Scriptures of the Old Testament: "For whatever things were written before were written for our learning, that we through the patience and comfort of the Scriptures might have hope" (Romans 15:4). Speaking of God's dealings with the Israelites during the wilderness journey, Paul affirms: "Now all these things happened to them *as examples*, and they were written for our admonition, upon whom the ends of the ages have come" (1 Corinthians 10:11, emphasis added).

In Israel's history we can trace the providential workings of God. We can follow also a pattern, or type of things spiritual, concerning Christ and his church—things to come. Who can read the history of Joseph without reflecting upon the circumstances surrounding the life, suffering, death and resurrection of the Lord Jesus Christ? Born among brethren and persecuted in infancy, he finds sanctuary in Egypt, is sold by someone close to him, falsely accused, treated as an outcast, envied and persecuted, yet remains upright and blameless through trials and imprisonment; he is raised up to the right hand of power and glory and given a wife; the hostility of his fellow Israelites leads to blessing for the Gentiles; we see him distributing life-giving resources, receiving his brethren again through repentance and providing a home of plenty, safety and peace for all persons under his charge.

Joseph displays a deep spiritual discernment regarding the providence of God. Speaking to his brothers he says, "You meant evil against

---

[11] Line from a hymn of that name by Amelia M. Hull (c. 1832).

me; but God meant it for good, in order to bring it about as it is this day, to save many people alive" (Genesis 50:20). Joseph skilfully distinguishes between the wicked purposes in the minds of his brothers and the gracious purpose in the mind of God. The seriousness and evil of their deeds is not reduced in the slightest degree. The selling of Joseph was a despicable crime. Yet, at one and the same time, he was sold by the will of God. The Lord did not permit Joseph's death; the Lord did permit Joseph's enslavement. The Lord "used" the expression of human hostility for his own greater purposes: "Joseph was sold by the wicked consent of his brethren, and by the secret providence of God."[12]

Years later, a similar crime would be perpetrated, but this time upon the only begotten Son of God. He was betrayed by his "brethren" and sold, not to slavery, but to death. Following Christ's resurrection and the outpouring of the Holy Spirit at Pentecost, the apostle Peter views the Saviour's death from two vastly different perspectives: "Jesus of Nazareth…being delivered by the determined purpose and foreknowledge of God, you have taken by lawless hands, have crucified, and put to death" (Acts 2:22–23).

As with Joseph's words, so with the apostle Peter's: no lessening of guilt is permitted. The Lord of glory was falsely accused, disgracefully tried, unlawfully sentenced and viciously executed by corrupt men.

Having traced the central theme of the Old Testament revelation of Christ by means of Christophanies and types, we still need to explore one further area, that of *prophecies*. In the numerous Messianic predictions of the Old Testament we find the clearest, most detailed anticipation of Christ and his church.

PROPHECIES

"The chief object of prophecy," declares Ernest Hengstenberg, "was to prepare the way for Christ, that, when He should come, He might be identified by a comparison of the prediction with its fulfilment."[13] "For the testimony of Jesus is the spirit of prophecy" (Revelation 19:10). Like a skilful artist, God begins with light sketches which to the

---

[12] John Calvin, *A Commentary on Genesis* (1554; Edinburgh: Banner of Truth Trust, 1965), 487.

[13] Hengstenberg, *Christology of the Old Testament*, 10.

onlooker may appear quite indistinct and unrecognizable. Little by little, colour and detail are added—nothing is rushed—until it is quite obvious what the finished product will be like. The lack of clarity and the shortage of specific detail must not be misconstrued as marks of error. Nothing is calculated to mislead. The great Artist has the finished picture in his mind's eye.

As Patrick Fairbairn, Geerhardas Vos and others have shown, there is a fundamental connection throughout. Fairbairn speaks of "the inter-connected and progressive character of prophecy" and uses the analogy of an acorn and an oak tree:

> At first, the word of God is as a seed, it may be of the oak, or of any other plant, in which the whole majestic form and various parts of the future lie undisclosed, ready to reveal themselves when the times and the seasons, and other conditions which God has appointed to determine its being, shall have taken their course. And there is no break, nor leap, nor start in its course, which proceeds by a slow, and sweet, and beautiful progression, to perfect that purpose or word of God, which said at the beginning, "Let the earth bring forth grass, the herb that yields seed, and the fruit tree that yields fruit according to its kind, whose seed is in itself."[14]

Vos insists that "in the seed-form the minimum of indispensable knowledge was already present."[15] From the first moment of creation, God has one overriding thought in his mind—his Son and his people. Even as God creates Eve from the side of Adam and presents her back to him, so we glimpse the creation of a people through the Son to be returned to him, bound to him by love in the closest of ties, for all eternity. The centre and soul of the Old Testament is the same as that of the New Testament. It is Christ and his church.

In the Old Testament, it is evident that a divinely determined principle of selectivity is in operation. In the formula, "Thus says the

---

[14] Patrick Fairbairn, *Prophecy: Viewed in Respect to Its Distinctive Nature, Its Special Function, and Proper Interpretation* (1865; Grand Rapids: Baker, 1976), 178.

[15] Geerhardas Vos, *Biblical Theology: Old and New Testaments* (1948; Edinburgh: Banner of Truth Trust, 1975), 7.

Lord," there is a single principle, a single understanding of all prophetic revelation which left the prophets and the people in no doubt concerning the divine disclosure: "no prophecy of Scripture is of any private interpretation, for prophecy never came by the will of man, but holy men of God spoke as they were moved by the Holy Spirit" (2 Peter 1:20–21).

If the *key*, then, for an orderly and progressive arrangement of the subjects, themes and teachings of the Old Testament *is Christ and his church*, then a related question arises: Were the Old Testament authors consciously aware of this theme? Did the prophets understand what they uttered? The apostle Peter provides the answer. Writing to new covenant believers in the dispersion he says,

> Of this salvation the prophets have inquired and searched carefully, who prophesied of the grace that would come to you, searching what, or what manner of time, the Spirit of Christ who was in them was indicating when He testified beforehand the sufferings of Christ and the glories that would follow. To them it was revealed that, not to themselves, but to us they were ministering the things which now have been reported to you through those who have preached the gospel to you by the Holy Spirit sent from heaven—things which angels desire to look into (1 Peter 1:10–12).

It would seem that not only the *prophets* wanted to understand God's purposes in Christ—the *angels* in heaven were also intrigued by what God was doing and revealing to the Old Testament church (Romans 16:25–26; Ephesians 3:9). Yet while the prophets studied the revelation at the time to understand its meaning and its application, they were not ignorant of the general drift or scheme which united their words with the past and pointed on toward the future.

By theophany, type and prophecy the way is prepared for the coming of the Son of God to earth. Israel's history is itself part of the prophetic preparation. With Patrick Fairbairn we affirm: "Christ...is the end of the *history* as well as of the *law* of the Old Testament" (emphasis added).[16]

---

[16] Fairbairn, *The Typology of Scripture*, 72.

The author of Hebrews welds together the revelation of God in the Old Testament and the revelation of God in Christ when he says, "God, who at various times and in various ways spoke in time past to the fathers by the prophets, has in these last days spoken to us by His Son" (Hebrews 1:1–2).

The history of Israel is the history of the Old Testament church preparing for the coming of the Redeemer. It also provides analogies and insights into the New Testament church in its conflicts and ultimate victory in Christ. Since the days of Eve, the church (i.e. the Old Testament church) has been "with child"—crying "out in labour and in pain to give birth" (Revelation 12:2). Satan has been constantly active seeking to destroy "her child [i.e. Christ] as soon as it was born" (Revelation 12:4). Once the child-king is born, he is "caught up to God and to His throne" (Revelation 12:5). Unable to molest the child further, Satan turns his attention back to the woman (now the New Testament church) who "fled into the wilderness, where she has a place prepared by God, that they should feed her there" (Revelation 12:6).

There is a living *union* between the Old Testament church and the New Testament church. The unity of the people of God in all ages is not simply the participation in a common salvation. It is an integral unity which means that the blessings of the inheritance promised to the remnant in the Old Testament are blessings shared by the church in the New. We share the same faith, the same hope, as the believing Jews of the Old Testament. United under our common Head, we will *together* inherit the promised blessings: "And all these, having obtained a good testimony through faith, did not receive the promise, God having provided something better for us, that they should not be made perfect apart from us" (Hebrews 11:39–40).

It is not only our Lord and Saviour who has this solid bond with the past, and especially with the history recorded in the books of the Old Testament (see Figure 1); we too have an unbroken (and unbreakable) link with Old Testament history. It is not only Christ who is to be seen there, it is his church also. Christians have an inseparable bond with the history of the Old Testament: "Israel's theology—and ours—is rooted in history."[17] Furthermore, the history of Israel is *our* history:

---

[17] Walter C. Kaiser Jr., *Toward an Old Testament Theology* (Grand Rapids: Zondervan, 1978), 41.

Figure 1. Chronology of the Old Testament

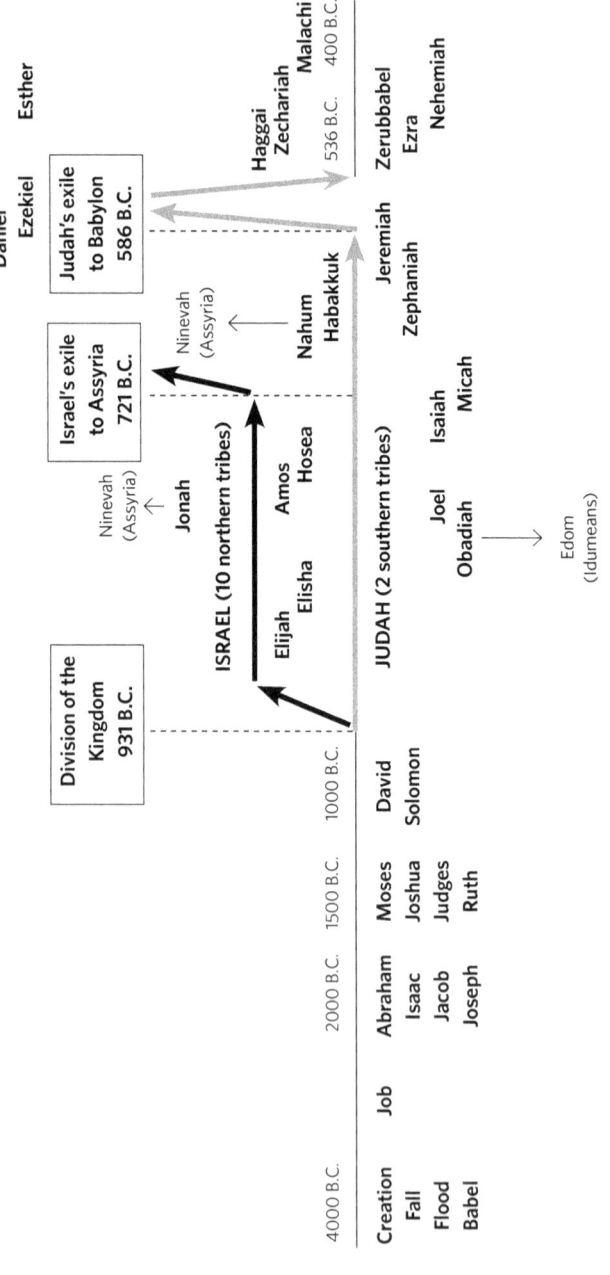

For you are all sons of God through faith in Christ Jesus. For as many of you as were baptized into Christ have put on Christ. There is neither Jew nor Greek, there is neither slave nor free, there is neither male nor female; for you are all one in Christ Jesus. And if you are Christ's, then you are Abraham's seed, and heirs according to the promise (Galatians 3:26–29).

Conclusion

The Bible's story is about Christ. History is *his story*. The Old Testament Scriptures outline the remarkable steps which the Father took to prepare for the coming of his Son. Those who believe the Old Testament Scriptures receive Jesus Christ as that long-awaited Son and deliverer (John 5:39–40,45–47). These sacred writings "are able to make you wise for salvation through faith which is in Christ Jesus" (2 Timothy 3:15). They act as "our tutor to bring us to Christ, that we might be justified by faith" (Galatians 3:24).

The Old Testament is the logical introduction, the firm foundation and the ultimate authority for the life of Christ recorded in the New Testament. The *whole* Bible is God's message about his Son, our Saviour. *God's chief purpose in writing this book was to reveal Christ.* The Old Testament is the *preparation* for Christ. The New Testament is the *manifestation* of Christ. The Scriptures reveal Christ from Genesis to Revelation. The entire Bible finds meaning in him. Jesus Christ is the origin, the substance and the object of all divine revelation:

> In a word, the blessed Redeemer, whom the Gospel reveals, is Himself the beginning and the end of the scheme of God's dispensations; in Him is found alike the centre of Heaven's plan, and the one foundation of human confidence and hope. So that before His coming into the world, all things of necessity pointed toward Him; types and prophecies bore testimony to the things that concerned His work and kingdom; the children of blessing were blessed in anticipation of His promised redemption; and with His coming, the grand reality itself came, and the higher purposes of Heaven entered on their fulfilment.[18]

---

[18] Fairbairn, *The Typology of Scripture*, 48.

As William Hendriksen asserts, no Old Testament book is "interpreted fully until it is viewed in the light of New Testament revelation."[19] The fulfilment is always greater than the promise, and the reality than the expectation. To the prophets of the Old Testament, the vision of the Coming One, the promised Seed, was indeed glorious. But greater far is that reality by which we now know the One who loved us and gave himself for us. The mystery of Christ as the Lamb of God who takes away the sin of the world could only be known in part by the church of the Old Testament.

Christ in all his fulness is presented in the Old Testament: Christ in his offices—as Prophet, Priest and King; Christ in his character—as holy, harmless, undefiled; Christ in his person—as God and man; Christ in his relation to God and humanity; Christ in his body the church; Christ as giving to God all that God requires from his people; Christ as bringing to his people all that they require from God; Christ seen in his suffering; Christ viewed in glory; Christ as the first and the last; the all in all to his people.

"The different books are but God's chapters in which He arranges and illustrates some one or more of these or other aspects of His Beloved."[20]

---

[19] William Hendriksen, *Survey of the Bible: A Treasury of Bible Information* (Welwyn: Evangelical Press, 1976), 298.

[20] Jukes, *The Law of the Offerings*, 18.

GENESIS

MEANING	AUTHOR	KEY THOUGHT
"origins"	**Moses** *(commonly accepted)*	**Beginning**

THEME

Human failure and God's glorious purpose

THEME VERSE
In the beginning, God created the heavens and the earth.
GENESIS 1:1

GENESIS / **SUMMARY**

PART 1 / **FOUR MOMENTOUS EVENTS** — 1:1–11:32

1. **Creation**
   a. Creation of the material universe — 1:1–25; 2:1–6
   b. Creation of the human race — 1:26–31; 2:7–25

2. **The Fall**
   a. Temptation, Fall and curse — 3:1–24
   b. Cain, Abel and Seth — 4:1–26
   c. Adam's descendants — 5:1–32

3. **The Flood**
   a. The wicked judged; the righteous saved — 6:1–22
   b. The great Flood — 7:1–8:19
   c. The rainbow covenant — 8:20–9:17
   d. Noah's descendants — 9:18–10:32

4. **Tower of Babel**
   a. An ungodly ambition — 11:1–9
   b. Shem's descendants — 11:10–32

PART 2 / **FOUR CHOSEN LEADERS** — 12:1–50:26

1. **Abraham**
   a. The call of Abraham — 12:1–20
   b. Abraham and Lot — 13:1–14:24
   c. Covenant promises: a son, the land and great prosperity — 15:1–17:27
   d. Abraham prays for Sodom and Gomorrah — 18:1–33
   e. The destruction of Sodom and Gomorrah — 19:1–38
   f. Life in Gerar and the birth of Isaac — 20:1–21:34
   g. The test of obedience in offering Isaac — 22:1–24
   h. Abraham purchases land to bury Sarah — 23:1–20
   i. Abraham's servant seeks a bride for Isaac — 24:1–67
   j. Abraham and Keturah — 25:1–6
   k. Abraham's death — 25:7–8

2. **Isaac**
   a. Isaac's birth   21:3
   b. Isaac's marriage to Rebekah   24:1-67
   c. The birth of twins sons Jacob and Esau   25:20-26
   d. Isaac's later years   26:1-35

3. **Jacob**
   a. Jacob's deceit to secure the birthright   27:1-46
   b. Jacob's vision of the heavenly ladder   28:10-22
   c. Life with Laban, Leah and Rachel   29:1-31:55
   d. Wrestling with God and man   32:1-32
   e. His brother Esau's family   36:1-43
   f. Jacob's journey to Egypt   46:1-47:31
   g. Jacob blesses Joseph's sons   48:1-22
   h. Jacob's last words to his twelve sons   49:1-33

4. **Joseph**
   a. Joseph's birth   30:1,22-24
   b. Conflict with his brothers   37:1-36
   c. A slave in Egypt   39:1-23
   d. Dreams in prison   40:1-23
   e. Joseph's rise to power   41:1-57
   f. Joseph's brothers travel to Egypt   42:1-45:28
   g. Joseph buries his father   50:1-21
   h. Joseph's death   50:22-26

GENESIS

The first five books of the Old Testament, Genesis, Exodus, Leviticus, Numbers and Deuteronomy, are known among the Jews as the *Torah* (meaning "law"). Among non-Jews they are known as the *Pentateuch* (from the Septuagint, the Greek translation of the Old Testament, meaning "five books") or simply "the Law."

Genesis is the first book of the Pentateuch, the first book of the Old Testament, the first book of the Bible. It holds a strategic and vital place in God's revelation. Here is the record of how Israel was selected from among the nations of the world to become the chosen people. The choice was not made on account of any merit or excellence on their part; it is, therefore, "the story of God's free grace in establishing Israel for Himself as His people."[1] Opening with the account of creation, the book concludes with the death of Joseph and with the Israelites established and prospering in the land of Egypt.

Genesis is in many respects the most important book in the Bible. As its name implies, it is the book of "beginnings," or the book of "origins." Without it, the origin of life, the birth of sin and the first promise of a radical solution would have remained a mystery and left the rest of the Scriptures seriously impoverished. Almost all the truths of God's revelation, the great doctrines which are afterward fully developed in the books of Scripture, are here in seed form.

GENESIS / **AUTHOR**

Of the five books traditionally ascribed to Moses, only Exodus is directly credited to him in Scripture (Mark 12:26). The other four—Genesis, Leviticus, Numbers and Deuteronomy—are not referred to individually by name. The Lord Jesus Christ and the New Testament writers do, however, make a number of collective references to the writings of Moses (Luke 16:29,31; 24:27,44; John 1:45; 5:45–47; 2 Corinthians 3:15).

Of ultimate concern is not the human author but the assurance that this book is part of the Scriptures breathed out by God (2 Timothy 3:16). That the ultimate authorship is divine, all biblical writers are

---

[1] H.C. Leupold, *Exposition of Genesis*, 2 vol. (Grand Rapids: Baker, 1942), 1:9.

agreed. The Lord Jesus clearly accepted Genesis as written by God, as we see in his debate with the Pharisees on the issue of divorce:

> The Pharisees also came to him, testing him, and saying to him, "Is it lawful for a man to divorce his wife for just any reason?" And he answered and said to them, "Have you not read that he who made them at the beginning 'made them male and female,' and said, 'For this reason a man shall leave his father and mother and be joined to his wife, and the two shall become one flesh'? So then, they are no longer two but one flesh. Therefore what God has joined together, let not man separate" (Matthew 19:3–5).

The reliability of the early history which Moses records is often challenged on the ground that the events in the opening chapter occurred 2,500 years, and those in the closing chapter took place at least 300 years, before the time of Moses. There is, however, no biblically based reason to assume that written records had not been produced earlier. Moses may have in fact made use of existing manuscripts, records, as well as oral traditions, in his compilation. He certainly had the qualifications for the task—for he "was learned in all the wisdom of the Egyptians, and was mighty in words and deeds" (Acts 7:22). More importantly, Moses was singularly favoured by God:

> If there is a prophet among you,
> I, the Lord, make Myself known to him in a vision;
> I speak to him in a dream.
> Not so with My servant Moses;
> He is faithful in all My house.
> I speak with him face to face,
> Even plainly, and not in dark sayings;
> And he sees the form of the Lord (Numbers 12:6–8).

The contents of Genesis were revealed by God. As the Lord Jesus Christ promised the assistance of the Holy Spirit to aid the memories of his apostles (John 14:26), so God could easily ensure the accuracy of what was transmitted down the years until a written form was adopted. And as the Lord Jesus Christ promised his apostles further revelations by his Spirit of "things to come" (John 16:13), so God could effortlessly reveal "things to come" to Abraham, Isaac, Jacob and Moses. Geerhardus Vos speaks for all Bible-believing Christians when he insists that "revelation" implies an infallible communication: "If God be personal and conscious, then the inference is inevitable that in every mode of self-disclosure He will make a faultless expression of His nature and purpose. He will communicate His thought to the world with the stamp of divinity on it."[2]

GENESIS / **HISTORICAL SETTING**

The book of Genesis covers a period in excess of 2,200 years, from the days of creation (4000+ B.C.) to the death of Joseph (1804 B.C.).

GENESIS / **OUTLINE**

The first eleven chapters are governed by four momentous events: Creation, the Fall, the Flood and the Tower of Babel. The second half of the book, the remaining thirty-nine chapters, is taken up with the biographies of four major personalities: Abraham, Isaac, Jacob and Joseph.

PART 1 / **FOUR MOMENTOUS EVENTS (1:1–11:32)**

1. Creation

Genesis opens with the declaration: "In the beginning God created the heavens and the earth" (1:1; cf.[3] Psalm 19:1–6; 24:1; 33:6–9). Here is the only correct and satisfactory information concerning prehistoric times. Acceptance of the doctrine of creation is, however, dependent upon the disposition of the heart. It is 'by faith we understand that the worlds were framed by the word of God' (Hebrews 11:1). The teaching of Scripture is clear and unequivocal: "that God created the universe on six successive days, limited by morning and evening, six real, ordinary days like our days of twenty-four hours."[4]

---

[2] Geerhardas Vos, *Biblical Theology: Old and New Testaments* (1948; Edinburgh: Banner of Truth Trust, 1975), 11.

[3] "cf." means "compare with."

[4] Homer C. Hoeksema, *'In the Beginning God…'* (Grand Rapids: Reformed Free Publishing Association, 1966), 45. Hoeksema enumerates the various alternative "interpretations" of creation and demonstrates their weakness and inadequacy.

In the first two chapters information is supplied which forms the backdrop for all subsequent events. Human beings are shown to be the high point of God's creative work. They, of all creation, bear the image of God (1:26–27). Of all created beings it is only human beings who are capable of a deep relationship with God. This is our outstanding privilege. Created to enjoy fellowship with God, to rule over the rest of creation as his vice-regents, to produce children and to enjoy the fruit of the earth—the conditions of life for the first human beings were idyllic. Only one restriction had been placed upon them by God: "Of every tree of the garden you may freely eat; but of the tree of the knowledge of good and evil you shall not eat, for in the day that you eat of it you shall surely die" (2:16–17).

2. The Fall

In spite of this serious warning, the first human beings, Adam and Eve, disobey through unbelief. Their relationship with the Creator is never to be the same again—until the Restorer comes and permanently corrects the problem at source. The changes which take place as a result of this second momentous event, the Fall, cannot be overstated. In Genesis, the "wiles of the devil" (Ephesians 6:11) are exposed. Here there is a clear indication of how the Evil One operates. Studying Genesis should mean that "we are not ignorant of his devices" (2 Corinthians 2:11). He calls into question the Word of God: "Has God indeed said…?" (3:1). He casts doubt on its trustworthiness, denies its truth: "You will not surely die. For God knows that in the day you eat it your eyes will be opened, and you will be like God, knowing good and evil" (3:4–5).

When Adam and Eve respond to the insidious insinuations of Satan and rebel against God, the results are catastrophic. God keeps his word. The death penalty is enforced. From that moment, the human body is subject to decay. And not only Adam and Eve and their posterity are to suffer: "For the creation was subjected to futility, not willingly" (Romans 8:20).

Exclusion from the Garden of Eden is only the beginning. Humanity now has a sinful bias, and that sinful nature, which was not there at creation, is soon exhibited in hatred and violence. Adam and Eve are to witness the appalling results of their transgression when their older son murders his younger brother. The issue is really between

Cain and the Lord, not between Cain and his brother. But because "The LORD respected Abel and his offering" (4:4), Cain takes out his anger upon his brother (1 John 3:12). The first murder graphically illustrates the corrupting power of sin that now flows through humanity—from the Fall.

Following Abel's death, a third son is born to Adam and Eve. The line is traced through Seth showing the early ancestors of the promised Seed (3:15; see Figure 2).

The descendants of Cain prove to be as ungodly as their father. In Lamech the ungodliness of the Cainite line appears in his defiance and arrogance in abusing the words of the Lord (4:24). The wickedness of humanity continues its downward spiral, reaching such depths that "The LORD was sorry that he had made man on the earth, and he was grieved in his heart" (6:6). The third momentous event is on the horizon—judgement!

3. The Flood

The Flood destroys every living thing except those who are saved in Noah's ark—for "Noah found grace in the eyes of the LORD" (6:8). "By faith Noah, being divinely warned of things not yet seen, moved with godly fear, prepared an ark for the saving of his household, by which he condemned the world and became heir of the righteousness which is according to faith" (Hebrews 11:7)

The dimensions of the ark are supplied by the Lord. It would have been quite unlike the representation given in most illustrations. Longer than a football pitch, it was three hundred cubits long, fifty cubits wide and thirty cubits high (approximately 459 x 75 x 44 feet, or 140 x 23 x 13.5 metres, giving a volume of 1.5 million cubic feet, or 43,500 cubic metres—see Figure 3). Built with three floors, the ark had room for 432 double-decker buses or 125,000 sheep! This would have been enough room for pairs of all living land-dwelling animals and also some prehistoric kinds. Designed as it was to float rather than to sail, marine experts say that these are the best proportions possible in order to ride storm waves with maximum stability.[5]

---

[5] *Our World*, No. 18 (Creation Resources Trust, Somerset, England); *Creation ex nihilo Technical Journal*, Vol. 19, No. 2 (August 2005): 16–19.

Figure 2. The line of descent from Adam to Noah

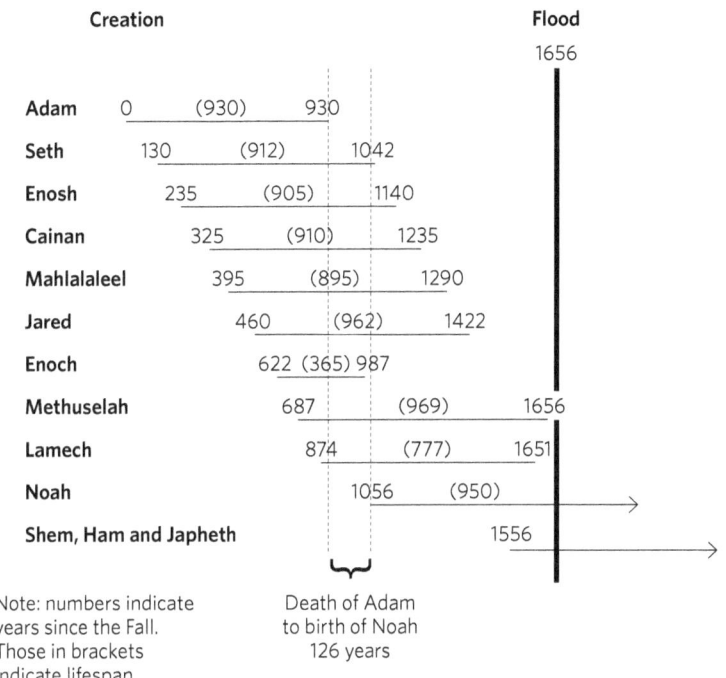

Adam lived 930 years (Genesis 5:5) and Methuselah lived 969 years (Genesis 5:27). Together they spanned the whole period from the Fall to the Flood, with an overlap of 243 years. Adam would often tell of the events in the Garden of Eden. In ten generations, Noah was the first one not to know Adam personally!

Figure 3. The dimensions of Noah's ark

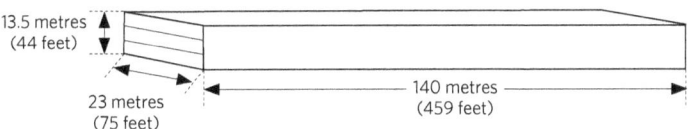

Although the dimensions of the ark are stated in the Scriptures, the actual shape is not given.

The mercy of God is shown in that Noah was "a preacher of righteousness" (2 Peter 2:5), and declared the judgement of God well before the event.

Following the Flood there is the establishment of the covenant with Noah and creation (9:9–11). Some time later an incident, brought about as a result of Noah's intoxication and Ham's lack of discretion, is to have far-reaching implications for the sons of Noah and their descendants. The ancestral line of the promised Seed—that is Christ—is to pass through Shem (Luke 3:36). The words of Noah to this son have a prophetic character. The opening phrase indicates that true religion will be preserved in the descendants of Shem: "Blessed be the Lord, the God of Shem" (9:26). This is the second Messianic prophecy (the first is recorded in 3:15). The families of the earth will be blessed only through their association and relationship with the descendants of Shem. In connection with the descendants of Shem the descendants of Japheth will be received among the true worshippers of God (9:27).[6]

4. The Tower of Babel

The Tower of Babel is built on "a plain in the land of Shinar" (11:2), probably located in ancient Babylonia in southern Mesopotamia. It symbolizes godless arrogance. In an attempt to make a monument of unsurpassed proportions, "a tower" is planned "whose top is in the heavens," so that the architects can "make a name" for themselves (11:4).

Apparently quite aware that God had said, "Be fruitful and multiply, and fill the earth" (9:1), these people react and, filled with self-importance, commence to build a construction which would bind them together so that they should not "be scattered abroad over the face of the whole earth" (11:4).

The Lord prevents the proceedings by the simple expedient of confusing "their language, that they may not understand one another's speech" (11:7). The basic languages of the world come into being. Unable to communicate, the builders disperse. The project is discontinued. They separate into their various language groups.

---

[6] For a detailed argument see Ernest W. Hengstenberg, *Christology of the Old Testament and a Commentary on the Messianic Predictions* (1847; Grand Rapids: Kregel, 1970), 24–25.

Figure 4. The line of descent from Shem to Abraham

	Flood						
Shem -98			(600)			502	
Arphaxad		2	(438)		440		
Shalah		37	(433)		470		
Eber		67	(464)				531
Peleg		101	(239)	340			
Reu		131	(239)	370			
Serug		163	(230)	393			
Nahor		193	(148)	341			
Terah		222	(205)		427		
Abraham		292	(175)		467		
Isaac			392	(180)		572 →	

Note: numbers indicate years since the Flood. Those in brackets indicate lifespan.

Death of Shem

These four major occurrences—creation, the Fall, the Flood and the Tower of Babel—form the backdrop for all subsequent history. Human rebellion, foolishness, spiritual blindness and religious incompetence find their first expression and explanation here in Genesis. These are the dominant issues in the first eleven chapters of this book.

PART 2 / **FOUR CHOSEN LEADERS (12:1–50:26)**

Against the backdrop of human rebellion and sin, Genesis presents the beginnings of divine activity. Plans, promises, covenants and the provision of a wonderful solution for the human predicament are initiated. The family line of Shem serves to introduce Terah's eldest son, Abram (11:10–26). (See Figure 4.)

The second part of Genesis records the biographies of Abraham, Isaac, Jacob and Joseph. God's dealings with these men are highly significant. From the time reached at the conclusion of the book of

Genesis, and thereafter, the Lord will be known as "the God of Abraham, the God of Isaac, and the God of Jacob" (Exodus 3:6; cf. Matthew 22:31–32).

1. Abraham

The story of Abraham in this book is by no means a full biography. Only the main features of his life are noted. The selection of material is based upon the central theme—the early preparation for the coming of the promised Seed (3:15), who is to be the Son of God, Jesus the Christ.

Abraham is chosen from an idolatrous background. His father Terah "served other gods" (Joshua 24:2).

The Lord's call to Abraham to move out to an unnamed destination demanded considerable trust and confidence. Abraham was to travel almost 1,000 miles from Ur to Haran, and then on to Canaan (see Map 1). He is the first one to be called a *Hebrew* (`*Ibrîy* meaning "one from beyond"—14:13).

Whether Abraham became a believer in Ur or in Haran is not stated. It is clear, however, that he was a believer before he left Haran (Hebrews 11:8).

Abraham's initial call includes promises of personal blessing, numerous offspring, a great name and his being made a blessing to "all the families of the earth" (12:2–3). On arrival in Canaan, the Lord adds the blessing of the land (12:7). A few years later, after the division between the shepherds of Lot and the shepherds of Abraham, the Lord indicates the extent of the land promised to Abraham and reinforces his promise of numerous offspring (13:14–17). The promise of descendants and the gift of land is repeated and confirmed by a dramatic covenant (15:1–21). The involvement of Hagar to bear the offspring seems to have been entirely Sarah's idea and may have been motivated by a misguided attempt to fulfil the promise of God regarding a son for Abraham (16:1–16). Thirteen years later the Lord appears to Abraham and reinforces his promises of offspring, adding that the covenant and the promise of the land of Canaan as a possession are "everlasting," that God "will be *their* God" (suggesting a close personal relationship) to Abraham and his descendants, that Sarah will be the mother of the promised son and that Abraham and Sarah's natural descendants will include royalty (17:1–21). In Genesis 18 the promise of a son and a

Map 1. The journeys of Abraham

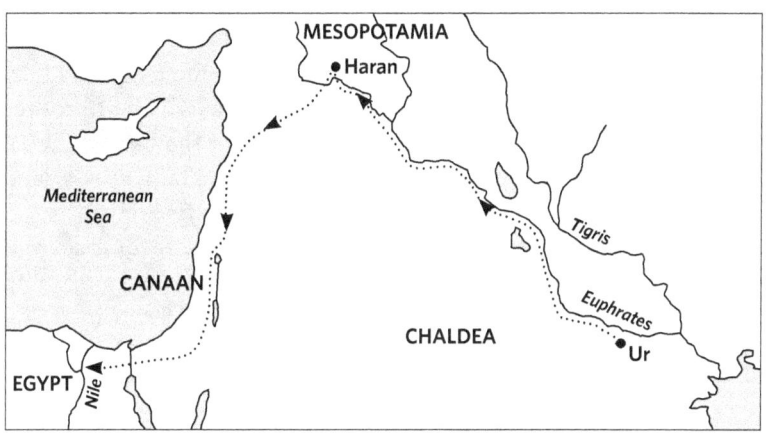

multitude of descendants is repeated to Abraham and Sarah. Some years later, after the successful test of obedience in the offering of his son Isaac, the promises of blessing are given once again to Abraham: "descendants as the stars of the heaven and as the sand which is on the seashore," together with victory over their enemies and blessing for all nations of the earth (22:17–18).

These great promises to Abraham are in one sense only a qualifying of the original promise to Adam and Eve (3:15). They merely mark out "a particular channel, through which divine grace should flow in raising up a spiritual seed, to resist and baffle and drive out the tempter."[7]

2. Isaac

The prophetic disclosures successively made to Isaac and Jacob (26:3–4; 28:13–15) are little more than renewals of the original promise to Abraham. Ernest Hengstenberg concludes: "The undeniable meaning of these promises made to the patriarchs is, that through their posterity salvation should be conferred upon all the nations of the earth. The nature of this blessing, however, is not accurately defined."[8]

---

[7] Patrick Fairbairn, *Prophecy: Viewed in Respect to Its Distinctive Nature, Its Special Function, and Proper Interpretation* (1865; Grand Rapids: Baker, 1976), 181.

[8] Hengstenberg, *Christology of the Old Testament*, 26.

The son of Abraham and Sarah receives the name Isaac (meaning "laughter") since his father and mother laughed on hearing that Sarah was to give birth to a son when they were both well advanced in years (17:17; 18:10–15). Incredulous laughter turns to the laughter of joy (21:6). Isaac is the long-awaited son of promise. His half-brother Ishmael seems to have resented Isaac's arrival in the family (21:9). Probably when Isaac is in his teens, he is taken by his father to the land of Moriah to be sacrificed. The Lord intervenes (22:1–2,11–12).

Abraham takes great care in providing a suitable wife for Isaac, and while theirs is an arranged marriage, Isaac clearly loves his wife Rebekah (24:67). Isaac and Rebekah have twin sons, Jacob and Esau. In mid-life, famine drives Isaac to Gerar. Here he repeats his father's earlier deception by insisting that his wife is his sister (26:7–11; cf. 12:19; 20:2). Following a fraud perpetrated by Jacob by which he obtains the blessing of the firstborn, Isaac sends his son away to Padan Aram. Twenty years later he sees his son return prosperous and with a large family. Isaac lives 180 years.

3. Jacob

Jacob (meaning "supplanter" or "deceiver") receives his name following the unusual nature of his birth (25:26). He is a meek and quiet-tempered man who appreciates the peaceful life of a shepherd. In contrast, his brother Esau is a fiery personality and loves hunting. Esau shows disdain for his own birthright as the firstborn, by flippantly selling it to Jacob for a bowl of stew. He thereby reveals his total lack of spiritual interest and his disregard for the promises of God.

Spurred on by his mother, Jacob fraudulently obtains his father's blessing. When Esau discovers the deception, he is very angry and vows to kill Jacob (27:41). Jacob leaves in fear for his life. On the pretext of seeking a wife, Jacob is dispatched to Padan Aram to the home of his uncle Laban. Because of their deception, mother and son are separated and Rebekah dies years before Jacob returns.

Before setting out for Padan Aram, Jacob received "the blessing of Abraham" from his father Isaac (28:3–4). On the journey, the Lord appears to him in a dream, reinforces the divine promise and assures Jacob of divine protection (28:10–15). Once in Padan Aram, "the deceiver" is himself deceived. Jacob labours seven years for the hand of Rachel only to be tricked by Laban into marrying her older sister

Leah. Not content with one wife, Jacob labours a further seven years for Rachel, whom he loves. Jacob is constantly cheated in his wages and it is only through the providence of God that he prospers. After twenty years, Laban's sons become more and more critical of Jacob. Laban too is increasingly ill-disposed toward him. Under divine instruction Jacob takes his family and livestock and returns home to the land of promise (31:3).

The turning-point of Jacob's life comes at Peniel, where he is humbled by the Angel (Hosea 12:3–5). He turns from his old ways of craftiness and deceit and begins to rely solely upon the Lord in prayer.

Jacob's home life is frequently traumatic: the tensions between his two wives, the distress of Rachel at her childlessness, the incident surrounding his daughter Dinah, the corruption of Reuben, the violence of Simeon and Levi and the loss of his favourite son Joseph, presumed dead for so many years. But the Lord is with him. Jacob's latter days are calm, happy and prosperous in the land of Egypt with his extended family.

Jacob functions as a prophet when, on his deathbed, he blesses his twelve sons (49:1–28). Bypassing Reuben, Simeon and Levi, he addresses his fourth son as the heir of the promise (verses 9–12). To Judah is given the blessing of the firstborn. His will be the family from which the promised Seed, the Shiloh, will be born.[9] Following the blessing Jacob gives instruction for his burial back in the promised land. Upon his death, his son Joseph makes the necessary arrangements (50:2–13).

4. Joseph

The fourth person whose history is recorded in some detail in the book of Genesis is Joseph. Whereas the line of promise was to pass from Abraham through Isaac, Jacob and Judah, it is not to Judah that detailed attention is given. It is one of his younger brothers whom the Lord uses to illustrate forcefully how he keeps his promises. God keeps his covenant with Abraham, Isaac and Jacob in the life of Joseph, whose experiences in Egypt are recalled by the psalmist:

---

[9] For an explanation of the name "Shiloh" see page 63.

> Moreover He called for a famine in the land;
> He destroyed all the provision of bread.
> He sent a man before them—
> Joseph—who was sold as a slave.
> They hurt his feet with fetters,
> He was laid in irons.
> Until the time that his word came to pass,
> The word of the Lord tested him.
> The king sent and released him,
> The ruler of the people let him go free.
> He made him lord of his house,
> And ruler of all his possessions,
> To bind his princes at his pleasure,
> And teach his elders wisdom.
>
> Israel also came into Egypt,
> And Jacob dwelt in the land of Ham (Psalm 105:16–23).

To Jacob, the famine is an added affliction following the loss of his beloved son. Nevertheless God uses the one to provide for the other. In later life, godly Joseph will trace the providential hand of God and say to his brothers, "You meant evil against me; but God meant it for good, in order to bring it about as it is this day, to save many people alive" (50:20).

God's dealings with these four great men—Abraham, Isaac, Jacob and Joseph—are concisely traced by Stephen before the Jewish council in Jerusalem (Acts 7:1–16).

From the historical outline, we turn to the spiritual message of the book of Genesis.

GENESIS / **CHRIST AND HIS CHURCH**

Genesis is packed full of Christological significance.

As Creator God reveals himself in the mysterious plurality of his being: "Let *us* make man in our image" (1:26, emphasis added). Clarity is given in the New Testament, where it is revealed that God the Father and "the Son of his love" were co-Creators (Colossians 1:13,16–17; Hebrews 1:2–3; John 1:1–3).

From the Fall, the Creator is Lord over two kingdoms: the kingdom of nature and the kingdom of grace. In the first he is *Elohim*—the Creator, Preserver and Ruler. In the second he is also *Jehovah*—the Saviour, Guardian and Friend. All his arrangement and organization of the universe have the ultimate goal to prepare, establish and confirm the kingdom of grace in humanity. "As mercy presupposes misery, so grace presupposes sin."[10] Christ has been given all authority over the kingdom of nature to ensure the well-being of his kingdom of grace (Ephesians 1:22; Matthew 28:18).

THEOPHANIES

The Angel of the LORD appears in the pages of Scripture in such a way that his deity cannot be denied. Here is the Son of God appearing momentarily in human form before his incarnation.[11] Appearing to Abraham's second "wife" Hagar, he is called "the angel of the LORD" four times (16:7,9,10,11). Moses the historian identifies him as "the LORD [YHWH] who spoke to her" (16:13). Hagar speaks of him as "God" (16:13). Moses records the testimony of Jacob: "Then the Angel of God spoke to me in a dream, saying… 'I am the God of Bethel'" (31:11,13). Years later, when Jacob blesses Joseph, he speaks of the "God, before whom my fathers Abraham and Isaac walked, the God who has fed me all my life long to this day" as "the Angel who has redeemed me from all evil" (48:15,16). This is further confirmed by the prophet Hosea, who declares of Jacob:

He took his brother by the heel in the womb,
And in his strength he struggled with God.
Yes, he struggled with the Angel and prevailed (Hosea 12:3–4).

---

[10] Ernest W. Hengstenberg, *History of the Kingdom of God under the Old Testament*, vol. 1 (Edinburgh: T & T Clark, 1877), 2.

[11] For a fuller treatment of theophanies as appearances of the Son of God, see James A. Borland, *Christ in the Old Testament: A Comprehensive Study of Old Testament Appearances of Christ in Human Form* (Chicago: Moody, 1978), 34–49.

TYPES

Adam "is a type of him who was to come" (Romans 5:14),[12] that is, Christ. The first Adam is to be followed by the last Adam. The apostle Paul quotes Genesis 2:7: "The first man Adam became a living being," and adds, "The last Adam became a life-giving spirit" (1 Corinthians 15:45). Adam is treated by God as the representative head of the whole human race. The punishment which the Lord laid upon Adam was laid upon *all* humanity (Romans 5:12). What Adam did brought guilt upon all human beings, since all human beings are united to him by birth (all who are born are "in Adam"). The Lord Jesus Christ, as the second Adam, is treated in the same manner. He is the representative head of his people. What he did brought blessing upon all human beings united to him (all who are twice-born, as evidenced by repentance and faith, are "in Christ").

Adam and Eve in their relationship are a type of Christ and his church (2:20–24; Ephesians 5:28–32). In the forming of Eve from Adam's side, and in the exclusive love of Adam for Eve as part of his own flesh, Christ is seen in his exclusive and jealous love for his church (2 Corinthians 11:2). The New Testament reveals the Lord Jesus as the Bridegroom who has come to claim his people as his bride (John 3:29–30; cf. Revelation 19:6–9).

The sabbath rest after the six days of creative work is a *type* of the blessings enjoyed by believers in Christ (2:2–3; cf. Hebrews 4:1–10). The promised rest symbolized in creation was not fulfilled in Canaan (Joshua 23:1); otherwise David "would not afterward have spoken of another day" (Hebrews 4:8; cf. Psalm 95:7–11). The remaining "rest" (Hebrews 4:9—the Greek word *sabbatismos* means a "sabbatism" or a "sabbath rest") is not realized until the believer rests by faith in Christ (Hebrews 4:10; Matthew 11:28; Ephesians 2:8–9).

The temptations of Eve bear a strong connection with the Lord's temptations. Satan appealed to "the lust of the flesh, the lust of the eyes, and the pride of life" (1 John 2:16). This is evident in Eve's thoughts, "that the [forbidden] tree was good for food, that it was pleasant to the eyes, and a tree desirable to make one wise" (3:6). The

---

[12] For an explanation of the meaning of the word "type," see the introductory chapter, "The central theme of Old Testament Scripture," 28.

same parallels are discernible in the temptations of Christ—"the lust of the flesh" (cf. Luke 4:2-3), "the lust of the eyes" (cf. Luke 4:5-7) "and the pride of life" (cf. Luke 4:9-11). While the devil still uses the same three-pronged attack on the Lord's people, it is obvious that the temptations of our Lord were tailored specifically for him. Twice Satan confronted the Lord with the challenge: "If you are the Son of God...."

The delivery of Noah and his family in the ark is seen as a type of the believer's union with Christ in baptism (6:14-8:19; cf. 1 Peter 3:20-21). The Lord determined to punish humanity for its great wickedness (6:5-7). He set a day for the Flood and then proceeded to warn the people through the preaching of Noah (2 Peter 2:5). The people took no notice of the warning (cf. Luke 17:26-27). The ark symbolizes Christ as the only means of salvation from the judgement of God (cf. Acts 4:12). It is later prophesied, "A man will be as a hiding place from the wind, and a cover from the tempest" (Isaiah 32:2). The ark had only one door (cf. John 10:7). The ark was entered by faith (Hebrews 11:7). The ark took the full force of the storm (cf. Psalm 69:1-2; 42:7).

The building of the Tower of Babel, "whose top" was intended to be "in the heavens," was foiled by the Lord. Only one bridge between heaven and earth is possible. Jacob is privileged to dream about the ladder which is a type of Christ (11:1-9; 28:12-17; cf. John 1:51). "The stairway-tower of Jacob's dream was God's answer to the tower of Babel. The top of it did reach to heaven, for God was the builder, not man. God alone establishes communication between heaven and earth."[13] On the Day of Pentecost there was an anticipation of the ultimate restoration of one common language throughout the regenerated earth (Acts 2:6-11).

In *Melchizedek*, there is a type of Christ in his unique role as king and priest of God Most High (14:18-20; Psalm 110:1-4; Hebrews 7:1-3). He is "king of righteousness" and "king of peace." He holds the unique office of royal priest and is superior to Abraham and, therefore, by implication, to the Aaronic or Levitical priesthood (Hebrews 7:4-10). It is later predicted that Messiah, under the title of "the Branch," will build the temple of the Lord and be "a priest on his throne, and the counsel of peace shall be between them both"

---

[13] Edmund P. Clowney, *The Unfolding Mystery: Discovering Christ in the Old Testament* (Leicester: Inter-Varsity Press, 1988), 64.

(Zechariah 6:12–13). In other words, there will be perfect harmony between Christ's kingly rule and his priestly office. As the royal priest, he will promote the peace of his people.

In *Ishmael and Isaac*, the hostility of unregenerate Israelites toward spiritual children of God is symbolized (21:9–10; cf. Galatians 4:21–31). This is reminiscent of the hostility felt by Cain toward Abel (4:8; cf. 1 John 3:11–15).

While there are many more links which may be located between the book of Genesis and Christ and his church, one further reference will suffice for this overview—*Joseph* as a type of Christ. Many lessons may be drawn from the character and experiences of Joseph.

George Lawson notes,

> there is very remarkable similarity between the character of Joseph and that of Christ, as well as between the events of their lives—only an allowance must be made for the incomparable excellency of our great Redeemer above all the sons of men. As the shadow is to the body, so were all the types and figures of our Lord Jesus Christ to Him, whom they represented.[14]

Resemblances of a more or less typical character cannot fail to be observed between Joseph and Christ, and between his varied life and Christ's, "by the most literal and unimaginative commentator."[15] We see him rejected and despised by his brethren; sold; becoming a servant; severely tempted yet without yielding to sin; falsely accused; offering no defence; cast into prison; suffering at the hands of Gentiles; innocent yet suffering; winning the respect of his jailer; numbered with transgressors; a blessing to one and judgement on the other; delivered from prison by the hand of God; the revealer of secrets; warning of impending danger and the steps to take to prepare for it; exalted to the right hand of the king; given a wife by the king; thirty years old when he begins his life's work; making bread available for a starving world.

---

[14] George Lawson, *Lectures on the History of Joseph* (1807; London: Banner of Truth Trust, 1972), 1. In this book Lawson does not develop the notion of Joseph as a type of the Lord Jesus Christ.

[15] Robert Candlish, *Studies in Genesis* (1868; Grand Rapids: Kregel, 1979), 608–616.

Joseph's words to his brothers sum up his experience and also the experiences of the Israelites in Egypt in later years: "But as for you, you meant evil against me; but God meant it for good, in order to bring it about as it is this day, to save many people alive" (50:20). These words also sum up our Lord's experiences at the hands of the high priest and the Sanhedrin: "Him, being delivered by the determined purpose and foreknowledge of God, you have taken by lawless hands, have crucified, and put to death" (Acts 2:23).

PROPHECIES

1. The promised Seed

The first prophecy comes immediately after the Fall. Even as the living God is pronouncing judgement upon Adam and Eve for their wilful disobedience, he includes a wonderful promise (3:15). This first prophecy concerning the promised "seed" is indistinct. The only factor that is clear is the certainty of victory for the seed of the woman. It is not explicitly stated whether the fulfilment will come through some peculiarly gifted race, or by a single individual from among the descendants of the woman. This prophecy concerning a seed, a descendant or descendants, is the reason why genealogies and ancestral lines are given such prominence in Genesis. The line of descent of the following men is distinctly recorded in order to see God's promise fulfilled: Adam (5:1); Noah (6:9); the sons of Noah (10:1); Shem (11:10); Terah, the father of Abraham (11:27); Ishmael (25:12); Isaac (25:19); Esau (36:1,9); Jacob (37:2). These serve to prove that God has not forgotten his initial promise.

The Hebrew word translated *seed* (*zera`*) is ambiguous. It may refer to one individual, or it may refer to a group. Genesis does not resolve the question. It simply shows that the chosen line is Abraham, Isaac and Jacob. Even in the New Testament the ambiguity is perpetuated. The plural and singular are traceable:

> 1. The seed are *all the true children of God*. At first it seems that the seed of Abraham (in the New Testament the Greek word for seed is *sperma*) refers to the physical descendants of Abraham (Luke 1:55; John 8:33,37; Acts 7:5–6; Romans 11:1; 2 Corinthians 11:22; Hebrews 11:18). The apostle Paul, however, broadens the

promise to immense proportions by arguing that "the seed of Abraham" includes only those Hebrews who share his faith and also all Gentiles who share that faith (Romans 4:13–16; 9:6–8; Galatians 3:7,26–29). The early recipients of the promise could not have imagined the remarkable way in which the Lord would fulfil his word!

2. At the same time the New Testament argues that the promised seed *refers to Christ*. Peter implies this as he preaches in the temple at Jerusalem shortly after the Pentecost experience (Acts 3:25–26). Paul argues strongly that the word "seed" in Genesis is not a grammatical plural and so refers to Christ (Galatians 3:16); yet at the same time, within a few verses, he interprets "the seed of Abraham" as composed of all believers (Galatians 3:29). It is evident that the collective function of *zera`* (*seed*) "allows the writer to refer to the group or to a representative individual of that group." [16] The ambiguity of the original promise is further reinforced by Paul when he makes evident allusion to Genesis 3:15 in saying to the Christians at Rome, "the God of peace will crush Satan under your feet shortly" (Romans 16:20).[17]

2. The promised land

The land is an important motif throughout the Scriptures. Adam and Eve were driven from their homeland as a result of their rebellion and sin (3:23–24). Years later the land of Canaan was given to Abraham and his descendants for their possession (12:7; 13:15). But Abraham only received title to a small plot of that land during his lifetime. He purchased the cave of Machpelah from Ephron the Hittite, son of Zohar (23:3–18). "And after this Abraham buried Sarah his wife in the cave of the field of Machpelah, before Mamre (that is, Hebron) in the land of Canaan. So the field and the cave that is in it were legally transferred to Abraham by the sons of Heth as property for a burial place" (23:19–20).

The New Testament leaves us in no doubt that Abraham had his eyes set on a distant and spiritual fulfilment of the promise which was going to be no less real, and no less material:

---

[16] Thomas E. McComiskey, *The Covenants of Promise: A Theology of the Old Testament* (Nottingham: Inter-Varsity Press, 1985), 20.

[17] Vos, *Biblical Theology*, 43.

By faith he [Abraham] sojourned in the land of promise as in a foreign country, dwelling in tents with Isaac and Jacob, the heirs with him of the same promise; for he waited for the city which has foundations, whose builder and maker is God.... These all died in faith, not having received the promises, but having seen them afar off, they were assured of them, embraced them, and confessed that they were strangers and pilgrims on the earth. For those who say such things declare plainly that they seek a homeland. And truly if they had called to mind that country from which they had come out, they would have had opportunity to return. But now they desire a better, that is, a heavenly country. Therefore God is not ashamed to be called their God, for he has prepared a city for them (Hebrews 11:9–10,13–16).

3. The promised blessing

The promises made to Abraham were also made to Christ before his incarnation (Galatians 3:16). "I will establish my covenant between me and you and your descendants after you in their generations, for an everlasting covenant, to be God to you and your descendants after you" (17:7).

The promised blessing is a deep personal relationship with the living God. It is a full restoration of the intimate bond and friendship that existed between the Lord and Adam and Eve in the earliest days. In Genesis, the glorious characteristics of salvation in Christ are set before us in symbolic form. From the very beginning, it is God who takes the initiative to deal with the problem of sin. God himself clothes Adam and Eve after their sin (3:21). The clothing is made of skin. The death of an animal is required. God provides a covering. Years later Isaiah will say:

> But we are all like an unclean thing,
> And all our righteousnesses are like filthy rags;
> We all fade as a leaf,
> And our iniquities, like the wind,
> Have taken us away (Isaiah 64:6).

Isaiah will also say:

> I will greatly rejoice in the LORD,
> My soul shall be joyful in my God;
> For He has clothed me with the garments of salvation,
> He has covered me with the robe of righteousness (Isaiah 61:10).

Only in this way could humanity's shame be covered and sinners be made fit to stand in the presence of God. God is operating on the basis of his abiding principle: "Without shedding of blood there is no remission" (Hebrews 9:22). Was the animal that died a lamb? Genesis does not say, but it would be entirely in harmony with the flow of Scripture if this were the case.

The first biblical statement regarding a lamb appears in Genesis 4 in relation to Cain and Abel and their offerings in worship. Judged from the standpoint of the record of revelation up to that point in history, it would seem quite arbitrary for the Lord to receive Abel's offering of a lamb and reject Cain's offering of vegetables. The unfolding significance of a lamb as sacrifice is indisputable (Exodus 12:3,5–13; John 1:29; Revelation 5:6), but was Abel blessed merely on the basis of a coincidence? He was a shepherd. He brought a lamb and was consequently accepted. Cain, a horticulturist, brought vegetables and was rejected. This might be seen to suggest that God deals with people in a somewhat arbitrary fashion.

The truth, however, is far different, as the New Testament later makes clear. In the letter to the Hebrews it is said, "By faith Abel offered to God a more excellent sacrifice than Cain, through which he obtained witness that he was righteous" (Hebrews 11:4). In Scripture, *faith* is never a matter of chance. It is never a "leap in the dark," as some have erroneously taught. It is always the right response to God's Word—spoken or written. If Abel brought the right offering "by faith," then the Lord must have previously revealed the kind of offering which would be acceptable. Abel, then, is seen as believing the Word of God and being obedient in coming to God in God's own way. Cain, with the hard heart of unbelief, wanted to come to God on his own terms. He wanted to use his own means in finding acceptance. These two then become symbolic, on the one hand, of the true believer coming to God by the means he has provided, and, on the other, of the unbeliever trying to find acceptance on his own basis.

This interpretation finds further confirmation in the fact that the Lord provided *coverings of skin* for Adam and Eve in replacement of their coverings of vegetation (3:21; cf. 3:7). Even though there is no *recorded* institution of a sacrificial system, Noah offered animal sacrifices (8:20), and Abraham built altars (12:7,8; 13:18).

Further confirmation that God had revealed his will with regard to sacrifice is shown when Abraham's son Isaac accompanies his father to the land of Moriah to offer a burnt offering to the Lord, and he asks, "Where is the lamb for a burnt offering?" (22:7). From Abraham come the prophetic words, "God will provide for himself the lamb for a burnt offering" (22:8). On that particular occasion a ram is provided, not a lamb. The words of Abraham are to find a glorious fulfilment nearly two thousand years later when the Lamb of God offered himself in that same geographic area. What God requested from Abraham, but did not allow him to fulfil, God did when he gave up his Son, his only Son Jesus, whom he loves (cf. 22:2).

A further prophecy of Christ is given by Jacob on his deathbed. Giving prophetic blessing to the twelve tribes through his twelve sons, Jacob says of his fourth son:

> The sceptre shall not depart from Judah,
> Nor a lawgiver from between his feet,
> Until Shiloh comes;
> And to him shall be the obedience of the people (49:10).

The Hebrew word *Shîylôh* (*Shiloh*) means "pacifier," "peacemaker" or "man of rest."[18] From the tribe of Judah a great peacemaker will arise. Years later Isaiah predicts:

> For unto us a Child is born,
> Unto us a Son is given;
> And the government will be upon His shoulder.
> And His name will be called
> Wonderful, Counselor, Mighty God,

---

[18] For the interpretation of "Shiloh" see Leupold, *Exposition of Genesis*, 2:1178-1185.

Everlasting Father, Prince of Peace.
Of the increase of His government and peace
There will be no end,
Upon the throne of David and over His kingdom,
To order it and establish it with judgment and justice
From that time forward, even forever.
The zeal of the LORD of hosts will perform this. (Isaiah 9:6–7).

God kept his word given through Jacob. The tribe's capacity for rule and sovereignty was not lost. The tribe of Judah did not lose its identity, as did the other tribes of Israel. Though perilously close to annihilation in the dark days of the Babylonian exile (Esther 3:13), God ensured their survival (Esther 4:13–14). It was not until about forty years after the death and resurrection of Christ that the Jewish nation was entirely destroyed (A.D. 70). By then the promise had been fulfilled. Shiloh had come, to whom "the obedience of the people" is to be. The promised Son had come down from heaven, suffered, bled and died, and in his last resurrection appearance revealed to his aged apostle the fulfilment of the prophecy.

In Revelation, John records seeing a vision of the heavenly order (Revelation 4–5). He hears a question ring out: "Who is worthy to open the scroll and to loose its seals?" In other words, "Who can bring about the will and purpose of God on earth? Who can bring the world to its God-appointed end?" There is a painful silence which causes John to weep until one of the elders says to him, "Do not weep. Behold, the Lion of the tribe of Judah, the Root of David, has prevailed to open the scroll and to loose its seven seals" (Revelation 5:5).

When John looks up he does not see a lion; he sees a lamb—with the marks of death upon it (Revelation 5:6). The Lion of Jacob's prophecy (49:9–10) is none other than "the Lamb of God who takes away the sin of the world!" (John 1:29). Two great types of Christ are united—the Lion is the Lamb!

GENESIS / **CONCLUSION**

Genesis is packed full of good things from the Lord. Four momentous events overshadow the first section of the book; four great men dominate the pages of the latter. In and through it all, God is at work.

Human sin is repugnant to the holy God. Punishment is well deserved by every person, young or old. Yet God's grace triumphs, for "Where sin abounded, grace abounded much more" (Romans 5:20). Faced with human inability, weakness and sinfulness, the Lord achieves his purposes. He has made his plans; nothing will thwart him.

Genesis is a treasury of spiritual gems. Here, all the major doctrines are to be found "in germ form" and attest to its divine authorship. The truths which are embodied here are expanded and developed throughout the rest of the Bible. Here is evidence that this book "is given by inspiration of God" (2 Timothy 3:16). Here is demonstrated the truth: "Prophecy never came by the will of man, but holy men of God spoke as they were moved by the Holy Spirit" (2 Peter 1:21). Who but the One who knows the end from the beginning could have provided such a reliable introduction?

> For I am God, and there is no other;
> I am God, and there is none like Me,
> Declaring the end from the beginning,
> And from ancient times things that are not yet done,
> Saying, "My counsel shall stand,
> And I will do all My pleasure" (Isaiah 46:9–10).

Through the ups and downs, the rebellions and sin, judgements and punishment, God has been working. A chosen people, the Israelites, have been established in the land of Egypt. But that is not to be their homeland. God has promised them the land of Canaan. As he prophesied to Abraham, "Know certainly that your descendants will be strangers in a land that is not theirs, and will serve its people and be afflicted by them four hundred years. And also the nation whom they serve I will judge; afterward they shall come out with great possessions" (15:13–14).

Three hundred years and more are to pass before there dawns the next great epoch in God's unfolding purposes—moving ever on toward the coming of Christ for his church.

GENESIS / **APPLICATION & REFLECTION**

1. Sovereign free choice

Each book of the Bible has a "prominent and dominant theme."[19] Historically considered, the book of Genesis is the book of beginnings, but viewed doctrinally, it is seen to be the book that deals with election—God's free and sovereign choice. In Genesis, God chooses Shem from the three sons of Noah as the one from whose line, ultimately, the Saviour will come; God chooses Abraham from an idolatrous people, and makes him the father of the chosen nation; God passes by Ishmael in favour of Isaac (Romans 9:7); he calls Jacob and not Esau (Romans 9:10-13); he appoints Joseph from all the twelve sons of Jacob/Israel to be the honoured instrument in providing for the family during famine, raising him to the second place of rule and authority in all Egypt; and, finally, he passes by the elder of Joseph's sons and grants the blessing of the firstborn to Ephraim (48:13-20). Time and again, the principle of God's sovereign choice is illustrated in the book of Genesis. Clear teaching regarding the sovereignty of God cannot be avoided by any who read the first book of the Bible.

2. Only by grace

The story of Genesis is the story of God's free grace (love and favour toward the undeserving). Having passed the death sentence upon Adam and Eve for their rebellion and sin, the Lord keeps his word. "Sin entered the world, and death through sin, and thus death spread to all men, because all sinned" (Romans 5:12). Yet, even as he pronounces judgement against them, the Lord gives a gracious promise. God will put enmity between the seed of the serpent and the seed of the woman. God will ensure the victory for the seed of the woman. When corruption is so widespread that God regrets having created human beings and determines, as a just punishment, to destroy every living thing, one man—Noah—finds grace in his eyes (6:8). In the face of total destruction, grace prevails and one family is saved. When human pride, arrogance and godlessness reach new heights, God punishes the people by scattering them over the earth. But by sovereign grace, God chooses and calls Abraham. The corruption and evil of Sodom and Gomorrah result in the Lord's raining down "brimstone and fire...from the LORD out of the heavens," overthrowing "those cities, all the plain, all the inhabitants of

---

[19] Arthur W. Pink, *Gleanings in Exodus* (Chicago: Moody Press, 1972), 7.

the cities, and what grew on the ground" (19:24-25). Yet grace prevails in the rescue of Lot. Grace overrules nature in the gift of a son to Abraham and Sarah (Romans 4:19-21). With Elmer Martens we conclude, "The gospel of God's intervention is unmistakable."[20]

3. Justification by faith

In Genesis the truth of justification by faith is first made known: "And he [Abraham] believed in the LORD, and he accounted it to him for righteousness" (15:6). God's dealings with Abraham were not on account of Abraham's obedience, or service, or love, but on account of *his faith*. Abraham's own body might be dead and Sarah long past the age of childbearing, yet Abraham was fully convinced that God had power to keep his word. As God accounted righteousness to Abraham, Abraham evidently had none of his own. Abraham, the sinner, was *declared* righteous. Believing God, he had righteousness reckoned to his account.

Christians enjoy the same blessing, but with one important difference: Abraham trusted God and looked *forward* to the promised son; we trust God and look *back* and see the glorious fulfilment in the promised Son. While Abraham had believed in the Lord for many years (Hebrews 11:8), it is here revealed that the faith which was "counted for righteousness" was the faith which believed what God had said concerning the promised seed. Abraham believed the promise of God which pointed to Christ.[21] Justification by faith is first indicated in the Scriptures in connection with the Saviour, in order that no one should separate justification from him.[22] There is no justification apart from Christ (Acts 13:38-39).

When Paul demonstrates that justification by faith alone is not a novel idea, but one that has always been the case since the Fall, he uses the stalwarts of the faith, Abraham and David. Of Abraham he says,

> For what does the Scripture say? "Abraham believed God, and it was accounted to him for righteousness." Now to him who works, the wages are not counted as grace but as debt. But to him who does not

---

[20] Elmer A. Martens, *Plot and Purpose in the Old Testament* (Leicester: Inter-Varsity Press, 1981), 9-30.
[21] Arthur W. Pink, *Gleanings in Genesis* (Chicago: Moody Press, 1922), 168.
[22] Leupold, *Exposition of Genesis*, 479.

work but believes on him who justifies the ungodly, his faith is accounted for righteousness.(Romans 4:3-5).

While the people of the Old Covenant period had a far less distinct picture of the Messiah than believers who are under the New Covenant, the essence of their faith was just the same—that is, "trust in God's grace and power to bring deliverance from sin."[23]

4. Prevailing prayer

The importance and value of prayer are indicated in Genesis. Abraham prayed for the righteous in Sodom and Lot was spared (18:22-32; 19:15-16). Abraham prayed to God and the life of Abimelech was spared (20:7,17). Abraham's servant prayed for guidance in the choice of a bride for Isaac and God answered his prayer (24:12-15). "Isaac pleaded with the LORD for his wife, because she was barren; and the LORD granted his plea, and Rebekah his wife conceived" (25:21). Jacob wrestled with God and prevailed (32:28).

> Jacob's victory was not, of course, a conquest. He had not mastered the Angel of God. Lame and helpless, he could only cling to the One who had laid hold of him. His victory was a victory of faith. He did not let go because he *could* not. God's blessing was all his hope and desire. Faith wins when it knows that all is lost, and clings to God alone. "Israel," the name God gave to Jacob, reflects this ambiguity. Normally it would be taken to mean "God Prevails." But the Lord turns the meaning around as He gives the name to Jacob: Jacob has prevailed with God. In that name Jacob's desperate faith is acknowledged by the Lord.[24]

While God is the sovereign Lord, "who works all things according to the counsel of his will" (Ephesians 1:11), and "does whatever he pleases" (Psalm 115:3), he nevertheless honours the prayers of his people. "The effective, fervent prayer of a righteous man avails much" (James 5:16).

---

[23] Vos, *Biblical Theology*, 44.
[24] Clowney, *The Unfolding Mystery*, 73.

EXODUS

MEANING	AUTHOR	KEY THOUGHT
"departure"	**Moses** (see Mark 12:26)	**Redeemed by blood**

THEME

Delivery from slavery and laws for life

THEME VERSE

You in Your mercy have led forth
The people whom You have redeemed...
EXODUS 15:13

EXODUS / **SUMMARY**

Introduction		1:1-7

PART 1 / **SLAVERY** — 1:8-4:17

a.	Oppression in Egypt	1:8-22
b.	The early life of Moses	
	a. His birth and adoption	2:1-10
	b. His attempt to assist his kinsmen	2:11-14
	c. His flight to Midian	2:15-20
	d. His marriage	2:21-22

Forty years pass (Acts 7:30)

c.	The Lord remembers his covenant with Abraham	2:23-24
d.	The call of Moses at the burning bush	3:1-10
e.	Moses' difficulties and God's remedies	3:11-4:17

PART 2 / **CONFRONTATION** — 4:18-12:30

a.	The return of Moses to Egypt	4:18-31
b.	Freedom demanded, oppression increased	5:1-21
c.	Moses' complaint and God's response	5:22-6:13
d.	The families of Moses and Aaron	6:14-27
e.	Aaron speaks for Moses before Pharoah	6:28-7:6
f.	Aaron's rod	7:8-13
g.	Conflict with Pharoah and the ten plagues	7:14-11:10
h.	The institution of the Passover	12:1-28
i.	The last plague	12:29-30

PART 3 / **LIBERATION** — 12:31-18:27

a.	The Exodus	12:31-42
b.	Regulations for Passover	12:43-51
c.	Experiences on the way to Mount Sinai	13:1-18:27

PART 4 / **LAW AND ORDER** — 19:1–40:38

a. Arrival at Sinai: God speaks with Moses — 19:1–25
b. The Ten Commandments — 20:1–26
c. Laws concerning servants, violence, control of animals, property, moral and ceremonial justice, Sabbaths, three annual feasts — 21:1–24:18
d. Direction for building the tabernacle — 25:1–27:21
e. Garments for the high priest — 28:1–43
f. Consecration of Aaron and his sons — 29:1–46
g. Altar of incense, ransom money, laver and oil — 30:1–38
h. Builders for the tabernacle and the Sabbath law — 31:1–18
i. The worship of the golden calf — 32:1–35
j. Command to leave Sinai — 33:1–6
k. Moses meets with the Lord — 33:7–23
l. New tablets of stone and the covenant renewed — 34:1–35
m. Preparation and erection of the tabernacle — 35:1–40:38

EXODUS

At the close of the book of Genesis, God's people were enjoying life in Egypt. Their days of famine were over and they were benefiting from the comfort and security of a new land. The Egyptians had accepted and respected them on account of all that Joseph had done for their nation. The book of Exodus opens three-and-a-half centuries later with a brief reference to the members of Jacob's family who had joined Joseph in Egypt. In the intervening years the experiences of the Israelites have changed dramatically. From respect, friendship and appreciation, the attitude of the Egyptians toward the Israelites has turned to dislike, distrust and persecution. The turning point is noted in the words: "Now there arose a new king over Egypt, who did not know Joseph" (1:8).

The Israelites went into Egypt as an extended family of seventy people (Genesis 46:27); they came out as a nation of almost two million men, women and children.[1] Once favoured friends, they had now become feared foes. They entered as honoured relatives of the prime minister of all Egypt; they left as the fugitive slaves of a despotic and oppressive government.

EXODUS / **AUTHOR**

Our Lord places the authorship of Exodus beyond all dispute. Replying to a trick question of the Sadducees concerning the resurrection, he says, "But concerning the dead, that they rise, have you not read in the book of Moses, in the burning bush passage, how God spoke to him, saying, 'I am the God of Abraham, the God of Isaac, and the God of Jacob'? He is not the God of the dead, but the God of the living. You are therefore greatly mistaken." (Mark 12:26–27; cf. Luke 20:37–38).

---

[1] The figure is calculated as 1,734,540 in James G. Murphy's *A Critical and Exegetical Commentary on the Book of Exodus* (1866; Minneapolis: Klock and Klock, 1979), 131.

EXODUS / **HISTORICAL SETTING**

The overriding theme of the book of Exodus is *deliverance*. The events recorded cover a period of Israel's history from slavery in Egypt to emancipation and consolidation on Mount Sinai (approximately 1526–1446 B.C.). The book opens in darkness and gloom, yet ends in glory. "It commences by telling how God *came down in grace* to deliver an enslaved people, and ends by declaring how God *came down in glory* to dwell in the midst of a redeemed people."[2] This portion of Israel's history is intimately tied up with the life of its central figure, Moses. Whereas Joseph was the man raised up by God as the deliverer of his people on their *entry* into Egypt, Moses was the man raised up by God four centuries later as the deliverer of his people on their *exit* from Egypt.

At the time of his death, "Moses was one hundred and twenty years old…. His eyes were not dim nor his natural vigour abated" (Deuteronomy 34:7). His life falls naturally into three distinct periods of forty years' duration: with Pharaoh's daughter in the royal court of Egypt (2:2–15); with Jethro in the land of Midian (2:16–4:19); and with the children of Israel in Egypt and in the wilderness (Exodus 4:20–Deuteronomy 34:5). Robert Lee summarizes the life of Moses like this: firstly, forty years thinking he was somebody; secondly, forty years learning he was a nobody; and, thirdly, forty years secondly discovering what God can do with a nobody.[3]

EXODUS / **OUTLINE**

After a brief introduction setting the scene, the book of Exodus records the history of Israel in four sections, the first two occurring in Egypt and the last two in the wilderness: slavery, confrontation, liberation and law and order. The first eighty years in the life of Moses fit within the first section of slavery in Egypt. The last forty years cover the three remaining more detailed sections—first in Egypt, then on the journey in the wilderness, and finally at Mount Sinai.

---

[2] Robert Lee, *The Outlined Bible: An Outline and Analysis of Every Book in the Bible* (London: Pickering and Inglis, 1930), analysis no. 2.
[3] Lee, *Outlined Bible*, analysis no. 2.

PART 1 / **SLAVERY (1:8-4:17)**

After a brief introduction indicating the growth in the Israelite population in Egypt, Moses the historian introduces the conditions of acute persecution. Fearing the rising numbers and the force of arms which this could represent, Pharaoh and the Egyptian authorities take steps to try to influence the birthrate of the Hebrews. Initiating a process of hard labour, they subject the Israelites to demanding tasks. The Egyptians "made their lives bitter with hard bondage—in mortar, in brick, and in all manner of service in the field" (1:14). When it is evident that this procedure is not having the desired effect, Pharaoh turns to more drastic measures. The Hebrew midwives, Shiphrah and Puah, are commanded to kill all male children at birth. Fearing God more than they fear the king, they let the boys live. In answer to criticism, they claim that the Israelite mothers spend less time in labour and give birth *before* the midwives arrive.

Into this dreadful situation a boy is born to a Levite couple, Amram and Jochebed (6:20). The mother conceals the child in their house for three months. Changing the hiding place to a waterproof basket in the bullrushes leads to discovery by Pharaoh's daughter. By a remarkable providence, the life of Moses is spared. The child is adopted; his own mother rears him; he eventually takes his place as a royal prince under the guardianship of Pharaoh's daughter. In consequence, "Moses was learned in all the wisdom of the Egyptians, and was mighty in words and deeds" (Acts 7:22). The education and upbringing Moses receives in the Egyptian court provide him with rich intellectual resources which are to stand him in good stead for the task to which the Lord calls him later. Nevertheless, Moses evidently considered himself to be lacking in communication skills (4:10).

When he is forty years old, Moses visits his Israelite brethren and events are set in motion which are to culminate in his flight from Egypt into the land of Midian (Acts 7:23–29). He sees an Egyptian guard beating an Israelite. The only way Moses can restrain the aggressor is to kill him. The only witness to the incident is the man on whose behalf he intervenes! The following day Moses sees two Hebrews fighting. It is not sufficient that they are a people beaten by the Egyptians; they are also beating each other! When Moses tries to stop the fight, he discovers that his killing of the Egyptian is well known. The Hebrew he had rescued on the previous occasion had evidently informed on him. What is more, the news is not kept within the Israelite community. Pharaoh is informed, and Moses is sought on a charge of murder. He flees from Egypt to the land of Midian, settles with the priest Jethro, whose daughter he marries, and has two sons.

Moses spends the next forty years as a shepherd in Midian. It is likely that those years of quiet reflection gave him a spiritual depth which it might have been difficult to acquire in all the worldly activity of a pagan palace.[4]

At the age of eighty, Moses is called to the service of God. The third period of forty years in his life begins. The cry of the Israelites in their bondage in Egypt has been heard: "So God heard their groaning, and God remembered His covenant with Abraham, with Isaac, and with Jacob. And God looked upon the children of Israel, and God acknowledged them" (2:24–25).

Through the miraculous burning bush, God makes Moses aware of his "life's work." At eighty, Moses is to deliver the Israelites from their bondage and slavery in Egypt (Acts 7:30–34). God always has a man or woman prepared for his work, but they are not always willing to serve him. Moses is reluctant to begin his difficult assignment. He presents many excuses. He is a reluctant leader. Yet what the Lord later says to Jeremiah might equally have been said to Moses:

> Before I formed you in the womb I knew you;
> Before you were born I sanctified you;
> And I ordained you a prophet (Jeremiah 1:5).

God's providential dealings with Moses have prepared him for his ministry. Moses is to prove a faithful servant in the household of God (Hebrews 3:5).

Moses has to convince the Israelites, as well as Pharaoh and the Egyptian authorities, that his assignment is from the Lord. In order to do this, God gives him power to perform three miracles—turning his rod into a snake, making his hand leprous and turning water taken from the river into blood. Claiming a lack of eloquence, Moses is given his older brother Aaron to be his assistant and his official mouthpiece.

---

[4] Raymond Brown, *Let's Read the Old Testament* (London: Victory Press, 1971), 9.

PART 2 / **CONFRONTATION (4:18–12:30)**

Returning to Egypt, Moses and Aaron convince the Israelite leadership of their divine commission. The two brothers then visit Pharaoh with the request that they might take the Israelites into the wilderness to hold a service of worship. They are under no obligation to explain the ulterior motive behind their request. Pharaoh's response is to increase the workload for the Israelites who, in turn, react against Moses. Moses remonstrates with the Lord, who graciously reinforces his promise to deliver the children of Israel from the Egyptian bondage:

> I am the LORD. I appeared to Abraham, to Isaac, and to Jacob… I have also established my covenant with them, to give them the land of Canaan…. And I have also heard the groaning of the children of Israel…and I have remembered my covenant…. I will take you as my people, and I will be your God…. And I will bring you into the land which I swore to give to Abraham, Isaac, and Jacob; and I will give it to you as a heritage: I am the LORD (6:2–8).

With this statement the relationship of God to the patriarchs, described in Genesis, is reaffirmed. The triple promise of seed, land and blessing was established in a covenant given to Abraham at the age of ninety-nine (Genesis 17:1–8), reiterated to Isaac (Genesis 26:3) and to Jacob (Genesis 28:14; 35:9–12). By the time of the Exodus, the first facet of the promise, that of seed (offspring, or descendants), has been realized. The families of Israel have been exceptionally fruitful (1:7). Fulfilment of the remaining parts of the promise, land and blessing, is now to be undertaken.

The ten plagues of Egypt

Over a period of about nine months, ten terrible plagues come upon the Egyptians. Throughout them all, the Israelites are protected.

1. The Nile is turned into blood—Pharaoh's heart grows hard (7:20,22).
2. Frogs cover the land—Pharaoh begs, promises freedom, hardens his heart again (8:6,8,15).

3. Lice on humans and animals—Pharaoh's heart grows hard (8:17,19).
4. Thick swarms of flies—Pharaoh bargains, hardens his heart again (8:24,28,32).
5. The livestock of the Egyptians die—Pharaoh's heart becomes hard (9:6,7).
6. Boils on humans and animals—the Lord hardens Pharaoh's heart (9:10,12).
7. Thunder, hail and fire—Pharaoh apologizes, promises, hardens his heart (9:23,27,28,34).
8. Locusts over all the land—Pharaoh begs, but the Lord hardens his heart (10:13,16-17,20).
9. Three days of thick darkness—Pharaoh bargains, but the Lord hardens his heart (10:22,24,27).
10. Death of all Egypt's firstborn—Pharaoh commands the Israelites to leave Egypt (12:29,31).

The most serious of the ten plagues of Egypt is kept till last. The wrath of God comes upon the Egyptians and the eldest son in every home dies on an appointed night (4:22-23). At the same time God calls for faith and obedience from his people Israel. The only way they are able to escape the coming judgement is to believe and obey the word of the Lord.

The Hebrews are instructed to take an unblemished lamb, offer it as a sacrifice, paint its blood on the doorposts and lintels of their homes, and cook and eat the flesh that very night. "And when I see the blood, I will pass over you; and the plague shall not be on you to destroy you when I strike the land of Egypt" (12:13).

PART 3 / **LIBERATION (12:31-18:27)**

The last devastating plague, the death of the firstborn throughout all Egypt, results in the command of Pharaoh that the Israelites should leave immediately. The great migration of just under two million people begins (see Map 2). The Israelites are miraculously led by a pillar of cloud by day and a pillar of fire by night.

When the Egyptians recover from the shock surrounding the departure of the Hebrew slaves, the army is dispatched and pursues them as far as the Red Sea. With the great sea before them, the wilderness to their left and to their right, and the Egyptians on the skyline behind them, the people react with great fear and bitterly criticize Moses. Moses responds by telling them, "Do not be afraid. Stand still, and see the salvation of the Lord, which He will accomplish for you today. For the Egyptians whom you see today, you shall see again no more forever. The LORD will fight for you, and you shall hold your peace" (14:13–14).

They are warned against panic. God delivers them in a remarkable and most unexpected manner—the sea divides and the children of Israel pass through the midst of the sea on dry ground, and the waters are a wall to them on either side.

The Lord hinders the Egyptian army as they try to follow over the bed of the Red Sea. Their chariot wheels come off, "so that they drove them with difficulty" (14:25). Returning the sea to its normal flow kills all the soldiers. Israel is free. Moses leads the people in a song of thanksgiving and praise to the Lord.

The two-month journey to Sinai continues in the Wilderness of Shur. At Marah the Israelites complain that the water is bitter and unfit to drink. The Lord shows Moses how to make it sweet. At Elim they enjoy a pleasant oasis. In the Wilderness of Sin they begin to grumble again, regretting having left the meat and bread of Egypt. The Lord provides quail and manna in abundance. At Rephidim, the people once more contend with Moses about the lack of water. A desperately needed supply miraculously flows from the rock struck by Moses. The Amalekites attack but are defeated. Success is attributed to the arms of Moses being held up by Aaron and Hur (to show the importance of prayer and reliance upon the Lord).

The arrival of his wife, his two sons and his father-in-law Jethro from Midian leads to some sound advice that eases the workload for Moses. A large number of assistants are appointed to make judgement in simple cases, thus leaving Moses free to tackle only the more serious problems which arise among the people.

PART 4 / **LAW AND ORDER (19:1–40:38)**

In the third month after leaving Egypt, the Israelites arrive at Mount Sinai. Over a period of ten months, events are to occur here which will have profound influence upon the whole of God's dealings with his

Map 2. Israel's journey from Egypt to Mount Sinai

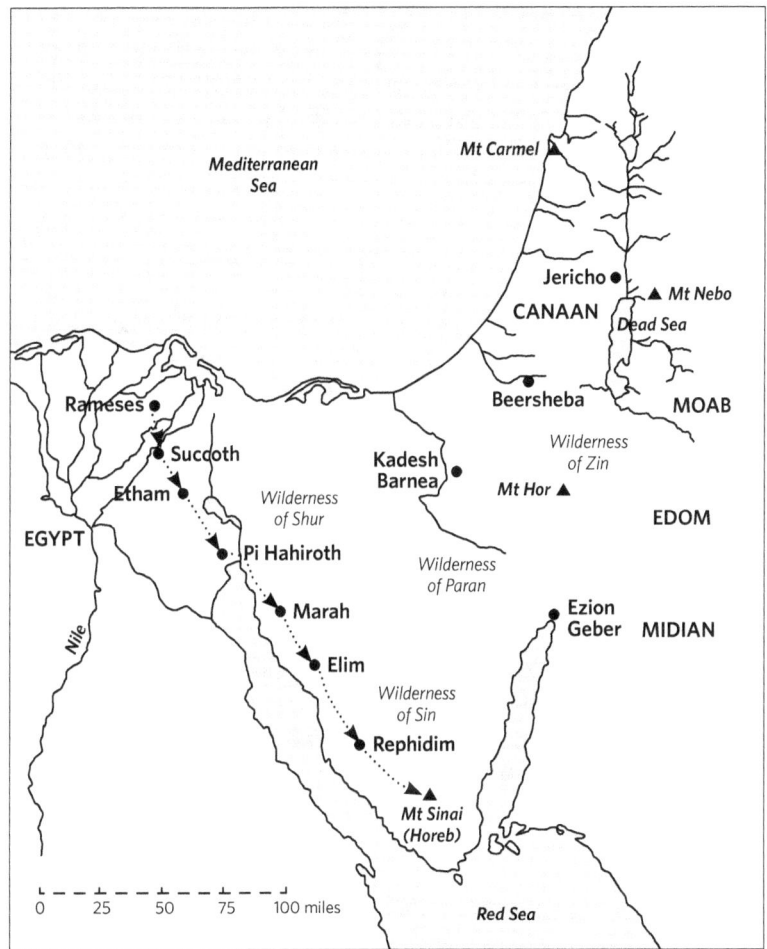

people. All subsequent divine revelation throughout the Scriptures will connect in some measure with this encounter. On Mount Sinai, God gives Moses the particulars of his law and instructions about the detailed design and construction of the tabernacle.

The law of Moses

In the history of the world nothing has happened, with the exception of the incarnation and the cross, which is so significant, so solemn, so profound, as the giving of the law by God himself at Sinai.[5] The ethos in which the law was given is striking. There was the warning of instant death to any person or animal that touched the mountain or its base. This was accompanied by "thunderings and lightnings, and a thick cloud on the mountain; and the sound of the trumpet was very loud, so that all the people who were in the camp trembled" (19:16). It was essential for humanity to learn the nature of God's holiness and the character of human sinfulness. The Lord uses various means to instill a right appreciation of the moral gulf that exists between the Creator and his human creatures.

The law makes sin recognizable for what it is. By this the Israelites could see their corruption and sense their misery. God's commandments are addressed to the heart. The commandments require not only outward actions, but also inward affections; they require not only the outward act of obedience, but also the inward affection of love. The law of God forbids not only the act of sin, but the desire and inclination: "Man's law binds the hands only, God's law binds the heart."[6]

The covenant established with Moses (19:5) is a continuation of the one established first with Noah and then later with Abraham. In the covenant with Moses, the Lord keeps his promise made 400 years earlier (Genesis 15:13). Through Moses, God provides additional instructions to show the Israelites how they are to conduct themselves as the people of God—as God's "special treasure…above all people.… a kingdom of priests and a holy nation" (19:5–6). Here the Lord sets out the principles and rules by which he will govern his people. Israel is to be governed, not by a democracy, the rule of the majority; nor by an aristocracy, the rule of the few; but by a theocracy, the rule of God. Consequently the Old Covenant law is an intermingling of moral, civil and ceremonial laws.

The Ten Commandments summarize the duties of the Israelites as the people of God (20:1–17).

In the wisdom and grace of God, that which most glorifies the Lord also tends most to the good of his people. The Lord gives laws which,

---

[5] F.B. Meyer, *Devotional Commentary on Exodus* (Grand Rapids: Kregel Publications, 1978), 219.

[6] Thomas Watson, *The Ten Commandments* (1692; London: Banner of Truth Trust, 1959), 45.

when obeyed, would be most beneficial for the Israelites.

> The LORD came from Sinai…
> From his right hand
> Came a fiery law for them.
> Yes, He loves the people (Deuteronomy 33:2–3).

Love *from* God provided the law; love *for* God seeks to fulfil the law (Psalm 119:97,101; cf. John 14:15).

The tabernacle

Central to the worship life of the Israelites was to be "the tabernacle of the tent of meeting" (39:32). At the heart of the tabernacle was the altar of sacrifice. A tribe was selected and ordained to function as priests. Men had served in this capacity before the establishment of the priesthood under Aaron (19:22,24). Abel, Noah, Abraham and Jacob functioned in a priestly capacity when they built altars and offered sacrifices to the Lord (Genesis 4:4; 8:20; 22:13; 31:54). These *occasional* priests were now to be replaced by a *hereditary* priesthood to carry out all the services associated with the tabernacle and the worship of God.

God's design for the tabernacle, entrusted to Moses on Mount Sinai, was to be followed to the letter (25:9). The people contributed materials, skills and labour. The outer courtyard was a fenced rectangle with one wide door for entry (27:9,13,16).[7] In the courtyard stood the altar for animal sacrifices, constructed of acacia wood overlaid with bronze. Between the tabernacle proper and the altar stood the laver of bronze, a large bowl filled with water for the priests to wash their hands and their feet before entering the enclosed tabernacle (30:17–21). (See Figures 5 and 6.)

In the tabernacle proper there were two rooms, "the holy place and the Most Holy" (26:33), separated by a thick veil. In the first room, the holy place, "the sanctuary" (Hebrews 9:2), stood three items: the lampstand, the table of shewbread and the altar of incense. The solid

---

[7] Kiene gives the conversion of the old Hebrew cubit as 52.52 cm or 20.7 inches. Paul F. Kiene, *The Tabernacle of God in the Wilderness of Sinai* (Grand Rapids: Zondervan, 1977), 30.

gold lampstand, with its seven branches (25:31–40; 26:35), burned day and night and gave light to the holy place. The table of shewbread was made of acacia wood overlaid with gold (25:23–30). Newly baked bread was placed on the table on the Sabbath and replaced every seven days. The twelve loaves, representing the tribes of Israel, were a thank offering placed, or "shown," before the face of the Lord continually. The altar of incense was also made of acacia wood overlaid with gold (30:1–10). The name *altar* links it with the altar of sacrifice. The atonement was symbolized in the altar of sacrifice reconciling the Israelite with God. The altar of incense represented the reconciled Israelites in their prayer and worship ascending to the Lord.[8]

The second room, the Most Holy, the Holy of Holies or "the Holiest of All" (Hebrews 9:3), housed the ark of the covenant, also called the ark of the Testimony (26:34). The ark contained "the golden pot that had the manna, Aaron's rod that budded, and the tablets of the covenant" (Hebrews 9:4).[9] This inner room was entered only once a year by the high priest on the Day of Atonement to sprinkle the sacrificial blood upon the mercy seat (Leviticus 16;14–15; Hebrews 9:7).

The ark of the covenant, made of acacia wood, was overlaid with pure gold, inside and out. The lid of the ark was the mercy seat made of pure gold with two golden cherubim on either end facing the mercy seat (25:10–22):

> Draw a straight line from the centre of the Gate to the Mercy-Seat. You go through the Altar, through the Laver, through the Door; you pass the Table of Shewbread on your right hand, and the golden Lampstand on your left; through the Altar of Incense, through the Veil, to the Ark, covered by the Mercy-Seat, in the Holy of Holies. This is the true Pilgrim's Progress from the camp outside to the immediate presence of God.[10]

---

[8] According to Hebrews 9:4 in the RAV, the altar of incense is located inside the Holy of Holies. The literal words of Hebrews 9:4 are "having a golden censer" (AV). The censer from the altar was taken into the Holy of Holies once a year on the Day of Atonement (Leviticus 16:12–13). The altar remained outside the Holy of Holies.

[9] When the ark was eventually housed in the temple at Jerusalem, it contained only the two slabs of stone upon which were written the Ten Commandments (1 Kings 8:9).

[10] C.L. Maynard, cited by A.M. Hodgkin, *Christ in All the Scriptures* (London: Pickering and Inglis, 1907), 21.

Figure 5. Plan of the tabernacle to scale

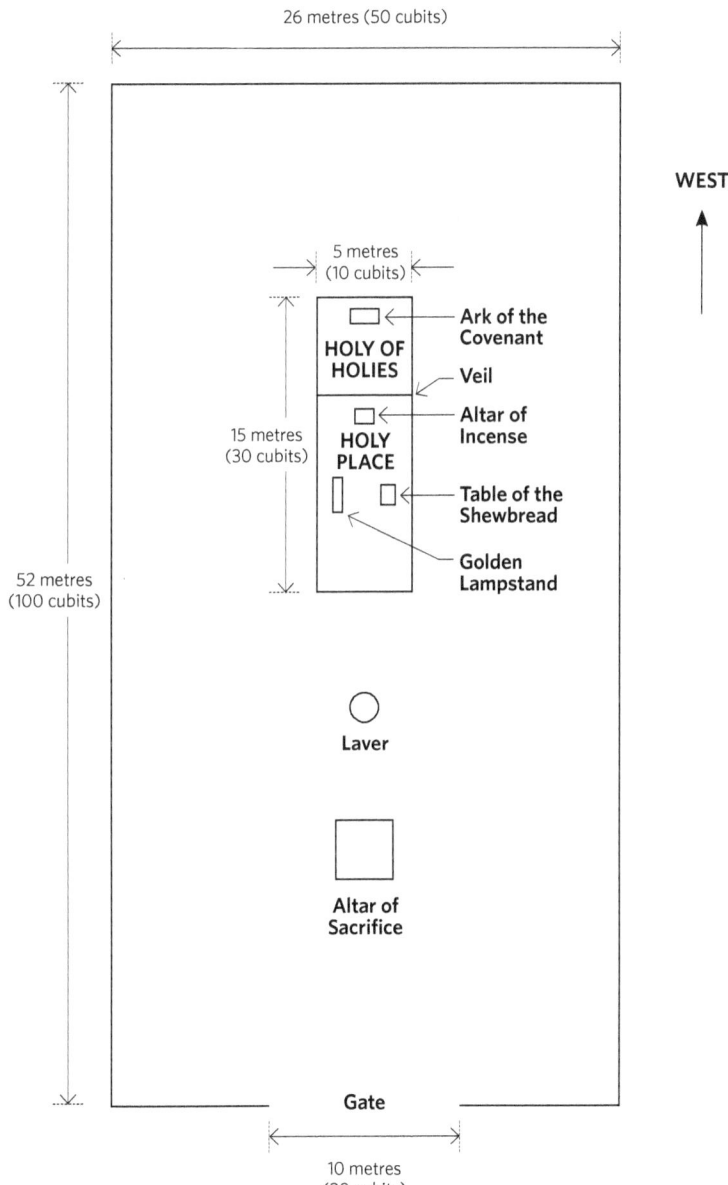

Measurement conversion: 1 cubit = 52.52 cm or 20.7 inches

On completion of all the work, the tabernacle was consecrated by the Lord:

> Then the cloud covered the tabernacle of meeting, and the glory of the LORD filled the tabernacle. And Moses was not able to enter the tabernacle of meeting, because the cloud rested above it, and the glory of the Lord filled the tabernacle (40:34–35).

EXODUS / **CHRIST AND HIS CHURCH**

In 1 Corinthians 10, the apostle Paul refers back to the events covered by the book of Exodus. He speaks of the Israelites being under the cloud, passing through the sea, drinking from the rock. Some of those Israelites became idolaters; others committed sexual immorality; still others, he says, tempted Christ and were destroyed by serpents, and numerous individuals murmured and complained against God. Paul sums up all these references in this way: "Now all these things happened to them as examples, and they were written for our admonition, upon whom the ends of the ages have come. Therefore let him who thinks he stands take heed lest he fall" (1 Corinthians 10:11–12).

TYPES

So much in this book of Exodus has a spiritual message and application for Christians: "For whatever things were written before were written for our learning, that we through the patience and comfort of the Scriptures might have hope" (Romans 15:4). Exodus is packed full of Christological significance.

- *Israel's bondage* in Egypt (1:11–14) is a symbol of the sinner's slavery to sin (Romans 6:17–18).
- The *Passover Lamb* (12:5,7,13) is a type of Christ[11] and his precious blood (John 1:29; 1 Peter 1:19; 1 Corinthians 5:7; Revelation 5:6). Not one of its bones shall be broken (12:46; cf. Numbers 9:12; Psalm 34:20; John 19:36).

---

[11] A type is a figure, episode or symbolic factor resembling some future reality in such a way as to foreshadow or prefigure it (see pages 28–32).

Figure 6. The tabernacle in the wilderness

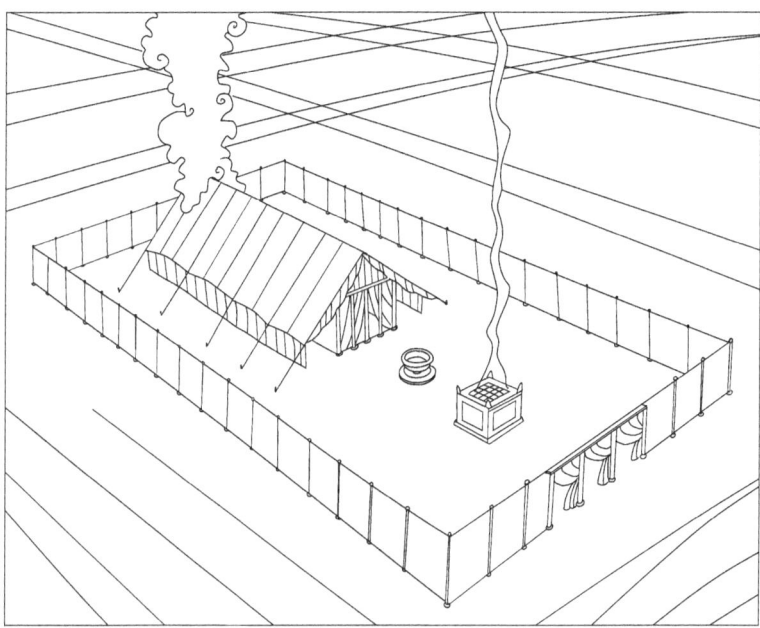

- The *pillar of cloud and fire* (14:19; cf. 13:21–22) is a type of Christ's presence with his people (John 14:18; Matthew 28:20).
- The *song of Moses* (15:1–19) is a type of songs of spiritual victory (Revelation 15:3–4).
- The *mixed multitude* (12:38) symbolizes the regenerate and unregenerate in the visible church (Matthew 13:24–30,36–43).
- The *waters of Marah and Elim* (15:23–27) are a type of bittersweet experiences in the Christian life (1 Peter 1:6).
- The *manna* (16:4) is a type of Christ, the bread of life (John 6:31–35).
- *Water from the rock* (17:6) is a type of Christ, who provides living water (1 Corinthians 10:4; John 4:10; 7:37–39).

The tabernacle

The earthly tabernacle was built to God's exact specifications (25:9). It was designed to represent spiritual realities (Hebrews 8:5). The person and work of the Lord Jesus Christ are prefigured in the construction, materials and furnishings of the tabernacle in the wilderness.[12] The tabernacle in the wilderness represents our Saviour's incarnation on earth: "And the Word became flesh and dwelt among us, and we beheld His glory, the glory as of the only begotten of the Father, full of grace and truth" (John 1:14—the Greek word translated *dwelt* is from a root word meaning *tabernacled*).

All the beauty of the earthly tabernacle was internal. Viewed externally it was a long, dark-coloured, unattractive tent of badger skin. Inside it was beautiful in the extreme, glistening with gold and exquisitely coloured tapestries. Here is the ordinary, plain, external appearance and extraordinary internal beauty of Christ (Isaiah 53:2; 52:14; Hebrews 7:26; 4:15; 1 John 3:5). Not only is there an absence of all sin in Christ; there is also a positive holiness and righteousness. He is *Jehovah Tsidkenu*, "the LORD our Righteousness" (Jeremiah 23:6); for he is altogether righteous. He is righteous in name, righteous in deed, righteous in mind, righteous in heart; he is righteous altogether—through and through, inside and out.

The *altar of sacrifice* speaks of the atoning work of the Saviour and the fellowship with God which we enjoy through him (Hebrews 13:10; 1 John 1:7).

The *ark* containing the unbroken law of God speaks of Christ, who alone kept it utterly and completely in spirit and in letter (Psalm 40:8; cf. Hebrews 10:5-7).

The *mercy seat* over the ark was covered with gold to symbolize God's royal throne. To those who come to God through Jesus Christ, that royal throne of judgement is none other than the mercy seat. We are justified freely by His grace through the redemption that is in Christ Jesus, whom God set forth as a propitiation by His blood" (Romans 3:24-25). The Greek word translated *propitiation* is from *hilasterion* meaning "mercy seat" (cf. Hebrews 9:5).

> In the court stood the altar of burnt offering and the laver, pointing forward to Christ through whose blood we are justified and through whose Spirit we are sanctified. In the holy place were to be found the table of shewbread, the seven-branched lampstand,

---

[12] For a detailed study of the furnishings and materials used in the tabernacle as representing the character and work of Christ, see Kiene, *The Tabernacle of God in the Wilderness*, 9-162.

and the altar of incense, respectively foreshadowing Christ as our Bread of Life, our source of Light, and our Intercessor. Finally, there was the Holy of Holies with its ark of the covenant, containing the law. But between the Glorious Presence and God's holy law which man had transgressed was the blood-sprinkled cover, the "mercy seat," an appropriate symbol and type of Christ, our Atonement. The Holy of Holies was the image of heaven itself; the ark, a symbol of God's throne. The entire tabernacle, being the abode of Jehovah, was a beautiful and most appropriate prophecy of Christ, in whom all the fulness of the Godhead dwells bodily.[13]

The priesthood

On Mount Sinai, God gave Moses the details of the Old Covenant law. He also directed Moses about the particular construction of the tabernacle and its furnishings. The third area of instruction given on the holy mount concerned the establishment of a priesthood.

The priestly line of Aaron foreshadows the work of the Lord Jesus Christ as the great High Priest for his people. Aaron and his sons are mentioned twenty-four times in this book of the Scriptures. Neither Aaron nor Christ is self-appointed (28:1; cf. Hebrews 5:4–6). The Lord Jesus Christ is now in heaven for "we have a great High Priest who has passed through the heavens" (Hebrews 4:14). His service is not yet completed; he is needed to function as our High Priest. His service as High Priest will continue until the whole church is complete and delivered safely to the Father (Hebrews 7:25).[14]

Clothing for the high priest

In the book of Exodus, detailed attention is given to the making of clothing and ornaments for the high priest to wear (see Figure 7). A number of Bible scholars, past and present, have seen significance and meaning in these articles, drawing comparison with the person

---

[13] William Hendriksen, *Survey of the Bible: A Treasury of Bible Information* (Welwyn: Evangelical Press, 1976), 212–213.

[14] The consecration of the high priest (29:1–37) and his sacred duties, together with their rich significance in relation to the Lord Jesus Christ, will be considered in detail in the next chapter on the book of Leviticus.

and work of the Saviour.[15] A word of caution must, however, be expressed. While the parallels may well be intended by the Lord, there is no clear New Testament warrant for being dogmatic on all details.

The *high priest's garments* (28:1–43; 39:1–31) may be seen to set forth the varied excellencies and glories of our High Priest, Jesus Christ.

God uses types as pictures to teach his people what would otherwise be virtually incomprehensible. Not only do the furnishings of the tabernacle add to the vision of Christ's glory, but the clothing of the high priest speaks much of Christ. God designed each part of the clothing and ornaments "for glory and for beauty" (28:2). But this was not in order that Aaron might appear admirable, magnificent or stunning—though he did. It was designed to represent the glories of the Lord Jesus Christ. Of that there can be no doubt. Every brilliant colour shone and the richest jewels dazzled.

> The rainbow's varied hues, the sun's meridian light, seemed to concentrate in a human form. Earth brought her best. Art framed them with a Spirit-given skill…. This workmanship would never have seen birth, except to show His all-surpassing worth.[16]

The *tunic* was made of finely woven linen. It covered the whole body from the neck to the feet, and the arms down to the wrists. It was worn next to the skin. The spotless pure cotton was of the finest possible quality. This symbolizes the personal perfection and purity of our Saviour, from head to toe.

The *robe* was slightly smaller than the tunic and worn over it. It did not cover the arms and reached only just below the knees. This robe was entirely blue. Blue is the colour of the sky. By this colour the heavenly origins of the Lord are displayed.

The *ephod* was a tunic shorter than the robe, like a tabard, or two aprons, one covering the front, the other covering the back, with broad shoulder straps for support (28:7). It was a mixture of dazzling colour—"gold and blue and purple and scarlet thread, and fine linen

---

[15] See Kiene, *The Tabernacle of God in the Wilderness*, 162–173; Henry Law, *The Gospel in Exodus* (1855; London: Banner of Truth Trust, 1967), 134–139; Arthur W. Pink, *Gleanings in Exodus* (Chicago: Moody Press, 1972), 259–272.

[16] Law, *Gospel in Exodus*, 134.

thread, artistically woven" (28:6). The most skilful artisans worked these materials. This embroidery may be intended to signify the fact that all rare and beautiful graces are beautifully combined in the person of Jesus Christ.

The *belt* (band) for the ephod, made of the same material and design, was fastened around the waist, holding the ephod, the robe and the tunic (28:8). This belt signifies service. It speaks of the Lord Jesus Christ in all his matchless perfections demonstrating his peerless character, serving and ministering for his church and to his church (Matthew 20:28; cf. John 13:4).

The *breastplate*, made of the same material and design, was worn over the ephod, above the belt (28:15). Composed of two pieces of cloth the same size, it was fastened together at the bottom and formed a kind of pocket in which were placed the Urim and Thummim. It measured a handspan across and a handspan down.

Figure 7. The elaborate and symbolic garments of the high priest

On the front of this richly embroidered breastplate, twelve precious stones were set, each one representing one of the tribes of Israel. This signifies how much the church is loved. We who are the Lord's have been loved "with an everlasting love" and with lovingkindness God has drawn us to himself (Jeremiah 31:3). We are always upon the heart of our High Priest, our Lord and Saviour. Christ Jesus the great High Priest knows his own, loves his own, prays for his own, guards his own, cherishes his own, delights in his own.

The *turban* of fine white linen is surrounded with a belt of blue.

(Does this suggest that all our Saviour's thoughts are centred in heaven?) On this a golden plate is fixed, engraved with the words: "Holiness to the LORD" (28:36). So everything that Jesus Christ is, what Jesus thinks, what Jesus has done and is doing, and all his people in him, are "Holiness to the LORD."

EXODUS / **CONCLUSION**

The great theme of the book of Exodus is redemption accomplished. Responding to the cries of the Israelites in slavery under the Egyptians, God comes down to rescue his people. They are liberated, led through the wilderness and taught the fundamentals of God-honouring behaviour—in society, home and personal life. Here the foundational truths of salvation are established, not so much in the form of explicit and systematic doctrine, but rather through types, symbols and Israel's history. In the book of Exodus, the glorious types of our Saviour and Redeemer, the Lord Jesus Christ, shine forth. We meet him on every page, in every event. The New Testament guards us against excess and error by leading us to see, with the eye of faith, the Christ who is "in all the Scriptures" (Luke 24:27). We see Christ as the spotless Lamb, the water-giving Rock, the manna from heaven, the cloud and fire of the constant presence of the living God. We see him at Sinai—in the tabernacle, the altar, the shewbread, the lampstand, the veil, the ark, the mercy seat—in the priesthood, its garments and breastplate.

In Exodus we see our deliverance from the slavery of sin (Romans 6:6), and our hazardous journey to the promised land (1 Peter 1:4–6), following after the Lord Jesus Christ (Hebrews 12:1–2).

Through the law of God at Sinai, the people were taught the need for the tabernacle and all that it represents. The law serves to highlight human inability, guilt and sin. The tabernacle, with its furnishings, priesthood and ceremonies, is a type, a preparation for the one sacrifice and the one High Priest, who having "by himself purged our sins" (Hebrews 1:3), has entered the heavenly sanctuary bearing his own precious blood on behalf of his people. He is "able to save to the uttermost" because he lives forever to make intercession for us (Hebrews 7:25).

The book of Exodus points distinctly and unwaveringly to Jesus Christ, the Son of God!

EXODUS / **APPLICATION AND REFLECTION**

The opening books of the Bible contain much more than an inspired history of events that happened thousands of years ago. They are filled with illustrations and pictures of the great doctrines of our faith which are explained and amplified in the New Testament.

1. Redemption

Each book of the Bible has a *prominent* and *dominant theme*. As we noted in the previous chapter, historically considered, the book of Genesis is the book of beginnings, but viewed doctrinally it is seen to be the book which deals with election—God's free and sovereign choice. Historically, the book of Exodus deals with the deliverance of Israel from Egypt, but viewed doctrinally it is concerned with redemption. Just as the first book teaches that God elects, or chooses, for salvation, so the second book teaches how God saves: by redemption—that is, by costly deliverance. Exodus is therefore a powerful illustration, or type, of that redemption from sin which comes through the incarnation, suffering and sacrificial death of the Lord Jesus Christ.[17]

Taking the theme of redemption, A.W. Pink bases his outline on one verse:

You in Your mercy have led forth
The people whom You have redeemed;
You have guided them in Your strength
To Your holy habitation (15:13).

From this Pink draws out a fivefold division for the book of Exodus:

The structure of the book of Exodus

1. The need for redemption—a people enslaved	Exodus 1-6
2. The might of the Redeemer—displayed in the plagues	Exodus 7-11
3. The character of redemption—purchased by blood, emancipated by power	Exodus 12-18
4. The duty of the redeemed—obedience to the Lord	Exodus 19-24
5. The provision made for the failures of the redeemed—tabernacle and services	Exodus 25-40

---

[17] Pink, *Gleanings in Exodus*, 7.

2. Faith and obedience

These two, faith and obedience, belong together: "faith without works is dead' (James 2:20). The obedience of the Hebrew slaves made their deliverance possible (12:7,13). God told them what they had to do and they acted upon it. Obedience to the gospel is essential to salvation (Hebrews 5:9; cf. 1 Peter 4:17). Paul, the great champion of justification by faith alone, speaks of the "obedience to the faith" (Romans 1:5; 16:26). Biblical writers use the word "faith" in two different ways. It is used *objectively*, as in "the faith which was once for all delivered to the saints" (Jude 3). In this usage it is the body of truth, the doctrines given by God. The translation of Romans 1:5 in the Revised Authorized Version would then be correct, namely "obedience to the faith"—in other words, obedience to the fundamental doctrines of Christianity which a regenerate person exhibits. Alternatively, "faith" may be understood *subjectively* as the impulse of a regenerate soul: "By grace you have been saved through faith, and that not of yourselves; it is the gift of God" (Ephesians 2:8). Consequently Romans 1:5 would then be understood as "the obedience of faith," meaning the obedience to the Word of God which true faith produces. Either way, it amounts to much the same thing. Scripture testifies clearly that God-given faith obeys the doctrines of God's Word. There is no real conflict between Paul and James. Paul is as convinced as James that genuine faith produces obedience (James 2:26).

3. Prevailing prayer

When the Amalekite soldiers came to intercept the Israelite travellers, Moses knew that this emergency situation called for prayer. Moses' arms upheld (17:12) are symbolic of mutual support in prevailing prayer (Acts 2:42; 4:23-31; Ephesians 6:18-19; James 5:16-18).

4. The law

The law of Sinai was a burden placed upon the Israelites. It was impossible, even for the most devout and zealous, to keep it. The law made the Israelites conscious of their inability and sinfulness and caused them to seek mercy from God through the appointed sacrificial system. They waited "for the consolation of Israel" and longed for the coming of the promised deliverer (Luke 2:25; Galatians 3:24). The Old Covenant could not bring salvation, but those who trusted in the mercy of God were forgiven in anticipation of the death of Christ. The law of Moses was holy (Romans 7:12) and spiritual (Romans 7:14), but "weak through the flesh" (Romans 8:3). Sinners have no ability to obey the whole of the law of God, which is why God gave the promise of a new covenant at the same time as he gave the Old Covenant law: "The Lord your God will circumcise your heart and the heart of your descendants, to love the Lord your God with all your heart and with all your soul, that you may live" (Deuteronomy 30:6). This promise was to be amplified by the prophets. For example, "I will give you a new heart and put a new spirit within you.... I will put My Spirit within you and cause you to walk in My statutes, and you will keep My judgements and do them" (Ezekiel 36:26-27). Everything in the command was to be fulfilled in the promise.

In the New Covenant, the Lord keeps his promises given through Moses and the prophets. Nearly 1,500 years after Sinai, at the Jerusalem Council in the early years of the Christian church, the relation of believers to the law of Moses comes under discussion. The apostle Peter resists the imposition of the law of Moses upon Gentile converts in words that are highly instructive:

> Now therefore, why do you test God by putting a yoke on the neck of the disciples which neither our fathers nor we were able to bear? But we believe that through the grace of the Lord Jesus Christ we shall be saved in the same manner as they (Acts 15:10-11).

Peter claims that such a requirement would offend God. He calls it a weight that no Jew could bear. He emphasizes that, whether Jew or Gentile, the way of salvation is now the same: we are saved by grace alone, through faith alone, in Christ alone! "But some of the sect of the Pharisees who believed rose up, saying, 'It is necessary to circumcise them, and to command them to keep the law of Moses'" (Acts 15:5). To these Pharisees, it seems to have been less important that Jews become Christians than that all nations should become Jews. Peter insists that requiring Gentiles to obey the law of Moses is to *test* or *tempt* God. Peter's argument is plain: circumcision and the observance of the law of Moses cannot be necessary for Gentile converts because God has acknowledged them (Acts 15:7-9). The Lord demonstrated his acceptance of Gentiles, uncircumcised and without the law of Moses, when his Holy Spirit descended upon Cornelius, his family and his friends (Acts 10:44-48). To require Gentiles to obey the law of Moses would not only tempt God, it would put an impossible yoke upon Gentile believers. A yoke is an emblem of slavery (1 Timothy 6:1). From Sinai onward, the law was a yoke. The history of Israel from Sinai to Christ was a record of heartache and struggle under the weight. They often broke the yoke and burst the bonds in rebellion and transgression (Jeremiah 5:5). Even for the godly, the law of Moses was a stern disciplinarian to prepare them to receive Christ that they might be justified by faith in him alone (Galatians 3:24). If this yoke could not be borne by those Jews at the council nor by their fathers[18] (Acts 15:10), then it follows that the law of Moses should no longer be required of anyone, Jew or Gentile, since converted Jews now "believe that through the grace of the Lord Jesus Christ" they will be saved in the same manner as Gentiles (Acts 15:11).

So the apostle Peter settles the debate by asserting, in effect, that salvation is by grace alone through faith alone in Christ alone. The reasoning of Acts 15 would seem to answer the issue for all time. Sadly that is not the case. Since the days of the New Testament the relationship of the law of Moses to Christians, whether Jew or Gentile, has been the focus of widely differing opinions often resulting in a considerable lack of Christian charity.

The difficulty centres in the meaning and definition of "the law of Moses." What is "the yoke" of Acts 15:10 which is not to be imposed upon Gentile believers? Some maintain that the yoke "is not the moral law, and the just restraints of religion; but the ceremonial laws and customs of the Jews."[19] Others insist that the yoke is not "circumcision, but the Mosaic law in general, and that viewed chiefly as a condition of salvation.... The law, indeed, itself was a heavy burden, but it was insupportable when regarded as a condition of salvation."[20] But it is difficult, if not impossible, to see how either of these interpretations can be derived from the words of Peter.

Calvin, with characteristic clarity and forcefulness argues:

> it is easy to gather from the actual situation that he [Peter] is not speaking about ceremonies alone...not only holy men, but also a great many hypocrites acquitted themselves correctly and punctiliously in the outward observation of the rites. Yes, and what is more, it would

---

[18] This is not a reference to Abraham, Isaac and Jacob—for whom circumcision was not a yoke but a promise—but the fathers since the time of Moses. See Paton J. Gloag, *A Critical and Exegetical Commentary on the Acts of the Apostles*, 2 vol. (1870; Minneapolis: Klock and Klock, 1979), 2:73.

[19] Albert Barnes, *Notes, Explanatory and Practical, on the Acts of the Apostles* (London: Routledge and Sons, n.d.), 238.

[20] Gloag, *Acts of the Apostles*.

not be such a difficult thing to satisfy the moral law, if it were satisfied with bodily obedience only, and did not demand spiritual righteousness. For it is given to many to control their hands and feet, but it is really extremely hard to manage all the affections, so that perfect self-restraint and purity reign in the soul as well as in the body. Accordingly it is ridiculous for people to limit Peter's word to ceremonies.... When he says that they were unable to bear the yoke of the Law, it is established that it is impossible to keep the Law.[21]

Many of the Puritans viewed the Ten Commandments as the moral law of God.[22] They then reasoned that this moral law is still in force for believers. The law, they asserted, is only abolished in regard to justification and in reference to its curse. In other respects, "Believers are to make great use of the moral law."[23]

It is argued by some Christians that the yoke, the law of Moses, was completely superseded by the incarnation, suffering, death, resurrection and ascension of the Lord Jesus Christ, followed by the sending of the Holy Spirit to establish the New Covenant: "For the law was given through Moses, but grace and truth came through Jesus Christ" (John 1:17). The Christian, in distinction from the believing Jew under the Old Covenant, is freed from all responsibilities to obey Moses. The Christian loves and obeys Jesus Christ (Romans 7:1–6; John 14:15). Freed from the heavy and burdensome law of Moses, the New Covenant believer is constrained by the love of Christ (2 Corinthians 5:14). He or she is never antinomian (without moral law) but is always "under law toward Christ" (1 Corinthians 9:21, see context).[24]

No man who lived under the Old Covenant ever fulfilled the law of Moses, and in that sense really bore its yoke. That is why the Old Covenant had its Day of Atonement and its many arrangements with offerings and sacrifices to remove sins. All these sacrifices were *types* of the sacrifice of Christ, and through faith the Old Covenant believer was linked to the Promised One, that is, Christ himself. For the intolerable yoke of the law, the Saviour

---

[21] John Calvin, *The Acts of the Apostles 14–28* (1554; Edinburgh: Saint Andrew Press, 1966), 37–38.
[22] Watson, *The Ten Commandments*, 6.
[23] Watson, *The Ten Commandments*, 45.
[24] It is not the purpose of this book to argue for one position in preference to another, merely to illustrate the diversity of opinion that exists among Bible-believing scholars and teachers.

substituted his gospel yoke, a wonderful yoke which itself bears every believer.[25] Jesus invites: "Come to Me, all you who labor and are heavy laden, and I will give you rest. Take My yoke upon you and learn from Me, for I am gentle and lowly in heart, and you will find rest for your souls" (Matthew 11:28-29).

Paul shows the connection between circumcision and the Old Covenant law when he warns the Christians of Galatia, "Stand fast therefore in the liberty by which Christ has made us free, and do not be entangled again with a yoke of bondage" (Galatians 5:1; cf. verses 2-3). In accord with the apostle Peter at the Jerusalem Council, Paul insists that the only remedy that is effective for salvation is "faith working through love" (Galatians 5:6).

The Lord Jesus criticized the scribes and Pharisees, "for they bind heavy burdens, hard to bear, and lay them on men's shoulders" (Matthew 23:4). The one and only means of salvation ordained by God is "'the grace of the Lord Jesus,' and not...observance of the law. Even in the Old Covenant the saving means was the Old Testament gospel and promise of the Messiah, and not the law."[26] Nothing, be it the law of the rabbis, or the law of Moses, or anything else, must be added "to the sole-sufficing grace of the only Saviour."[27]

---

[25] R.C.H. Lenski, *The Interpretation of the Acts of the Apostles* (Minneapolis: Augsburg Publishing House, 1961), 604.

[26] Lenski, *The Interpretation of the Acts of the Apostles*, 604–605.

[27] Rudolf Stier, *The Words of the Apostles* (1869; Minneapolis: Klock and Klock, 1981), 239.

LEVITICUS

MEANING	AUTHOR	KEY THOUGHT
"referring to the Levites"	**Moses** *(commonly accepted)*	**God is holy**

THEME

Worshipping and serving the Lord

THEME VERSE
"You shall be holy, for I the Lord your God am holy."
LEVITICUS 19:2

LEVITICUS / **SUMMARY**

PART 1 / **THE LAW OF SACRIFICE**   1:1-7:38

a.	The burnt offering	1:1-17
b.	The cereal offering	2:1-16
c.	The peace offering	3:1-17
d.	The sin offering	4:1-35
e.	The trespass offering	5:1-19
f.	Conditions necessitating atonement	6:1-7
g.	Regulations for the burnt offering	6:8-13
h.	Regulations for the cereal offering	6:14-23
i.	Regulations for the sin offering	6:24-30
j.	Regulations for the guilt offering	7:1-10
k.	Regulations for the peace offering	7:11-21
l.	Prohibition of fat and blood	7:22-27
m.	Further regulations for peace offerings	7:28-38

PART 2 / **THE CONSECRATION OF PRIESTS**   8:1-10:20

a.	Preparation for anointing	8:1-5
b.	The anointing ceremony	8:6-13
c.	The consecration sacrifice	8:14-36
d.	Instructions about sacrifices	9:1-7
e.	Aaron and his sons begin their duties	9:8-24
f.	The fate of Nadab and Abihu	10:1-7
g.	Prohibitions against drunkenness of priests	10:8-11
h.	Rules regarding eating consecrated food	10:12-20

PART 3 / **CLEAN AND UNCLEAN**   11:1-15:33

a.	Clean and unclean species	11:1-47
b.	Purification after childbirth	12:1-8
c.	Laws concerning leprosy	13:1-14:57
d.	Purification after secretion	15:1-33

PART 4 / **THE DAY OF ATONEMENT**   16:1-34

PART 5 / **THE LAW OF HOLINESS**   17:1-25:55

    a. The blood of sacrifice for the people 17:1-16
    b. Religious and ethical laws and punishment 18:1-20:27
    c. Principles of priestly holiness 21:1-22:33
    d. Festivals and special days 23:1-43
        (1) Sabbath rest 23:1-3
        (2) The Feast of Passover 23:5
        (3) The Feast of Unleavened Bread 23:6-8
        (4) The Feast of Firstfruits 23:9-14
        (5) The Feast of Pentecost 23:15-22
        (6) The Feast of Trumpets 23:23-25
        (7) The Day of Atonement 23:26-32
        (8) The Feast of Tabernacles 23:33-43
    e. Oil and bread for the sanctuary 24:1-9
    f. The penalty for blasphemy and other offences 24:10-23
    g. Sabbatical and jubilee years 25:1-55

PART 6 / **PROMISES, WARNING AND APPENDIX 26:1-27:34**

LEVITICUS

> Pursue...holiness, without which no one will see the Lord (Hebrews 12:14).

Leviticus (meaning, "pertaining to the Levites") is the third of the first five books of the Bible known as the Pentateuch. As we have seen, viewed historically, the first book, Genesis, is the book of beginnings; viewed doctrinally it is the book of election—God sovereignly choosing as he wills. The second book, Exodus, viewed historically, deals with the deliverance of Israel from Egypt, whereas doctrinally it deals with redemption. As the first book of the Bible teaches that God elects, or chooses, those who shall be saved, so the second instructs as to how God saves—that is, through the payment of a ransom. The third book, Leviticus, teaches the holy requirements of God in worship and life, and the gracious provisions he has made to meet those requirements. Viewed historically, the book of Leviticus is an account of the institution of an elaborate sacrificial system and the inauguration of a meticulous priesthood. From the doctrinal perspective it is profound teaching concerning the work of the Lord Jesus Christ as sacrifice and High Priest.[1]

LEVITICUS / **AUTHOR**

"Now the LORD called to Moses, and spoke to him..." (1:1). There are two clear implications from this statement: firstly, that which follows is from Moses; and, secondly, it was not the product of his mind and thinking, but the revelation of almighty God to him. While these words strictly refer only to the section of the book which immediately follows (1:1–3:17), nevertheless, the same or a similar expression is used no less than fifty-six times in the twenty-seven chapters. It seems not unreasonable, therefore, to conclude that they cover the entire book. The contents of Leviticus are God's Word communicated to, and through, his servant Moses. The Lord Jesus speaks of Moses as the recipient of God's Word contained in Leviticus when, having healed a

---

[1] Arthur W. Pink, *Gleanings in Exodus* (Chicago: Moody Press, 1972), 7.

leper, he says, "See that you tell no one; but go your way, show yourself to the priest, and offer the gift that Moses commanded, as a testimony to them" (Matthew 8:4). Such a command is found only in Leviticus (14:2–10).

The Bible does not inform us whether or not Moses wrote down every word himself, or whether the Spirit of God directed and inspired other people, in the days of Moses or afterward, to commit these laws to writing (cf. Ezra 6:18). The important point, as always, is knowing with confidence that they form part of the inspired Scriptures given by God.

That God is the ultimate author of Leviticus is confirmed, if such confirmation is needed, by the Lord Jesus Christ. For instance, in justifying his disciples for plucking ears of corn on the Sabbath day, he refers to the example of David, who ate the shewbread, "which was not lawful for him to eat, nor for those who were with him, but only for the priests" (Matthew 12:4). The law of which our Lord speaks is found only in Leviticus (24:9). Such a reference is only relevant on the assumption that Jesus regarded the prohibition of the shewbread as having the same inspired authority as the obligation of the Sabbath. In other words, it is clear that Jesus regards both the Levitical law and the Sabbath law as from God.

A second confirmation is also related to the Sabbath, this time when Jesus refers to Moses as having renewed the institution of circumcision originally given to Abraham (John 7:22–23). As before, divine authority is seen to be behind the command. But this renewal of circumcision is not found in the Pentateuch except in Leviticus (12:3). From these examples it is clear that the Lord Jesus Christ "believed, and intended to be understood as teaching, that the law of Leviticus was, in a true sense, of Mosaic origin, and of inspired, and therefore infallible, authority."[2] Andrew Bonar says there is no book in the whole of the Scriptures "that contains more of the very words of God than Leviticus. It is God that is the direct speaker in almost every page.... This consideration cannot fail to send us to the study of it with singular interest and attention."[3]

---

[2] Samuel H. Kellogg, *The Book of Leviticus* (1899; Minneapolis: Klock and Klock, 1978), 10.

[3] Andrew A. Bonar, *A Commentary on Leviticus* (1846; Edinburgh: Banner of Truth Trust, 1966), 1.

LEVITICUS / **HISTORICAL SETTING**

The laws of Leviticus were given in the wilderness. The book covers a period in Israel's history of less than two months at the beginning of the second year after the Exodus from Egypt: from the first day of the first month to the twentieth day of the second month (Exodus 40:17; Numbers 10:11—c.1445 B.C.). The book is closely connected with Exodus and Numbers but, unlike those books, Leviticus contains only a small amount of historical narrative (8–10; 24:10–23).

There is a natural flow from Exodus to Leviticus. This is highlighted in the closing words of the former and the opening words of the latter: "Then the cloud covered the tabernacle of meeting, and the glory of the LORD filled the tabernacle…" "Now the LORD called to Moses, and spoke to him from the tabernacle of meeting, saying…" (Exodus 40:34; Leviticus 1:1).

At Sinai the Israelites are organized into a *theocracy*—the Lord is to govern his people *personally*. Basic laws are given covering moral, civil and ceremonial duties (Exodus 20–24). The covenant between God and Israel is confirmed. The tabernacle is constructed. Before the Lord continues to lead the Israelites to the promised land, he provides detailed instruction as to how worship is to be conducted in the tabernacle. An elaborate sacrificial system is instituted together with a series of annual festivals. These remind the Israelites of the past and point to the future.

LEVITICUS / **OUTLINE**

There is a clear and simple structure: ceremonies and laws are set out in a straightforward manner. The emphasis throughout Leviticus is on the holiness of God: "You shall be holy, for I the LORD your God am holy" (19:2; cf. 11:45). The underlying purpose is to provide guidelines to the priests and people for the appropriate worship of God. At the root of the concept of holiness is *separation*. The Israelites are to understand that they are separated *by* God, *to* God and *for* God. Their view of worship is to extend beyond the confines of the tabernacle and embrace *every aspect* of their lives. Their behaviour is to reflect the distinction and dignity of their relationship with the living God (20:26). It is this personal relationship which is the key and motivation for their obedience and faithfulness: "I am the LORD your God. You shall therefore…" (11:44; cf. 18:2–5; 19:2–4).

PART 1 / **THE LAW OF SACRIFICE (1:1–7:38)**

The sacrificial system formed the core of Israel's public worship. It is surprising that there is no explanation regarding the meaning of the ceremonies. It seems to be taken for granted that the original participants understood the significance and only needed to be reminded of the correct procedures. The meaning of sacrifice as a whole, and of individual sacrifices in particular, can be determined by the symbolism employed and how they were used in worship.[4] Two emphases are apparent: (1) sin must be pardoned and removed and (2) lost fellowship with God must be restored and preserved. The New Testament, especially the letter to the Hebrews, enables Christians to understand the meaning and relevance of the sacrifices both in their original context and for today.

God is holy and he will not permit sin and uncleanness in his presence. In order to establish a relationship between God and sinners, a sacrifice has to be made substituting a pure life for a sinful one. Throughout the Old Testament period, animals (without moral discernment and therefore free from moral responsibility and from guilt) were used as the substituted sacrifice to atone for sin. Atonement—"at-one-ment"—means the reconciling through substitution of those who have been estranged. God is righteously angry with sinful humans; sinful humans are hostile toward the holy God. The atonement, or reconciling sacrifice, brings harmony through the removal of sin and guilt. The life of the animal is accepted in the place of the life of the sinner (Hebrews 9:22). The punishment of death for sin is exacted on the substitute. The sacrificed animal does not in fact remove sin but symbolizes the one who successfully accomplishes this great purpose (Hebrews 10:4,10).

A progression may be traced in the offerings of Leviticus: atonement, consecration, fellowship and preservation. The *burnt offering* (1:1–17) is the sacrifice for atonement. This is the major sacrifice since

---

[4] Raymond B. Dillard and Tremper Longman III, *An Introduction to the Old Testament* (Leicester: Apollos, 1995), 76–77.

it *initiates* a right relationship between God and sinners. The sacrificial animal or bird has to be without blemish. The connection of the sinner with the sacrifice is visualized when "he shall put his hand on the head of the burnt offering, and it will be accepted on his behalf to make atonement for him" (1:4). The whole of the creature, with the exception of the skin (7:8), is sacrificed to God by fire.

A right relationship is first established by God through the burnt offering, the atonement. The justified sinner, now declared righteous through the atoning sacrifice, gratefully responds in bringing the *cereal offering* (2:1–16; 6:14–23), signifying the consecration of the whole life to the service of God. Once reconciled to God, the pardoned sinner responds with wholehearted commitment.

The best grain is carefully and thoroughly sieved. Oil is poured upon it. Incense is then added to a small amount of this mixture and burned, usually with the burnt offering. The remaining oil and flour is then given to the priests as food.

A right relationship having been established between God and the sinner, and the forgiven sinner having responded with wholehearted devotion, the *benefits* of this fellowship are now to be experienced. So the third offering, the *peace offering* (3:1–17; 7:11–34), signifies the enjoyment of the reconciled relationship. Unlike the burnt offering, where the whole of the animal was consumed in the fire upon the altar, in this sacrifice only the fat surrounding the internal organs and also the kidneys are burnt (3:3–5). The rest, the flesh, is cooked and eaten by the priests and people (7:15, 31–34). Fellowship with God means fellowship also with God's people.

The fourth and fifth sacrifices provide for those who have already been reconciled to God through the atoning sacrifice. These offerings symbolize the maintenance of the already established relationship. The *sin offering* (4:1–35; 6:24–30) serves to *maintain* the relationship where sin has been committed unintentionally. This offering is the basis of restoration. In a similar way the *guilt offering* (5:1–19; 7:1–10) also serves to maintain an existing relationship. The difference is seen in the emphasis placed upon the notion of "trespass." This relates to an invasion of the rights of others, divine or human. Idolatry, for example, is a trespass against God, an invasion of his rights, in that it robs him of the worship, offerings and tithes that are rightfully his. The same Hebrew word for *trespass* is also used in connection with adultery (Numbers 5:12, cf. AV). Marital unfaithfulness involves the invasion of the rights of the spouse. Every trespass is a sin, but not every sin is a trespass. In this fifth sacrifice relating to the invasion of the rights of others there must not only be the removal of the sin but also compensation for the damage caused.[5]

PART 2 / **THE CONSECRATION OF PRIESTS (8:1-10:20)**

Along with the sacrificial system, the priesthood is a prime concern of Leviticus, as its name implies ("pertaining to the Levites," i.e. the priests). Priests functioned as *mediators*. They represented God to the people and the people to God.

Moses prepares and anoints Aaron and his sons for the priesthood on the basis of previous instructions (Exodus 29:1-36; 40:12-15). These are elaborate and detailed in order to instill into the minds of priests and people the entire holiness and spotless purity of the Lord of glory. No one is to rush carelessly into the presence of the Almighty. No one may approach him without being thoroughly washed, without wearing spotlessly clean clothing, without the provision of an appropriate sacrifice—that is, one that God has authorized. The priestly garments and the ceremony of anointing with oil linked these men with the tabernacle as separated exclusively to the service of God.

Aaron and his sons commence their duties. The strictness of the Lord in relation to the functioning of the priests is brought home dramatically when two of Aaron's sons, Nabad and Abihu, offer "profane fire before the LORD, which he had not commanded them" (10:1). They are immediately slain and the Lord utters a solemn warning:

> By those who come near Me
> I must be regarded as holy;
> And before all the people
> I must be glorified (10:3).

Priests are appointed by God to protect his honour and glory and promote his holiness among the people. This is to be achieved through

---

[5] Kellogg, *The Book of Leviticus*, 156.

their personal example, meticulous service and regular instruction (10:11).

PART 3 / **CLEAN AND UNCLEAN (11:1–15:33)**

The laws of purity emphasize the holiness of God. Holiness in God's people concerns the body as well as the soul. It is evident that the hygiene laws inculcated a sense of responsibility to live in a wholesome manner before the Lord. They also served to protect the Israelites from many of the diseases common to other nations of the time (Exodus 15:26).[6]

The criteria used to distinguish between clean and unclean animals, between clean fish and unclean crustaceans, is not readily apparent. Many theories have been presented. It is quite possible that the Lord made an arbitrary distinction on purpose! Though there was nothing morally different between one animal and another, the fact that God made a distinction meant that the Israelites must regard them as such. Consequently they would be faced with the issue of clean or unclean every day of their lives. In preparing meals the dominant thought would not be, "Is this healthy?" or "Is this nutritious?" but rather, "Is this kosher? Is this permitted, or is this forbidden, *in the sight of the living God*?"

Following the list of clean and unclean species, the Lord gives directions for purification after childbirth, procedures in cases of leprosy in people, clothing and buildings, and cleansing after bodily secretions of various kinds. Holiness in the people of God involves pure food, pure bodies, pure homes and pure habits.

PART 4 / **THE DAY OF ATONEMENT (16:1–34)**

Central to the worship of God was the sacrificial system. At the heart of the sacrificial system was the annual Day of Atonement (*Yom Kippur*). Only on this day could the high priest enter into the Holy of Holies, the most holy place of the tabernacle. This was a day of solemn

---

[6] For a Christian doctor's perspective on the benefits of the laws of Moses to the health of the nation, see S.I. McMillen, *None of These Diseases* (London: Marshall Morgan and Scott, 1966).

reflection, a day of humbling before the Lord. The people were to reflect deeply upon the seriousness of sin. This was the only day of the year where fasting was compulsory. All other annual festivals and feast days had an atmosphere of celebration, of rejoicing. While the sense of God's holiness would be impressed upon the people, there was nevertheless the triumphant note that the Lord had provided the means for forgiveness: "For the life of the flesh is in the blood, and I have given it to you upon the altar to make atonement for your souls; for it is the blood that makes atonement for the soul" (17:11).

This Day of Atonement was the high point of all sacrifices. It was intentionally comprehensive. Here was provision for any and every sin not covered by the specific offerings detailed in the first seven chapters.

PART 5 / **THE LAW OF HOLINESS (17:1–25:55)**

The people of God are to ensure holiness in life. They are to separate themselves from the practices of the surrounding nations. The key to this section is found in the eighteenth chapter:

> According to the doings of the land of Egypt, where you dwelt, you shall not do; and according to the doings of the land of Canaan, where I am bringing you, you shall not do; nor shall you walk in their ordinances. You shall observe My judgments and keep My ordinances, to walk in them: I am the LORD your God (18:3–4).

The Israelites were to maintain a distinctive lifestyle. This was to be achieved by obedience to the laws that God gave through his servant Moses. They were not only to abstain from food forbidden by God (11:1–47), they also had to prepare and consume permitted food in a way that was pleasing to God. They were to avoid even the appearance of following the idolatrous practices of the surrounding heathens. To kill an animal in the open field might have given the impression that they were pouring the blood on the ground and thereby sacrificing to "field-devils" (17:3–7).[7] Consequently, all animals permitted for food

---

[7] C.F. Keil and F. Delitzsch, *Commentary on the Old Testament: Vol. 1: The Pentateuch* (Grand Rapids: Eerdmans, 1980), 407.

were to be slaughtered at the door of the tabernacle. Their blood was to be sprinkled on the altar of burnt offering and the fat parts burnt "for a sweet aroma to the LORD" (17:6). Only then, after the priest had taken his appropriate portion, were the people to eat the flesh. (The diet of the Israelites contained very little meat. It was eaten mainly on feast days,[8] so the restrictions here were not really a burden upon the people.)

The Israelites were not to consume blood, otherwise they would be excommunicated—driven from the community of Israel. Eating carrion (dead and rotting flesh) carried with it a day-long penalty with appropriate washings. These laws were not intended simply to supplement the food laws of chapter eleven. They raised the eating of food into an act of worship. This had two implications: (1) it kept the Israelites from participating in idolatrous sacrificial meals and (2) it reminded them that their daily food was provided for them by the Lord.

The Israelites were also to be distinct in their sexual relationships. Incest—that is, physical intimacy with those who constitute close family, either by blood or marriage—was forbidden. Homosexuality was designated "an abomination"; bestiality was classed as a "perversion" (18:22,23). The penalty for these corruptions was excommunication—permanent banishment (18:29).

This section includes a list of various moral and ceremonial laws followed by specified punishments (19:1–20:27).

The holiness required of priests receives special attention (22:1–16). They were the appointed leaders and needed to set a good and godly example to the people. The laws concerning defilement through contact with a dead body and restrictions regarding marriage were stricter for them than for the Israelite population as a whole.

Festivals and special days

The seventh day of each week was to be kept as "a *Sabbath* of solemn rest" (23:3; cf. Exodus 20:8–11). The day was to be kept free from work, in accordance with God's example at creation (Exodus 31:12–17). The Sabbath principle was also to be applied to the land once the Israelites were settled (25:2–7; Exodus 23:10–11).

---

[8] Bonar, *A Commentary on Leviticus*, 321.

On the evening of the fourteenth day of the first month (Hebrew: *Abib*, corresponding to our March/April) the *Feast of the Passover* was to be commemorated with the eating of a lamb (23:5; cf. Exodus 12:1–28). This reminded the Israelites of God's deliverance of their ancestors from Egyptian slavery, passing over their homes and destroying the firstborn in Egypt (Exodus 12:27).

On that evening, no leaven was to be consumed—in fact none was to be found in their homes. The *Feast of Unleavened Bread* was to be observed for seven days (23:6–8; cf. Exodus 12:15–20, 13:3–10; Numbers 28:17–25). This served to remind the Israelites of the haste and distress with which their ancestors departed from Egypt (Exodus 12:39).

During the Feast of Unleavened Bread, on the day after the Sabbath, the *Feast of Firstfruits* (a sheaf of firstfruits was used as a wave offering, 23:15) was to be celebrated (23:9–14). This was the day when they were to bring the firstfruits of the early (barley) harvest. In this way the Israelites would offer the first cut of harvest to the Lord as an expression of gratitude and thanksgiving for his daily provision of their food.

Seven weeks later, the Israelites were to celebrate the *Feast of Weeks*, also known as Pentecost (23:15–22). Falling on the fiftieth day (seven weeks, or the seventh of the seventh days) calculated from the Feast of Firstfruits, this was the firstfruits of the late (wheat) harvest, the main harvest (Numbers 28:26).

Each year on the first day of the seventh month the *Feast of Trumpets* was observed (23:23–25; Numbers 29:1–6) to announce the dawn of the sabbatical month. Nine days later the *Day of Atonement* was to be enacted (23:26–32), to make atonement for the priests and people (16:1–34). When the sacrificial blood was shed, the work of the priest was not over. The blood had to be taken beyond the veil into the Holy of Holies, there to be sprinkled upon the mercy seat over the ark of the covenant (16:14). Every fifty years, a *jubilee year* was observed from the Day of Atonement. This was calculated on the sabbath principle (23:3) and applied to the sabbath of sabbath years (seven times seven). All land taken in payment of debt had to be returned to its rightful owner. All servants had to be released so that they could return to their own plots of land (25:8–17).

Five days after the Day of Atonement, the *Feast of Tabernacles* was to be observed (23:33–43). The festivities included the construction of shelters, or booths, in which the people slept for seven nights. Over the seven days, seventy bullocks were sacrificed: thirteen on the first day, twelve on the second, eleven on the third, and so on (Numbers 29:12–38). This feast is also called "the Feast of Ingathering" (Exodus 23:16) and marked the end of the year's harvest of barley, wheat and grapes (Deuteronomy 16:13). The law of Moses was to be read every seventh year during the time of this feast (Deuteronomy 31:9–13). The Feast of Tabernacles reminded the Israelites in a graphic manner that their ancestors had been homeless wanderers in the desert, and the Lord had protected and provided for them.

Attendance at three of the festivals (held initially in the tabernacle, the tent of meeting, and later in the temple) was compulsory to all male adults—the Feast of Unleavened Bread (including Passover and Firstfruits), the Feast of Pentecost and the Feast of Tabernacles (Deuteronomy 16:16).

PART 6 / **PROMISES, WARNING AND APPENDIX (26:1-27:34)**

The whole of the law is summed up in the first two verses of Leviticus 16—idolatry is forbidden and the pure worship of the Lord is required (26:1–2). Following the fiery death of two of Aaron's sons, the priests would have been in no doubt about the seriousness of obedience.

LEVITICUS / **CHRIST AND HIS CHURCH**

The importance of the book of Leviticus is evident from the use made of it by the Lord Jesus and the writers of the New Testament.[9] Whereas some books of the Bible, such as Isaiah and Psalms, abound in prophecies concerning the Lord Jesus Christ and his church, the book of Leviticus bursts with typology. It is essentially and intentionally a book of types.[10] Here are vivid pictures illustrating wonderful truths about the Saviour and his people.

---

[9] There are about forty special references to Leviticus.
[10] A type is a figure, episode, or symbolic factor resembling some future reality in such a way as to foreshadow or prefigure it (see pages 28–32). Two books of particular help are: (i) Andrew Bonar, *A Commentary on Leviticus*. C. H. Spurgeon recommended this book as: "Very precious. Mr Andrew Bonar has a keen eye for a typical analogy,

TYPES

The Epistle to the Hebrews is the New Testament counterpart to Leviticus, containing the explanation of so many of the types found there. The manner in which that letter was composed suggests that it was not a new idea to understand the ceremonies of the Old Covenant as illustrations of something more glorious to come.

1. The sacrifices as types of Christ and his church

In Leviticus, we find demonstrated the horror and consequences of sin and the nature of the sinner before a holy God. But there is also grace, amazing grace, and a vivid picture of the Saviour of sinners. Leviticus reveals, in vivid picture language, the glorious person and work of our Saviour. The use of types or symbols is part of God's design before the full revelation in his Son. The blood of bulls and goats cannot make atonement for sin (Hebrews 10:4). Yet the blood of sacrificial animals does convey significance. It serves as a sign, "a symbol that points beyond itself to the reality of Christ's atoning sacrifice."[11] The blood of animals with which the earthly tabernacle was purified prefigured "better sacrifices than these"—that is, the Lord Jesus Christ our Saviour, who "has appeared to put away sin by the sacrifice of Himself" (Hebrews 9:23,26). The Levitical law at its best is only "a shadow of the good things to come" (Hebrews 10:1).

The *burnt offering* is the sacrifice for atonement offered to God by fire. This is the sacrifice of substitution establishing a right relationship with God (2 Corinthians 5:21). The fire symbolizes the wrath of God, for, "Our God is a consuming fire" (Hebrews 12:29). The Saviour experienced hell while still alive on the cross. His devastating agony is expressed in his cry: "My God, My God, why have You forsaken Me?" (Matthew 27:46). "For Christ also suffered once for sins, the just for the unjust, that he might bring us to God" (1 Peter 3:18). It

---

but he always keeps the rein upon his imagination, and is therefore safe to follow. He is a master in Israel." (ii) Andrew Jukes, *The Law of the Offerings*. This is also recommended by Spurgeon: "A very condensed, instructive, refreshing book. It will open up new trains of thought to those unversed in the teaching of the types." See *Commenting on Commentaries* (1876; Edinburgh: Banner of Truth Trust, 1969), 60–61.

[11] Edmund P. Clowney, "Preaching Christ from All the Scriptures," in Samuel T. Logan Jr., ed., *The Preacher and Preaching: Reviving the Art in the Twentieth Century* (Phillipsburg: Presbyterian & Reformed, 1986), 175.

is the living God "who has reconciled us to himself through Jesus Christ" (2 Corinthians 5:18). He demonstrated "his righteousness, that He might be just and the justifier of the one who has faith in Jesus" (Romans 3:26).

The *cereal offering* signifies the consecration of the whole life to the service of God. When Christ came into the world he said, "A body You have prepared for Me.... Behold, I have come...to do Your will, O God" (Hebrews 10:5,7). The Son of God says, "Here am I and the children whom God has given Me" (Hebrews 2:13). Accepted believers respond in Christ; we "walk in love, as Christ also has loved us and given Himself for us, an offering and a sacrifice to God for a sweet-smelling aroma" (Ephesians 5:2). We present our "bodies a living sacrifice, holy, acceptable to God" which is our "reasonable service" (Romans 12:1). Our bodies are holy because of the consecration of the Holy Spirit (represented by the oil of the cereal offering) and "acceptable to God" because God "has made us accepted in the Beloved" (Ephesians 1:6).

The *peace offering* signifies the enjoyment of our reconciled relationship. The Lord Jesus exhibited a deep fellowship with God the Father throughout the whole of his earthly life. He yielded to God what he most desires, "truth in the inward parts" (Psalm 51:6). He "poured out his soul unto death" (Isaiah 53:12). He "humbled Himself and became obedient to death, even the death of the cross" (Philippians 2:8). Christ is our peace offering, "having made peace through the blood of his cross" (Colossians 1:20). Consequently the "Prince of Peace" (Isaiah 9:6) bequeaths peace to all his followers (John 14:27). "Therefore, having been justified by faith, we have peace with God through our Lord Jesus Christ" (Romans 5:1).

The fourth and fifth sacrifices provide for those who have already been reconciled to God through the atoning sacrifice. These offerings symbolize the maintenance of an already established relationship. The *sin offering* and the *guilt offering* maintain the reconciled relationship. The purpose of the atonement is to free sinners from the "law of sin and death" (Romans 8:2). We are urged not to present our "members as instruments of unrighteousness to sin," but to yield them "as instruments of righteousness to God" (Romans 6:13). But who is able? Thank God there is, even so, the assurance that "if anyone sins, we have an advocate with the Father, Jesus Christ the righteous. And He

Himself is the propitiation[12] for our sins" (1 John 2:1–2).

The whole sacrificial system of the Old Covenant is abolished. Every detail of every offering pointed to some aspect of the perfect sacrifice of Christ. In the humble, obedient life of Christ, culminating in a holy sinless death, the sacrifices instituted in Leviticus are rendered obsolete. When Christ came into the world he said, "Behold, I have come to do Your will, O God," from which the writer to the Hebrews concludes: "He takes away the first that He may establish the second. By that will we have been sanctified through the offering of the body of Jesus Christ once" (Hebrews 10:9–10).

> Not all the blood of beasts,
>   On Jewish altars slain,
> Could give the guilty conscience peace,
>   Or wash away the stain.
>
> But Christ, the heavenly Lamb,
>   Takes all our sins away;
> A sacrifice of nobler name
>   And richer blood than they.
>
> My faith would lay her hand
>   On that dear head of thine,
> While like a penitent I stand,
>   And there confess my sin (Isaac Watts).

"What we have in type in Leviticus, we have in reality in the Cross of Christ."[13]

2. The priesthood as types of Christ and his church

The contrast between the earthly and the heavenly priesthood is brought out in detail in Hebrews (see Table 3).

---

[12] The self-sacrifice of Christ's holy, obedient life meets all the requirements of God's righteousness and justice. God is *entirely* satisfied. Believers are no longer children of wrath, but children of grace.

[13] A.M. Hodgkin, *Christ in All the Scriptures* (London: Pickering and Inglis, 1907), 24.

Table 3. The contrast between the earthly and heavenly priesthoods

Earthly priests	Christ, the heavenly Priest
are sinners, they offer sacrifice for their own sins first (Hebrews 9:7)	is "holy, harmless, undefiled, separate from sinners" and has no sin for which to atone (Hebrews 7:26; cf. 1 John 3:5)
die and need to be replaced (Hebrews 7:23)	lives for ever (Hebrews 7:24-25)
entered the Holy of Holies once a year (Hebrews 9:7)	entered heaven's Holy of Holies and stayed there, having "sat down at the right hand of the Majesty on high" (Hebrews 7:27; 1:3)
carried the blood of goats and calves (Hebrews 9:12-13)	presented his own precious blood (Hebrews 9:12)
brought the sacrifices for sins (Hebrews 5:1)	is the sacrifice for sins; High Priest and sacrifice are one, it is he "who through the eternal Spirit offered himself without spot to God" (Hebrews 9:14; cf. John 10:17-18)
repeated the sacrifices daily (Hebrews 10:11)	"offered one sacrifice for sins forever" (Hebrews 10:12)
offered sacrifices that could not take away sin (Hebrews 10:4)	offered the perfect sacrifice for sin (Hebrews 9:26; 1 John 1:7; 1 Peter 1:19)

His one surrender of Himself as the atoning Lamb, forever quenched all wrath, forever took away all curse, forever satisfied all claims, forever saved the family of faith, forever opened heaven, forever vanquished hell. To add to infinite perfection is impossible. Woe be to them who think such offering incomplete![14]

The Levitical priesthood and sacrifices are gone, but the spiritual truth they represent stays forever. There is no entry into the kingdom of God, no enjoyment of everlasting bliss and happiness, without the services of a high priest and mediator bearing a sacrifice for sin:

---

[14] Henry Law, *The Gospel in Exodus* (1855; London: Banner of Truth Trust, 1967), 133.

But Christ came as high priest of the good things to come, with the greater and more perfect tabernacle not made with hands, that is, not of this creation. Not with the blood of goats and calves, but with his own blood he entered the Most Holy Place once for all, having obtained eternal redemption (Hebrews 9:11–12)

The Lord Jesus Christ "loved us and washed us from our sins in his own blood" (Revelation 1:5). We are "a holy priesthood, to offer up spiritual sacrifices acceptable to God through Jesus Christ" (1 Peter 2:5). The Christian church does not *have* a priesthood; it *is* a priesthood. As priests believers have direct access to God, speak to God on behalf of others and speak to others on behalf of God (1 Peter 2:9–10).

3. The festivals as types of Christ and his church

As with the various sacrifices of Leviticus, so too with the different festivals—all are types of Christ and his church. Festival, new moon or sabbaths, are "a shadow of things to come, but the substance is of Christ" (Colossians 2:17). Our task now is to discern the spiritual significance of the annual festivals (see Table 4).

The *Feast of Passover* finds its glorious fulfilment in the sacrifice of the true paschal Lamb, the Lord Jesus Christ (1 Corinthians 5:7; John 1:29,36; 19:36; 1 Peter 1:18–19). Uniting the Feast of Passover and the *Feast of Unleavened Bread*, and replacing them, is the New Covenant symbolic meal of bread and wine—representing the body and blood of the Saviour (Matthew 26:17–18,26–28; John 6:33–35,48–58). His is the pure life—"holy, harmless, undefiled" (Hebrews 7:26). We, his followers, are to "keep the feast, not with old leaven, nor with the leaven of malice and wickedness, but with the unleavened bread of sincerity and truth" (1 Corinthians 5:8).

Linked with the Feast of the Passover and the Feast of Unleavened Bread is the *Feast of Firstfruits*. It was on this day of the year that the Lord Jesus arose from the dead, becoming "the firstfruits of those who have fallen asleep" (1 Corinthians 15:20). His resurrection is the sign and seal of the resurrection of all who believe in him (1 Corinthians 15:23; cf. John 6:39–40; 1 Thessalonians 4:14,16–17).

Exactly seven weeks later the *Feast of Pentecost* is observed.

Jewish tradition links the celebration of Pentecost with the giving of the law to Moses. William Arnot draws a Christian parallel from this tradition:

> At the feast of the Passover, the lamb was slain; at the feast of Pentecost, the law was given. Coincident with the slaying of the lamb was the death of Christ; coincident with the giving of the law was the descent of the Spirit.... On the first Pentecost the law was written on tables of stone; on the last Pentecost came the Spirit, whose office it is to write that law on the living tables of the heart.[15]

While being an attractive idea, this theory has one major flaw: there is no evidence to be found in either the Old or the New Testament for linking Pentecost to the giving of the law.

A more satisfactory approach is to look at the connection between the Feast of Pentecost and *the coming of the Holy Spirit*. It was on the Day of Pentecost that the Holy Spirit first descended to bring the promised blessing of the New Covenant to the nations of the earth (Acts 2:1–4). The Lord Jesus had to die in order to produce the harvest (John 12:24). Following his death, resurrection and glorification, the Holy Spirit was sent from heaven (John 7:39). The great harvest of the nations was to begin (Matthew 28:18–20; Acts 1:8; Luke 10:2; John 4:35–38; cf. Acts 2:41; 4:4; 5:14). Ingathering will be achieved through the worldwide proclamation of the gospel, the Word of God (Acts 2:6–11; 1 Peter 1:23,25; Revelation 7:9).

The seventh month of the religious calendar of the Israelites (September/October) was to form a high point of the year. It began with the *Feast of Trumpets* on the first day, followed by the *Day of Atonement* on the tenth day. From the fifteenth day, the *Feast of Tabernacles* was observed for seven days. These festivals combine to make a powerful symbol of the finished work of Christ which culminates in his return to establish his everlasting kingdom on earth. The sound of trumpets is associated with the return of the Lord Jesus Christ (Matthew 24:31; 1 Corinthians 15:52; 1 Thessalonians 4:16).

---

[15] William Arnot, *Studies in Acts: The Church in the House* (1883; Grand Rapids: Kregel Publications, 1978), 38–39.

Table 4. The feasts of the Israelites (Leviticus 23)

	Feast	Day/ Month	Meaning for Israel	Meaning for Christians	Biblical references
v.3	Sabbath	every seventh day	God's rest after creation	Salvation rest in Christ	Hebrews 4:8-10; Matthew 11:28-30
v.5	Passover	14th day of the first month	Deliverance from Egypt (death of lamb)	Deliverance from sin (death of Christ)	1 Corinthians 5:7; 1 Peter 1:19; John 1:29; 19:31,36
vv. 6-7	Unleavened Bread	15th day of the first month (7 days)	Haste of departure from Egypt	Sinless life of Christ	Hebrews 7:26; 1 Corinthians 5:7-8
vv. 10-11	Firstfruits	16th day of the first month	First crop early (barley) harvest	Resurrection (Christ, the firstfruit from the dead)	Matthew 28:1,6; 1 Corinthians 15:20,23
vv. 15-16	Weeks (Pentecost)	50th day from Firstfruits	First crop main (wheat) harvest	The Spirit comes: power for world evangelization	Acts 2:1-4; 1:8; Matthew 28:18-20
v.24	Trumpets	1st day of the seventh month	Sabbatical month	Announcing the imminent return of Christ	1 Corinthians 15:52; Matthew 24:31; 1 Thessalonians 4:16
v.27	Day of Atonement	10th day of the seventh month	Humbling— reconciliation through sacrifice	Humbling— reconciliation through Christ's sacrifice	1 John 1:6-9; Romans 5:11; 2 Corinthians 5:19
v.34	Tabernacles (Booths)	15th of the seventh month (7 days)	End of all harvests	New heavens and a new earth	2 Peter 3:13; Revelation 21:1-4

Note: The Jewish day was calculated from evening to evening, that is, sunset to sunset (cf. Genesis 1:5,8,13).

Christ is the atoning sacrifice (Hebrews 9:26). On the Day of Atonement the high priest carried a censer of burning coals into the Holy of Holies. Once inside, he sprinkled incense upon the coals so that "the cloud of incense may cover the mercy seat" (Leviticus 16:12–13).

> Thus Jesus fills the heavens with fragrance. His precious intercession sheds precious odours round. He pleads that all His work on earth is done. He spreads His wounded hands. He shows His wounded side. He proves that every term of the vast covenant of grace is kept, that sin is punished, and His people free… "Who shall lay anything to the charge of God's elect?"[16]

The constant theme of the Levitical sacrifices is atonement through substitution—sin is removed by being carried by another (2 Corinthians 5:21). The scapegoat released into the wilderness emphasizes the point:

> Aaron shall lay both his hands on the head of the live goat, confess over it all the iniquities of the children of Israel, and all their transgressions, concerning all their sins, putting them on the head of the goat, and shall send it away into the wilderness by the hand of a suitable man. The goat shall bear on itself all their iniquities (Leviticus 16:21–22).

The seventy bullocks sacrificed at the Feast of Tabernacles are thought to represent the seventy nations of the earth.[17] The one bullock additional to the seventy and sacrificed on the eighth day would then be understood to represent Israel. The final church will be composed "of all nations, tribes, peoples, and tongues" (Revelation 7:9). This feast points to the end of the journey, the prosperous and peaceful life of the new world (2 Peter 3:13; Revelation 21:1–4), following the return of the Lord Jesus.

The Old Testament saints looked upon a hidden Saviour. The prophets struggled to understand the meaning and the timing "of the

---

[16] Law, *The Gospel in Exodus*, 131.
[17] Rudolf Stier, *The Words of the Lord Jesus*, Vol. 5 (1874; Edinburgh: T & T Clark, 1985), 278.

sufferings of Christ and the glories that would follow" (1 Peter 1:11). We "look upon an unveiled Saviour; and, going back to the Old, we can see far better than the Jews could, the features and form of Jesus the Beloved, under that veil."[18]

LEVITICUS / **CONCLUSION**

Leviticus begins after redemption is known, and speaks of things connected with the access of a chosen people to God.... Christ in His work is the sum and substance of these types, it is Christ as discerned by one who already knows the certainty of redemption: it is Christ as seen by one, who, possessing peace with God and deliverance, is able to look with joy at all that Christ has so fully been for him. Christ as the priest, the offerer, the offering; Christ as meeting all that a saved sinner needs to approach to God; Christ for the believer, and all that Christ is to the believer, as keeping up his communion with God; this is what we have distinctly set forth in the varied types of Leviticus. Exodus gives us the blood of the lamb, saving Israel in the land of Egypt. Leviticus gives us the priest and the offerings, meeting Israel's need in their access to Jehovah.[19]

Leviticus teaches laws to establish Israel's physical, moral and spiritual well-being. The law of Leviticus was intended to prepare Israel for its world mission. Through Israel, the unapproachable holiness of God was to be communicated to the nations. He is still exactly what he was when he spoke to Moses on Mount Sinai or called to him out of the tent of meeting. The God of the New Testament is no different from the God of the Old. He is just as holy as he was then, just as intolerant of sin, just as merciful to the penitent sinner who trusts in the appointed blood of atonement as he was then. The message of Leviticus is loud and clear: "Without shedding of blood there is no remission" (Hebrews 9:22), and at the same time, by God's gracious provision, *with* the shedding of blood there is full remission.

---

[18] Robert Murray M'Cheyne, cited by Bonar, *A Commentary on Leviticus*, 8.
[19] Jukes, *The Law of the Offerings*, 33–34.

The works of the Lord are great,
Studied by all who have pleasure in them.
His work is honourable and glorious,
And His righteousness endures for ever.
He has made His wonderful works to be remembered;
The Lord is gracious and full of compassion (Psalm 111:2–4).

LEVITICUS / **APPLICATION & REFLECTION**

1. Holiness

The stress which this book places upon sacrifices is calculated to impress upon the reader two great truths: the holiness of the Lord and the sinfulness of humanity. No one can approach the living God except on the grounds of atonement. The seriousness of sin is evident in the number and nature of the sacrifices. It is also apparent in the punishments that the Lord specifies for wrongdoing.

There are those who are uncomfortable with the severity of some of the laws in Leviticus, and what seem to them to be the arbitrary and even trivial character of other requirements. They judge that these appear to them to be irreconcilable with both the mercy and the dignity and majesty of God.[20]

The severity of the penalties which were attached to the Levitical laws are consistent with the impeccable holy character of God. Liberal-minded critics may call these punishments harsh, but they underestimate the seriousness of sin, and how repugnant and insulting sin really is to the all-holy and all-glorious God (cf. Habakkuk 1:13). Even what we dare to call "small" sins are singularly offensive to one who is morally perfect and unspeakably pure! No one can deny that Leviticus impresses the Israelite, and every serious reader, with God's absolute intolerance of sin and impurity (cf. 1 Corinthians 6:9-10; Galatians 5:19-21; Romans 1:18-32).

But in Leviticus, the very book which emphasizes the message from heaven that "without shedding of blood there is no remission" (Hebrews 9:22), we see revealed with equal clarity and force that *with* shedding of blood there *is* full remission of sins for every believing penitent. "For I will forgive their iniquity, and their sin I will remember no more" (Jeremiah 31:34) is clearly the promised implication within the sacrificial system. Even under the Old Covenant, believers may rejoice and praise God for the reality of pardon: "As far as the east is from the west, so far has He removed our transgressions from us" (Psalm 103:12).

2. Worship

"God is a Spirit, and those who worship Him must worship in spirit and truth" (John 4:24). Leadership in worship and teaching is still a serious responsibility. Those who teach the people of God "shall receive a stricter judgement"

---

[20] Kellogg, *The Book of Leviticus*, 4.

(James 3:1). "Let all things be done decently and in order" (1 Corinthians 14:40).

It is interesting to note that, for a book so full of Christology, there is no reference in Leviticus to the Holy Spirit. Yet that is not surprising. The Holy Spirit's main task is not to draw attention to himself, but to glorify Christ (John 16:13-14).

3. Separation

The apostle Peter quotes Leviticus when he urges Christians to live as obedient and transformed children of God: "As He who called you is holy, you also be holy in all your conduct, because it is written, 'Be holy, for I am holy'" (1 Peter 1:15-16; cf. Leviticus 11:44,45; 19:2).

God makes the distinction between clean and unclean foods to symbolize the necessity of separation from ungodliness and corruption (20:22-26). The detailed regulations emphasize the importance of both inward *and* outward purity. They instil the conviction that believers are to be separate from all that is ungodly and impure—a thought that permeates the whole of the Old and New Testaments (2 Corinthians 6:14-18).[21]

Under the New Covenant, the distinction between foods as clean or unclean has been abrogated (Acts 10:9-16). We receive our food with thanksgiving to God, "for it is sanctified by the word of God and prayer" (1 Timothy 4:5). In matters of food and drink there is, nevertheless, an abiding principle which governs the manner and the amount of that which we consume: "'Whether you eat or drink, or whatever you do, do all to the glory of God" (1 Corinthians 10:31). All areas of daily life are important to the Lord: whether in food or drink, in clothing or behaviour; whether single or married; whether in family, in church, or in the world; whether domestic, agricultural, trade or business, "Let us cleanse ourselves from all filthiness of the flesh and spirit, perfecting holiness in the fear of God" (2 Corinthians 7:1).

---

[21] Cf. Leviticus 26:12; Jeremiah 32:38; Ezekiel 37:27; Isaiah 52:11; Ezekiel 20:34, 41; 2 Samuel 7:14.

NUMBERS

MEANING	AUTHOR	KEY THOUGHT
"numbering" Israel	**Moses** *(commonly accepted)*	**Trials in the wilderness**

THEME

Unbelief bars entrance to abundant life

THEME VERSE

Do not harden your hearts, as in the rebellion,
As in the day of trial in the wilderness.
PSALM 95:8

NUMBERS / **SUMMARY**

PART 1 / **PREPARATION FOR LEAVING SINAI** 1:1–10:10

a.	The first census: the tribes of Israel	1:1–4:49
b.	Various regulations	5:1–6:27
c.	Offerings at the dedication of the altar	7:1–89
d.	The candlestick, consecration of Levites and rules concerning their service	8:1–26
e.	Second Passover, cloud and trumpets	9:1–10:10

PART 2 / **SINAI TO THE PLAINS OF MOAB** 10:11–21:35

a.	Preliminary movement from Sinai	10:11–36
b.	Unrest among the tribes	11:1–15
c.	Provision of quail	11:16–35
d.	Miriam's leprosy	12:1–16
e.	The twelve spies	13:1–14:45
f.	Miscellaneous commands	15:1–41
g.	Korah, Dathan and Abiram	16:1–17:13
h.	The service of the priests and Levites	18:1–32
i.	The law of purification	19:1–22
j.	Miriam's death; Moses again strikes the rock	20:1–13
k.	Edom's refusal to let Israel pass; Aaron's death	20:14–29
l.	The journey to the plains of Moab	21:1–35

PART 3 / **EVENTS ON THE PLAINS OF MOAB** 22:1–36:13

a.	Balaam: the foreign prophet who blesses Israel	22:1–24:25
b.	Immorality, idolatry and the zeal of Phinehas	25:1–18
c.	The second census: the new generation	26:1–65
d.	Inheritance rights of daughters; Joshua to succeed Moses	27:1–23
e.	Regulations concerning offerings; vows of the women	28:1–30:16

f.	War against Midian	31:1-54
g.	Inheritance in Transjordan	32:1-42
h.	Israelite encampments	33:1-49
i.	Division of the territory; cities for Levites; cities of refuge; marriage of heiresses	33:50-36:13

NUMBERS

The title "Numbers" is likely to provoke a reaction of anticipated boredom. Derived from the Septuagint, the name conjures up thoughts of endless lists and registers. While the book does contain records of families, names and duties to perform, it also holds considerable interest for the Christian who begins with the conviction that "All Scripture is given by inspiration of God, *and is profitable*" (2 Timothy 3:16, emphasis added). There is much Christological interest contained in its pages, such as the smitten rock, the bronze serpent and the cities of refuge. There are also many spiritual lessons of great relevance to the Christian life. It would be better known by its Hebrew name *bemidhbar*, which means simply, "In the wilderness," for this is the setting: from the Wilderness of Sinai (1:1) to the Wilderness of Paran (10:12) and on to the plains of Moab (22:1).

The book of Numbers records a pathetic story. It carries various details about the wanderings of the Israelites in the wilderness. Here is the account of their frequent lapses into idolatry and immorality, together with God's judgement upon them for their sins. It covers the forty years in which the vast majority of the adults who left Egypt died in the wilderness through unbelief and disobedience (Hebrews 3:17–19).

NUMBERS / **AUTHOR**

The journeys of the children of Israel were recorded by Moses (33:2). There are no other references that indicate Moses as the author of this book, though he is frequently mentioned as receiving communication directly from God (1:1; 2:1; 3:5,11,14,40,44; 4:1,17,21, etc.,—more than eighty references in all). While attributing the authorship to Moses we note that it is extremely unlikely that Moses wrote about his own humility! (12:3) This was probably added by Joshua or a later editor.[1]

---

[1] E.J. Young maintains that Moses could have written these words. See Edward J. Young, *An Introduction to the Old Testament* (Grand Rapids: Eerdmans, 1949), 86.

Table 5. Timeline of the completion of the tabernacle and its dismantling

Second year out of Egypt

Occasion	Day	Month	Reference
Tablernacle erected	1	1	Exodus 40:2,17
Passover celebrated	14	1	Numbers 9:2-3,5
Census ordered	1	2	Numbers 1:1-2
Tabernacle dismantled	20	2	Number 10:11

NUMBERS / **HISTORICAL SETTING**

The book of Exodus closed with the establishment of the children of Israel as a theocratic nation. A year after the departure from Egypt, the tent of meeting was completed: "and the glory of the LORD filled the tabernacle" (Exodus 40:34). Two weeks later, the Israelites celebrated, for the second time, the Passover instituted in Egypt as an annual memorial (Exodus 12:14,24; Numbers 9:2–3,5). Leviticus links Exodus and Numbers in stipulating in great detail the manner and mode of worship and service for the Lord. The laws of Leviticus regulate the lifestyle of the Israelites in preparation for their entry into the land of Canaan. The bulk of the information in Leviticus was given over a seven-week period spanning the completion of the tabernacle to its dismantling for transportation (Exodus 40:17; Numbers 10:11; see Table 5).

The book of Numbers overlaps part of the period covered by Leviticus, though with a different purpose in mind. Here, the preparation for leaving the Wilderness of Sinai is recorded, followed by the journey to Kadesh Barnea. After the failure of the Israelites to occupy Canaan, they are consigned to thirty-eight more years of wandering in the wilderness. When the punishment has been exacted by God upon the unbelieving adult males and they have died in the wilderness, the events which took place on the plains of Moab on the threshold of the promised land form the concluding section of the book. Numbers covers the years 1445–1406 B.C.

NUMBERS / **OUTLINE**

The flow of history and the unfolding of revelation are seen clearly in the Pentateuch. Genesis is the book of beginnings and teaches God's sovereignty in choosing whom he wills. Exodus deals with the deliverance of Israel from Egypt and teaches how God redeems and delivers his people from the bondage of sin. Leviticus elucidates the holy requirements of God in worship and fellowship and the gracious provisions he has made to meet these requirements. Numbers follows, not just in chronological order, but also in thematic and theological sequence. This is the record of Israel's walk and warfare in the wilderness. Through this historic record, Christians are taught spiritual lessons as to how believers pass through this life, with its sin and trials, with their repeated failures always without excuse, yet nevertheless experiencing God's faithfulness and longsuffering.[2]

God had given a promise to Abraham:

> I will establish my covenant between me and you and your descendants after you in their generations, for an everlasting covenant, to be God to you and your descendants after you. Also I give to you and your descendants after you the land in which you are a stranger, all the land of Canaan, as an everlasting possession; and I will be their God (Genesis 17:7–8).

From Egypt the Israelites are being led by the Lord to the land promised to their fathers—to Abraham (Genesis 12:7; 13:15,17; 15:7; 17:7–8), to Isaac (Genesis 26:3–4), to Jacob (Genesis 28:13; 35:12; 48:3–4) and to their descendants (Exodus 12:25).

PART 1 / **PREPARATION FOR LEAVING SINAI (1:1–10:10)**

This first section covers a period of nineteen days from the 1st to the 20th of the second month of the second year after the departure from Egypt. The Lord requires a census to be taken exactly one month after the erection of the tabernacle. The first and the second census of Israel which the Lord ordered are both for the purpose of recording the number of men of twenty years and over, capable of military service (1:3; 26:2). This suggests an estimated total population of roughly two

---

[2] Arthur W. Pink, *Gleanings in Exodus* (Chicago: Moody Press, 1972), 7.

million.[3] For the Lord to miraculously feed such a vast company in the wilderness for forty years was no minor achievement.

The opening chapters provide information about the composition and numerical strength of the various tribes. Distinct places are assigned to each tribe while they are in the camp and also as they are on the move. The tabernacle is always to be central. Encamped, three tribes are located on each of the four sides of the tent of meeting. On the move, six tribes, those to the east and south, move out first. The tabernacle follows. The six remaining tribes, those dwelling to the west and north, bring up the rear.

As well as marching instructions, God provides rules to govern the spiritual welfare of his people. To assist Aaron and the priests in the duties and responsibilities of the tabernacle, the tribe of Levi is separated instead of the firstborn of every family of all twelve tribes (3:5–13).

The Lord is never merely concerned with the spiritual realm. He is equally concerned with the physical and moral welfare of his people. Contact with certain diseases would expose the people to obvious dangers, so strict laws of quarantine are laid down (5:1–4). Provision is also made for establishing innocence or guilt in the case of suspected infidelity (5:11–31). Because family life is so very important to God, he gives laws to protect and promote the stability of the family.

On a brighter note, when any of the Israelites have real cause for thanksgiving, then they can take "the vow of a Nazirite" (6:1–21). This vow involves abstinence from eating or drinking anything produced from grapes, such as wine, vinegar, grape juice, fresh grapes or raisins. Vines are a symbol of the settled life. To refrain from the produce of the vine emphasizes the pilgrim nature of a godly life. They are also not to cut their hair nor go near a dead body. Letting the hair grow is probably to give public indication of the vow. During this period such people are to be regarded as "separated" or "consecrated" to the Lord (6:8–9).

In relation to the second celebration of the Passover, a question arises about what to do if someone is ceremonially unclean, for example, by touching a corpse. Moses turns to the Lord and receives instruction for the people (9:1–14). The Passover is a festival to remember

---

[3] C.F. Keil and F. Delitzsch, *Commentary on the Old Testament: Vol. 3: The Pentateuch* (Grand Rapids: Eerdmans, 1980), 5.

what great actions God has performed in the past. God also provides guidance for the present. In the daytime, the pillar of cloud represents God's guiding presence. At night, the symbol is a pillar of fire (9:15–23; cf. Exodus 13:21–22). When the cloud moves—then, and only then— the people are to move.

Two silver trumpets are made so that they can be blown when it is necessary to gather the people together (10:1–10). Different sounds on the trumpets indicate different messages for the people. At this point the Lord also provides Hobab, evidently a highly skilled Midianite guide (10:29–32). So together with the cloud of his presence, God provides a human guide.

PART 2 / **SINAI TO THE PLAINS OF MOAB (10:11-21:35)**

The children of Israel have been in the wilderness for fourteen months when instructions are given to move north in the direction of the promised land. The camp at Mount Sinai, which has been their home for almost a year, is dismantled and once more the huge company is on the move. After walking for three days, the people begin to display a spirit of unrest. The adults in this huge company are prone to murmuring and disobedience (cf. Exodus 15:24; 16:20; 17:3). They forget their former hardships and the extraordinary kindness the Lord has shown toward them. They look back to their life in Egypt and long for those former days. They talk about the food they used to eat when they were in that land—the fish, cucumbers, melons, leeks, onions and garlic. They remember the delicious savouries—but forget the disastrous slavery. This time, the Lord reacts to their grumbling, and the fire of his judgement strikes the outskirts of the camp (11:1). He further responds to their criticism by giving them plenty of meat and predicts that they will react by gorging themselves on quail for a whole month until they are literally sick of the meat (11:19–20).[4] The Lord's anger is expressed toward those who "yielded to craving" and he strikes them with a great plague (11:33–34).

The journey which should have taken eleven days (Deuteronomy 1:2) takes over a month. Eventually they arrive at Kadesh Barnea.

---

[4] This was not the first time that the Lord provided quail in the wilderness (Exodus 16:12–13; cf. Psalm 105:40).

Map 3. Israel's journey from Mount Sinai to the plains of Moab

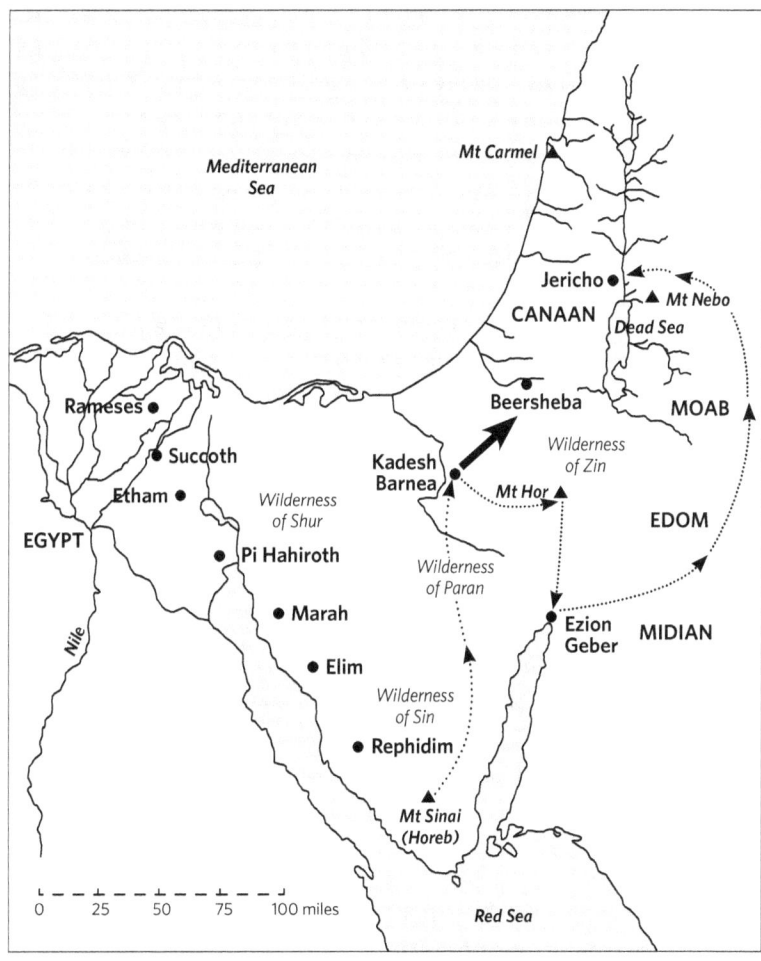

....▶ Likely route from Mt Sinai to Kadesh Barnea
➤ Entry of the spies to investigate the promised land
....▶ Journey from Kadesh Barnea to the plains of Moab, across from Jericho

Timeframes
Six weeks journeying to Mt Sinai (Exodus 19:1)
Almost a year camped at Mt Sinai (Numbers 10:11)
Over a month journeying from Mt Sinai to Kadesh Barnea
Six weeks spying out the promised land (Numbers 13:2)
Thirty-eight years wandering in the wilderness

Approaching Canaan from the south, Moses sends spies from the Wilderness of Paran into the promised land to reconnoitre the area (13:2; see Map 3). The spies spend almost six weeks walking through the land of Canaan and then return to their own people at Kadesh. The reports these men bring back test the faith and confidence of the Israelites. From a human perspective, the odds are overwhelmingly against them. Ten spies give a bad report and discourage the Israelites. Two spies, Caleb and Joshua, though realistic about the strength of the enemy, nevertheless encourage the people to invade the land:

> The majority declared the land to be fair and beautiful, but impossible of possession, because of the giants and the walled cities. The men of the minority also saw the giants, and the walled cities, but they saw God. The majority had lost the clear vision of God, and therefore were filled with fear by the Anakim and the walled cities. With the loss of clear vision there was the loss of perfect confidence.[5]

Moses and Aaron join Joshua and Caleb in trying to persuade the people to trust the Lord and enter Canaan. Joshua publicly voices his confidence in God: "If the LORD delights in us, then he will bring us into this land and give it to us, 'a land which flows with milk and honey'"(14:8; cf. Exodus 3:8).

The people respond by accepting the report of the ten spies. *This is the great turning-point in the history of Israel.* The people will not go up and take the land of Canaan. Here is the tragic failure of the mass of the people at Kadesh Barnea. They are lost—in sight of home. What a catastrophy! Unbelief debars them from the promised land. The reluctance of the vast majority to listen to the voice of the Lord, to be confident in his promises and to obey his command, in spite of the obstacles, results in serious punishment:

> The carcasses of you who have murmured against me shall fall in this wildernes…. Except for Caleb…and Joshua…. But your little ones, whom you said would be victims, I will bring in, and

---

[5] G. Campbell Morgan, *Student Survey of the Bible* (Iowa Falls: World Bible Publishers, 1993), 35–36.

they shall know the land which you have despised.... And your sons shall be shepherds in the wilderness forty years, and bear the brunt of your infidelity, until your carcasses are consumed in the wilderness. According to the number of the days in which you spied out the land, forty days, for each day you shall bear your guilt one year, namely forty years, and you shall know my rejection (14:29–34).

And so the Israelites are destined to spend a further thirty-eight years in aimless wandering in the wilderness between the Mediterranean Sea and the two large forks of the Red Sea. Their history during this period is one of unbelief and fear, of quarrels and division, of rebellion and strife.

Forty years in the wilderness
Little is recorded about the events during those long years in the wilderness. When the thirty-eight years of judgement and punishment are ended, the people return again to Kadesh Barnea (20:1). Six-hundred thousand fighting men died during those years. Some were killed in the futile attack on the Amalekites, as Moses prophesied (14:40–45); others died under the direct judgement of God (16:31–32,35), or as a result of the plague (16:49) or by suffering snake bites (21:6), while the remainder died of natural causes.

In spite of the discontent and complaining of the Israelites, the Lord provides for them, often miraculously: "If we are faithless, he remains faithful; he cannot deny himsel" (2 Timothy 2:13).

At Kadesh Barnea, an event occurs which is to have serious implications for Moses and Aaron. The Lord is once more to supply water for the vast company as he had done at Rephidim (20:7–12; cf. Exodus 17:1–7). The people, desperate for water, criticize Moses and Aaron. The two brothers respond by seeking God in prayer:

> So Moses and Aaron went from the presence of the assembly to the door of the tabernacle of meeting, and they fell on their faces. And the glory of the LORD appeared to them.
> Then the LORD spoke to Moses, saying, "Take the rod; you and your brother Aaron gather the congregation together. Speak to the rock before their eyes, and it will yield its water; thus you

shall bring water for them out of the rock, and give drink to the congregation and their animals." Moses took the rod from before the LORD as He commanded him.

And Moses and Aaron gathered the assembly together before the rock; and he said to them, "Hear now, you rebels! Must we bring water for you out of this rock?" Then Moses lifted his hand and struck the rock twice with his rod; and water came out abundantly, and the congregation and their animals drank (Numbers 20:6–11).

Moses does not obey the Word of the Lord. Instead of *speaking* to the rock with the rod of God in his hand, as God directed him, he speaks to the congregation with caustic words demonstrating considerable impatience. While the words do not actually express doubt and unbelief, they are highly inappropriate. Years later the psalmist explains what happened:

They angered Him also at the waters of strife,
So that it went ill with Moses on account of them;
Because they rebelled against His Spirit,
So that he spoke rashly with his lips (Psalm 106:32–33).

Contrary to the instructions of the Lord, Moses *strikes* the rock twice with the rod, as though it somehow depended on human exertion and not on the power of God alone, or as if the promise of God would not have been fulfilled without all the smiting on his part. In the ill will expressed in his words, the weakness of faith is displayed. This normally faithful servant of God, worn out with the numerous temptations, allows himself to be overcome, so that he stumbles and does not honour the Lord before the people. Moses discredits the Lord in his harsh words and rash action. The sin is all the more grievous because Moses is the leader of the people and he acts unworthily of his office. God punishes him by withdrawing his office from him before he has finished the work entrusted to him. He is not to lead the congregation over Jordan. He will not set foot in the promised land (27:12–14).

In some ways the behaviour of Moses is understandable. Forty years earlier, the Lord had promised to bring water from a rock. On that occasion Moses was commanded to "strike the rock, and water will come out of it, that the people may drink" (Exodus 17:6). This servant of God, noted for his scrupulous care in communicating the details of God's law, forgets himself for a moment, with serious consequences.

The Israelites move and journey south-east to Mount Hor. Aaron is succeeded in the office of high priest by his son Eleazar just before he dies on Mount Hor. Following thirty days of mourning for their departed leader, the children of Israel resume their travels. They travel south to Ezion Geber on the tip of the Red Sea before passing west then north to go around the land of Edom (see Map 3).

The journey from Mount Hor takes them in the opposite direction to the land of Canaan, and "the soul of the people became very discouraged on the way" (21:4). Rebellion erupts again in the ranks. Once more the people sin against the Lord. They are critical of the food the Lord supplies for them. They have come to loathe what they now describe as "this worthless bread" (21:5). Responding to their murmuring and complaining, God sends swift punishment—a plague of poisonous snakes. The camp of the Israelites is overrun and many people are bitten and die. In desperation, the people acknowledge their sin and plead with Moses to pray for them. Moses accedes to their request and in answer to his prayers the Lord provides a means of healing that requires faith and obedience. A bronze serpent is to be made and erected in the centre of the camp with instructions that anyone bitten by a snake should look at the bronze serpent and healing will then be assured (21:4-9).

The children of Israel continue their journey. Rapidly moving from one camp to another, they progress toward the promised land. As they approach the land of the Amorites they seek permission to pass through the territory without conflict. They are happy to give an undertaking of noninterference but Sihon king of the Amorites will not hear of it. He fights against Israel and is defeated. Og, the king of Bashan, also seeks to resist Israel's passage through his land. He too suffers defeat.

PART 3 / **EVENTS ON THE PLAINS OF MOAB (22:1-36:13)**

The children of Israel arrive on the threshold of the promised land—"in the plains of Moab on the side of the Jordan across from Jericho"

(22:1). Balak, the king of Moab, becomes increasingly disturbed. He does not want Israelites as his neighbours. He is well aware of the defeat of the kings, Sihon and Og. Balak's strategy, however, is significantly different. He sends for Balaam, a non-Israelite prophet, to curse the Israelites as they draw close to his realm. The Lord overrules and Balaam, rather than cursing, blesses Israel instead (22:1–24:25).

Although the Lord continually performs marvellous deeds for his people, they still fall to the temptations of the flesh and indulge in idolatry and immorality (25:1–18). What the enemy cannot achieve through force of arms, the devil can accomplish through subtle insinuation and corruption.

Forty years after the Exodus from Egypt, a new census is taken of the children of Israel (26:1–51; cf. 1:1–46). Excluding the tribe of Levi, there are now 601,730 males twenty years of age and older. Only two of the original men out of 603,550 of the first census (1:46) are still alive— Caleb and Joshua (26:64–65). These are the only two adult males of those who left Egypt who are to be allowed to enter into the promised land. The Lord keeps his word—of judgement as well as of promise.

A new leader is appointed for the second generation of wilderness Israelites (27:16–23). Joshua is to succeed Moses as their commander-in-chief. He will lead the nation into Canaan. From this point to the end of the book of Numbers, the outlook is positive. The second generation faces a new test of faith: will they willingly and wholeheartedly follow Joshua into Canaan?

The Lord listens to the concerns of the daughters of Zelophehad and a new law is enacted to safeguard the transference of inheritance to a daughter where there is no son (27:1–11). In several areas, for example those of ceremonies and vows, the law is finalized in preparation for settling in Canaan.

The book of Numbers concludes on the threshold of the promised land: "These are the commandments and the judgements which the LORD commanded the children of Israel by the hand of Moses in the plains of Moab by the Jordan, across from Jericho" (36:13).

NUMBERS / **CHRIST AND HIS CHURCH**

As in the wilderness days covered in Exodus, the tabernacle, the pillar of cloud, the pillar of fire, the manna and the water from the rock are all found here in Numbers. These signify the providence of God: the tabernacle and pillar represent God's presence; the manna and the water from the rock represent God's provision. All these have special importance in relation to Christ. He is the great *presence* of God *with* his people. He is the great *provision* of God *for* his people.

TYPES

In Numbers, there is a repeat of the command of God to bring *water from a rock* (20:7–11; cf. Exodus 17:5–6). On the first occasion Moses had to *strike* the rock (Exodus 17:6). On the second occasion he has to *speak* to the rock (20:8). The Hebrew for the first-mentioned rock [*tsuwr*] signifies low-lying bedrock, whereas the Hebrew for the second rock [*celà*] is a high and exalted rock. The rods which Moses is instructed to take with him are different. The first time, at the beginning of the wilderness journey, God told him, "Take in your hand your rod with which you struck the river" (Exodus 17:5). This rod was to strike the rock. The second time, forty years later, not long before the entry into the promised land, God told Moses to take a different rod. "So Moses took the rod *from before the* Lord *as He commanded him*" (20:8–9, emphasis added; cf. 17:10). This rod is not the rod of Moses but the rod of Aaron the priest ("before the Lord" in 20:9 means the same as "before the Testimony" in 17:10). To strengthen the concept of the priestly rod, this time Moses is to take Aaron with him (20:8). On the first occasion, Aaron is not mentioned!

The striking of the rock the second time is even more serious when its significance is understood. Paul says of the Israelites, "They drank of that spiritual Rock that followed them, and that Rock was Christ" (1 Corinthians 10:4). Christ is symbolized on both occasions: in the first striking of a low-lying (humble) rock as a Saviour "smitten by God, and afflicted...for our transgressions" (Isaiah 53:4–5). By his death, he supplies living water, spiritual life, to his needy people (John 4:10; 7:37–39; 19:34). The second rock denotes him as the exalted Saviour, the High Priest in heaven. He is not to be smitten twice.[6] "We have such a High Priest, who is seated at the right hand of the throne of the Majesty in the heavens" (Hebrews 8:1). He continually supplies the

---

[6] For detailed explanation of these types see Pink, *Gleanings in Exodus*, 136–140.

living water of spiritual life (Revelation 22:1,17).

On account of his disobedience, Moses is not permitted to enter the land of Canaan. In terms of spiritual analogy, it would not have been appropriate for him to enter the promised land. He represents the law (John 1:17). The law is not able to bring a sinner to heaven—only Christ is able to do that (Romans 8:1–4; 3:20–24; Galatians 2:19–21). Moses is replaced by Joshua (the Hebrew equivalent of the name "Jesus"), the captain who leads God's people home (Hebrews 12:1–2).

Another outstanding type of Christ found in the book of Numbers is the *bronze serpent* (21:6–9). It is the only occasion when the Lord God presents a type of his Son that is disturbing and offensive. Thoughts of a type of Christ here would be immediately dismissed if it were not for the fact that the Lord Jesus likens *himself* to the serpent raised up in the wilderness (John 3:14–15). The analogy is not simply that the Saviour would be nailed to a cross, as the snake was fastened to a pole, and erected for all to see. There is a far deeper meaning to this analogy. There are features about this period in Israel's history which shed a profound light on the crucified Christ. The people sin (21:5; cf. v.7). The Lord sends punishment (21:6). The people repent and seek forgiveness (21:7). The Lord provides the means of healing which requires faith and obedience (21:8).

The measures which the Lord adopts for healing of the snakebites are highly disturbing. The serpent is the symbol of everything that is evil from the first book of the Bible even to the last. It is the serpent in the Garden of Eden that Satan uses as his agent in tempting Adam and Eve to sin. In the book of Revelation, the devil is referred to as "that serpent of old" (Revelation 12:9). The associations could not be more unpalatable. Nevertheless, the Lord's self-identification with the serpent in the wilderness cannot be passed over lightly. He identifies himself with the solution to the problem of sin. That solution is itself related to the curse of God (the poisonous serpents). Christ is seen therefore as identified, at great personal cost, with the sin (2 Corinthians 5:21), with the curse (Galatians 3:13) and with the cure (John 3:14–16; cf. Numbers 21:9).

Where was the power of healing? It is clear that the power to heal did not reside in the serpent of bronze. There was no answer to that question until the day a young Jew was executed just outside the capital city of Judah.

A type of Christ is suggested in the *water of purification* (19:9–22). This was God's gracious provision for symbolic cleansing (cf. Ezekiel 36:25; Titus 3:5; John 13:8). The water contained the ashes of a red heifer offered as a burnt offering for sin. The water symbolizes cleansing; the ashes of the heifer represent the atoning sacrifice. Together these two point to "the blood of Jesus Christ" which "cleanses us from all sin" and "from all unrighteousness" (1 John 1:7,9).

The *cities of refuge* (35:9–34) remind Christians that the Saviour is our hiding place. Six cities were scattered throughout Israel—three on the west side of the River Jordan and three on its east side. They were to be easily accessible so that the one who had committed manslaughter could take sanctuary from the avenger of blood. In the same way, the Saviour is always within reach. In him, we hide. To him, we have "fled for refuge" (Hebrews 6:18), echoing the words of David who cried out, "Deliver me, O LORD, from my enemies; in You I take shelter" (Psalm 143:9). The apostle Paul says he has renounced all his natural advantages as a Hebrew:

> Yet indeed I also count all things loss for the excellence of the knowledge of Christ Jesus my Lord, for whom I have suffered the loss of all things, and count them as rubbish, that I may gain Christ and be found in Him, not having my own righteousness, which is from the law, but that which is through faith in Christ, the righteousness which is from God by faith (Philippians 3:8–9).

PROPHECIES

When Balak, the king of Moab, called in the non-Israelite prophet Balaam, he expected him to curse Israel and enable the Moabites to win a decisive victory. However, Balaam did not curse them but uttered four prophetic blessings upon Israel. The final prophecy includes these words:

> I see Him, but not now;
> I behold Him, but not near;
> A Star shall come out of Jacob;
> A Scepter shall rise out of Israel,
> And batter the brow of Moab,

> And destroy all the sons of tumult.
>
> And Edom shall be a possession;
> Seir also, his enemies, shall be a possession,
> While Israel does valiantly.
> Out of Jacob One shall have dominion,
> And destroy the remains of the city (24:17–19).

Sometime in the future, a powerful ruler will rise from the Israelites and win a remarkable victory over their enemies. The rising star represents the appearance of a glorious ruler or king, and this is confirmed by saying, "A sceptre shall rise out of Israel," for the sceptre is a symbol of dominion (Genesis 49:10). "By this Ruler, the Jews from the earliest times have understood the Messiah, either exclusively, or else principally, with a secondary reference to David."[7]

> The fulfilment of this prophecy commenced with the subjugation of the Edomites by David (2 Samuel 8:14; 1 Kings 11:15–16; 1 Chronicles 18:12–13), but it will not be completed till "the end of the days," when all the enemies of God and His Church will be made the footstool of Christ (Psalm 110:1).[8]

One of the reasons given by Ernest Hengstenberg for rejecting this prophecy as a prediction of Christ is that he feels "no evidence can be drawn from the New Testament."[9] This would appear to be an unusual oversight for such a scholar. At least two significant verses are to be found: "And so we have the prophetic word confirmed, which you do well to heed as a light that shines in a dark place, until the day dawns and the morning star rises in your hearts" (2 Peter 1:19); and, "I, Jesus, have sent My angel to testify to you these things in the churches. I am the Root and the Offspring of David, the Bright and Morning Star" (Revelation 22:16).

---

[7] Ernest W. Hengstenberg, *Christology of the Old Testament and a Commentary on the Messianic Predictions* (1847; Grand Rapids: Kregel, 1970), 34.

[8] Keil and Delitzsch, *Commentary on the Old Testament: Vol. 3: The Pentateuch*, 194; cf. Franz Delitzsch, *Messianic Prophecies* (Edinburgh: T&T Clark, 1880), 40–41.

[9] Hengstenberg, *Christology of the Old Testament*, 34.

This prophecy of Balaam may also be connected with the leading of the wise men by means of a star (Matthew 2:2,9). Christ is "the Bright and Morning Star." He is the Ruling Star out of Jacob.

NUMBERS / **CONCLUSION**

The Lord leads his people from the bondage of Egypt out into the great unknown with the promised land as the ultimate goal. The first phase of the wilderness journey requires trust and confidence in the Lord's leading and the Lord's providing. The second phase displays the failure of the vast majority of the Israelites through their unbelief and disobedience. The result is thirty-eight more years spent in the wilderness. The third and final phase shows a new generation following Joshua and Caleb and taking up positions for entry into the promised land.

God is concerned about the practical details of our everyday life. He cares about his people's well-being. He provides for their needs. He sustains them daily. He guides them repeatedly. He fights their battles. He frustrates their enemies. He is constantly close at hand. The thing that God cannot abide is sin. The thing that none can hide is sin. For, "Be sure your sin will find you out" (32:23).

NUMBERS / **APPLICATION AND REFLECTION**

Numbers is a bewildering book in many ways. Its style and arrangement are baffling:

> Lists of tribes are followed by accounts of historical events, regulations about sacrifice are given alongside details of intricate legal controversies. It is all very important as history, for we want to know the route of God's people as they made their way to the promised land, but what are the main lessons of this book for a Christian today?[10]

That this book is designed to be of benefit for Christians is beyond dispute (cf. 1 Corinthians 10:1-13). "For whatever things were written before were written for our learning, that we through the patience and comfort of the Scriptures might have hope" (Romans 15:4).

1. Prepared for service

The "numbering" which takes place is, in reality, a registration for service. It shows that every believer is a soldier and that every soldier has something to do (2 Timothy 2:3-4; Ephesians 6:13-17). It further demonstrates that there is strength in organization (2:1-34). God wants his work done, in the same way as he requires his worship to be conducted—"decently and in order" (1 Corinthians 14:40). Every believer has his or her special task to perform in the kingdom of God (Romans 12:4-8; 1 Corinthians 12:4-31; Ephesians 4:16). Special tasks require special talents: spiritual gifts and graces are more necessary than mental or physical qualifications.

2. Gifts for the work of God

The seventh chapter enumerates at great length the offerings of the tribal princes. They each brought exactly the same gifts. Rather than mentioning them as a whole, the narrative spells out each man's contribution individually. The repetition makes the point: "God delights to honour the gifts of His children."[11] The New Testament reinforces the same truth. The Lord Jesus

---

[10] Raymond Brown, *Let's Read the Old Testament* (London: Victory Press, 1971), 33-34.

[11] A.M. Hodgkin, *Christ in All the Scriptures* (London: Pickering and Inglis, 1907), 31.

takes special note of the poor widow placing her two mites in the treasury. He draws the attention of his disciples to her sacrificial giving (Mark 12:42-44). When a woman pours expensive perfume over his feet, the Lord Jesus defends her action and declares it to be the extravagance of faith and love (Luke 7:37-38,47).

The tithe (ten per cent of real income) became the standard for the Israelites in their giving (Genesis 14:20; 28:20-22; Nehemiah 10:38-39; Malachi 3:8-10; Proverbs 3:9-10). But the tithe was not the sum total of their giving. There were many other freewill contributions that the people made to the work of God.

If the principles of giving outlined in the New Testament were observed by the church, there would be no shortage of funds for ministry, evangelism or church-planting at home or abroad: "He who sows sparingly will also reap sparingly, and he who sows bountifully will also reap bountifully. So let each one give as he purposes in his heart, not grudgingly or of necessity; for God loves a cheerful giver" (2 Corinthians 9:6-7).

Tithing is a guideline, and only a guideline, for New Covenant believers. For some believers, the giving of ten per cent of income will involve real self-sacrifice. For others in the Western world, it is too easy and leaves far too much room for self-indulgence. To the Israelites the Lord said, "You shall remember the LORD your God, for it is He who gives you power to get wealth" (Deuteronomy 8:18). And to Christians, Paul sends the message:

> Command those who are rich in this present age not to be haughty, nor to trust in uncertain riches but in the living God, who gives us richly all things to enjoy. Let them do good, that they be rich in good works, ready to give, willing to share, storing up for themselves a good foundation for the time to come, that they may lay hold on eternal life (1 Timothy 6:17-19).

3. Grumbling

The first twenty-five chapters of the book of Numbers illustrate a disgruntled people. The Israelites were constantly moaning—about the journey, the desert, the food, the giants, their leaders. The book of Numbers might well be named "the book of murmurings," for it contains several major incidents of despondency and gloom. Seven distinct episodes of grumbling and complaining are noted from chapters 11 to 21. The children of Israel complained about:

- the journey (11:1-3)
- the food (11:4-6)
- the giants (13:33-14:3)
- their leaders (16:3)
- divine judgement (16:41)
- the desert (20:2-5)
- the manna (21:5; cf. 11:6)

From the many references to grumbling, murmuring and complaining which appear in Scripture, it might well be concluded that this is one of our major failings in the spiritual life. Paul writes:

> Do all things without complaining and disputing, that you may become blameless and harmless, children of God without fault in the midst of a crooked and perverse generation, among whom you shine as lights in the world, holding fast the word of life (Philippians 2:14-16).

4. Unbelief

This fourth book of the Pentateuch contains warnings regarding the dangers and serious consequences of sin and unbelief. The wilderness was the testing-ground of faith: "And you shall remember that the LORD your God led you all the way these forty years in the wilderness, to humble you and test you, to know what was in your heart, whether you would keep His commandments or not" (Deuteronomy 8:2).

Failure to trust God and enter into the promised land resulted in thirty-eight more years of wandering in the wilderness. Under the sentence of death through their unbelief, the large proportion was doomed to die for their sins there in the wastelands. They were not to enter the promised land.

> Beware, brethren, lest there be in any of you an evil heart of unbelief in departing from the living God... For who, having heard, rebelled? Indeed, was it not all who came out of Egypt, led by Moses? Now with whom was He angry forty years? Was it not with those who sinned, whose corpses fell in the wilderness? And to whom did He swear that they would not enter His rest, but to those who did not obey? So we see that they could not enter in because of unbelief. Therefore, since a promise remains of entering His rest, let us fear lest any of you seem to have come short of it. For indeed the gospel was preached to us as

well as to them; but the word which they heard did not profit them, not being mixed with faith in those who heard it (Hebrews 3:12,16-19; 4:1-2).

Illness and death are sometimes *directly* related to individual sin. Such is the connection in the case of the paralyzed man at the pool of Bethesda (John 5:1-15).[12] The same is true in the deaths of Ananias and Sapphira (Acts 5:1-11). Their instant deaths were the result of the immediate judgement of God. The link between sin and suffering, and sin and death, is such that Paul warns the Corinthians about insincerity at the Lord's Supper: "For he who eats and drinks in an unworthy manner eats and drinks judgement to himself, not discerning the Lord's body. *For this reason many are weak and sick among you, and many sleep*" (1 Corinthians 11:29-30, emphasis added).

All suffering, illness and death is related to sin (Romans 5:12; 6:23), but not all suffering, illness and death is *directly* related to specific sins committed by that individual. There is the classic case of Job, who suffered though he was righteous before God. There is the instance of the man born blind, where neither his parents nor himself were directly responsible for his affliction (John 9:2-3).

5. Pressing forward

As we read this story of the Hebrew people and their travels, our thoughts turn to our own walk with God. The Bible pictures the Christian life as a journey: "For here we have no continuing city, but we seek the one to come" (Hebrews 13:14). We are to live "as sojourners and pilgrims" (1 Peter 2:11). Having entered the narrow gate or door (which is Christ, John 10:9), we are to walk the "difficult...way which leads to life" (Matthew 7:13-14). When the apostle Paul pleads with the Christians at Ephesus "to lead a life worthy of the calling with which [they] were called," his actual words are, "*walk worthily*" (Ephesians 4:1). And again to the Corinthians he writes, "For though we *walk* in the flesh, we do not war according to the flesh" (2 Corinthians 10:3). "For we *walk* by faith, not by sight" (2 Corinthians 5:7). The Word of God recognizes that, as we walk, it is easy to take a wrong turn and lose our

---

[12] Is there an intended connection between this man's illness as a result of his sin (John 5:5,14) and the thirty-eight years spent by the children of Israel wandering in the wilderness because of their sin? A number of Bible scholars believe there is such a link.

sense of direction. This is what the book of Numbers is all about. In the period of history covered by this fourth book of the Bible, the children of Israel made a number of serious mistakes. These events and occurrences were recorded for our learning and instruction.

It is an insult to God to look back with longing to our old sinful, pre-conversion days. Within a relatively short time in the wilderness, the Israelites were looking back to their life in Egypt and hankering for those former days. They talked about the food they used to eat when they were in that land—the fish, cucumbers, melons, leeks, onions and garlic. They did not appreciate the blessings which they were experiencing—freedom from slavery, fellowship with God, miraculous provision of food and guidance, and the constant prospect of the promised land before them—"a land which flows with milk and honey" (14:8).

The Lord Jesus warned the Jews of his day to "remember Lot's wife," who looked back (Luke 17:32; cf. Genesis 19:17,26). He also said, "No one, having put his hand to the plough, and looking back, is fit for the kingdom of God" (Luke 9:62).

The Lord not only teaches the danger of looking back with longing, he also encourages believers to be constantly pressing forward: "forgetting those things which are behind and reaching forward to those things which are ahead, I press toward the goal for the prize of the upward call of God in Christ Jesus" (Philippians 3:13-14). When faced with seemingly insurmountable obstacles, such as giants and impregnable cities (13:28), the outcome will depend upon whether we see "the difficulties in the light of God, or God in the shadow of the difficulties."[13] The Lord wants realism in his people, but above all else he requires a strong confidence in his purposes and power (2 Kings 6:16). Let us run with patience, "looking unto Jesus" (Hebrews 12:2).

---

[13] Campbell Morgan, *Student Survey of the Bible*, 39.

DEUTERONOMY

MEANING **"second law"**	AUTHOR **Moses** *(common accepted)*	KEY THOUGHT **Obedience**

THEME

Preparation for entry into the promised land

THEME VERSE
By this word you shall prolong your days in the land which you cross over the Jordan to possess.
DEUTERONOMY 32:47

DEUTERONOMY / **SUMMARY**

PART 1 / **GOD'S ACTS** 1:1–4:43

    a. Review of divine guidance — 1:1–46
    b. Events from Kadesh to Bashan — 2:1–3:29
    c. Exhortation to obey the law — 4:1–43

PART 2 / **GOD'S LAWS** 4:44–26:19

    a. Introduction — 4:44–49
    b. Exposition of the Ten Commandments — 5:1–11:32
    c. Exposition of principal laws of Israel — 12:1–26:19
       (1) Centralization of worship — 12:1–32
       (2) Punishment for idolatry — 13:1–18
       (3) Dietary rules — 14:1–29
       (4) The slaves and the poor — 15:1–23
       (5) Three annual feasts — 16:1–17
       (6) Appointment of judges — 16:18–20
       (7) Prohibition of sacred trees and pillars — 16:21–22
       (8) Punishment for idolatry — 17:1–7
       (9) Court of appeal — 17:8–13
       (10) Choosing a king — 17:14–20
       (11) Priests, Levites and prophets — 18:1–22
       (12) Criminal laws — 19:1–21
       (13) Laws concerning future wars — 20:1–20
       (14) Murder; captive women; rights of firstborn — 21:1–23
       (15) Social and moral behaviour — 22:1–30
       (16) Rights of citizenship in the congregation — 23:1–25
       (17) Divorce; injustice to the poor; gleaning — 24:1–22
       (18) Corporal punishment; levirate marriage — 25:1–19
       (19) Thanksgiving and tithes — 26:1–19

PART 3 / **GOD'S COVENANT** 27:1–30:20

    a. The law enforced — 27:1–26
    b. Blessings and curses — 28:1–68

c.	The Sinai covenant renewed	29:1-29
d.	The blessing of returning to God	30:1-20

PART 4 / **GOD'S SERVANTS** — **31:1-34:12**

a.	The final counsel of Moses	31:1-21
b.	Commission of Joshua; instruction to the Levites	31:22-30
c.	The Song of Moses	32:1-47
d.	Moses to die on Mount Nebo	32:48-52
e.	Moses' final blessing on Israel	33:1-29
f.	The death of Moses	34:1-12

DEUTERONOMY

The name "Deuteronomy" derives from the Septuagint translation of the Old Testament. It means "second law" and came about because of a mistranslation of the phrase, "a copy of this law" (17:18). "Second law" suggests a new law in addition to the first one. This is not the case here. This book contains the original law given almost forty years earlier, repeated and amplified in preparation for the new generation of Israelites to enter into Canaan. It also includes a renewal of covenant obligations as Israel reaffirms a commitment to walk in obedience to the Lord. Under the Lord's direction, Moses also appoints his successor, the man who will lead Israel into the promised land.

In Exodus, Leviticus and Numbers, the Lord speaks directly to Moses, or through Moses to Israel. In Deuteronomy, Moses himself addresses Israel. The gist of his message is this: the Lord is a *unique* God, the God of heaven and earth, spiritual in his being; Israel is a *unique* people especially loved by the Lord. The relationship between God and Israel is *unique*: he is their Father; they are his children and must love him and serve him. Israel owes the Lord a great debt of gratitude.[1]

The book contains a number of discourses, or sermons, given by Moses, with a final chapter recording his death.

DEUTERONOMY / **AUTHOR**

No man was more qualified to receive revelations and instructions from God than "a prophet like Moses, whom the LORD knew face to face" (34:10). When it comes to any passage in the Pentateuch where the authorship of Moses is questioned there seems little to be gained from long and involved arguments in defence. Where the Bible speaks of Moses as the author, there the Christian reader will be content: "Whatever in Scripture—be it Old or New Testament—is directly or by clear implication ascribed to Moses should be assigned to his

---

[1] William Hendriksen, *Survey of the Bible: A Treasury of Bible Information* (Welwyn: Evangelical Press, 1976), 217–218.

authorship."[2] That the occasional insertion was made by later editors, adding a comment here or there to update or clarify geographical (3:13b–14) or historical (10:6–9) detail, does not undermine this position.[3] What is of paramount importance is that the real and ultimate Author of the whole of the Pentateuch is not in doubt—he is God the Holy Spirit (2 Peter 1:20–21; 2 Timothy 3:16). The record can therefore be trusted.

Deuteronomy makes it clear that its contents are substantially the work of Moses. For example:

> So Moses wrote this law and delivered it to the priests, the sons of Levi, who bore the ark of the covenant of the LORD, and to all the elders of Israel. And Moses commanded them, saying… So it was, when Moses had completed writing the words of this law in a book, when they were finished, that Moses commanded the Levites, who bore the ark of the covenant of the LORD, saying: "Take this Book of the Law, and put it beside the ark of the covenant of the LORD your God, that it may be there as a witness." (31:9–10, 24–26).

The Sadducees in New Testament times attributed the authorship of Deuteronomy to Moses (Mark 12:19; cf. Deuteronomy 25:5–6). There was no word to the contrary from the Lord Jesus Christ.

It has been suggested that the book of Deuteronomy may have been "a special favourite" of the Lord Jesus Christ in his childhood, youth and manhood.[4] To support this view, it is pointed out that the Saviour quoted *only* from this book in his conflict with Satan in the great temptations. He was in the wilderness preparing for his ministry of preaching, teaching and healing, spending almost six weeks fasting, and being tempted by Satan (Matthew 4:1–11; Luke 4:1–13; cf. Deuteronomy 8:3; 6:16; 6:13). A more likely explanation for his quotations exclusively from Deuteronomy is that the Lord was indicating the profound

---

[2] Hendriksen, *Survey of the Bible*, 210.
[3] For a brief examination of critical theory against Mosaic authorship, see Raymond B. Dillard and Tremper Longman III, *An Introduction to the Old Testament* (Leicester: Apollos, 1995), 93–97.
[4] Robert Lee, *The Outlined Bible: An Outline and Analysis of Every Book in the Bible* (London: Pickering and Inglis, 1930), analysis no. 5.

link between his period of trial in the wilderness (forty days and forty nights) and the wanderings of the Israelites in the wilderness for forty years.[5] Jesus is the Captain of our salvation (Hebrews 2:10 AV); he is the New Covenant Joshua, about to commence his ministry. He will do all that is necessary to gather his people together ready to lead them into the heavenly Canaan, the ultimate promised land.

DEUTERONOMY / **HISTORICAL SETTING**

The forty years of wandering in the wilderness have almost ended (1:3). Israel is camped in the plains of Moab on the east of the Jordan, across from Jericho. The adult generation of Israelites which left Egypt has died in the wilderness:

> For who, having heard, rebelled? Indeed, was it not all who came out of Egypt, led by Moses? Now with whom was [God] angry forty years? Was it not with those who sinned, whose corpses fell in the wilderness? And to whom did He swear that they would not enter His rest, but to those who did not obey? So we see that they could not enter in because of unbelief (Hebrews 3:16–19).

This was the punishment exacted by the Lord upon all those males over twenty years of age who refused to enter the promised land when the first opportunity arose. Caleb and Joshua, the two faithful spies who honoured God and trusted him, were rewarded by being given the distinction to lead Israel into Canaan.

This fifth book of the Pentateuch is a collection of the final addresses given by Moses to the Israelites in the plains of Moab: "These are the words which Moses spoke to all Israel on this side of the Jordan in the wilderness" (1:1). Deuteronomy begins where Numbers ended (cf. Numbers 36:13), and covers a period of about a month immediately prior to the successful crossing of the Jordan to take possession of Canaan. It is important that the law should be repeated and expounded

---

[5] R.C.H. Lenski at least concedes: "We read about other periods of precisely forty days in the Scriptures, so that it seems as though some mysterious law underlies this number." See R.C.H. Lenski, *The Interpretation of St. Matthew's Gospel* (1943; Minneapolis: Augsburg Publishing House, 1961), 141.

to the new generation before they make their entry into their own land. Moses prepares the people for two highly significant and imminent events: his death and the battles to gain the promised land.

The larger part of the contents of Deuteronomy was probably committed to writing soon after the addresses were given by Moses and shortly before his death (1406 B.C.). At 120 years of age, "His eyes were not dim nor his natural vigour abated" (34:7).

DEUTERONOMY / **OUTLINE**

PART 1 / **GOD'S ACTS (1:1-4:43)**

Moses summarizes the Lord's guidance from Horeb (Mount Sinai) to Kadesh Barnea. He once more reminds the people of the rebellion and unbelief of their parents who refused to enter into Canaan. This resulted in another thirty-eight years being spent in the wilderness. When the forty years of wandering in the wilderness came to an end, the Lord directed the Israelites back to Kadesh Barnea in preparation for taking the land of Canaan. From Kadesh Barnea, they moved in a roundabout way to the plains of Moab, on the east of the River Jordan opposite Jericho (see Map 3). En route the Lord gave them victory over the attacking forces of King Sihon and King Og. God also foiled the plans of Balak, king of the Amorites. The land east of Jordan was made secure so that the Israelites could proceed in crossing the river and taking Canaan.

Moses reminds the people of what the Lord has done in bringing them out of Egypt. He recounts the mighty deeds of God. God is about to fulfil another of his promises by giving them their own land (1:8). The threefold blessing which God gave Abraham concerned the promise of land, the promise of numerous descendants and the promise of outstanding blessing (Genesis 12:1-3,7). During the years spent in Egypt, the years covered by the book of Exodus, the family of Abraham increased rapidly through his grandson Jacob. The promise of numerous descendants was moving toward realization. In Deuteronomy, the Israelites are on the threshold of receiving the second part of the promise—their own land. The final aspect of the threefold promise is that in Abraham "all the families of the earth shall be blessed." That promise will await the coming of the Messiah with his worldwide blessing of salvation.

Moses urges the people to faithfulness and calls for their obedience to the Lord and his law (4:1–40). He then establishes three cities of refuge in the land to the east of Jordan, for those who commit manslaughter (that is, unintentional killing, as distinct from murder).

PART 2 / **GOD'S LAWS (4:44–26:19)**

This main section deals with a series of laws and exhortations about various aspects of life. Moses begins by expounding the Decalogue (the Ten Commandments) given by the Lord on Mount Sinai. He then reminds the congregation of their covenantal obligations to worship and serve the true God and instructs the Israelites to preserve these laws and communicate them to succeeding generations:

> Hear, O Israel: The LORD our God, the LORD is one! You shall love the LORD your God with all your heart, with all your soul, and with all your strength.
>
> And these words which I command you today shall be in your heart. You shall teach them diligently to your children, and shall talk of them when you sit in your house, when you walk by the way, when you lie down, and when you rise up (6:4–7).

These laws have not only to be taught; they have also to be obeyed. If the people do not obey, they will soon be drawn into idolatry instead of the pure worship of the living God. In order to remove the temptation to idolatry, the Israelites are commanded to exterminate the Canaanites. They are to be the instruments of God's righteous judgement against wicked and idolatrous nations (9:4–5).

Possessing and maintaining possession of the promised land is made dependent upon the loving obedience of the Israelites as the people of God (8:1; 11:8–9; 16:20). The people are reminded of the sins of past generations and warned about self-righteousness. They will owe their conquest and possession of Canaan, not to their own righteousness, but solely to the compassion and covenant faithfulness of the Lord.

Love and obedience will be rewarded with blessing (7:12–24; 11:1–25). Disobedience will bring a curse (11:28).

In expounding the main laws originally given at Sinai, Moses adds others that have direct relevance to living in a settled community in

Canaan. Worship will be in a central location appointed by God (12:1–28). Idolatry is a great evil (12:29–32) and must be dealt with decisively. Three cases are cited. The first is that of a false prophet who leads the people into idolatry. He is to be put to death (13:1–5). The second is that of a close member of the family who entices others to idolatry. The guilty party has to be stoned to death (13:6–11). The third case refers to a whole city that has been led into idolatry. Upon hearing an accusation, a full investigation has to be carried out. If the case is proven then all the inhabitants of that city are to be put to the sword (13:12–18).

In anticipation of the death of Moses, attention is given to providing orderly government for Israel by the establishment of judges, courts of appeal, priests, Levites, kings and prophets (16:18–18:22). Israel is a *theocracy*—a nation governed by God. The Lord does the choosing. Twenty-five times the verb *choose* occurs in this section, emphasizing the Lord's sovereign choice. God *chose* Israel. He *chose* the priests and the Levites (18:5). He will *choose* the place where he will be worshipped (12:26). He will *choose* a king (17:15).

In seeking to discern God's choice of a king the people are to note that the qualifications for kingship are quite strict:

1. He must be an Israelite.
2. He must not increase the number of horses because this may lead the Israelites back to Egypt (good horses were bred by the Egyptians—1 Kings 10:28).
3. He must not have many wives because they may turn his heart from the true God.
4. He must not amass silver and gold because these may make him self-sufficient, self-indulgent and arrogant.
5. He must have his own copy of the law and read it, meditate upon it and obey it (17:14–20).

When Israel comes into her own land, there will be need for further revelations from the Lord. The Lord will establish the prophetic office for this purpose. Detailed guidelines are laid down to distinguish the true from the false prophet. The nine abominations of the Canaanites, for which they are to be dispossessed, are spelled out (18:9–14). These practices must never be found among the people of God. The true prophet must be: firstly, an Israelite; secondly, like Moses, a mediator between God and the people; thirdly, one who speaks only the words of God; and, fourthly, one whose prophecies come true (18:15-22).

Once the land has been occupied, three cities of refuge are to be set up so that anyone guilty of manslaughter—that is, accidental, unpremeditated killing—might run there and be safe (19:1-7; cf. 4:41-43; Exodus 21:12-14; Numbers 35:9-34). Eventually, there would be six cities of refuge, three in the promised land and three across from the Jordan (Numbers 35:13-14).

Changing a neighbour's land boundaries is forbidden (19:14), and laws of witness are laid down (19:15-21). Even the principles governing warfare are spelled out (20:1-20). Only when the offer of peace has been rejected by the enemy should an attack be mounted (20:10-15).

The laws of Deuteronomy indicate that spirituality is not to be divorced from the rest of life. Love for God is to be expressed in *every* area of life: civil, domestic and personal. Numerous practical issues are covered, including the treatment of women captured in war, the inheritance rights of the firstborn, punishment for a disobedient son, the burial of criminals who have been hanged on a tree, respect for a neighbour's animals and property, various laws governing sexual behaviour, grounds for exclusion from the congregation, maintenance of cleanliness in the camp, treatment of runaway slaves, divorce and remarriage, freedom from military service for one year following marriage, articles taken as security against a loan, warnings against injustice, restrictions on corporal punishment, levirate marriage[6] and fighting and fraud (21:10-25:16). Instruction is also given that the Amalekites are to be destroyed because of their unprovoked attack upon Israel (25:17-19).

This section ends with rules about services of thanksgiving to God for his mercy and providence. Offerings of firstfruits and tithes are to be brought to the priest (26:1-15).

PART 3 / **GOD'S COVENANT (27:1-30:20)**

On entry into the promised land, the Israelites are to assemble in two companies, one upon Mount Gerizim and the other upon Mount

---

[6] The obligation of a man to marry his deceased brother's wife who has no son in order to maintain the family name and inheritance.

Ebal. Six tribes on Mount Gerizim are to speak blessings upon those who are obedient and believing (27:12; 28:1–14). Six tribes on Mount Ebal are to declare the curses that will fall upon those who are disobedient and unbelieving (27:13–26; 28:15–68). These blessings and curses are listed in detail to enforce the vital importance of obedience and faith.

The covenant renewed by Israel is not simply a commitment to the legal requirements of a contract (29:1–29).[7] It is the pledge and promise of a *living relationship* expressed in the loving, faithful commitment of both God and his people (6:5; 7:9,12–13; 11:1). "God's covenant with His people is a proclamation of His sovereignty and an instrument for binding His elect to Himself in a commitment of absolute allegiance."[8] Nevertheless the people are still responsible to choose to obey God.

The reiteration of the covenant is followed by an overview of covenantal promise (30:1–10).

The blessings God has promised will all be fulfilled; Israel will enter the land and drive out their enemies; God will set His name in their midst at the place of His choosing. But Israel will continue to rebel and the curses of the covenant will also be realized. The people will be driven from the land into exile. Then, after the blessings and the curses, God will gather His scattered people and circumcise their hearts to love the Lord with all their heart and soul, that they may live.[9]

PART 4 / **GOD'S SERVANTS (31:1–34:12)**

The closing chapters of this magnificent book direct our attention to two servants of God: Moses and Joshua. Moses is nearing the end of his days and he knows full well that his days of service are fast drawing

---

[7] The word "covenant" appears twenty-one times in Deuteronomy (seven times in chapter 29).
[8] Meredith G. Kline, cited by Irving L. Jensen, *Jensen's Survey of the Old Testament: Search and Discover* (Chicago: Moody, 1978), 131.
[9] Edmund P. Clowney, "Preaching Christ from All the Scriptures," in Samuel T. Logan Jr., ed., *The Preacher and Preaching: Reviving the Art in the Twentieth Century* (Phillipsburg: Presbyterian & Reformed, 1986), 168.

to a close: "Then Moses went and spoke these words to all Israel, and he said to them: 'I am one hundred and twenty years old today. I can no longer go out and come in. Also the Lord has said to me, "You shall not cross over this Jordan"'" (31:1–3).

The expression, "I can no longer go out and come in," is not an indication of infirmity and lack of mobility for, at his death, it is testified of Moses: "His eyes were not dim nor his natural vigour abated" (34:7). It means that he could no longer work for the nation (cf. Numbers 27:16–17).

The law is to be read every seven years (31:10–11). A copy of the completed law is to be placed beside the ark of the covenant (31:26).

The Song of Moses is a magnificent psalm that contrasts the faithfulness of God with the unfaithfulness of his people. Did Moses and Joshua sing this as a duet in the presence of the congregation? (32:44).

> Ascribe greatness to our God.
> He is the Rock, His work is perfect;
> For all His ways are justice,
> A God of truth and without injustice;
> Righteous and upright is He (32:3–4, part of the first stanza).

The four stanzas in Moses' song outline the entire history of Israel from start to finish: Israel's creation and gracious treatment (32:1–14); her ingratitude and apostasy (32:15–19); God's judgement (32:20–35); and Israel's salvation through the fire of judgement (32:36–43).[10]

Joshua is appointed as successor to Moses (31:3,23). He is to take up the mantle from Moses. He will take the Israelites into the promised land:

> Now Joshua the son of Nun was full of the spirit of wisdom, for Moses had laid his hands on him; so the children of Israel heeded him, and did as the Lord had commanded Moses.
> But since then there has not arisen in Israel a prophet like Moses, whom the Lord knew face to face, in all the signs and wonders which the Lord sent him to do in the land of Egypt,

---

[10] Franz Delitzsch, *Messianic Prophecies* (Edinburgh: T&T Clark, 1880), 41.

before Pharaoh, before all his servants, and in all his land, and by all that mighty power and all the great terror which Moses performed in the sight of all Israel (34:9–12).

There is no resistance in Moses the man of God, no resentment toward the Lord for his judgements. Moses dies, as he has lived, a spiritual giant. He dies "the death of the righteous" for, unlike Balaam, he has lived the life of the righteous (see Numbers 23:10).

The attitude of Moses is reflected in the death of Mr. Valiant for Truth in John Bunyan's *Pilgrim's Progress*. Just as he is about to cross the river he testifies to his friends:

> I am going to my Father's, and tho' with great difficulty I am got hither, yet now I do not repent me of all the trouble I have been at to arrive where I am. *My Sword* I give to him that shall succeed me in my Pilgrimage, and my *Courage* and *Skill* to him that can get it. My *marks* and *scars* I carry with me, to be a witness for me, that I have fought His battles, who now will be my Rewarder.[11]

DEUTERONOMY / **CHRIST AND HIS CHURCH**

Every book of the Pentateuch makes its distinct and lasting contribution to the unfolding of revelation and preparation for the coming of the Lord Jesus Christ. The book of Deuteronomy provides unique material in laying the foundation for the work of the Son of God who became Jesus the Christ.

PROPHECIES

1. The great Prophet

> The LORD your God will raise up for you a Prophet like me from your midst, from your brethren. Him you shall hear, according to all you desired of the LORD your God in Horeb in the day of the assembly, saying, "Let me not hear again the voice of the

---

[11] John Bunyan, *The Pilgrim's Progress: From This World to That Which Is To Come* (1676; Edinburgh: Banner of Truth Trust, 1977), 376.

Lord my God, nor let me see this great fire anymore, lest I die." And the Lord said to me: "What they have spoken is good. I will raise up for them a Prophet like you from among their brethren, and will put My words in His mouth, and He shall speak to them all that I command Him. And it shall be that whoever will not hear My words, which He speaks in My name, I will require it of him" (18:15–19).

When the book of Deuteronomy ends by declaring, "There has not arisen in Israel a prophet like Moses, whom the Lord knew face to face" (34:10), the way is paved for Israel to keep looking for the coming of "the Prophet." This explains the question of the priests and Levites, many years later, when they addressed John the Baptist and, among other things, asked, "Are you the Prophet?" (John 1:21). It also explains the reaction of the crowd when the Lord Jesus fed the 5,000: "Then those men, when they had seen the sign that Jesus did, said, 'This is truly the Prophet who is to come into the world'" (John 6:14).

We might have expected the Lord to have been delighted that they were beginning to see him as the promised Prophet. But he was not pleased. They had missed the point. What is the most significant part of being a prophet? Is it not *the words* that he speaks from God? (18:18–19). These men were rightly linking the miracles of Jesus with the credentials of Messiah and associating Messiah with "the Prophet," but they were not listening to his words. Miracles and wonders do not in themselves prove the authenticity of a prophet. That depends supremely upon *the content* of his teaching (13:1–4).

The priority for the Lord Jesus was *teaching*, not *miracles*. Just before the feeding of the 5,000, when he was followed by a great crowd, it is recorded that "He received them and spoke to them about the kingdom of God, and healed those who had need of healing" (Luke 9:11). Jesus is the Prophet. He speaks the authentic word from God. His words are life and death.

The promised Prophet is the promised Messiah

That the promised Prophet was linked in the thinking of the Jews to the promised Messiah is clear from the manner in which the apostle Peter and Stephen the martyr take this connection for granted (Acts 3:18,22; 7:37). Both take it as the general view held by all Jews. Neither of them considers it necessary to elaborate this point when affirming Jesus as the promised Messiah and the promised Prophet. It is also likely that Philip had this passage in Deuteronomy in mind when he found Nathanael and told him, "We have found him of whom *Moses in the law...wrote*—Jesus of Nazareth, the son of Joseph" (John 1:45, emphasis added).

Even the woman of Samaria, with her religious education that restricted her to receiving only the five books of Moses as the Word of God, was able to declare, "I know that Messiah is coming.... When He comes, He will tell us all things" (John 4:25). The connection with the concluding words of Deuteronomy 18:18 seems evident: "...and will put My words in His mouth, and He shall speak to them all that I command Him."

On the Mount of Transfiguration, the words of the Father from the cloud revealed the Messiah: "This is My beloved Son, in whom I am well pleased. Hear Him!" (Matthew 17:5). As the first sentence is a paraphrase of the prophecy in Isaiah 42:1, so the last instruction points to the great Prophet under consideration. To listen to Christ is to listen to "the Prophet." His words are life and death. It is crucial that he is heard. "Hear him!" says the Father.

When Jesus invited all who were thirsty to come to him and receive a constant "flow of living water," many of his hearers saw the link between the miraculous supply of water in the wilderness (Exodus 17:1–6; Numbers 20:7–12) and the promise of a prophet (18:15–19): "Therefore many from the crowd, when they heard this saying, said, 'Truly this is the Prophet'" (John 7:40).

2. The great curse

How significant that the altar of sacrifice for burnt offering and for peace offering was to be built upon Mount Ebal, the mountain of cursing (27:4–7,13–26). It points to the Lord Jesus Christ becoming accursed and replacing the curse upon his people by blessing. Deuteronomy is even more specific in relation to Christ's sacrificial work. This is the first time we hear of death by hanging on a tree:

> If a man has committed a sin deserving of death, and he is put to death, and you hang him on a tree, his body shall not remain overnight on the tree, but you shall surely bury him that day, so

that you do not defile the land which the Lord your God is giving you as an inheritance; for he who is hanged is accursed of God. (21:22–23).

The apostle Paul reveals the implications:

> For as many as are of the works of the law are under the curse; for it is written, "Cursed is everyone who does not continue in all things which are written in the book of the law, to do them." But that no one is justified by the law in the sight of God is evident, for "the just shall live by faith." Yet the law is not of faith, but "the man who does them shall live by them."
> Christ has redeemed us from the curse of the law, having become a curse for us (for it is written, "Cursed is everyone who hangs on a tree"), that the blessing of Abraham might come upon the Gentiles in Christ Jesus, that we might receive the promise of the Spirit through faith (Galatians 3:10–14).

This is the gospel: "Christ has redeemed us from the curse of the law, having become a curse for us" (Galatians 3:13). The law of Deuteronomy is preparation for the profound significance of the crucifixion. Believers are freed from the curse by the Saviour who became accursed. In the New Testament, five times the cross is spoken of as "a tree" (Acts 5:30; 10:39; 13:29; Galatians 3:13; 1 Peter 2:24). The apostles Peter and Paul obviously see the immense importance of the link between the cross of Christ and the curse of Deuteronomy 21:22–23. Yet this still leaves the question: Why did God choose to single out this death—death by hanging on a tree—as the one to be particularly and specifically accursed? Why not death by stoning? Why not death by fire? Why not death by drowning? Why death upon a tree? Why did the Lord isolate this mode of death as the special one to be accursed? Clearly it was to prepare for the cross, with the humiliation and shame experienced by the Saviour. But is there more to be discovered here?

Why should *tree* be used in place of *cross*? Why should the sinner who had committed a sin worthy of death be hanged upon a tree? What association would Moses have been able to form? He could certainly think about the significance of a tree. The prophets "enquired and searched diligently" to understand words given to them by God

(1 Peter 1:10–11). Moses was the historian of Genesis. He had recorded the first "sin to death" (Romans 6:16). That first sin of all sin was associated with a tree. Moses had noted that two special trees were planted in the Garden of Eden: "And out of the ground the LORD God made every tree grow that is pleasant to the sight and good for food. The tree of life was also in the midst of the garden, and the tree of the knowledge of good and evil" (Genesis 2:9).

"The tree of the knowledge of good and evil" was to Adam and Eve the tree of death.[12] Contact with that tree brought the sentence of death. From that moment they had to be kept from the tree of life:

> Then the LORD God said, "Behold, the man has become like one of Us, to know good and evil. And now, lest he put out his hand and take also of the tree of life, and eat, and live forever"—therefore the LORD God sent him out of the garden of Eden to till the ground from which he was taken. So He drove out the man; and He placed cherubim at the east of the garden of Eden, and a flaming sword which turned every way, to guard the way to the tree of life (Genesis 3:22–24).

The Lord Jesus Christ is *the tree of life* who dies upon *the tree of death*. He is cut down, cast into Marah, the waters of the bitterness of God's wrath (Exodus 15:25). On the way to Golgotha, having been unjustly sentenced to death, the Lord Jesus Christ carried his cross to the place of execution. Along the way he passed a group of women who were weeping for him. The Lord told them not to weep for him, but rather to weep for themselves because they were going to face dreadful days ahead. He went on to say, "For if they do these things in the green wood, what will be done in the dry?" (Luke 23:31). The Greek word translated here as *wood* is the same one that is translated as *tree* in Galatians 3:13, where we read, "Cursed is everyone who hangs on a tree" and, in 1 Peter 2:24, where the apostle says that Christ "himself bore our sins in his own body on the tree."

In his words to the women Jesus is drawing a contrast between *green* wood and *dry* wood. Dry wood burns and is consumed easily. Green

---

[12] Rudolf Stier, *The Words of the Apostles* (1869; Minneapolis: Klock and Klock, 1981), 90.

wood is wet and does not burn easily. If the Gentile Romans will crucify the Lord Jesus, dealing so with a green and yielding tree, what will they do to the Jews, who are a hard and unyielding dry tree? John Calvin delves deeper:

> [Jesus] takes an everyday simile to show that they cannot avoid the divine fire lighting on them and at once devouring them in its flame. We know how dry wood is usually thrown first on the fire, but if the wet and green wood is already alight, there will be far less delay for the dry.[13]

Divine judgement is falling on the Lord Jesus Christ. He is to be crucified "by the carefully planned intention and foreknowledge of God" (Acts 2:23)—he who is the green wood; the young tree; ever yielding to the Father, ever obedient to the Law; without sin; without fault; without flaw.

> Jesus suffered the agonies of hell especially on Calvary, but when that suffering was finished he sat down at the right hand of the Father, full of glory, honour and power. But for the impenitents the suffering will never end: Jerusalem's fall will be only a foretaste of their everlasting damnation.[14]

DEUTERONOMY / **CONCLUSION**

The book of Deuteronomy is not merely a repetition of things commanded and done as already recorded in Exodus, Leviticus and Numbers. It is rather

> a description, explanation, and enforcement of the most essential contents of the covenant revelation and covenant laws, with emphatic prominence given to the spiritual principle of the law and its fulfilment, and with a further development of the

---

[13] John Calvin, *A Harmony of the Gospels: Matthew, Mark and Luke*, vol. 3 (Edinburgh: St Andrew Press, 1972), 191–192.

[14] William Hendriksen, *The Gospel of Luke* (Edinburgh: Banner of Truth Trust, 1979), 1025.

ecclesiastical, judicial, political, and civil organization, which was intended as a permanent foundation for the life and well-being of the people in the land of Canaan.[15]

In some respects Deuteronomy portrays what an ideal Israel should be. It presents an Israel with "one God, one people, one land, one sanctuary, and one law."[16] The church of Jesus Christ as revealed in the New Testament embodies this same sense of unity. In his high priestly prayer, the Lord Jesus prayed that his people might be one (John 17:21). And the apostle Paul reiterates this singular concord in the church: "There is one body and one Spirit, just as you were called in one hope of your calling; one Lord, one faith, one baptism; one God and Father of all, who is above all, and through all, and in you all" (Ephesians 4:4–6).

---

[15] C.F. Keil and F. Delitzsch, *Commentary on the Old Testament: Vol. 3: The Pentateuch* (Grand Rapids: Eerdmans, 1980), 270.
[16] Dillard and Longman, *An Introduction to the Old Testament*, 102.

DEUTERONOMY / **APPLICATION AND REFLECTION**

1. Moses and Christ

Moses is one of the greatest of all the Old Testament characters: he had a profound and lasting impact upon the whole nation of Israel. He was the nation's leader, lawgiver, prophet and historian. No Israelite ever questioned what he wrote. Appeal was made to his law as the final arbitrator in all disputes. Born of Hebrew stock, educated in the Egyptian court, having forty years' communion with the Lord in the solitude of the district of Midian, no one was more suited as the mouthpiece of the living God.

Though not permitted to lead Israel into the promised land, a greater honour awaited him many years later. On the Mount of Transfiguration he was privileged to stand once more on the earth, this time in the company of the prophet Elijah and the apostles Peter, James and John. The greater honour still was to be standing there in the presence of the Lord Jesus Christ and discuss the Saviour's death (*exodos*—literally, *departure*, Luke 9:31). They were talking about the crucifixion!

The writer to the Hebrews indicates some of the comparisons and contrasts between Moses and the Lord Jesus (Hebrews 3:1-6) and also gives this testimony of him: "Moses indeed was faithful in all his house as a servant, for a testimony of those things which would be spoken afterwards" (Hebrews 3:5).

The contrast between that which Moses and Christ each represent is brought out in the words of the apostle John: "For the law was given through Moses, but grace and truth came through Jesus Christ" (John 1:17). With this distinction in mind, it is interesting to consider the latter days of Moses, especially with regard to his being a symbol, or type, of the law of God.

Moses, as the representative of the law, could not lead the children of Israel into the promised land.[17] "For what the law could not do in that it was weak through the flesh, God did by sending His own Son in the likeness of sinful flesh" (Romans 8:3-4; cf. 3:21-22). A new leader was necessary. In the providence of God, the man appointed was Joshua (the Hebrew form of the Greek name "Jesus"). He was to take up the mantle from Moses. At 120 years of age, Moses' "eyes were not dim nor his natural vigour abated" (34:7), for the law of God never loses its strength. Moses was buried in an

---

[17] A.M. Hodgkin, *Christ in All the Scriptures* (London: Pickering and Inglis, 1907), 37.

unknown grave (34:6). In like manner, believers "have become dead to the law through the body of Christ" (Romans 7:4; cf. vv.1-3). "For Christ is the end of the law for righteousness to everyone who believes" (Romans 10:4).

2. Instructing the young

The necessity of godly parenting, by example and by education, is delightfully expressed:

> Hear, O Israel: The LORD our God, the LORD is one! You shall love the LORD your God with all your heart, with all your soul, and with all your strength.
> And these words which I command you today shall be in your heart. You shall teach them diligently to your children, and shall talk of them when you sit in your house, when you walk by the way, when you lie down, and when you rise up (6:4-7).

The apostle Paul reinforces the duty of parents to train their children in the ways of the Lord (Ephesians 6:4). "Children are a heritage from the LORD" (Psalm 127:3). With such a blessing comes serious and sober responsibility. The Lord "seeks godly offspring" (Malachi 2:15). The Christian home is to be a loving centre of education—training children up in the things of God. They are to be taught and guided in how to live life *with* God and live life *for* God.

3. Things to remember

The key word in Deuteronomy is *remember* (occurring fourteen times). In order to promote obedience, God calls upon the people to recollect the events and experiences of the past. This word invites the children of Israel to look over their shoulder. They are told that they must not forget that God has done great things for them. Years later, David will compose many psalms which remind the Israelites of God's mercy and goodness in many wonderful and tangible ways. For example:

> One generation shall praise Your works to another,
> And shall declare Your mighty acts.
> I will meditate on the glorious splendor of Your majesty,
> And on Your wondrous works.
> Men shall speak of the might of Your awesome acts,

And I will declare Your greatness.
They shall utter the memory of Your great goodness,
And shall sing of Your righteousness (Psalm 145:4-7).

In the wilderness Moses called the people to remember:

- the giving of the law on Mount Sinai (also called Horeb—4:9-10)
- the covenant of the LORD (4:23);
- their slavery in Egypt (5:15)
- their great deliverance (7:18)
- the providence of God in the wilderness (8:2-6)
- their rebellion and sin (9:7)
- the punishments inflicted by God (24:9)
- their history (32:7)

Christians are also to remember. With spiritual insight, believers can remember that once we were slaves of sin and the Lord our God brought us "out from there by a mighty hand and by an outstretched arm" (5:15; cf. Romans 6:17-18). We are to remember the injunctions of Scripture:

> Beloved, I now write to you this second epistle (in both of which I stir up your pure minds by way of reminder), that you may be mindful of the words which were spoken before by the holy prophets, and of the commandment of us, the apostles of the Lord and Savior (2 Peter 3:1-2).

4. Obedience

Together with *remember*, there are other key words such as *hear* (over thirty times) and *do* (about 100 times). Obedience from the Israelites does not *earn* the favour of God, but is required because they already enjoy his favour. They are not expected to purchase their redemption by obedience, but to obey *because* they are already redeemed. Time and again they are told that God loves them and has chosen them. Because he loves them and has chosen them he took them out of bondage in Egypt. He has made them his special people; therefore they should respond by loving him in return, by being holy, and by keeping his laws.

This same order, grace then good works, is also emphasized in the New Testament: "For by grace you have been saved through faith, and that not of yourselves; it is the gift of God, not of works, lest anyone should boast. For we are His workmanship, created in Christ Jesus for good works" (Ephesians 2:8-10; cf. Titus 2:13-14).

Possessing the land of promise and keeping it were dependent upon the obedience of the children of Israel to the commandments of God. The obedience which the Lord requires is not servile obedience. It is to be obedience motivated and promoted by love. The word *love*, as expressing the relationship between God and his people, occurs only once in Exodus, when God declares that he shows "mercy to thousands, to those who love [Him] and keep [His] commandments" (Exodus 20:6). It is applied to the relationship between people in Leviticus: "You shall love your neighbour as yourself" (Leviticus 19:18; cf. v. 34). The word *love* is a lonely stranger in the first four books. Everything is changed in the book of Deuteronomy.

Its supreme and overwhelming message is that of love. To understand this will enable us to state the permanent values, and to deduce the living message... God's love of man is the motive of His government; and...man's love of God is the motive of his obedience.[18]

---

[18] G. Campbell Morgan, *Student Survey of the Bible* (Iowa Falls: World Bible Publishers, 1993), 45–46.

JOSHUA

MEANING	AUTHOR	KEY THOUGHT
"Jehovah is salvation"	**Joshua** *(predominantly)*	**Trusting brings victory**

THEME

Success and failure in the life of faith

THEME VERSE

Be strong and of good courage; do not be afraid, nor be dismayed, for the LORD your God is with you wherever you go.
JOSHUA 1:9

JOSHUA / **SUMMARY**

PART 1 / **ENTRY INTO THE PROMISED LAND**   1:1-5:12

a.	Confirmation of Joshua's leadership	1:1-9
b.	Preparation for crossing the Jordan	1:10-18
c.	Spies sent into Jericho	2:1-24
d.	Israel crosses the Jordan	3:1-17
e.	Two piles of memorial stones	4:1-5:1
f.	Second generation circumcised	5:2-12

PART 2 / **CONQUEST OF THE PROMISED LAND**   5:13-12:24

a.	Commander of the Lord's army	5:13-6:5
b.	The fall of Jericho (central Canaan)	6:6-27
c.	Achan's disobedience	7:1-26
d.	Conquest of Ai (central Canaan)	8:1-29
e.	Covenant renewed at Shechem	8:30-35
f.	Treaty with the Gibeonites	9:1-27
g.	Victory at:	
	a. Gibeon (southern Canaan)	10:1-27
	b. Makkedah (southern Canaan)	10:28-43
	c. Merom (northern Canaan)	11:1-15
h.	Summary of the conquest	11:16-12:24

PART 3 / **DIVISION OF THE PROMISED LAND**   13:1-22:34

a.	An unfinished task	13:1-7
b.	Distribution of the land:	
	a. Reuben, Gad and East Manasseh	13:8-33
	b. Judah	14:1-15:63
	c. Ephraim and West Manasseh	16:1-17:18
	d. The remaining seven tribes	18:1-19:51
c.	The cities of refuge	20:1-9
d.	The cities of the Levites	21:1-45
e.	Transjordan: tribes return to the east	22:1-34

PART 4 / **THE LAST DAYS OF JOSHUA**   **23:1–24:33**

a. Joshua's last address to the leaders   23:1-16
b. Joshua's last address to the people   24:1-28
c. Death of Joshua   24:29-31
d. Bones of Joseph   24:32
e. Death of Eleazar   24:33

JOSHUA

The book of Joshua records one of the most interesting and important periods in Israel's history. It deals with the establishment of the children of Israel as a nation in their own land. Genesis provides the *prophecy*, and the other four books of Moses provide the *preparation*. The first section of our Bibles, the Pentateuch (the first five books), is followed by the twelve historical books (Joshua to Esther).

The book of Joshua represents a distinct turning-point. It marks the end of Israel's trials and wanderings in the wilderness, and at the same time sets out the beginning of their new life as a settled community in their own land. What the Lord began in the great Exodus from Egypt he now completes in the settlement of Israel in the promised land.

JOSHUA / **AUTHOR**

In its present form, the book cannot have been written by Joshua, for it includes records of events which did not take place until after his death. Among these are the conquest of Debir (Kirjath Sepher) by Othniel (15:15–17) and of Leshem by the Danites (19:47). The accounts of the death of Joshua and of Eleazar show that the book is later than Joshua's time.[1] Jewish tradition maintains that Eleazar added the account of Joshua's death, and that Phinehas added the account of Eleazar's death.) Another pointer that the final composition may have been made by a later editor or compiler is the frequent expression "to this day" (4:9; 5:9; 6:25; 7:26; 8:28; 13:13; 15:63). Within the book itself, there is no evidence upon which to reject Joshua's authorship of the major part. Alternatively, a historian could have used substantial written or spoken material from Joshua (see 18:8–9; 24:26), adding other information to amplify or clarify (e.g. 10:13). Confidence in this portion of God's Word, as in any other, does not depend upon its human author. The divine origin is not in question.

The book of Joshua may therefore be trusted as a reliable and trustworthy record.

---

[1] Edward J. Young, *An Introduction to the Old Testament* (Grand Rapids: Eerdmans, 1949), 163.

Joshua's original name was *Hoshea* (Numbers 13:8; Deuteronomy 32:44), which literally means "salvation." During the wilderness journey, Moses renamed him *Jehoshua* (*Joshua* is a contracted form), meaning, "Jehovah is salvation" (Numbers 13:16).

Joshua was born in the land of Egypt and, with the sole exception of Caleb, he was the only adult Israelite in the great Exodus who survived the forty years of wandering in the wilderness and entered Canaan. He is first mentioned in Exodus 17:9, where Moses instructs him: "Choose us some men and go out, fight with Amalek." At this point, there is no indication of Joshua's parentage, early history or his piety, yet from this brief statement we can form some idea of the man. It is evident that Joshua had already attracted the attention of Moses and gained his confidence as a man of courage and competence, suited to be a captain over others. There was an immediate response from Joshua, for the next verse reads, "So Joshua did as Moses said to him, and fought with Amalek" (Exodus 17:10). Success was on Joshua's side, for "Joshua defeated Amalek and his people with the edge of the sword" (Exodus 17:13). This first mention of Joshua seems to set the tone and content of his future work for the Lord as captain of the people of God, successfully winning victories over God's enemies. Later the Lord gave him illumination, wisdom and authority to lead the whole congregation (Numbers 27:18–23).

Joshua was a great ruler, and because of his wisdom and godliness, he commanded the respect of all his subjects (Deuteronomy 34:9). He maintained order and discipline, putting the worship of God central in the nation's government and life. He encouraged the people to greater godliness. He was also a great military leader, using his God-given talents of wisdom, confidence and courage to outwit his enemies.

JOSHUA / **HISTORICAL SETTING**

Five-hundred-and-fifty years earlier, the Lord had led Abraham away from his home in Ur of the Chaldeans to the land of Canaan (Genesis 11:31; 12:1). Once in Canaan, the Lord gave Abraham a solemn promise: "To your descendants I will give this land" (Genesis 12:7). There was, however, to be a time lapse. The Lord revealed to Abraham the extent of the intervening years:

> Know certainly that your descendants will be strangers in a land that is not theirs, and will serve them, and they will afflict them four hundred years. And also the nation whom they serve I will judge; afterward they shall come out with great possessions (Genesis 15:13–14).

Twenty-four years after leaving Haran, the Lord amplified and confirmed his earlier promise:

> And I will establish My covenant between Me and you and your descendants after you in their generations, for an everlasting covenant, to be God to you and your descendants after you. Also I give to you and your descendants after you the land in which you are a stranger, all the land of Canaan, as an everlasting possession; and I will be their God (Genesis 17:7–8).

The book of Genesis ends with the settlement of the Israelites in Egypt. Exodus takes up the history with a brief mention of the intervening 400 years. From being treated as honoured guests in the land of Egypt, the Israelites become persecuted slaves. Exodus records how the Lord delivers his people and leads them from Egypt, through the Red Sea and the wilderness to arrive, after six weeks or so, at Mount Sinai in Horeb, where they receive the Ten Commandments. Leviticus takes up the story of the eleven-month stay at Mount Sinai, with the construction of the tabernacle, the establishment of an elaborate sacrificial system and the inauguration of detailed annual festivals. Numbers records the dismantling of the tabernacle at Sinai, the journey to Kadesh Barnea, the failed entry into the promised land, thirty-eight further years of wandering in the wilderness, and finally the trek around Edom and Moab to arrive on the plains of Moab. Deuteronomy continues the history of the Israelites with the preparation of the new generation for entry into the promised land, concluding with the appointment of Joshua as the new national leader and the death of Moses.

The book of Joshua spans a period of about twenty-four years, from the death of Moses on Mount Nebo, east of the River Jordan, to the settlement of Israel in her tribal districts (1406–1376 B.C.). It is a story of a military campaign led by Joshua, Moses' successor, in which Israel gains possession of Canaan. The land promised to Abraham's descendants extended from the "river of Egypt to the great river, the River Euphrates" (Genesis 15:18). The land promised to the Israelites in the days of Moses and Joshua extended from the "Red Sea to the Sea of the Philistines, and from the desert to the River [Euphrates]" (Exodus 23:31; Joshua 1:4). This places Israel between Egypt, the one world power on her southwestern border, and Babylon, the power on her eastern side.

Joshua is an aggressive book; consequently, it has been suggested that Joshua bears the same relationship to the five books of Moses that the Acts of the Apostles holds to the four Gospels.[2] The invasion of Canaan and the wars with the Canaanites indicate God's horror and hatred of sin. The Canaanites were so immersed in sin, and so given over to sin and vices of the most awful nature, that God's wrath burned against them.

The behaviour of the Canaanites was bad in the time of Abraham. At that time God predicted that it would grow worse; when it reached an all-time low, God would move in judgement against them. To Abraham God said, "But in the fourth generation they shall return here, for the iniquity of the Amorites [note: all the Canaanites are represented by their strongest family] is not yet complete" (Genesis 15:16). The invasions under Joshua show that the iniquity and wickedness of the Canaanites had by now reached the point where divine tolerance would bear with it no longer. During the four intervening centuries, between Abraham and Joshua, these wicked nations had forfeited their right to live. They were now to be replaced by the Israelites.[3]

Is it only the Canaanites who are to be singled out for this kind of judgement? History shows that the righteous government of God extends over *all* nations. Each is punished when its wickedness has come to the full—not necessarily punished to the same extent, nor in the same way, but punished as God sees fit. The Canaanites were not only idolaters; they were guilty of practices that were even regarded among other heathens as abhorrent and debasing. Furthermore, this generation of Israelites was probably the godliest in all their long history as a nation (24:31). They burned with a holy zeal—not only

---

[2] Robert Lee, *The Outlined Bible: An Outline and Analysis of Every Book in the Bible* (London: Pickering and Inglis, 1930), analysis no. 6.

[3] H.C. Leupold, *Exposition of Genesis*, 2 vol. (Grand Rapids: Baker, 1942), 1:486.

against their pagan enemies, but also against their dishonest and wayward brethren (as in the case of Achan—7:10–26). Later generations of Israelites were themselves to be severely punished when they turned away from the Lord and began to practise abominations:

> "Shall I not punish them for these things?" says the LORD.
> "And shall I not avenge Myself on such a nation as this?"
> (Jeremiah 5:9).
>
> Righteousness exalts a nation,
> But sin is a reproach to any people (Proverbs 14:34).

It is to be noted that not all Israel's enemies were defeated. Some of the cities within the boundaries were not taken until the days of David and Solomon. This may be partially explained by the failure of the Israelites fully to obey God's commands. At the same time, it is recorded that God designed a delay: "I will not drive them out from before you in one year, lest the land become desolate and the beasts of the field become too numerous for you. Little by little I will drive them out from before you, until you have increased, and you inherit the land" (Exodus 23:29–30). Perhaps the delay was intended to span more than the seven years of warfare under Joshua.

JOSHUA / **OUTLINE**

The book of Joshua is the record of the conquest of Canaan. Under the leadership of Joshua, Israel makes a carefully planned and well-executed invasion of the land. Joshua's skills in military strategy are displayed when, having been instructed by God to enter Canaan via Jericho, he proceeds to drive a wedge through central Canaan, separating the territory to the north from that to the south. He then moves in on the nearest enemies to the south. Having conquered them, he turns his attention to the enemies further afield in the north. There are many enemies in the land of Canaan. As well as the Canaanites, there are the Hittites, Amorites, Perizzites, Hivites, Jebusites, Geshurites, Gazites, Ashdodites, Ashkelonites, Gittites, Ekronites, Avites, Gebalites and others (Exodus 3:8; Joshua 13:2–6).

PART 1 / **ENTRY INTO THE PROMISED LAND (1:1-5:12)**

The book opens with the Lord's directions to Joshua, who had already been designated as the successor of Moses. God directs Joshua to lead the children of Israel into the promised land. The Lord promises Joshua that he will have success. In fact, the Lord says, "No man shall be able to stand before you all the days of your life; as I was with Moses, so I will be with you. I will not leave you nor forsake you" (1:5). Responding to the command, Joshua immediately begins to make the necessary preparations. Although the Lord has given him a solemn promise that he will be invincible, Joshua still sees the necessity of thoughtful planning and precise strategy on his part. He gives instructions to the people to make ready for the crossing of the Jordan; he reminds the tribes of Reuben, Gad and the half tribe of Manasseh of their promise to assist the other tribes in the conquest of Canaan (see Map 3), and he sends two spies into Jericho to reconnoitre the city.

Jericho is situated two hours' journey to the west of the Jordan. The two spies enter the city and take lodgings at the home of Rahab the prostitute. Staying overnight in such a house would not draw attention to the men or create suspicion. The house was also located on the city wall. This would facilitate an easier escape if their identity and mission became known, as in the event it did. Rahab shows herself as a true friend to the people of God. She informs the spies that the inhabitants are afraid of Israel because their God, Jehovah, "is God in heaven above and on earth beneath" (2:11). She demonstrates her true faith in the Lord God by concealing the spies at great personal risk (Hebrews 11:31).[4] The two Israelites promise to safeguard Rahab and her household when the attack is launched on the city provided she hangs a scarlet cord from her window. They then escape to the mountains and hide for three days until their pursuers return to Jericho. When it is safe they make their way back to the Jordan and to the camp of the Israelites.

The following day, having received the report from the spies, Joshua moves the whole company to the banks of the Jordan. Three days are spent in final preparation and prayer. The Israelites move out with the priests bearing the ark of the covenant in front of them (3:14). Whereas Moses divided the waters of the Red Sea with his rod, Joshua divides

---

[4] Loyalty to the Lord is more important than loyalty to one's nation.

the waters of the Jordan river with the ark of the covenant, the appointed symbol of the presence of almighty God since the covenant established on Mount Sinai. When the feet of the priests touch the waters of the Jordan, a pathway is made through the river. Although the river is in full flood, the Lord, by a remarkable miracle, makes a wide passage for the Israelites. The priests stand on firm, dry ground in the middle of the riverbed until all the people have passed over. Twelve stones from the dry riverbed are set up in the middle of the Jordan, and another twelve are erected as a permanent monument on the western bank. As soon as the priests come up out of the riverbed, the waters return to their natural flow.

Aware that the Lord's promise of preservation and victory depends upon obedience to the law of God (1:7–9), Joshua ensures that the generation born in the wilderness receives the covenant sign of circumcision. Although all those who came out of Egypt had been circumcised, the practice had not been carried out during the years in the wilderness (5:5). This may have been due to the judgement of God upon the grumbling unbelieving adult generation that left Egypt: "their children bore the reproach…by being denied the 'token' or 'sign of the covenant' (Genesis 17:11)."[5] Now in the promised land, the new generation is under the blessing of God, and it is appropriate for the rite to be administered once more.

After a few days' rest, the Israelites keep the Feast of Passover. In their first Passover celebration in the land of Canaan, they sample the produce of their new land. The miraculous supply of manna ceases forever on the following day.

PART 2 / **CONQUEST OF THE PROMISED LAND (5:13–12:24)**

The Angel of the Lord appears to Joshua to encourage him to proceed with the conquest of Canaan. Joshua is instructed as to how the Israelites are to proceed. Jericho is a strong and secure fortress city. It is to be taken with the aid of an outstanding miracle. With the ark of the covenant at the head, the army of Israel is to march in silence around the city walls once a day for six days. On the seventh day, they are to march around the walls seven times. On the final circuit, the priests

---

[5] Arthur W. Pink, *Gleanings in Joshua* (Chicago: Moody Press, 1964), 1324.

Figure 8. Military strategy in taking the city of Ai

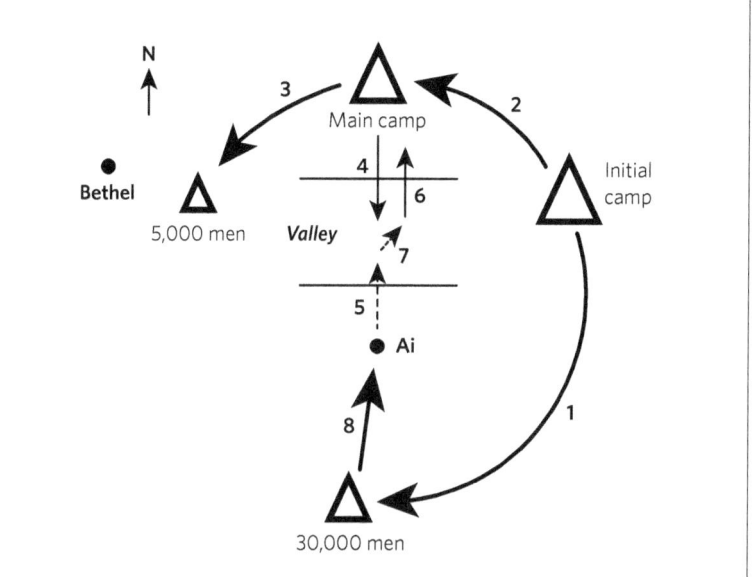

Key based on Joshua 8:1-23
1. 30,000 men are sent by night to lie in ambush near to the city (vv. 2-4,9).
2. Early the following morning, Joshua leads the main forces to the north (vv. 10-11).
3. A small contingent is sent to guard the approach from Bethel to Ai (v. 12).
4. The Israelites advance into the valley (v. 13).
5. The King of Ai sees the advance and leads his forces out to meet it (v. 14).
6. With the arrival of the enemy, the Israelites turn back as though retreating (v. 15).
7. The King of Ai and his forces pursue the Israelites (v. 16).
8. The signal is given and the men in ambush take the city and set fire to it (vv. 18-19). The men of Ai see the smoke. They turn back toward their city only to be trapped in a pincer movement by the Israelites (v. 22).

are to blow the trumpet and the people are to shout. The walls of the city will fall down and the soldiers are to move in to kill the enemy and destroy the city. Joshua obeys the Lord and the city is taken. Only Rahab and her household are spared, for the Israelites honour the promise made by the two spies (2:14; 6:25).

Later, in moving out from Jericho against the town of Ai, the Israelites are to learn that they will only succeed if they are faithful and obedient to the Lord. They cannot win victories in their own strength. Although the inhabitants of Ai are few, the Israelite forces sent against them are defeated. The Lord informs Joshua that his instructions are not being respected. This leads to the public exposure and execution of Achan and his family. A new attack is mounted against Ai and the Israelites win a decisive victory (8:1–23; see Figure 8). After the capture of Ai, Israel has established a firm foothold in central Canaan. Joshua is therefore able to proceed with the building of an altar on Mount Ebal in accordance with the instructions received from Moses (8:30–35; Deuteronomy 27:5–8).

News of the victories of the Israelites in taking the cities of Jericho and Ai soon spreads to the surrounding Canaanites. Their kings form an alliance against the Israelites. One tribe, the Hivites, does not join this coalition. They choose rather to adopt a more subtle approach. Travelling from their major city, Gibeon, six miles southwest of Ai and five miles northwest of Jerusalem, a few of their number come to the Israelites pretending to be ambassadors who have travelled many miles in order to form a treaty with Israel. Without enquiring from the Lord, Joshua agrees to a pact. When the deception is uncovered, the Gibeonites have to be spared because of the oath that Joshua has made, but are consigned to a life of servitude under the Israelites.

News of the treaty between the Gibeonites and the Israelites comes to the attention of Adoni-Zedek, the Amorite king of Jerusalem. He gathers another four Amorite kings to form an army to punish the Gibeonites, and to check the advance of the Israelites. In the event Israel triumphs. The Lord fights for them, casting down large hailstones which kill many of the enemy (10:11) and answering Joshua's prayer:

> "Sun, stand still over Gibeon;
> And Moon, in the Valley of Aijalon."
> So the sun stood still,
> And the moon stopped,
> Till the people had revenge
> Upon their enemies.
>
> …And there has been no day like that, before it or after it, that the LORD heeded the voice of a man; for the LORD fought for Israel (10:12–14).

Map 4. Conquest of the promised land

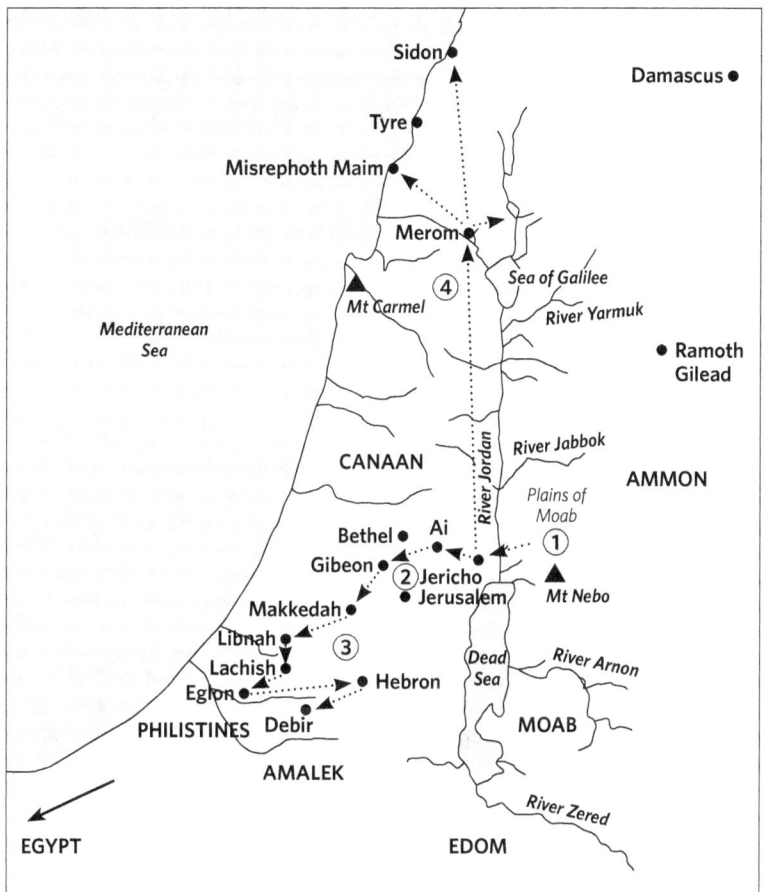

1. Joshua leads the Israelites over the River Jordan and on to take the city of Jericho.
2. After an abortive attempt to take Ai, the city falls to the Israelites.
3. The Israelites move against the southern tribes of the Canaanites and subdue them.
4. The Israelites move against the northern tribes and—with miraculous help—win decisive victories.

The five Amorite kings are defeated and executed. Having conquered the armies, Joshua then proceeds to secure their cities (see Map 4). Moving further south, the Israelites win victory after victory until they control the southern region as far as Kadesh Barnea (10:41–42).

The Canaanite tribes to the north hear of Israel's successes and organize a joint army, comprising thousands of fighting men, to resist

Israel. Mounting a surprise attack, the Israelites, though seriously outnumbered, are nevertheless victorious: "the LORD delivered them into the hand of Israel, who defeated them" (11:8). Joshua succeeds in subduing the northern territory. Canaan belongs to Israel. Seven years of heavy fighting have come to an end. Joshua and his army have conquered thirty-one kings (12:24).

PART 3 / **DIVISION OF THE PROMISED LAND (13:1–22:34)**

The Israelites are allotted portions of land as their inheritance. The Lord had given specific and detailed instruction as to ownership, sale and redemption of the land (Leviticus 25:23–28). An intermingling of justice and mercy is embodied in these laws. Any inclination toward capitalism is curbed, and no allowance is made for state ownership. No one could take advantage for long over another who had fallen on hard times.

Although some of the towns and villages within the boundaries of Canaan are still to be conquered, the Lord issues instructions for the distribution of the land to the individual tribes of Israel (13:1–7; cf. Judges 1:27–36; see Map 5).

The tribes of Reuben and Gad had very large flocks and herds, and the land on the east of the Jordan was rich in excellent pastureland. Their leaders had asked Moses and Eleazar the priest for permission to take that area as their inheritance (Numbers 32:1–5). Although the land on the east of the Jordan formed part of the original territory promised to Abraham (Genesis 15:18)—a promise later reiterated to Moses (Exodus 23:31)—the Reubenites and Gadites were being motivated by materialistic considerations similar to those which influenced Lot and failed to take other important factors into account (Genesis 13:10–13); the eastern territory requested by half the tribe of Manasseh, the tribe of Gad and the tribe of Reuben was to be constantly troubled by Moabites to the south, Canaanites and Syrians to the north and Ammonites, Midianites and Amalekites from the eastern deserts.

Moses had agreed to the request from the three tribes on condition that their fighting men accompany the remaining tribes until they had all inherited their lands.

The names of the twelve tribes to whom land is apportioned differ slightly from the names of Jacob's twelve sons. There are two reasons

Map 5. Division of the promised land

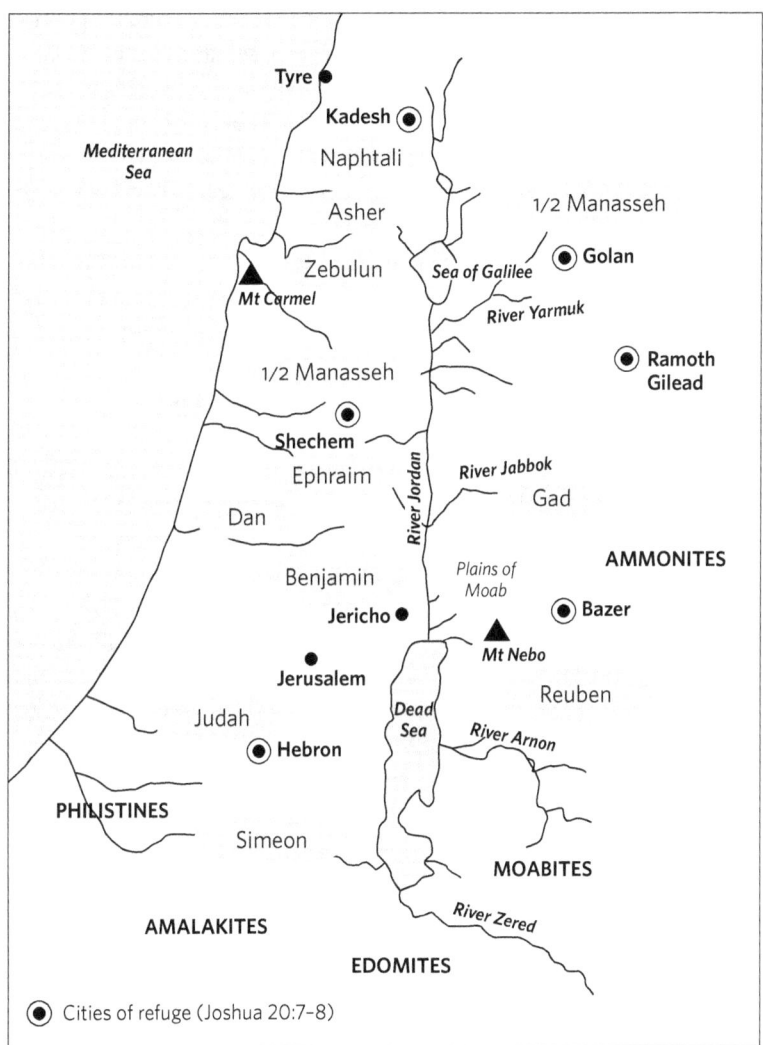

for this discrepancy. Firstly, the tribe of Levi does not inherit a tract of land in the same way as the other tribes. Soon after the Exodus, the Levites became a tribe of priests—as their inheritance they receive forty-eight cities and the surrounding land, dotted among the land apportioned to the other tribes (21:41). Six of these cities are designated as "cities of refuge" for the protection of those who commit manslaughter (20:1-9; cf. Numbers 35:9-15). Secondly, the tribe of Joseph does not appear. Instead, that tribe receives a double portion through the tribes of Joseph's two sons Manasseh and Ephraim. Consequently, the number of tribal territories still remains as twelve.

Once the distribution of the land to the west of the Jordan has been accomplished, the fighting men from the two and a half tribes whose inheritance is on the east of Jordan (Reuben, Gad and half of Manasseh) return home. They erect an impressive altar by the eastern banks of the River Jordan. The tribes of Reuben and Gad call the altar "Ed"(meaning "witness"): "For it is a witness between us that the LORD is God" (22:34). Several years then pass without comment.

PART 4 / **THE LAST DAYS OF JOSHUA (23:1-24:33)**

Joshua's final addresses to the leaders and to the people form a natural conclusion to the book as a whole. He gathers the leaders of the tribes together and reminds them of God's purposes and blessings.

Joshua reiterates the history of Israel from the days when the Lord brought Terah and Abraham from idolatry beyond the River Euphrates. He then urges the Israelites once more to be obedient and faithful to the Lord: "Now therefore, fear the LORD, serve Him in sincerity and in truth, and put away the gods which your fathers served on the other side of the River and in Egypt. Serve the LORD!' (24:14).

He calls upon the Israelites to remember their covenant obligations. The living God has established his covenant with them. He has kept his promises and blessed them. He will also keep his threats and punish them if they transgress the covenant of the Lord their God and turn away to other gods (23:15-16). They must not fail in their responsibilities. Their enjoyment of the promised land depends upon their faithfulness to the Lord.

Implicitly undergirding Joshua's address is the threefold covenant promise given to Abraham of a vast number of descendants, of possessing their own land and of enjoying singular blessing in relationship with the living God. Failure to keep the covenant will result in suffering and death, the loss of their land, and the great displeasure of God.

Joshua and the people renew their covenant to serve the Lord.

Joshua dies at the age of 110, after having driven out most of the Canaanites from the new land of Israel.

JOSHUA / **CHRIST AND HIS CHURCH**

THEOPHANIES

After the celebration of the Passover and before the invasion of Jericho, Joshua is confronted with an intriguing figure who introduces himself as "Commander of the army of the LORD" (5:14). Joshua is by Jericho, in all probability trying to work out his strategy. It is surprising that Joshua responds to this "man" by falling to the ground and worshipping him. Such behaviour from one who is so evidently God-fearing and walking in the law of the Lord can only mean that Joshua understands this "man" to be the Angel of the LORD who is to be treated as God himself! There is "no hesitation on his part in yielding to Him the Divine honour due to the Most High."[6] Joshua would have known of the Angel's visit to Abraham and to Hagar, and of the Angel's wrestling with Jacob at Peniel. Now he sees the Angel of the LORD for himself. Having fallen to the ground, Joshua seeks instruction from this exalted being. He is told to take his sandals from his feet (5:15; cf. Exodus 3:5), for he is in the presence of Deity. The Lord then instructs Joshua as to how he is to take the impregnable city of Jericho (6:1–5). Jehovah is to fight for him.

At Jericho, and in several later battles, the Son of God fought with a sword; now, since the days of the New Covenant, he fights with the sharp two-edged sword of the Spirit, which is the Word of God (Revelation 19:15; cf. Hebrews 4:12; Revelation 1:16; 2:12,16).

TYPES

There are no direct prophecies concerning the Lord Jesus Christ in the book of Joshua. There is however, in the person of *Joshua*, an allusion to a type of Christ. The name Joshua means "Jehovah is salvation." It is the Hebrew equivalent of the Greek name *Iesous*, meaning *Jesus*. In his role as captain over the people of God, leading them safely into the promised land, Joshua is a type of the one who, as "captain of their salvation," will bring "many sons to glory" (Hebrews 2:10, AV; cf.

---

[6] William G. Blaikie, *The Book of Joshua* (1908; Minneapolis: Klock and Klock, 1978), 130.

2 Corinthians 2:14; Hebrews 4:8–10). The inheritance that Jesus gives is not just the tract of land between the Mediterranean Sea and the desert, the Red Sea and the River Euphrates, but the "new heavens and a new earth in which righteousness dwells" (2 Peter 3:13; Revelation 21:1–4).

Crossing Jordan is a type of the believer's dying with Christ (1 Corinthians 10:2; Romans 6:3–4).

The *scarlet cord* (2:18) which the spies required as a sign also seems to be significant. There may be an allusion to the precious blood of Christ by which we are safe and saved (Hebrews 10:19; cf. Exodus 12:13).

Canaan—A type of heaven or of the Christian life?

Canaan has been regarded as a type of heaven to which the church is journeying through this wilderness. However, there is difficulty in making too strong an association between the promised land of Canaan and heaven. Heaven will not be a place of fighting, but of eternal rest and blessedness. In a sense, it is legitimate to view Canaan as the end of the trials in the wilderness. But a slightly different perspective provides a more satisfactory application. When viewed in the light of all the battles that are recorded in the book of Joshua then *entry into Canaan* may be better seen as personal conversion—entering into Christ. The battles which occur in Canaan are then seen as typical of spiritual battles in the Christian life. The *conquest of Canaan* typifies victories over spiritual enemies (2 Corinthians 10:3–5; Ephesians 6:12). The *partial subjugation of the Canaanites* typifies the existence of besetting sins which remain unconquered (Hebrews 12:1).

In Genesis, we hear the promises of God that there will be a country, and a people chosen to inherit that country. In Exodus, we see our unconverted self, in bondage to sin and Satan. In Leviticus, we hear God speaking, making known his holy requirements. In Numbers, we find ourselves in a great howling wilderness, which is what the world appears to those who have been awakened by the Spirit of God. In Deuteronomy, the strictness and spirituality of the law is revealed. This shatters self-righteousness and reveals that someone other than Moses must become the captain of our salvation if ever we are to arrive in the promised rest. That rest prefigures Christ:

For if Joshua had given them rest, then He would not afterward have spoken of another day. There remains therefore a rest for the people of God. For he who has entered His rest has himself also ceased from his works as God did from His.

Let us therefore be diligent to enter that rest, lest anyone fall according to the same example of disobedience (Hebrews 4:8–11).

Entry into Canaan was a time of *new beginnings*. There was a *new generation*, for all the adults who left Egypt died in the wilderness (Numbers 14:29–32). There was a *new leader*: Joshua replaced Moses, for grace achieves what the law could never accomplish. There was a *new sphere of life*: the wilderness was replaced by the land of Canaan. Here is a spiritual picture of those who have passed through a period of conviction for sin, who have felt the terrors of the law and have now been brought to put their trust in Jesus Christ.[7] At conversion we enter into rest in Christ.

After conversion, there is the blessing of victory, of resting, with the heavenly "Joshua," who is the Lord Jesus Christ, the captain of our salvation (Hebrews 2:10, AV). There is also a note of battle: "The flesh lusts against the Spirit, and the Spirit against the flesh; and these are contrary to one another, so that you do not do the things that you wish" (Galatians 5:17). Paul brings these two elements, victory and fighting, fighting and victory, into stark relief in Romans 7 and 8:

> For the good that I will to do, I do not do; but the evil I will not to do, that I practice. Now if I do what I will not to do, it is no longer I who do it, but sin that dwells in me.
>
> I find then a law, that evil is present with me, the one who wills to do good. For I delight in the law of God according to the inward man. But I see another law in my members, warring against the law of my mind, and bringing me into captivity to the law of sin which is in my members. O wretched man that I am! Who will deliver me from this body of death? I thank God—through Jesus Christ our Lord!
>
> So then, with the mind I myself serve the law of God, but with the flesh the law of sin.

---

[7] Pink, *Gleanings in Joshua*, 13.

There is therefore now no condemnation to those who are in Christ Jesus, who do not walk according to the flesh, but according to the Spirit (Romans 7:19–25; 8:1).

The military campaign under Joshua "typifies the warfare of the spirit. The Canaanites represent our lusts, besetting sins and spiritual enemies, and in the record we discover the *secret of an all-conquering life*."[8] "One man of you shall chase a thousand, for the LORD your God is He who fights for you, as He has promised you. Therefore take diligent heed to yourselves, that you love the LORD your God" (23:10–11).

The Canaanites were only partially subdued, not totally eradicated! We must "lay aside every weight, and the sin which so easily ensnares us, and let us run with endurance the race that is set before us, looking unto Jesus, the author and finisher of our faith" (Hebrews 12:1–2).

JOSHUA / **CONCLUSION**

This book has many lessons for Christians today.

Firstly, it shows that being a child of God is not easy. Let us note that there is a battle to be fought, a race to be run, a crown to be won. This will influence our evangelism. We shall not present an "easy" faith with a weak commitment. Following Christ means a daily self-denial, a daily taking up of our cross, a being crucified to the world and the world being crucified to us (Mark 8:34; Galatians 6:14). Faith and obedience must never be parted.

Secondly, and at the other extreme, neither is the Christian life one of constant defeats. While the warfare is fierce against the world, the flesh and the devil, nevertheless there is a note of triumph. "For whatever is born of God overcomes the world. And this is the victory that has overcome the world—our faith. Who is he who overcomes the world, but he who believes that Jesus is the Son of God?" (1 John 5:4–5). "Who shall separate us from the love of Christ? Shall tribulation, or distress, or persecution, or famine, or nakedness, or peril, or sword? …in all these things we are more than conquerors through Him who loved us" (Romans 8:35,37).

---

[8] Lee, *The Outlined Bible*, analysis no.6.

Joshua is a book about a land and a people. The land is an inheritance promised by God, waiting to be occupied. The people are the elect nation of God, facing human obstacles in the way of taking the land. And the obstacles are the occasion for battle—a holy war—designed by God to remove the idolatrous and corrupt enemies from the land. It is for this reason that Joshua is called the "Book of Conquest."[9]

Blessed be the God and Father of our Lord Jesus Christ, who according to His abundant mercy has begotten us again to a living hope through the resurrection of Jesus Christ from the dead, to an inheritance incorruptible and undefiled and that does not fade away, reserved in heaven for you, who are kept by the power of God through faith for salvation ready to be revealed in the last time.

In this you greatly rejoice, though now for a little while, if need be, you have been grieved by various trials, that the genuineness of your faith, being much more precious than gold that perishes, though it is tested by fire, may be found to praise, honor, and glory at the revelation of Jesus Christ, whom having not seen you love (1 Peter 1:3–8).

---

[9] Irving L. Jensen, *Jensen's Survey of the Old Testament: Search and Discover* (Chicago: Moody, 1978), 137.

JOSHUA / **APPLICATION AND REFLECTION**

1. Revelation
One notable fact concerning this book is its introduction to a new method of teaching. Up to this time, God had spoken through dreams, visions and ministering angels; from this point, he communicates primarily through the Book of the Law written by Moses, and Joshua is urged to obey it:

> Be strong and of good courage, for to this people you shall divide as an inheritance the land which I swore to their fathers to give them. Only be strong and very courageous, that you may observe to do according to all the law which Moses My servant commanded you; do not turn from it to the right hand or to the left, that you may prosper wherever you go. This Book of the Law shall not depart from your mouth, but you shall meditate in it day and night, that you may observe to do according to all that is written in it. For then you will make your way prosperous, and then you will have good success. Have I not commanded you? Be strong and of good courage; do not be afraid, nor be dismayed, for the LORD your God is with you wherever you go (1:6-9).

In the book of Joshua, God's major means of communication is the Word which has already been transmitted, but there are periods in history, and in the unfolding of revelation, when God uses other methods of communication. With Moses, he spoke face to face (Deuteronomy 34:10). There are times when the Lord has used dreams, visions and ministering angels. At other times he has spoken through prophets (Hebrews 1:1). In our day he communicates through the written Word, the Bible, and the Spirit of God opens our minds and hearts to the meaning and message of the Scriptures (John 16:13).

2. Models of faith
Israel at the battle of Jericho and Rahab the prostitute are presented in the New Testament as examples of faith (Hebrews 11:30-31). Rahab is also found among the ancestors of the Lord Jesus (Matthew 1:5). Some time after the fall of Jericho, she married Salmon of the tribe of Judah and gave birth to a son, Boaz, who eventually married Ruth the Moabitess. So Rahab was ultimately Ruth's mother-in-law! This illustrates how the grace of God triumphs over sin. The Saviour is the friend of sinners and not ashamed to call us his brethren (Matthew 11:19; Hebrews 2:11).

Another example of faith found in the pages of the book of Joshua is that of Caleb. With Joshua he had stood against the ten spies who, through lack of faith and confidence in God, talked the Israelites out of entering the promised land (Numbers 14:6-10). Though Joshua has been elevated to the highest position of responsibility in the nation, there is not the slightest indication of a bad spirit in Caleb. He could have been disgruntled that Joshua had such authority. When aged eighty-five, Caleb, with humility, reminds Joshua of the promise made to him by Moses forty-five years earlier (14:6-15). Joshua honours the pledge of Moses and it is recorded: "Hebron therefore became the inheritance of Caleb the son of Jephunneh the Kenizzite... because he wholly followed the LORD God of Israel" (14:14; cf. Numbers 32:11-12). A glorious testimony to Caleb's faith and obedience is recorded for posterity!

Caleb's ancestry is of interest, for when he accompanied Joshua and the other ten spies to reconnoitre Canaan, he represented the tribe of Judah (Numbers 13:6). He also appears as a regular member of the family of Judah in the tribal record (1 Chronicles 4:15). Yet he is described as "the son of Jephunneh the Kenizzite" (14:6,14).[10] The family was of Canaanite extraction, yet Caleb is not himself spoken of as a Kenizzite but simply "the son of Jephunneh the Kenizzite." So it would seem that Jephunneh joined the Israelites, was accepted as a member of the children of Israel, and consequently brought up his sons, Caleb and Kenaz, as full members of the tribe of Judah. So Caleb's family were originally outside the covenant family of Israel and, like Rahab before and Ruth afterward, they were incorporated because of their faith and allegiance to the true God, the God of Israel. This provides further illustration of the ease with which outsiders could be assimilated into the commonwealth of Israel and share in the covenants of promise—through faith (cf. Ephesians 2:12-13).

3. Separation

The incident with the Gibeonites warns of two dangers: the possibility of deception by unbelievers, and the consequences of unholy alliances. The Israelites entered into a treaty with the Gibeonites without first seeking the

---

[10] "It was not customary to distinguish Israelites in this way, but only those who had come among them from other tribes, like 'Heber the Kenite,' 'Jael, the wife of Heber the Kenite' (Judges 4:11,17), Uriah the Hittite, Hushai the Archite, etc." See Blaikie, *The Book of Joshua*, 263.

counsel of the Lord (9:14-15). This is a warning to the church of God in all ages to beware of the trickery and cunning craftiness of the world that often seeks a peaceful coexistence with the church, and even acceptance into it, whenever it is to its advantage to do so.[11] Paul warns the Ephesians, and their elders, of the enemy within as well as without (Ephesians 4:14; Acts 20:29-30). The Lord also taught the parable of the wheat and tares to illustrate that believers are not always capable of detecting unbelievers among them (Matthew 13:36-43).

Unholy alliances also include marriage to unbelievers. The Lord warns the Israelites of the serious problems that will arise if they disobey his command and marry peoples of other nations:

> Therefore take careful heed to yourselves, that you love the LORD your God. Or else, if indeed you do go back, and cling to the remnant of these nations—these that remain among you—and make marriages with them, and go in to them and they to you, know for certain that the LORD your God will no longer drive out these nations from before you. But they shall be snares and traps to you, and scourges on your sides and thorns in your eyes, until you perish from this good land which the LORD your God has given you (23:11-13).

4. Ministry support

The tribe of Levi did not receive a division of land in the same way as the other tribes of Israel. After the settlement, the ten tribes together with Manasseh and Ephraim allocated cities and surrounding land to the Levites. In total, they were provided with forty-eight cities and so they lived dispersed throughout the other tribes (Numbers 35:1-8). The Levites also received a generous portion of the heave and wave offerings as their food, as well as the best of the oil, the wine and the firstfruits, with the tithes of the children of Israel (Numbers 18:9-19,24; Deuteronomy 18:1-3). In this way, they were sustained by the gifts of the people. In this, the Levites are a type of the ministers of the gospel in the Christian era. The apostle Paul points out this comparison: "Do you not know that those who minister the holy things eat of the things of the temple, and those who serve at the altar partake of the offerings of the altar? Even so the Lord has commanded that those who

---

[11] O. Gerlach, cited by Carl F. Keil, *The Books of Joshua, Judges and Ruth* (Grand Rapids: Eerdmans, 1950), 95.

preach the gospel should live from the gospel" (1 Corinthians 9:13-14).

While points of comparison are legitimately drawn between the Levites of old and present-day ministers of the gospel, there are marked differences which must not be overlooked. The likeness is shown in terms of material support, not in regard to their function or task. Unlike Christian ministers, Levitical priests were not commissioned to evangelize—that was the work of the prophets. Gospel ministers are not priests, do not offer sacrifices (except sacrifices of devotion and praise which *all* Christians are to render—Romans 12:1; 1 Peter 2:5), and are not intermediaries between God and sinners any more than any other believers (1 Peter 2:9).

Where possible, ministers of the gospel are not to entangle themselves "with the affairs of this life" (2 Timothy 2:4). The Lord provides for the support of the ministry through the gifts and kindness of the brethren: "Let him who is taught the word share in all good things with him who teaches" (Galatians 6:6).

> Thus it is laid down as an unchanging principle that spiritual benefits demand a temporal return. Not that any price can be put upon the invaluable ministry of the Gospel, but that those whom God has set apart to preach it have a just claim for generous compensation. And that not in the way of charity or gratuity, but as a *sacred debt*—a debt which professing Christians fail to discharge at the peril of their souls. For let none be deceived: if they fail to support the Gospel, God will severely chastise them.[12]

Such gifts in support of the ministry are "a sweet-smelling aroma, an acceptable sacrifice, well pleasing to God" (Philippians 4:18).

---

[12] Pink, *Gleanings in Joshua*, 388.

JUDGES

MEANING	AUTHOR	KEY THOUGHT
"deliverers" and "rulers"	**Unknown** *(probably Samuel)*	**Rebellion and repentance**

THEME

Causes and cure in backsliding

THEME VERSE
In those days there was no king in Israel; everyone did what was right in his own eyes.
JUDGES 17:6; 21:25

JUDGES / **SUMMARY**

PART 1 / **INTRODUCTION AND INTERPRETATION 1:1–3:6**

a.	The Lord consulted and the result	1:1–10
b.	Incomplete conquests within Canaan	1:11–36
c.	The Angel's rebuke and Israel's repentance	2:1–5
d.	Joshua's death and the pattern of Israel's subsequent history	2:6–23
e.	Israel's repeated failure	3:1–6

PART 2 / **WAVES OF OPPRESSION FOLLOWED BY DELIVERY**   3:7–16:31

1. From the north
- a. Oppression of Cushan-Rishathaim, king of Mesopotamia (eight years)   3:7–8
- b. Othniel delivers Israel (forty years)   3:9–11

2. From the southeast
- a. Oppression by Eglon, king of Moab, with Ammon and Amalek (eighteen years)   3:12–14
- b. Ehud delivers Israel (eighty years' rest)   3:15–30

3. From the west
- a. Oppression by the Philistines   3:31
- b. Shamgar delivers Israel   3:31

4. From within the north
- a. Oppression by Jabin, king of Canaan (twenty years)   4:1–3
- b. Deborah, with Barak, delivers Israel (forty years' rest)   4:4–5:31

5. From the east
- a. Oppression by Midian, Amalek and people of the East (seven years)   6:1–6
- b. A prophet's rebuke   6:7–10

    c.   Gideon delivers Israel (forty years' rest)   6:11–8:35

6. Civil war
    a.   Abimelech (Gideon's son) takes control
        by treachery (three years)   9:1–57
    b.   Tola saves Israel and judges
        (twenty-three years)   10:1–2
    c.   Jair judges Israel (twenty-two years)   10:3–5

7. From the east
    a.   Oppression by the Ammonites
        (eighteen years)   10:6–9
    b.   Israel's sorrow and the Lord's response   10:10–18
    c.   Jephthah delivers Israel and judges
        (six years)   11:1–12:7
    d.   Ibzan judges Israel (seven years)   12:8–10
    e.   Elon judges Israel (ten years)   12:11–12
    f.   Abdon judges Israel (eight years)   12:13–15

8. From the west
    a.   Oppression by the Philistines (forty years)   13:1
    b.   Samson begins to deliver Israel and judges
        (twenty years)   13:2–16:31

PART 3 / **EXAMPLES OF CORRUPTION WITHIN ISRAEL**   **17:1–21:25**

    a.   Personal and tribal idolatry   17:1–18:31
    b.   The evil of the mena of Gibeah   19:1–30
    c.   War between Israel and tribe of Benjamin   20:1–48
    d.   Drastic steps to preserve the tribe of
        Benjamin   21:1–25

JUDGES

The book of Judges takes up the history of the people of Israel where that of Joshua closes, with the death of Joshua, Israel's commander-in-chief (1:1; Joshua 24:29). Whereas Joshua recounts one of the high points in the spiritual state of the nation of Israel, Judges records one of the darkest periods of their history. Although Israel had conquered the whole land of Canaan in a general sense, there still remained pockets of enemy heathen nations here and there. The reasons given for the continuing existence of these enemies within the borders of Israel are: firstly, to test the obedience of the people to the laws of God (2:22; 3:4); and, secondly, in order that the new generation might learn how to fight (3:1–3). To "be taught to know war" (3:2) here means to learn to depend upon the Lord for help in fighting against the Canaanites. So both reasons blend into one—walking with God in obedience to, and dependence upon him and him alone. There were temptations all around them: temptations to intermarry with their heathen neighbours, temptations to establish close friendships with Gentiles, temptations through the beauty of the Canaanite women, the pomp and self-pleasing of their pagan religious rituals, the hope of learning the future by idolatrous divination and superstitious fears of the supposed gods of the localities in which they settled.[1] The Lord uses the nations who tempt the Israelites to periodically become the instruments of their punishment.

According to Robert Lee, the book of Judges is notable for several reasons. In the first place, it has two beginnings (1:1; 2:6). Secondly, it contains the first record in biblical history of the emergence of a woman into prominence and leadership of a nation (4:4–5). Thirdly, it contains the greatest and grandest battle song in the world (5:2–31). Finally, it contains the oldest known parable in the world (9:8–15).[2]

---

[1] Andrew R. Fausset, *A Critical and Expository Commentary on the Book of Judges* (1885; Minneapolis: James and Klock, 1977), 4. There is also a more recent Banner of Truth edition of this title available.

[2] Robert Lee, *The Outlined Bible: An Outline and Analysis of Every Book in the Bible* (London: Pickering and Inglis, 1930), analysis no. 7.

JUDGES / **AUTHOR**

The writer of this book is unknown. From the phrase found four times in the closing chapters—"In those days there was no king in Israel" (17:6; 18:1; 19:1; 21:25)—it seems evident that the book was written after the establishment of the monarchy (c. 1000 B.C., not long after the death in 1051 B.C. of Samson, the last main character of the book). It was probably written by Samuel the prophet, the last judge in Israel, during his partial retirement from the leadership of the people at the accession of Saul to the throne of Israel. According to the Jewish Talmud, "Samuel wrote the book which bears his name and the book of Judges and Ruth."[3]

JUDGES / **HISTORICAL SETTING**

The book of Judges covers a period of about 326 years from the death of Joshua (c. 1376 B.C.) to the rise of Samuel as a prophet of the Lord (c. 1050 B.C.). It portrays a series of relapses into idolatry on the part of God's people. These are followed by invasion of the promised land and periods of oppression by their enemies. The history centres around the personalities of the heroic judges who were raised up to become deliverers of Israel whenever the people sincerely repented of their sins. The dark side of their disobedience is especially emphasized in the record.

From the attention given to Israel's repeated backsliding and spiritual failure, the impression may be given that Israel was almost constantly in a bad relationship with the Lord. This is not the case. Of the years mentioned in this book, Israel enjoyed the majority of the time in faithfulness to the one true God—at least externally and formally.[4] It is also to be noticed that only certain areas had international

---

[3] *Baba Bathra* 14b, cited by Edward J. Young, *An Introduction to the Old Testament* (Grand Rapids: Eerdmans, 1949), 169.
[4] The discrepancy between 340 years (1390 B.C. to 1050 B.C.) and 410 years (sum total of years related in the book of Judges) is explained in that the rule of the judges overlapped. The Bible presents three different historic periods which must be reconciled with the inspired record in the book of Judges: 300 years (Judges 11:26), 480 years (1 Kings 6:1) and 450 years (Acts 13:20). See Leon J. Wood, *The Distressing Days of the Judges* (Grand Rapids: Zondervan, 1975), 10–17; and Carl F. Keil, *The Books of Joshua, Judges and Ruth* (Grand Rapids: Eerdmans, 1950), 277–292.

problems at any one time. The problem may be located at one time in the north, at another time in the south, or then again in the west or east. Where the tribes are at least outwardly showing allegiance to the true God, their history passes without comment. A study of the dates would seem to show that the Israelites maintained an outward loyalty to Jehovah for the larger part of the time. This is not evident from a casual reading of the book of Judges.

The judges

The book receives its title from the rulers or judges who led Israel during this period. The term "judge" had a broader meaning at that time than its English counterpart has today. These judges were not merely civil magistrates who administered justice and adjudicated disputes. Primarily, they were "deliverers…endued with the Spirit of God [3:10; 6:34; 11:29; 13:25], who were called upon to deliver and to govern the people" in times of spiritual decline and enemy oppression.[5] Though the judges were given spiritual powers, it is evident that the possession of supernatural gifts was not always accompanied by a right use of those gifts.

Gideon introduced the golden ephod and brought disaster upon his family and people (8:27). Jephthah brought heartache into his family circle when he made a rash vow (11:30–31,34–40). He also gratified his own violent spirit in taking revenge on Ephraim (12:1–6). The history of Samson, the last judge, illustrates both the strength and weakness of Israel: strength when separated to God, utter weakness when the relationship with God became severed by lust. Samson brought heartache to his godly parents through his lust and arrogance.

These judges are not to be confused with the judges set up by Moses following the advice received from Jethro, his father-in-law (Exodus 18:21–23; cf. Deuteronomy 1:13,16–17; 16:18–20). The men appointed by Moses were to judge in the sense of making a decision between two or more alternative possibilities. Those men were like magistrates and their role was very different from that of the judges here in the book of that name. The latter are *shophetim*, commissioned by God to deliver the Israelites from the oppression of their enemies, usually by war, and then to rule the people during the era of peace that followed (2:16;

---

[5] Young, *An Introduction to the Old Testament*, 170.

3:9).[6] God's "eternal principle is, when His people return to Him in penitence, He returns to them in mercy."[7]

God's salvation and God's righteousness go hand in hand:

Rain down, you heavens, from above,
And let the skies pour down righteousness;
Let the earth open, let them bring forth salvation,
And let righteousness spring up together.
I, the LORD, have created it (Isaiah 45:8).

Consequently these individuals were judges of righteousness not only *in* Israel, but *for* Israel. The divine principle in dealing with Israel is summed up in chapter 2:

Nevertheless, the LORD raised up judges who delivered them out of the hand of those who plundered them. Yet they would not listen to their judges, but they played the harlot with other gods, and bowed down to them. They turned quickly from the way in which their fathers walked, in obeying the commandments of the LORD; they did not do so. And when the LORD raised up judges for them, the LORD was with the judge and delivered [saved] them out of the hand of their enemies all the days of the judge; for the LORD was moved to pity by their groaning because of those who oppressed them and harassed them. And it came to pass, when the judge was dead, that they reverted and behaved more corruptly than their fathers, by following other gods, to serve them and bow down to them. They did not cease from their own doings nor from their stubborn way (2:16–19).

The number of judges

There is a difference of opinion as to how many individuals are to be identified in this book as judges. One commentator favours eight on the strict usage of the word "judge." Another says twelve by adding Ehud, Shamgar, Deborah and Gideon. Others say fourteen by including

---

[6] Irving L. Jensen, *Jensen's Survey of the Old Testament: Search and Discover* (Chicago: Moody, 1978), 152.
[7] Fausset, *Commentary on the Book of Judges*, 1.

Barak with Deborah, and Abimelech the usurper. Leon Wood favours fourteen by excluding Barak who, he says, merely assisted Deborah, and Abimelech who was a usurper, and including instead Eli the priest and Samuel the prophet. Wood then divides the fourteen into eight major and six minor judges. The major ones he sees as Othniel, Ehud, Deborah, Gideon, Jephthah, Samson, Eli and Samuel, while the six minor ones are Shamgar, Tola, Jair, Ibzan, Elon and Abdon.[8]

It is probably wisest not to try to identify with exactness who is to be regarded as a judge, but to recognize that in the period known as "the days of the judges" a number of men and one woman are presented as heroes of Israel. Some are said to be endued with the Holy Spirit to achieve great exploits: Othniel, Gideon, Jephthah and Samson. Some go down in history as people of great faith: Gideon, Barak, Samson and Jephthah (Hebrews 11:32).

In the book of Judges itself, some are mentioned as judging but not recorded as delivering (Jair, Ibzan, Elon and Abdon). Others delivered Israel but are not said to have judged (Ehud, Shamgar and Gideon). Samson is stated to have been a judge but only to have begun to deliver Israel (13:5). Those said to have both judged *and* delivered (or saved) Israel are Othniel, Deborah, Tola and Jephthah.

The majority of the judges were local or national heroes raised up to deliver the Israelites. They continued their rule after the end of the war. None of them established a hereditary rule; there was no dynasty, no family succession. Each judge delivered only part of Israel: Shamgar, the southwest district; Deborah, together with Barak, and Gideon, northern Israel; Jephthah, the eastern side of the Jordan; and Samson, the midwest territories of Judah and Dan.

JUDGES / **OUTLINE**

At first sight, the book seems confusing and quite disorderly. It is not in chronological order. If it were to be given in correct sequence of events then it would begin with 2:6–9; followed by 1:1–2:5; then to 2:10–13; followed by chapters 17–21, and finally the section from 2:14–16:31. The Holy Spirit's concern in this book is not primarily *historical* but *spiritual*.

---

[8] Wood, *Distressing Days of the Judges*, 6–7.

PART 1 / **INTRODUCTION AND INTERPRETATION (1:1–3:6)**

The theological explanation for Israel's history during this period is bound up with the covenant that God had made with their fathers (2:20). Through unfaithfulness to God in turning to worship and serve other gods, Israel breaks its solemn historic covenant. This brings the disapproval and punishment of God upon them. They suffer under God's righteous anger until they cry out to the Lord and he sends delivery once again.

To enjoy the blessing of God, the Israelites must be faithful to him. The promises of blessing from God in the covenant with Abraham (Genesis 15), and the obligations of faithfulness and obedience from Israel in the covenant with Moses (Exodus 6:2–8; 19:5–6; 20:1–17), form the central core by which the history of Israel is to be interpreted.

When the Israelites seek guidance and the help of the Lord, he responds powerfully on their behalf. It is clear from the book of Judges that Israel as a nation fails to obey the Lord in some important areas. The promised land has been given to them, but they have not carried out their instructions to drive out the Canaanites (1:21,27,29–33). Though the Lord has been entirely faithful in honouring his part of the covenant, they have not kept their side. Time and again, the tribes of Israel fail to complete their assignment—for whatever reason, whether out of pity for the Canaanites, or from a feeling of power in subduing them and using and abusing them as forced labour, or from sympathy toward their religious beliefs and practices, or in thinking they knew better than the Lord and the divinely appointed leadership. It seems clear that they deliberately ignored God's command to destroy the Canaanites.

For their failure and disobedience, the Israelites are rebuked by "the Angel of the Lord" (2:1–5). The phrase, "The Angel of the Lord came up from Gilgal to Bochim" (2:1) is not an indication of any journey he made, but to connect this event with the last time the Angel appeared—to Joshua at Gilgal, just before the invasion of Jericho (Joshua 5:13–15).

The people respond to the Angel's rebuke with tears of repentance. They are so overcome with sorrow and penitence that they rename the place Bochim, meaning "weeping."

With the death of Joshua and all the elders who served with him, the people of Israel go into serious moral and spiritual decline (2:11–23).

PART 2 / **WAVES OF OPPRESSION FOLLOWED BY DELIVERY (3:7-16:31)**

All the history in the book of Judges is accurate history, but the arrangement is not based on chronology (the sequence of events); instead it is presented in a repeated sequence of *sin > oppression > delivery*. This recurring pattern is often called a cycle and further defined as having five steps: "sin, servitude, supplication, salvation, and silence,"[9] or "rest, rebellion, retribution, repentance and restoration."[10] The problem with these distinctions is that every episode related in Judges does not *necessarily* contain evidence of each stage of the cycle. It may therefore be more accurate to describe the recorded history as a "downward spiral."[11]

There is a general pattern discernible:

1. The children of Israel do evil in the sight of the Lord (3:7,12; 4:1; 6:1; 10:6; 13:1). What this evil consists of is summarized as breaking covenant with the Lord (2:1–2), turning from him, worshipping and serving other gods, and friendship and intermarriage with the Canaanites (2:11–3:7).
2. In response to this evil, the anger of the Lord burns hot. He withdraws his protection and power from the Israelites and sends fierce foreign oppressors against them (3:8,12; 4:2; 6:1; 10:7; 13:1).
3. Eventually, under the oppressors, the Israelites repent and cry to God for help (3:9,15; 4:3; 6:6–7; 10:10).
4. The Lord responds to their repentance by raising up judges to deliver them from their oppressors and to lead them back to a life of fellowship with him (3:9,15; 10:12). The deliverer is sometimes declared to be empowered by the Spirit of God, as in the case of Othniel (3:10), Gideon (6:34), Jephthah (11:29) and Samson (13:25; 14:6,19).

---

[9] Bruce Wilkinson and Kenneth Boa, *Talk Thru the Old Testament* (Nashville: Nelson, 1983), 62.

[10] Jensen, *Jensen's Survey of the Old Testament*, 158.

[11] Raymond B. Dillard and Tremper Longman III, *An Introduction to the Old Testament* (Leicester: Apollos, 1995), 125.

5. The enemy is subdued, the Israelites are delivered and a period of peace usually follows (3:11,30; 5:31; 8:28). Upon the death of the judge the people revert back to idolatry and immorality. The sequence begins over again.

The downward spiral

The first judge of Israel is *Othniel* (3:9–10), Caleb's nephew and son-in-law (1:13). He is a fine example of what a judge/deliverer should be—raised up by the Lord, empowered by the Holy Spirit, a highly capable and experienced soldier (Joshua 15:16–17). He leads Israel in a successful war with Mesopotamia (see Map 6). Upon his death the downward spiral of Israel begins in earnest.

Israel "again did evil in the sight of the Lord" (3:12).

The second deliverer, *Ehud*, though raised up by the Lord, is not said to be endued with the Spirit of the Lord, nor is there any comment to indicate whether he has a personal relationship with the Lord. Ehud is of the tribe of Benjamin (3:15). Like so many of his tribe, he is left-handed (20:15–16), a feature which enables him to take King Eglon by surprise, and stab him to death. After the deed, Ehud escapes and rallies his men, who proceed to win an overwhelming victory against their oppressors.

The third deliverer is *Shamgar* (3:31). During eighty years of national rest, the spiritual and moral tone of the nation deteriorates. This time the Lord uses the Canaanites, under King Jabin, to punish the Israelites from within their own land (4:2–3). These were the people whom the Lord had told the Israelites to destroy! (Deuteronomy 20:17). Jabin reigned at Hazor, eight miles west northwest of Merom, in the land given to Naphtali. For twenty years, the children of Israel in the northern region suffer painfully under the powerful army of Jabin's general, Sisera.

Responding to the cry of the people, the Lord inspires as deliverer one who is already functioning as a judge in the central region just a mile or two south of Bethel in the territory of Ephraim—*Deborah* the prophetess, wife of Lapidoth. Deborah was not the first prophetess in Israel,[12] but she was the first prophet, male or female, since Moses.

---

[12] Miriam was the first prophetess (Exodus 15:20). After Deborah there were others such as Huldah (2 Kings 22:14) and Anna (Luke 2:36).

Deborah also has the distinction of being "the first and only woman ever to exercise civil authority in Israel."[13]

Forty years of peace ensue. Extended peace is once more attended by increased laxity in matters spiritual and moral: "And the children of Israel did evil in the sight of the LORD" (6:1).

This time, the Lord uses the Midianites as the taskmasters to bring Israel to her knees.[14] Repeatedly invaded, the Israelites eventually return in sorrow to the living God. The Lord responds, not by sending an immediate deliverer as previously, but by first sending a prophet. This unnamed prophet delivers a message designed to make the people aware of their sins, in order that they may understand the reason for their suffering. The prophet also acts as a herald preparing the way for the Lord's deliverer, *Gideon*, the "mighty man of valour" (6:12) of the tribe of Manasseh.

The "Angel of the LORD" visits Gideon (6:11). This manifestation was unusual for that period. Previous men, Othniel, Ehud and Barak, had been moved by the Spirit of God, but Gideon is privileged to see a Christophany.

Although Gideon has genuine faith in the living God (Hebrews 11:32) it is intermingled with unbelief. In spite of the visit of the Angel of the LORD, he needs constant reassurance. His forces number 32,000 and the opposition has 135,000 (7:3; 8:10). He asks the Lord for a sign to confirm his Word (6:36–37). Not content with one miracle, he asks for another (6:39). Despite these misgivings, he has outstanding confidence in the power and purposes of God. With just 300 men, Gideon defeats the vast army of the Midianites.

On his return home, the people of Israel offer Gideon a hereditary throne (8:22). He shows commendable modesty and humility by refusing, on the grounds that the Lord is the true King of Israel. While Moses had given directions for the appointment of a king over Israel (Deuteronomy 17:14–20), the ideal was for Israel to function under a direct theocracy—that is, the rule of God (1 Samuel 12:12,17). Commendable as this refusal is, Gideon falls into a more subtle temptation. Requesting the gold earrings taken from the slaughtered enemy, he

---

[13] Gordon J. Keddie, *Even in Darkness: Judges and Ruth Simply Explained* (Welwyn: Evangelical Press, 1985), 49.

[14] Descendants from Abraham's son Midian, born to Keturah (Genesis 25:2).

Map 6. Israel's oppressors in the days of the Judges

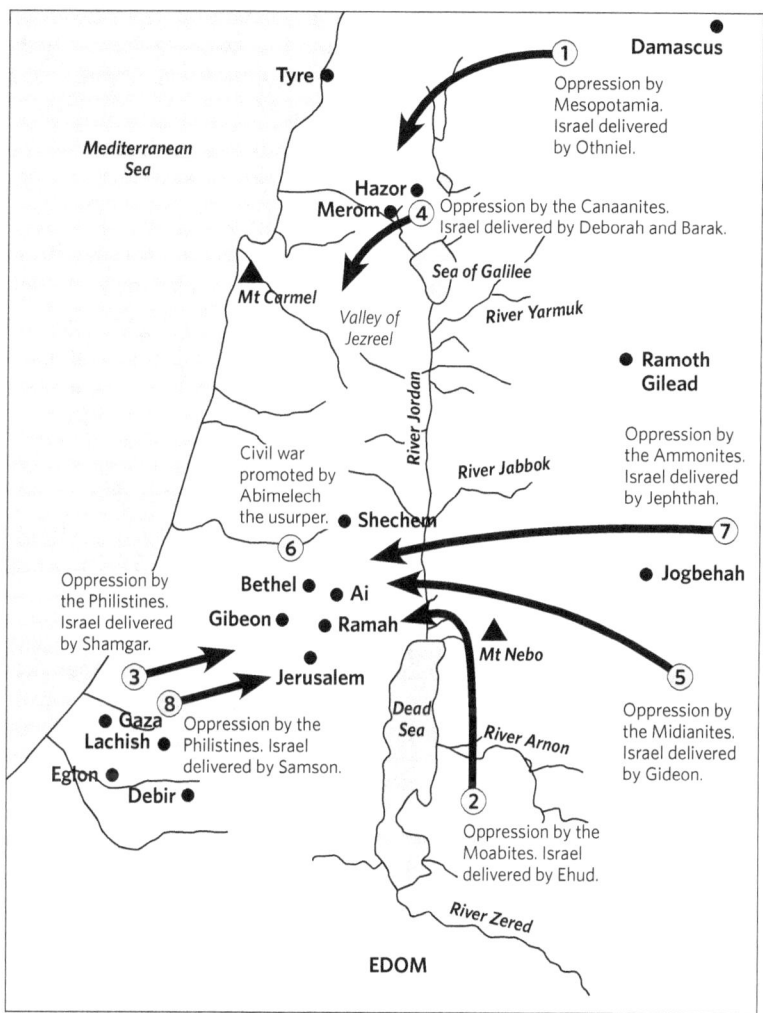

uses this vast quantity of gold to have an ephod (high priest's tunic) made (Exodus 28:5–14), which he houses in his hometown of Ophrah. Gideon has formed wrong conclusions from a series of events: he had been visited by the Angel of the LORD; he had been commissioned to deliver Israel; his gift had been accepted as a sacrifice by fire; under God's instruction he had built an altar to the Lord and sacrificed a bullock using the wood from the idolatrous image; and he had subsequently received several revelations from the Lord. Gideon wrongly concludes from these events that he is to serve as a high priest to Israel. The Word of God does not permit him to serve in this capacity; he does not fulfil the requirements. The high priest must be a descendant of Aaron and is appointed to function in the tabernacle at Shiloh (Joshua 18:1; Judges 18:31). Gideon sins on both counts. The people also sin in accepting Gideon's ephod as approved by God. The priesthood at Shiloh may have been abused by men of low calibre at the time, but this did not justify Gideon in making his own substitute. This sin brings serious repercussions upon Gideon's family and upon the Israelites in years to come. It opens the way for disregarding strict obedience to the revealed will of God, leading the nation to fall back into the worship of Baal upon Gideon's death (8:33). Further blots upon an otherwise upright character are Gideon's numerous wives and a concubine (8:30–31).

After Gideon's death, his son Abimelech seizes power. He is not a deliverer but an oppressor from within. He murders seventy of his half brothers to establish himself as king over Israel (9:1–6). Only one brother, Jotham, escapes death. On Mount Gerizim, Jotham declares a parable of curse against the people of Shechem and against Abimelech. Abimelech the usurper rules in Shechem for three years and then dies a humiliating death: "Thus God repaid the wickedness of Abimelech.... And all the evil of the men of Shechem God returned on their own heads, and on them came the curse of Jotham the son of Jerubbaal" (9:56–57).[15]

After Abimelech two judges are briefly mentioned, *Tola* and *Jair* (10:1–5). After some years of relative calm in the nation, the spiritual and moral state of the nation once more deteriorates: "Then the children of Israel again did evil in the sight of the LORD...and they forsook the LORD and did not serve him" (10:6).

In his anger, the Lord sends the Philistines from the southwest and the Ammonites from the east to harass and oppress the children of Israel for eighteen years. Eventually the people acknowledge their wickedness in turning from the true God to idols. They cry out to the Lord that he may have mercy upon them and deliver them. The Lord refuses to help. "Such repulse is but intended to quicken and to

---

[15] Jerubbaal is another name for Gideon (6:32).

deepen repentance."[16] The people show true contrition. They destroy their idols, cease to practise idolatry and recommence with seriousness the worship of Jehovah.

Battle lines are drawn between the Ammonite army at Gilead and the Israelites at Mizpah, and *Jephthah* becomes commander-in-chief. He is successful in battle and wins a decisive victory over the Ammonites.

Following the death of Jephthah three men judge Israel: *Ibzan*, *Elon* and *Abdon* (12:8–15). Whether they function concurrently with other judges in different areas of Israel is not made clear. Upon the death of Abdon, deterioration once more takes place: "Again the children of Israel did evil in the sight of the LORD" (13:1). The Israelites repeatedly fail to see the connection between their faithfulness and obedience to the Lord, on the one hand, and their security and well-being as a nation, on the other.

This time, the Lord uses the Philistines to the southwest of Israel to punish his people. Israel is to face forty years of affliction, its longest period throughout the whole time of the judges. During this period, the Lord raises up a man who will "begin to deliver Israel out of the hand of the Philistines" (13:5).

Unlike his great predecessors, *Samson* gathers no army, nor brings remarkable delivery for the children of Israel. With superhuman power he single-handedly performs exploits among the Philistine enemy, illustrating what all Israel could achieve if only they would rely upon the Lord and the strength of his might.

Samson's birth is announced in an unusual manner. His parents are visited by the Angel of the LORD (13:3; cf. Genesis 18:10). Their son is to be consecrated to the Lord: "No razor shall come upon his head, for the child shall be a Nazirite to God from the womb; and he shall begin to deliver Israel" (13:5). The Angel implies the strongest connection between the former and the latter: success in his work will depend upon Samson's adherence to the prescribed lifestyle (Numbers 6:1–8). Whereas this vow of separation was normally of temporary duration, for Samson it is to be lifelong. These outward forms are intentionally to be matched by true inner dedication to the Lord. In this, Samson did not always succeed. He is the epitome of "the weak strong man."

---

[16] Luke H. Wiseman, *Practical Truths from Judges* (1874; Grand Rapids: Kregel, 1985), 230.

Samson is full of self-indulgence. In this respect, he is a living symbol of the spiritual corruption of the nation as a whole (2:17; 8:27,33). Lust and love for forbidden women lead to Samson's ultimate downfall. He falls in love with Delilah, a Philistine woman. Eventually succumbing to Delilah's pleas, Samson discloses the secret of his strength. He is overpowered, blinded and made a slave in a prison workhouse. But his hair grows again and his strength returns once more.

Taken to the temple of Dagon, the god of the Philistines, Samson is paraded before a vast crowd of spectators. Making one last request for power from the Lord, Samson dies—taking over 3,000 Philistines with him. He is more successful in death than in life (16:30).

> Samson, when strong and brave, strangled a lion; but he could not strangle his own love. He burst the fetters of his foes, but not the cords of his own lusts. He burned up the crops of others, and lost the fruit of his own virtue when burning with the flame enkindled by a single woman.[17]

PART 3 / **EXAMPLES OF CORRUPTION WITHIN ISRAEL (17:1-21:25)**

The purpose of this section appears to be that of illustrating the extent to which the Hebrews have transgressed the Ten Commandments and the Book of the Covenant. The evils which result when "everyone did what was right in his own eyes" (21:25) include theft (17:2), idolatry (17:5), immorality (19:2), homosexuality (19:22) and mass abduction (21:23).

Micah

An Ephraimite named Micah builds a shrine, makes an ephod to wear so that he might determine the will of God, sets up idols and establishes one of his sons as his priest. A little later, a Levite from Bethlehem travelling in the area is invited to lodge with Micah and offered the position of family priest. Micah foolishly concludes that the presence of a Levitical priest, in spite of the idolatrous paraphernalia, will ensure the Lord's blessing upon him (17:13).

---

[17] Ambrose, cited by Keil, *The Books of Joshua, Judges and Ruth*, 417–418.

The Benjamites

Around the same time, another Levite, from Ephraim, travelling with his concubine, stops at the Benjamite city of Gibeah to spend the night. The men of Gibeah surround the house and demand the Levite be sent out to them for their perverted purpose. God's nation of Israel has become as evil as Sodom (cf. Genesis 19:5–8). The Levite's concubine is instead handed over to the perverted mob. Discovering her dead the following morning, the Levite transports her body back to the mountains of Ephraim.

Once at home he dismembers her body into twelve parts and sends these to the twelve tribes.

Outraged by the incident at Gibeah, the leaders of the tribes gather together at Mizpah to determine what course of action to take against the men of Gibeah. They form a representative force that is dispatched to Gibeah. Once they arrive at the city, word is sent for the Benjamites to deliver up the perpetrators of the atrocious crime. The Benjamites refuse, choosing to side with the evil men of their community. The other tribes of Israel are forced to confront the whole tribe of Benjamin.

In the first battle, Israel suffers very heavy losses: 22,000 men are killed. In the second battle, Israel is defeated again, this time with a loss of 18,000 soldiers. Then at the third attempt, the Benjamites are defeated and routed. Eventually only 600 men remain of the tribe of Benjamin. The question inevitably rises as to why the Israelites experience two defeats and such heavy losses when they are seeking to obey the law of God in respect to purging the land. The answer is not immediately obvious. Careful examination reveals that the Israelites do not consult the Lord in an appropriate manner. Commendable as it is that they consult God at Bethel, their sin is "the state of mind with which they had entered upon the war, their strong self-consciousness, and great confidence in their own might and power."[18] Their first consultation with the Lord only asks, "Which of us shall go up first to battle against the children of Benjamin?" (20:18). The second, though accompanied by weeping before the Lord, raises the question: "Shall I again draw near for battle against the children of my brother Benjamin?" (20:23). On both occasions, the Israelites are confident in their own strength and their greater numbers. It is only when they humble

---

[18] Keil, *The Books of Joshua, Judges and Ruth*, 452.

themselves before the Lord and acknowledge their weakness and inadequacy, with fasting, penitence and sacrifice, that they rise successfully above the Benjamites. The final battle sees the defeat of the tribe of Benjamin to such an extent that the tribe is very nearly annihilated. Only 600 men remain of the whole tribe! Drastic steps are taken to provide the remaining Benjamites with virgin wives from other tribes.

The book of Judges documents the weakness and waywardness of the Israelites during the period between the death of Joshua and the establishment of the monarchy in Israel. Preparation is made for Israel to have a king in the repeated reference, "In those days there was no king in Israel" (17:6; 18:1; cf. 19:1; 21:25), and summed up in the final verse of the book: "In those days there was no king in Israel; everyone did what was right in his own eyes" (21:25). When the Israelites did what was right in their own eyes it was invariably what was evil in the sight of the Lord.

JUDGES / **CHRIST AND HIS CHURCH**

THEOPHANIES

The book of Judges contains three Christophanies: "the Angel of the LORD" rebukes the Israelites (2:1–5); appoints Gideon to his work as judge and deliverer of Israel (6:11–24); and informs Manoah's wife that she will bear a son, whom she calls Samson (13:3–5,9–23). In the last of these visitations, when asked his name, the Angel replies, "Why do you ask my name, seeing it is wonderful?" (13:18). This is not the proper name of the Angel of the LORD so much as an expression of the uniqueness of his character—"absolutely and supremely wonderful" (cf. Isaiah 9:6).[19] God *alone* is described in such terms. When Manoah offers food prepared for the Angel as a burnt offering, "the Angel of the LORD ascended in the flame of the altar" (13:20). From this miracle, Manoah and his wife knew that their visitor was none other than the Angel of the LORD. The deity of the Angel is confirmed beyond all doubt in the words of Manoah: "We shall surely die, because we have seen God!" (13:22). With spiritual logic, his wife reassures him that they will not die.

---

[19] Keil, *The Books of Joshua, Judges and Ruth*, 407.

TYPES

There are no obvious types of Christ in the book of Judges. Some commentators see Samson as a type of Christ but the arguments in favour are unconvincing.[20]

JUDGES / **CONCLUSION**

Judges is another great book of God. Here we see what happens when people disobey, or only partially obey, the Lord. When people do what they like instead of doing what God commands, it always leads to disaster. Problems arose for the Israelites when "everyone did what was right in his own eyes" (17:6; 21:25).

The Canaanites who were allowed to remain in the conquered land symbolize sinful tendencies and lusts remaining in the believer's heart and mind. Paul urges Christians to mortify (put to death) the sinful inclinations: "fornication, uncleanness, passion, evil desire, and covetousness, which is idolatry" (Colossians 3:5).

> If we wilfully spare a single Canaanite, or enter into a tacit agreement with the enemy, though we may perhaps not fail of heaven at last, we will have stripes of sorrow on our journey thither: "they shall be as thorns in your sides, and their gods shall be a snare unto you" [2:3, AV]. Our prospects will be dim, our usefulness will be impaired, our light will be turned into darkness, and our songs into dirges of lamentation; while the remorseless, tyrannous lust humbles us again and again, sinks us lower than the dust, and reduces us to exquisite and abject misery: the just penalty of refusing to take up the cross and deny self, that we might follow Christ.
>
> Merciful Lord! Deliver me and Thy whole Church from the humiliation and bitterness of being subject to the Canaanite![21]

---

[20] Fausset, *Commentary on the Book of Judges*, 224–225,255,262–263.
[21] Wiseman, *Practical Truths from Judges*, 63.

JUDGES / **APPLICATION AND REFLECTION**

1. The human heart is prone to wander away from God

There is a potential prodigal in the heart of every believer. We find it hard to believe some of the things God teaches. We find it hard to obey some of the commandments he gives. We find it hard to walk in holiness and subdue self-interest and deny ourselves sinful pleasures. We find it hard to pray as we ought, to read Scripture as we should, to attend worship as God directs. We find it hard to love our brethren as our Saviour requires. We find it hard to seek the lost, share the gospel, do good to all, to love our neighbour. In a hundred-and-one ways, it is evident that our greatest enemy is *within*. It is our self. My greatest enemy is me! "The heart is deceitful above all things, and desperately wicked" (Jeremiah 17:9). "For the good that I will to do, I do not do; but the evil I will not to do, that I practice" (Romans 7:19).

> Oh to grace how great a debtor
>   Daily I'm constrained to be!
> Let that grace, Lord, like a fetter,
>   Bind my wandering heart to thee.
>
> Prone to wander, Lord, I feel it,
>   Prone to leave the God I love;
> Take my heart, O take and seal it,
>   Seal it for thy courts above! (Robert Robinson)

2. God pursues and restores his backslidden people

In this book of the Bible, there are seven accounts of backsliding, seven periods of oppression, seven cries to God and seven deliveries:

> Thus they were defiled by their own works,
> And played the harlot by their own deeds.
>
> Therefore the wrath of the LORD was kindled against His people,
> So that He abhorred His own inheritance.
> And He gave them into the hand of the Gentiles,
> And those who hated them ruled over them.
> Their enemies also oppressed them,
> And they were brought into subjection under their hand.

Many times He delivered them;
But they rebelled in their counsel,
And were brought low for their iniquity.

Nevertheless He regarded their affliction,
When He heard their cry;
And for their sake He remembered His covenant,
And relented according to the multitude of His mercies (Psalm 106:39-45).

"Those whom the Lord loves He disciplines" (Hebrews 12:6). Affliction is good for the soul. The psalmist declares: "Before I was afflicted I went astray, but now I keep Your word" (Psalm 119:67). In love and grace toward his wayward people, the Lord "commands and raises the stormy wind" so that:

Their soul melts because of trouble.
They reel to and fro, and stagger like a drunken man,
And are at their wits' end (Psalm 107:26-27).

God's people get into difficulties in numerous ways. They reach a point of desperation. Four times in Psalm 107 we read the words: "Then they cried out to the LORD in their trouble, and He delivered them out of their distresses" (vv. 6,13,19,28). There are repeated statements in the book of Judges that Israel cried out to the Lord and he heard them and rescued them: "When the children of Israel cried out to the LORD, the LORD raised up a deliverer for the children of Israel, who delivered them" (3:9; cf. 3:15; 4:3; 6:6-7; 10:10). The testimony of David is: "This poor man cried out, and the LORD heard him, and saved him out of all his troubles" (Psalm 34:6).

God calls his people to faithful obedience. Nevertheless, if they wander from him, or wilfully turn from him, there is a way back. They can cry out to the Lord in times of affliction and distress. "Cast your burden on the LORD, and He shall sustain you" (Psalm 55:22). "God...gives grace to the humble," so cast "all your care upon him for he cares for you" (1 Peter 5:5,7).

3. Vows to the Lord

Jephthah made a rash vow. The words he used meant that he had in mind the possibility of a human being coming to meet him.[22] Making a vow is not

---

[22] Keil, *The Books of Joshua, Judges and Ruth*, 389.

unlawful, but Jephthah seems to have shown a distinct lack of faith. The Spirit of God had come upon him—that should have been enough to assure him of victory. Maybe he foolishly thought that by promising some great sacrifice to God, he would somehow make sure of success. Vows ought not to be made *in order to* obtain God's favour and blessing, but to *witness* to our gratitude and thankfulness.

> When you make a vow to the LORD your God, you shall not delay to pay it; for the LORD your God will surely require it of you, and it would be sin to you. But if you abstain from vowing, it shall not be sin to you (Deuteronomy 23:21-22).
>
> Do not be rash with your mouth,
> And let not your heart utter anything hastily before God.
> For God is in heaven, and you on earth;
> Therefore let your words be few.
> For a dream comes through much activity,
> And a fool's voice is known by his many words.
>
> When you make a vow to God, do not delay to pay it;
> For He has no pleasure in fools.
> Pay what you have vowed.
> It is better not to vow than to vow and not pay.
>
> Do not let your mouth cause your flesh to sin, nor say before the messenger of God that it was an error. Why should God be angry at your excuse and destroy the work of your hands? (Ecclesiastes 5:2-6)
>
> It is a snare for a man to devote rashly something as holy,
> And afterwards to reconsider his vows (Proverbs 20:25)

When a vow is made, the promise ought to be fulfilled (Numbers 30:2). But there are exceptional promises, such as that of Herod (Mark 6:23-27), involving the life or welfare of another human being, where breaking the vow would involve less sin than keeping it. In such a case, it is necessary to withdraw from the vow and seek pardon for having rashly made it. Jephthah was wrong to make the vow he did. Human sacrifice was abhorrent to the Lord (Leviticus 18:21; 20:2-5). God would have seriously disapproved of such action. In those early days, human sacrifices were never heard of among the Israelites. Such practices were only introduced to Jerusalem by the godless kings, Ahaz and Manasseh (2 Kings 16:3; 21:6). They were not even the general practice among the heathens.

Andrew Fausset argues in defence of Jephthah on the following lines: Firstly, Jephthah knew what he was doing right from the beginning. It was not a hasty vow. Secondly, Jephthah knew the Pentateuch well enough to know that human sacrifices were contrary to the law of God. Thirdly, if Jephthah had sacrificed his daughter he could not possibly have been listed as an example of faith among the heroes of Hebrews 11 (v.32). Fausset concludes by saying, "all the requirements of the case are fulfilled, if we suppose he devoted his only daughter to lifelong virginity as a spiritual burnt-offering consecrated to Jehovah."[23] This harmonizes with the sequel where Jephthah's daughter asks for permission to go away to the mountains, with her close female friends, to mourn her virginity (11:37-38). To mourn her virginity is not to mourn because she has to die a virgin, but because she has to live and remain a virgin.[24] The statement in verse 39 that "she knew no man" would be utterly superfluous if she had been put to death. She was to commit her life to a life of celibacy in the service of the tabernacle (cf. Exodus 38:8; 1 Samuel 2:22; Luke 2:37).

From that day, there was an annual remembrance of Jephthah's daughter (11:40). What the daughters of Israel gathered yearly to praise was her willingness to sacrifice forever her natural aspirations "from motives of filial obedience, patriotic devotion, and self-renouncing piety."[25] Literal burnt offerings could only be offered at the lawful altar and by the Levitical priests and they would never have consented to such an unlawful act. If Jephthah himself had offered her upon an altar of his own, then he would not have said, "It shall surely be the LORD's, and I will offer it up as a burnt-offering" (11:31).[26] E.J. Young suggests: "In fulfilment of the vow, he probably devoted her to perpetual virginity, but of this one cannot be certain."[27] Even this would be an abuse of his responsibility as a father. On the basis of 1 Samuel 12:11 and Hebrews 11:32, Leon Wood suggests that what he did with his daughter

---

[23] Fausset, *Commentary on the Book of Judges*, 204.
[24] Keil, *The Books of Joshua, Judges and Ruth*, 392.
[25] Fausset, *Commentary on the Book of Judges*, 205.
[26] Wiseman favours the view that the young woman was put to death (see Wiseman, *Practical Truths from Judges*, 266–268).
[27] Young, *An Introduction to the Old Testament*, 175.

"was something approved of God and that he was himself in right relation to God."[28] The true honour, however, must rest upon Jephthah's daughter. The Lord turned the foolish vow of a father into a glorious memorial to his mercy and grace "through the lovely submissiveness and self-sacrifice of a godly daughter."[29]

4. Strength and weakness

Sometimes the people of God are brought low so that all glory for achievements will be given to the Lord. Gideon's army was drastically reduced in size, "lest Israel claim glory for itself against [God], saying, 'My own hand has saved me'" (7:2). The same truth is underlined in the New Testament when Paul says,

> But God has chosen the foolish things of the world to put to shame the wise, and God has chosen the weak things of the world to put to shame the things which are mighty; and the base things of the world and the things which are despised God has chosen, and the things which are not, to bring to nothing the things that are, that no flesh should glory in His presence. But of Him you are in Christ Jesus, who became for us wisdom from God—and righteousness and sanctification and redemption— that, as it is written, "'He who glories, let him glory in the Lord" (1 Corinthians 1:27–31).

The divine power displayed in the judges culminates in Samson, who possessed his extraordinary power by virtue of being a Nazirite, consecrated to the Lord. In his natural character, he was a weak man. "In Samson we have the spectacle of a man in whom faith was mighty, but who, nevertheless, failed to subdue his own passions, and to keep his body under subjection."[30] We may see something here of an illustration of the believer with and without close fellowship with God. When weak and yet leaning hard upon the Lord, then we are strong:

> And He said to me, "My grace is sufficient for you, for My strength is made perfect in weakness." Therefore most gladly I will rather boast

---

[28] Wood, *Distressing Days of the Judges*, 289.
[29] Keddie, *Even in Darkness*, 85.
[30] Wiseman, *Practical Truths from Judges*, 293.

in my infirmities, that the power of Christ may rest upon me. Therefore I take pleasure in infirmities, in reproaches, in needs, in persecutions, in distresses, for Christ's sake. For when I am weak, then I am strong (2 Corinthians 12:9-10).

5. The weakness of the law

Since Phinehas the son of Eleazar was already functioning as high priest in the days of Joshua (Joshua 22:13,30-32; 24:33), the reference to Phinehas the priest (20:28) locates the appalling incidents of chapters 17-21 in the years immediately following the death of Joshua. The good days for Israel under Joshua's leadership evaporated soon after his death. The Israelites proved to be constantly attracted to, and influenced by, the idolatry and sexual perversion of the Canaanite fertility religions. The fact that Phinehas was the grandson of Aaron also indicates how quickly the Israelites departed from the covenant of the Lord at Sinai.

Throughout the book of Judges, the weakness of the law of Sinai is all too apparent. The apostle Paul explains the reason for this failure: "it was weak through the flesh" (Romans 8:3). Sinful human nature cannot obey the law. The law brings the knowledge of sin (Romans 3:20). Only drastic action by an intermediary, and drastic transformation within believers, can solve the problem. The Son of God provides the answer to the first and the Spirit of God provides the answer to the second:

> There is therefore now no condemnation to those who are in Christ Jesus, who do not walk according to the flesh, but according to the Spirit. For the law of the Spirit of life in Christ Jesus has made me free from the law of sin and death. For what the law could not do in that it was weak through the flesh, God did by sending His own Son in the likeness of sinful flesh, on account of sin: He condemned sin in the flesh, that the righteous requirement of the law might be fulfilled in us who do not walk according to the flesh but according to the Spirit (Romans 8:1-4).

RUTH

MEANING	AUTHOR	KEY THOUGHT
(after main character)	**Unknown** *(probably Samuel)*	**Kinsman-redeemer**

THEME

A stranger brought into the family of God

THEME VERSE
For wherever you go, I will go...
Your people shall be my people,
And your God, my God.
RUTH 1:16

RUTH / **SUMMARY**

PART 1 / **EMIGRATION TO MOAB**		**1:1-5**
PART 2 / **THE SAD RETURN TO JUDAH**		**1:6-22**
PART 3 / **RUTH AND BOAZ**		**2:1-4:17**
	a. Ruth meets Boaz	2:1-23
	b. Ruth follows advice	3:1-18
	c. Boaz redeems Ruth	4:1-12
	d. Marriage and the birth of a son	4:13-17
PART 4 / **ANCESTORS OF KING DAVID**		**4:18-22**

RUTH

The book of Ruth is a literary and spiritual gem. Alexander Schroder declares: "No poet in the world has written a more beautiful short story."[1] In the eighteenth century, Dr. Samuel Johnson read this book to his friends in a literary club in London. In his introduction, he did not disclose its title or origins but simply read through its pages. The people who listened responded with high praise. They thought it a recent composition and were outspoken in their appreciation and acclaim. Dr. Johnson then informed them that it was the book of Ruth which he had read to them from a book which they all despised—the Bible.[2]

The book of Ruth is a story about very ordinary people facing ordinary events. It tells of Naomi, a wife and mother bereft of husband and sons, who experiences great hardship in famine and bereavement, eventually being brought to a place of peace and security. It tells of Ruth, the foreign woman from Moab, who attaches herself to Naomi, her mother-in-law, and to Naomi's God, and receives immense blessing in later life. It tells of Boaz, Naomi's kinsman by marriage, who shows great kindness to Ruth and Naomi. By his obedience to the law of God and his respectful dealings with Ruth, Boaz becomes an honoured ancestor of the Lord Jesus Christ.

RUTH / AUTHOR

The writer is unknown. Jewish tradition accredits the book to the prophet Samuel. Judging from the first verse of this book, "Now it came to pass, in the days when the judges ruled" (1:1), and its last verse, "Obed begot Jesse, and Jesse begot David" (4:22), it must have been written when the rule of the Judges had ceased, at the introduction of the monarchy, and after the birth of David.

---

[1] David Atkinson, *The Message of Ruth: The Wings of Refuge* (Leicester: Inter-Varsity Press, 1983), 25.
[2] Robert Lee, *The Outlined Bible: An Outline and Analysis of Every Book in the Bible* (London: Pickering and Inglis, 1930), analysis no. 8.

RUTH / **HISTORICAL SETTING**

The book of Ruth illustrates a peaceful period during the time of the judges. Whereas Judges provides us with a bleak portrayal of spiritual conditions in the nation, Ruth paints another side to the picture: a time between the fighting and the wars; a time of calm and tranquillity in the life of the nation of Israel. The times covered by this book occurred during the first 100 years of "the days when the judges ruled" (1:1), some time after the Moabite oppression and delivery by Ehud (Judges 3:12–14,30). This is based on the fact that Ruth married Boaz, who was the son of Salmon and Rahab, the converted Canaanite prostitute (Matthew 1:5; Hebrews 11:31) and that Israel was not at war with Moab.[3]

These were real people, with real problems, real difficulties, real experiences, who enjoyed real blessing from God. The book of Ruth presents a brief picture of rural life in Israel during the thirteenth century B.C. There are the everyday routines of life: the need to work, the joys of the family, the pains of bereavement, parting from relatives and relationships with a mother-in-law.

RUTH / **OUTLINE**

This book is notable because it is the only instance in the Bible where a whole book is devoted to the history of a woman (the book of Esther contains far more than the history of Esther herself).

---

[3] The more usual practice is to calculate back from the birth of King David through Jesse and Obed, placing the marriage of Boaz and Ruth during the forty-year period of peace following Gideon's delivery of Israel (Carl Keil, Leon Wood, Gordon Keddie). This results in too many years to be filled by the lives of Rahab and Boaz. A more accurate way of calculation is to work forward from Rahab, who was at least in her teens when Israel invaded Jericho, and is unlikely to have been more than fifty when she gave birth to Boaz. That would make the latest time for his birth to be thirty-five years after the invasion. If Boaz then fathered Obed as late as his eightieth year, the very latest period into which the book of Ruth would fall is 105 years after possession of the land of Canaan—i.e. during the eighty years of rest following Ehud's delivery from the oppression of Moab.

PART 1 / **EMIGRATION TO MOAB (1:1-5)**

Elimelech and his wife Naomi of the tribe of Judah leave their home town of Bethlehem (i.e. Ephrath, Genesis 35:19) because of a severe famine and out of desperation, having lost their ancestral land in order to pay their debts. They journey east with their two sons, Mahlon and Chilion, crossing over the River Jordan and going down the west coast of the Dead Sea, over the River Arnon, and into the land of Moab.[4] Elimelech dies and the two sons marry women of Moab. After having been in the land of Moab for ten years, Mahlon and Chilion also die.

PART 2 / **THE SAD RETURN TO JUDAH (1:6-22)**

Naomi, left with two Moabite daughters-in-law, and hearing that the famine is over in Judah, decides to return to her own people. She urges her two daughters-in-law to return to their parental homes, and seeks God's blessing upon each one in finding a new husband and home. Tears flow as the three women contemplate separation. Both women propose to accompany Naomi back to Bethlehem. Naomi insists that they will have no benefit from remaining with her. She cannot herself provide any more husbands for them. Naomi urges them to return to their own people. Tears flow once more and Orpah bids farewell, but Ruth will not be parted from her mother-in-law, for she has been converted to faith in the God of Israel, the only true and living God. Ruth professes her allegiance to Naomi, to Naomi's people and to Naomi's God.

Seeing the determination in her daughter-in-law, Naomi realizes that further protestations on her part will be useless. The two women continue on their journey to Bethlehem.

On their arrival in Bethlehem, the local women are surprised to see Naomi returning after a ten-year absence. When they enquire, "Is this Naomi?" she takes the opportunity to testify to her great grief: "Do not call me Naomi [pleasant]; call me Mara [bitter], for the Almighty has dealt very bitterly with me" (1:20).

---

[4] The Moabites descended from Abraham's nephew Lot by his oldest daughter (Genesis 19:37; 11:27).

PART 3 / **RUTH AND BOAZ (2:1-4:17)**

It is harvest time when the two women arrive in Bethlehem. Ruth obtains permission from the servant in charge to follow the reapers in order to glean what remains in the fields. The law of God provides for those who are poor and strangers:

> When you reap the harvest of your land, you shall not wholly reap the corners of your field when you reap, nor shall you gather any gleaning from your harvest. You shall leave them for the poor and for the stranger: I am the LORD your God (Leviticus 23:22).

Boaz, a relative of Naomi by marriage, comes from the city, sees Ruth gleaning, and asks his servant about her. Hearing that she is Ruth the Moabitess who returned with Naomi, Boaz is pleased to assist her. He has heard of her reputation and seeks God's blessing upon her: "The LORD repay your work, and a full reward be given you by the LORD God of Israel, under whose wings you have come for refuge" (2:12).

Boaz encourages Ruth to stay with his young female workers. He takes steps with the men to ensure Ruth's safety and also to provide for more grain to be dropped for her to glean. Ruth works daily in the fields of Boaz through the barley harvest and the wheat harvest, probably for a period of just under two months.

Naomi's strategy

Naomi is concerned to provide some degree of security for her daughter-in-law Ruth.[5] Widows do not seem to have been included among those who could inherit property from a man who died without leaving a male heir (Numbers 27:8–11). On the basis of the provisions laid down in the law of God, Naomi seeks the restoration of her husband's land through property redemption and the continuance of her husband's name through levirate marriage.

The first part of the plan requires the buying back of the land:

---

[5] Naomi had prior legal claim to a kinsman-redeemer but gave this up in favour of Ruth.

> If one of your brethren becomes poor, and has sold some of his possession, and if his kinsman-redeemer comes to redeem it, then he may redeem what his brother sold. Or if the man has no one to redeem it, but he himself becomes able to redeem it, then let him count the years since its sale, and restore the balance to the man to whom he sold it, that he may return to his possession (Leviticus 25:25–27).

The second part of the plan requires the marriage of Ruth to a near kinsman:

> If brothers dwell together, and one of them dies and has no son, the widow of the dead man shall not be married to a stranger outside the family; her husband's brother shall go in to her, take her as his wife, and perform the duty of a husband's brother to her. And it shall be that the firstborn son which she bears will succeed to the name of his dead brother, that his name may not be blotted out of Israel. But if the man does not want to take his brother's wife, then let his brother's wife go up to the gate to the elders, and say, "My husband's brother refuses to raise up a name to his brother in Israel; he will not perform the duty of my husband's brother." Then the elders of his city shall call him and speak to him. But if he stands firm and says, "I do not want to take her," then his brother's wife shall come to him in the presence of the elders, remove his sandal from his foot, spit in his face, and answer and say, "So shall it be done to the man who will not build up his brother's house." And his name shall be called in Israel, "The house of him who had his sandal removed" (Deuteronomy 25:5–10).

The threshing-floor

Ruth follows Naomi's advice, bathes, dresses in her finest outfit and goes to the threshing floor to wait for Boaz to take a rest. Once he has fallen asleep, Ruth lies at his feet. A startled Boaz discovers Ruth at midnight. She identifies herself and adds, "Spread the corner of your garment over your maidservant" (3:9, alternative reading). This is not an invitation to immorality, but "a formal proposal of marriage couched in the picturesque language of the time."[6] Boaz, an honourable man of mature years (3:10), praises Ruth for having taken refuge with him, and promises to fulfil her wishes when he has satisfied himself that a closer relative will renounce his right and duty.

True to his word, Boaz takes the necessary steps required by the law of God to see that the land of Elimelech and the wife of Elimelech's son are redeemed by the next of kin. Finding the nearest kinsman to Elimelech, and in the presence of ten elders of the town, Boaz asks him if he will redeem the land of Elimelech. This the near kinsman is prepared to do. Then Boaz links the redemption of the land to the redemption of the family line. This second part the near kinsman will not fulfil since he fears it would jeopardize his existing inheritance (if Ruth bears a son, this kinsman and his family will lose a considerable amount of money in buying land that neither he nor his existing family can ever possess). Atkinson may well be right in his assessment:

> The kinsman was now placed in a predicament—which was exactly what Boaz had intended! Here Boaz' deep personal care for Ruth shines through. It was in order that he might marry her that Boaz had engineered this ploy, mentioning the land first, and Ruth afterwards. And his "masterstroke" came off. He skilfully used the possibilities of the law to place the nearest kinsman in an impossible position. The unnamed "goel" [i.e. kinsman-redeemer] now realized that he had two responsibilities and not one, and that both belonged together...he could hardly accept one without the other.[7]

Boaz steps into the breach, redeems the land and redeems Ruth by taking her to be his wife. As kinsman-redeemer, Boaz does not take possession of the land but holds it in trust for the first son born to Ruth. According to levirate law, that son would take the name and the inheritance of Mahlon, Ruth's first husband.

Boaz and Ruth have a son, Obed. He is to become the grandfather of King David (4:22).

---

[6] Gordon J. Keddie, *Even in Darkness: Judges and Ruth Simply Explained* (Welwyn: Evangelical Press, 1985), 121.
[7] Atkinson, *The Message of Ruth*, 113–114.

PART 4 / **ANCESTORS OF KING DAVID (4:18-22)**

The book of Ruth closes by showing how, in the providence of almighty God, the family fits into the ancestral line of the great King David (cf. Matthew 1:3-6).

RUTH / **CHRIST AND HIS CHURCH**

The New Testament does not provide a reference to Boaz as a type of Christ, nor to Ruth as a type of the church. With the benefits of the completed Scriptures, the position of Boaz and Ruth in this representative character seems unavoidable. As Jensen warns, "In a study of types, one should always be careful to make the antitype, not the type, the pre-eminent fact; and also to avoid forcing types for the mere sake of typology."[8]

TYPES

1. Ruth as a type of the Gentile church

Ruth symbolizes the Gentile portion of the church of Jesus Christ. Her story is a prophetic insight into God's love for the world beyond the Jews. It demonstrates his amazing grace in reaching out to those who are accursed. Ruth was a Moabitess. The *law* of God excluded her; the *grace* of God included her:

> An Ammonite or Moabite shall not enter the congregation of the LORD; even to the tenth generation none of his descendants shall enter the congregation of the LORD for ever, because they did not meet you with bread and water on the road when you came out of Egypt, and because they hired against you Balaam the son of Beor from Pethor of Mesopotamia, to curse you (Deuteronomy 23:3-4).

---

[8] Irving L. Jensen, *Jensen's Survey of the Old Testament: Search and Discover* (Chicago: Moody, 1978), 166.

Ruth was a stranger away from God

> At that time you were without Christ, being aliens from the commonwealth of Israel and strangers from the covenants of promise, having no hope and without God in the world. But now in Christ Jesus you who once were far off have been brought near by the blood of Christ.... Now, therefore, you are no longer strangers and foreigners, but fellow citizens with the saints and members of the household of God (Ephesians 2:12–13,19).

Ruth turns from father and mother, homeland and kindred

> If anyone comes to Me and does not hate his father and mother, wife and children, brothers and sisters, yes, and his own life also, he cannot be My disciple (Luke 14:26).

> Listen, O daughter,
> Consider and incline your ear;
> Forget your own people also, and your father's house;
> So the King will greatly desire your beauty;
> Because He is your Lord, worship Him (Psalm 45:10–11).

> And everyone who has left houses or brothers or sisters or father or mother or wife or children or lands, for My name's sake, shall receive a hundredfold, and inherit eternal life (Matthew 19:29).

It has been said that there is nothing in human literature more beautiful than Ruth's address to her mother-in-law:

> Entreat me not to leave you,
> Or to turn back from following after you;
> For wherever you go, I will go;
> And wherever you lodge, I will lodge;
> Your people shall be my people,
> And your God, my God.
> Where you die, I will die,
> And there will I be buried.

> The LORD do so to me, and more also,
> If anything but death parts you and me (1:16–17).

Ruth was poor and needy

> For when we were still without strength, in due time Christ died for the ungodly.... God demonstrates His own love toward us, in that while we were still sinners, Christ died for us (Romans 5:6,8).

Ruth was redeemed by union in marriage

> For I am jealous for you with godly jealousy. For I have betrothed you to one husband, that I may present you as a chaste virgin to Christ (2 Corinthians 11:2).

> Christ...loved the church and gave Himself for her, that He might sanctify and cleanse her with the washing of water by the word, that He might present her to Himself a glorious church, not having spot or wrinkle or any such thing, but that she should be holy and without blemish (Ephesians 5:25–27).

To "redeem" means to pay the price (to pay a ransom) necessary to buy the freedom of a captive or slave. Christians "were bought at a price" (1 Corinthians 6:20), at a very high price (1 Peter 1:19).

For those united with Christ, loneliness ceases; believers become fruitful and a blessing to others (John 15:4).

2. Boaz as a type of Christ

Boaz as the kinsman-redeemer is a type of Christ the Redeemer.

The kinsman-redeemer must be a blood relative

> But when the fullness of the time had come, God sent forth His Son, born of a woman, born under the law, to redeem those who were under the law, that we might receive the adoption as sons (Galatians 4:4–5).

Inasmuch then as the children have partaken of flesh and blood, He Himself likewise shared in the same…in all things He had to be made like His brethren, that He might be a merciful and faithful High Priest in things pertaining to God, to make propitiation for the sins of the people (Hebrews 2:14,17).

The kinsman-redeemer must be able to pay the price (2:1)
The expression "a man of great wealth" (2:1) sometimes means a valiant man: it is used of Gideon and Jephthah, each of whom is described as a "mighty man of valour" (Judges 6:12; 11:1). Sometimes it means a man of substance, as in Moses' prayer for Levi: "Bless his substance, LORD" (Deuteronomy 33:11). Sometimes it means riches, a word used several times by Isaiah (Isaiah 8:4; 61:6). It also carries the sense of moral worth—it is the word used by Boaz to commend Ruth when he says, "All the people of my town know that you are a *virtuous* woman" (Ruth 3:11). "In Boaz, therefore, we are introduced to a man of integrity, a man of influence, a man of means."[9] Yet a greater One than Boaz has come. "For you know the grace of our Lord Jesus Christ, that though He was rich, yet for your sakes He became poor, that you through His poverty might become rich" (2 Corinthians 8:9). "You were not redeemed with corruptible things, like silver or gold, from your aimless conduct received by tradition from your fathers, but with the precious blood of Christ, as of a lamb without blemish and without spot" (1 Peter 1:18–19).

The kinsman-redeemer must look with kindness upon the poor and needy (2:5)
The Lord Jesus is like the Good Samaritan who "came where he [the bruised and bleeding man] was. And when he saw him, he had compassion on him, and went to him and bandaged his wounds, pouring in oil and wine" (Luke 10:33–34). The four Gospels record a Saviour "who went about doing good and healing all who were oppressed by the devil, for God was with Him" (Acts 10:38). And, "when in penitence we come and lie at His pierced feet, and beseeching Him to spread over us the crimson mantle of His love, how immediate is His response."[10]

---

[9] Atkinson, *The Message of Ruth*, 59.
[10] Lee, *The Outlined Bible*, analysis no. 8.

The kinsman-redeemer must redeem people and property (4:5)
The kinsman-redeemer is one who redeems or recovers possession or ownership by payment of a price or by rendering service. In like manner, Christ redeems his people by giving his life for us (Titus 2:14), shedding his blood to pay the price for our release (Revelation 5:9). He also redeems creation (Romans 8:19–23). The Hebrew word for "kinsman-redeemer" appears over twenty times in the book of Ruth. In the RAV, it is translated as *kinsman, kinsmen, redeem, duty* or *right of redemption*.

The kinsman-redeemer must be willing to redeem (3:11; 4:9–10)

"Therefore My Father loves Me, because I lay down My life that I may take it again. No one takes it from Me, but I lay it down of Myself. I have power to lay it down, and I have power to take it again. This command I have received from My Father" (John 10:17–18).

Christ "loved me and gave Himself for me" (Galatians 2:20).

RUTH / **CONCLUSION**

The book of Ruth recounts the story of three ordinary people whose lives are interwoven by providence. First, we see Naomi the Israelitess, bereaved of husband and two sons, advising and helping Ruth and ultimately rejoicing in the birth of a grandson. Secondly, there is Ruth the Gentile, choosing to be faithful to the true God whatever the cost and personal inconvenience, seeking to be obedient to God and accepting Naomi's counsel and receiving blessing in union with Boaz. Finally, we are introduced to Boaz, the upright godly Israelite, without guile or deceit, full of respect for the laws of God, and full of benevolent love and friendliness toward a poor stranger.

Here is a beautiful picture of the behaviour of a woman of God, and the behaviour of a man of God. This book encourages the virtues of love and faithfulness in family relationships. It teaches purity and integrity in all relationships.

A stranger comes into the central line of the covenant people through marriage to a godly Israelite. Through these two, an aged

Israelitess, having passed through much hardship and suffering (famine and triple bereavement), eventually comes to a place of peace and contentment.

This book also presents the ancestry of David, but more especially the ancestry of David's Lord (Matthew 1:5–6). Here is a family tree that beautifully illustrates the amazing love of God and his unique redemptive work. Perez (4:18; Matthew 1:3) was one of the twins conceived as a result of an immoral union between Judah and his Canaanite daughter-in-law Tamar (Genesis 38). Rahab, the former prostitute, was adopted into the congregation of Israel (Joshua 6:25) and married Salmon. Ruth, the converted Moabitess, was taken by Boaz as his wife.

The blood of Ruth ran in the veins of the Lord Jesus Christ. The blood of the Lord Jesus Christ is the real redemption for Ruth.

RUTH / **APPLICATION AND REFLECTION**

1. Providence

The ordinary outworking of *providence* is the underlying thread of this book. Ruth's meeting with her kinsman-redeemer is described as being by chance: "And she happened to come to the part of the field belonging to Boaz" (2:3). The verse means the exact opposite of what it seems to say.[11] The clear implication is the involvement of the Lord in guiding and leading Ruth to meet her kinsman-redeemer.

> Trust in the LORD with all your heart,
> And lean not on your own understanding;
> In all your ways acknowledge Him,
> And He shall direct your paths (Proverbs 3:5-6).

God's name occurs twenty-three times in this brief book, and thus it instructs its readers concerning God's ongoing work in the life of ordinary people.[12] There are no miracles, no heavenly revelations, no prophetic disclosures, and yet there is the strong underlying sense of God's purpose and God's providence, or "providing," being unfolded. From "the illustration we are given of purity...faithfulness and loyalty, duty and love, the writer is wanting his readers to discern the hand of a God who cares, sustains and provides."[13] "And we know that all things work together for good to those who love God, to those who are the called according to His purpose" (Romans 8:28).

2. True conversion

Ruth the Moabitess is a unique illustration of God's grace extending *beyond* Israel. Here is the grace of God in all its splendour and glory. God so orders providence that Ruth comes from the outside. She is not seeking the true and living God. For in the natural state and condition, "There is no one who seeks after God" (Romans 3:11). She has not sought God. She has been sought *by* God. She has a Good Shepherd in heaven who leads her to the truth in his own inimitable fashion.

---

[11] Hals, cited by Raymond B. Dillard and Tremper Longman III, *An Introduction to the Old Testament* (Leicester: Apollos, 1995), 133.
[12] Dillard and Longman, *An Introduction to the Old Testament*, 133.
[13] Atkinson, *The Message of Ruth*, 27–28.

Ruth turns "to God from idols to serve the living and true God" (1 Thessalonians 1:9). The declaration, "Your people shall be my people, and your God, my God" (1:16), demonstrates her rejection of her past allegiances and commitments (Psalm 45:10). The Saviour says, "Everyone who has left houses or brothers or sisters or father or mother or wife or children or lands, for My name's sake, shall receive a hundredfold, and inherit everlasting life" (Matthew 19:29).

3. Love for God's people

Ruth's conversion from paganism to faith in the living and true God is evidenced by her love for the people of God. To Naomi she expresses her faith: "Your people shall be my people, and your God, my God" (1:16).

In the New Testament the apostle John develops the connection between love for God and love for those who are God's: "Everyone who loves Him who begot also loves him who is begotten of Him' (1 John 5:1). He also shows that this love for God's people is evidence of conversion: "We know that we have passed from death to life, because we love the brethren. He who does not love his brother abides in death" (1 John 3:14).

4. Signs of backsliding

Why did Naomi and her husband Elimelech leave Judah? Those who remained and lived through the famine seemed to have fared far better (1:6). Was it right to leave the land of promise? And why choose the land of Moab? The Moabites worshipped Chemosh and apparently offered human sacrifices (2 Kings 3:27). There was also widespread practice of Canaanite fertility rites. This was no place for a God-fearing man and his family. Moving to Moab may have been calculated to save lives, but the tragedy for this family was that all three males died in this foreign land.

There is no indication of Naomi's role in the move. She may have instigated the move, agreed with her husband's suggestion, or gone along out of respect for, and submission to, her husband. Nor is there any indication as to whether or not she was in agreement with her two sons marrying women of Moab contrary to the commandment of God (Deuteronomy 23:3).[14] There is, however, other clear evidence that she is in a poor spiritual state though

---

[14] Leon Wood argues that these two marriages did not contravene God's law. See Leon J. Wood, *The Distressing Days of the Judges* (Grand Rapids: Zondervan, 1975), 256–257.

she is not totally without some degree of faith in the true God.

The first obvious indication is in *the advice she gives to her two daughters-in-law*. After she has encouraged them both to go home to their parents, Orpah leaves and Ruth cleaves to her. Naomi then gives her the most staggering advice: "Look, your sister-in-law has gone back to her people and to her gods; return after your sister-in-law" (1:15). While it might be argued that Naomi is showing marked unselfishness in releasing her daughters-in-law, nevertheless she is tacitly recommending Ruth to return "to her gods." The words of Naomi imply that Ruth has been converted to faith in the God of Israel, the only true God. She has turned to the LORD. What Naomi is recommending is apostasy—turning back to her Moabite gods!

The second pointer to a poor spiritual state is in *Naomi's response to the providence of God*. To Orpah and Ruth, Naomi says, "It grieves me very much for your sakes that *the hand of the* LORD *has gone out against me!"*(1:13, emphasis added). And later, this spirit of resentment is present when she meets the women of Bethlehem:

> Do not call me Naomi [pleasant]; call me Mara [bitter], for the Almighty has dealt very bitterly with me. I went out full, and the LORD has brought me home again empty. Why do you call me Naomi, since the LORD has testified against me, and the Almighty has afflicted me? (1:20-21).

How different the response of godly Job at the news of the death of his whole family:

> Then Job arose, tore his robe, and shaved his head; and he fell to the ground and worshiped. And he said:
>
>> "Naked I came from my mother's womb,
>> And naked shall I return there.
>> The Lord gave, and the LORD has taken away;
>> Blessed be the name of the LORD."
>
> In all this Job did not sin nor charge God with wrong (Job 1:20-22).

The third feature which indicates something is not quite right with Naomi is the strategy she uses to enlist the help of Boaz. Naomi acknowledges the

Lord without really *actively* trusting in his providence. She has a belief in God, yet also there is an element of disobedience. There is an awareness of his law, but she forgets that the means used to achieve the ends are just as important to God as the ends themselves. The advice she gives to Ruth could have seriously compromised Ruth and Boaz, who were both virtuous people. It is not sound advice to creep into a man's "bedroom" and lie at his feet, even when that man has a fine moral and spiritual reputation. Their presence together through the night could well have been misconstrued. From a moral standpoint, this action promoted by Naomi and carried out by Ruth appears most unacceptable. Nevertheless, those familiar with the history of the time suggest that it would not have been judged so shocking by the customs of the people of Israel at that time.[15] But if that is so, why is Ruth so careful to leave the threshing floor before anyone could recognize her, and Boaz so insistent that her presence there that night should not be disclosed? (3:14).

We need to be alert to any signs of "departing from the living God" (Hebrews 3:12), such as finding excuses to miss worship, reluctance to be with the people of God, pulling out of church responsibilities, prayerlessness and not finding time to read and meditate upon the Word of God. Backsliding begins in the *heart*: leaving our first love (Revelation 2:4); losing the joy of the Lord (Psalm 51:12); or no longer delighting in the law of God (Psalm 1:2; Romans 7:22).

5. Women in the Bible

No impartial reader could ever conclude that the Bible has a low view of women. In studying the book of Judges, we noted that it contains the first record in history of the emergence of a woman into prominence and the leadership of a nation (Judges 4:4). Deborah is presented as a highly capable person and a judge in Israel in her own right.

Male chauvinism—the smug irrational belief in the superiority of men over women—is rebuked and corrected by the teaching, illustrations and examples found in the Word of God. There are occasional illustrations of chauvinism, as with Lot offering his daughters to the perverted crowd, or the Levite his concubine (Genesis 19:8; Judges 19:24). While such incidents are horrifying and inexplicable, there is no word of approval. That such things are recorded in Holy Scripture does not mean that the Lord sanctions these

---

[15] Carl F. Keil, *The Books of Joshua, Judges and Ruth* (Grand Rapids: Eerdmans, 1950), 483.

practices any more than he approved of the later vile behaviour of Lot's daughters, or Tamar's deceitful sin with her father-in-law (Genesis 19:31-36; 38:14-18). The Lord clearly assumes that his people will read the Scriptures with care and great thoughtfulness and so arrive at moral and spiritual conclusions that will be honouring to God.

Also rebuked and corrected is radical feminism, with its aggressive attack upon God as being against women. To maintain their cause, men and women of radical feminist persuasion have to overlook or twist the clear implications in the pages of this great book. They have to ignore, or to interpret in a distorted manner, the beautiful illustrations of godly women found here. The Bible portrays their character, their deeds and the respect which they gained among their fellow Israelites—both male and female.

Two of these outstanding godly women are Ruth and Esther. These two, each with a book bearing her name, shine out as examples of godliness, loyalty, devotion, obedience and service. They bring honour to God and provide a worthy example for all who follow after them—whether male or female. Ruth is the Gentile, Esther the Jew. Ruth, a Gentile, marries a Hebrew man. Esther, a Jewess, marries a Gentile king.

1 SAMUEL

MEANING	AUTHOR	KEY THOUGHT
"heard by God"	**Samuel**	**Heard by God**

THEME

The place and power of prayer in all experiences of life

THEME VERSE

For this child I prayed, and the Lord has granted me my petition which I asked of Him.

1 SAMUEL 1:27

1 SAMUEL / **SUMMARY**

PART 1 / **SAMUEL THE PROPHET**　　　　　　　**1:1–7:17**

    a. Samuel: given in answer to prayer　　　1:1–28
    b. Hannah's prophetic prayer　　　　　　　2:1–11
    c. The failure of Eli as judge and parent　　2:12–36
    d. Samuel's call and remarkable boyhood　　3:1–21
    e. The capture of the ark and the death of Eli　4:1–22
    f. The ark among the Philistines　　　　　5:1–12
    g. The ark returned to Israel　　　　　　　6:1–7:1
    h. The defeat of the Philistines through prayer　7:2–17

PART 2 / **SAUL, THE FIRST KING**　　　　　　**8:1–15:35**

    a. Samuel prayers concerning a king　　　8:1–22
    b. Saul chosen to be king　　　　　　　　9:1–26
    c. Saul anointed king　　　　　　　　　　9:27–10:27
    d. Saul delivers Jabesh Gilead　　　　　　11:1–15
    e. Samuel's last public address to the nation　12:1–25
    f. Saul's self-will and Samuel's prophecy　13:1–14
    g. Jonathan's victory over the Philistines　13:15–14:23
    h. Saul's rash oath　　　　　　　　　　　14:24–52
    i. Obedience is better than sacrifice　　　　15:1–35

PART 3 / **DAVID, THE GREATEST KING**　　　**16:1–31:13**

    a. David chosen and anointed　　　　　　16:1–13
    b. David: musician and armour-bearer　　　16:14–23
    c. David and Goliath　　　　　　　　　　17:1–58
    d. The friendship of David and Jonathan　18:1–5
    e. Saul's jealousy and attempt to kill David　18:6–30
    f. Saul persecutes David　　　　　　　　　19:1–17
    g. David's flight　　　　　　　　　　　　19:18–24
    h. Jonathan's loyalty and farewell　　　　　20:1–42
    i. David and the shewbread　　　　　　　21:1–9
    j. David flees to Gath　　　　　　　　　　21:10–15
    k. David in the Cave of Adullam　　　　　22:1–5

l.	Saul murders the priests and their families	22:6-23
m.	David rescues Keilah	23:1-29
n.	David spares Saul's life	24:1-22
o.	David and Abigail, the wife of Nabal	25:1-44
p.	David spares Saul's life again	26:1-25
q.	David flees again to the Philistines and is given a town	27:1-12
r.	War between Israel and Philistia: Saul consults a medium	28:1-25
s.	The Philistines remove David from the battlefield	29:1-11
t.	David's conflict with the Amalekites	30:1-31
u.	The death of Saul	31:1-13

1 SAMUEL

In the original Hebrew Bible 1 and 2 Samuel formed one book, as also did 1 and 2 Kings and 1 and 2 Chronicles. These three books were first divided by scholars working on the Septuagint, when they translated the Old Testament into the Greek language. The reason for the division in each case seems to have been that written Greek requires at least one third more space than Hebrew. The translators were consequently forced to divide each of Samuel, Kings and Chronicles into two, either because there was a limit to the length of scroll available, or in order to make the scrolls easier to handle.

Although this kind of biblical literature is generally classified among the historical books, the Jews listed them under the former prophets. The books from Joshua through to 2 Kings became known as "the former prophets," (see Figure 9) whereas later prophetic writings were gathered together under the heading of "the latter prophets." This shows that the Jews believed that God was speaking just as clearly through the historical events as through the overtly prophetic books.

1 SAMUEL / **AUTHOR**

Samuel, the prophet and judge, wrote the bulk of 1 and 2 Samuel, with Nathan and Gad completing it:

> Now the acts of King David, first and last, indeed they are written in the book of Samuel the seer, in the book of Nathan the prophet, and in the book of Gad the seer, with all his reign and his might, and the events that happened to him, to Israel, and to all the kingdoms of the lands (1 Chronicles 29:29–30).

The Jews regarded Samuel as a national leader, second only to Moses. The Lord also links Samuel with Moses as an intercessor when he addresses Jeremiah the prophet: "Then the LORD said to me, 'Even if Moses and Samuel stood before Me, My mind would not be favorable toward this people. Cast them out of My sight, and let them go forth'" (Jeremiah 15:1).

The connection between Samuel and Moses is not accidental.

Samuel was a prophet whose office, like that of all God's other prophets, can be traced back to the promise of God through Moses:

> I will raise up for them a Prophet like you from among their brethren, and will put My words in His mouth, and He shall speak to them all that I command Him. And it shall be that whoever will not hear My words, which He speaks in My name, I will require it of him (Deuteronomy 18:18–19).

This prophecy to Moses finds its ultimate fulfilment in Christ (Acts 3:22–23; John 5:45–47)

Samuel's role was to summon Israel back to the Old Covenant. The Israelites were a favoured people: the Lord loved them and had taken them as his own (12:22). Their responsibility was to respond to his great kindness by loving and obeying him (12:24–25). Samuel was personally committed to love God and to obey his law (12:3–5).

At the same time, the call of Samuel to be the prophet and judge of Israel formed a turning-point in the history of the Old Testament kingdom of God. As the prophet of Jehovah, Samuel was to lead the people of Israel out of the times of the judges into those of the kings, "and lay the foundation for a prosperous development of the monarchy."[1]

1 SAMUEL / **HISTORICAL SETTING**

First Samuel covers the history of Israel from the time of Eli the priest (c. 1060 B.C.) to the death of Saul (1010 B.C.). The book covers a period of transition. The rule of the judges draws to a close; the establishment of the monarchy is introduced. Two great institutions are now to be prominently brought forward and established, both marking a distinct advance in the history of Israel. These two institutions, the office of prophet and the office of king, are connected with the history of Samuel. This explains why the two books bear his name and why they do not close with the death of David, as might have been expected in a biography, or in a history of his reign.

---

[1] Carl F. Keil and Franz Delitzsch, *Biblical Commentary on the Books of Samuel* (Grand Rapids: Eerdmans, 1950), 13.

Figure 9. Harmony of Samuel, Kings, Chronicles, Ezra and Nehemiah

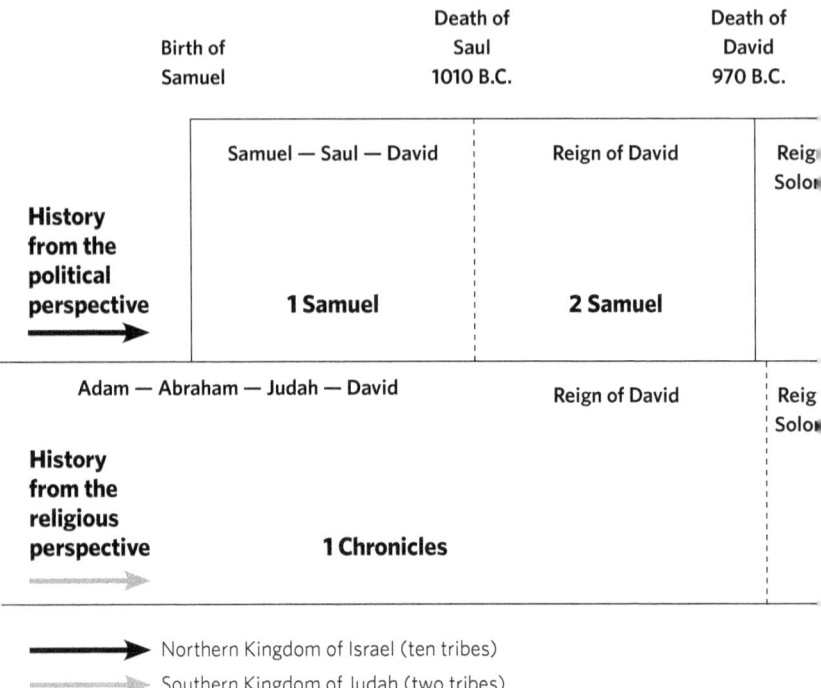

First Samuel centres around three main characters: Samuel, the last of the judges; Saul, the first of the kings; and David, Israel's greatest king. The history is not presented in a strictly chronological order. There are large gaps in the history of all three men. Long periods and important facts are omitted as the record is made. Sometimes the author refers back, providing the additional details later. As Alfred Edersheim explains, "All these peculiarities are not accidental, but designed, and in accordance with the general plan of the work."[2] As in other parts of Scripture, the record is governed by a purpose to provide

---

[2] Alfred Edersheim, *Israel under Samuel, Saul, and David, to the Birth of Solomon* (London: The Religious Tract Society, [1877?]), 2.

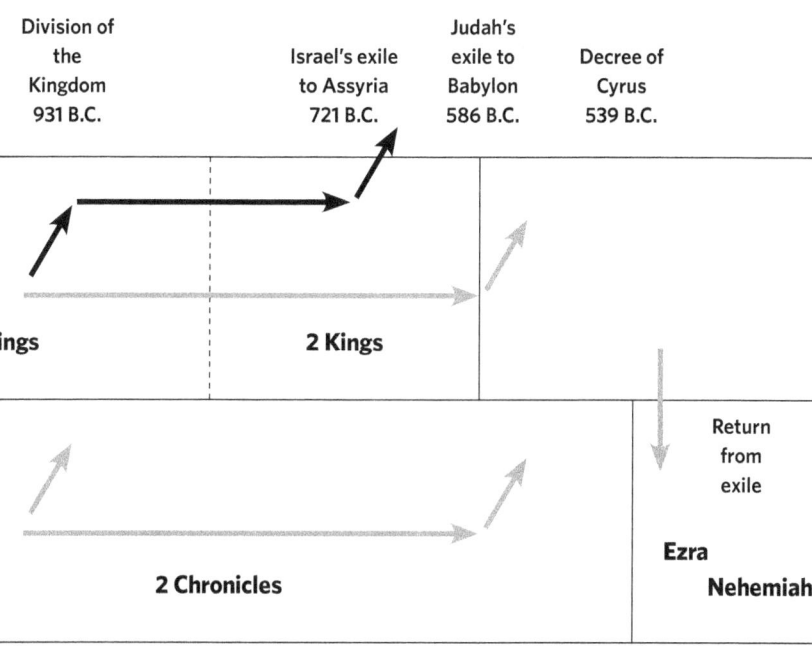

"*a history of the kingdom of God* during a new period in its development, and in a fresh stage of its onward movement toward the end."[3] The goal constantly in mind is the establishment of the kingdom of God in Christ—the priesthood of Eli, the prophetic order of Samuel and the kingly rule of David all point to this. This is always the Scriptures' chief end and goal. The reader is constantly urged to look for the Christ who is Prophet, Priest and King. The value of biblical history in the Old Testament is in what it teaches about the Saviour, and how it prepares for his coming.

---

[3] Edersheim, *Israel under Samuel, Saul, and David*, 2.

1 SAMUEL / **OUTLINE**

PART 1 / **SAMUEL THE PROPHET (1:1–7:17)**

The book of Judges ends with this disturbing comment upon the times: "In those days there was no king in Israel; everyone did what was right in his own eyes" (Judges 21:25; cf. 17:6; 18:1). The opening chapters of 1 Samuel give an account of life in Israel under the last two judges, Eli and Samuel. While the official capacity of Eli was that of a priest, and Samuel's was that of a prophet, they both functioned in positions of national leadership well beyond their religious duties. Eli "judged Israel forty years" (4:18). Samuel "judged Israel all the days of his life" (7:15).

Samuel is a child given by God in response to the persistent prayers of a barren wife. Consequently, his mother Hannah dedicates him to the Lord and, after a few years, she hands her young son into the care and training of Eli the priest. Samuel may legitimately perform priestly functions since he is a Levite by birth (1 Chronicles 6:34–38).

Hophni and Phinehas, two sons of Eli, behave wickedly. Because their father Eli rebukes them but does not restrain them, he comes under censure from the Lord. Samuel is called to the prophetic office while still a boy. His first duty is to confront Eli with the judgement of God. The Lord is with Samuel and within a short time he is recognized throughout the land as one "established as a prophet of the Lord" (3:20). A new period in the history of the kingdom of God has begun.

The Philistines are still occupying parts of Israel (cf. Judges 13:1). Growing stronger by the year, this enemy poses a serious threat to the children of Israel. In the first battle, the Israelites want the ark of the covenant among them as though its presence alone will somehow assure them of victory. The Philistines win the battle and capture the ark. Hophni and Phinehas, the two sons of Eli, and 30,000 Israelite foot soldiers are killed. When news is relayed to Eli that his sons are dead, and the ark captured, he falls backward from his seat and breaks his neck in the fall.

After Eli's grim death, responsibility as judge in Israel falls to Samuel. He is the last of the judges, but not a military judge—not ruling like Samson by physical strength, but by high spiritual qualities and prayer; not so much wrestling against flesh and blood as against principalities and powers, and the rulers of the darkness of this world, and spiritual wickedness in high places (Ephesians 6:12). In this respect, his function as judge blends with his work as prophet. In a real sense, he is the first of the prophets, for before him the prophetic office was more a casual illumination; under him it becomes a more steady and systematic light.[4] It is also probable that Samuel founded the school of the prophets mentioned in this book (10:5).

The presence of the ark of the covenant brings disaster upon thousands of Philistines. Eventually, it is returned to Israel. Samuel uses the occasion as an opportunity to call the people to repentance and prayer. The people respond, confess their sins and enjoy victory over the Philistines for the remaining years of Samuel's leadership (7:13).

PART 2 / **SAUL, THE FIRST KING (8:1-15:35)**

In his old age, Samuel appoints his two sons as successors to the office of judge, but they prove godless and dishonest. The people cry out to Samuel for a king to judge Israel "like all the nations" (8:5). The Lord chooses Saul as the first king of Israel. Industrious, generous, honest and modest, he is chosen by God to institute the monarchy.

Saul quickly vindicates his appointment as King of Israel, rallying the people and winning decisive battles against their enemies. However, when the Philistine army camps at Mishmash in preparation for battle, it seriously outnumbers Saul's army, whose men are afraid and deserting. After waiting seven days for the prophet Samuel, Saul wilfully oversteps his authority and, in direct contravention of the law of God, offers a burnt offering to the Lord. As soon as he has finished, the prophet Samuel arrives on the scene. What Saul has done in offering a sacrifice is so serious that he loses the perpetuity of his throne. He has demonstrated a lack of faith in God and disobedience to his Word. There will be no hereditary reign for his offspring, though Saul is not himself rejected. In spite of having only 600 men, Saul could have known great victory had he relied upon the Lord and been obedient to his commandments (13:13–15; cf. Gideon and his 300—Judges 7:7). Saul is the king after Israel's own heart (12:13): he offered sacrifices

---

[4] William G. Blaikie, *The First Book of Samuel* (1887; Minneapolis: Klock and Klock, 1978), 2.

to God, but not properly; he willingly fought against the enemies of Israel, but did not seek God's blessing before setting out; he trusted God until he saw his men deserting him; he believed in the outward forms of sacrifice without having internal faith, love and obedience. These reflect the character of Israel at the time. By contrast, Samuel announces that the hereditary throne is to pass to someone "after [God's] own heart" (13:14).

Saul's son Jonathan proves to be of a different character from what his father became. "Whatever fitness he might have shown for 'the kingdom,' had he been called to it, a more unselfish, warm-hearted, genuine, or noble character is not presented to us in Scripture than that of Jonathan."[5] Jonathan is a man of faith and courage. He is also a man of action. In his words to his armour-bearer, he displays his confidence in the Lord: "Come, let us go over to the garrison of these uncircumcised; it may be that the LORD will work for us. For nothing restrains the LORD from saving by many or by few" (14:6).

Further disobedience over Agag (15:9) results in the Lord's rejecting Saul as king:

So Samuel said:

> "Has the Lord as great delight in burnt offerings and sacrifices,
> As in obeying the voice of the LORD?
> Behold, to obey is better than sacrifice,
> And to heed than the fat of rams.
> For rebellion is as the sin of witchcraft,
> And stubbornness is as iniquity and idolatry.
> Because you have rejected the word of the LORD,
> He also has rejected you from being king" (15:22–23).

Saul's only excuse is that he "feared the people and obeyed their voice" (15:24).

---

[5] Edersheim, *Israel under Samuel, Saul, and David*, 65.

PART 3 / **DAVID, THE GREATEST KING (16:1–31:13)**

With the rejection of King Saul, the Lord directs the prophet Samuel to visit Bethlehem to anoint one of Jesse's sons as heir to the throne. David is anointed with oil and the Spirit of the Lord comes upon him from that day (16:13). He is not, however, to be revealed to Israel for some time, so he returns to his duties among his brothers.

Meanwhile, the Spirit of the Lord, who gives might and power and a sound mind, has departed from Saul. In the providence of God, this is to be the means of introducing David to the royal court. David, a skilful musician, is brought in to soothe Saul by playing the harp when he is troubled by "a distressing spirit from the Lord" (16:14,23).

Periodically, David returns home for rest and refreshment in the quiet solitude of the surroundings of Bethlehem (17:15), until he takes up Goliath's challenge. With courage inspired by a living faith, David confronts the giant: "You come to me with a sword, with a spear, and with a javelin. But I come to you in the name of the Lord of hosts, the God of the armies of Israel, whom you have defied" (17:45). David slays the giant. The Israelites are inspired, the Philistines dismayed. Israel rises up and wins a mighty victory.

From that day, a bond of extraordinary strength is established between David and Saul's son Jonathan. A pure, God-honouring relationship between two godly men with mutual respect and mutual affection is forged (18:3).

King Saul appoints David as a captain in his army and such is the popularity and success of this young officer that women sing,

"Saul has slain his thousands,
And David his ten thousands" (18:7).

In a fit of jealousy Saul twice attempts to kill him. Failing, Saul concludes that the Lord who has departed from him is now with David. He employs many schemes to seek to destroy David.

Taking painful leave of his great friend, David begins the life of the persecuted and hunted. He finds refuge in the Cave of Adullam. The solitude of the cave proves helpful to David in the exercise of the life of prayer and in living in utter dependence upon the Lord. Psalms 57 and 142 are composed here and indicate his confidence in the Lord.

Opportunities arise for David to easily take Saul's life, but David will not harm King Saul, "the anointed of the Lord" (24:6; 26:9,11), and he is even conscience-stricken at having cut off the corner of Saul's cloak. David seeks to convince Saul that he is in no danger whatsoever from him. Saul declares his appreciation and confesses his folly.

With all Saul's protestations, David remains certain that the king will not rest until he has sought him out and killed him (27:1). Failing to seek the Lord and depend upon him alone, David resolves to move out of Israel to the land of the Philistines.

Some time later, war is declared between the Philistines and the Israelites. Opposing camps are set up and King Saul, fearful of the prospect of war, seeks counsel from the Lord. But "The Lord did not answer him, either by dreams or by Urim or by the prophets" (28:6). In desperation, Saul disobeys the covenant law contained in the revealed Word of God and turns to a medium at En Dor (Leviticus 19:31). His wickedness is compounded when he asks her to "bring up Samuel" so that he can seek his advice and counsel.[6] Saul receives confirmation that God has rejected him and the news that he and his sons are soon to die in battle.

Assembling for battle with the Israelites, the Philistine princes take stock of their forces. Seeing David and his men at the rear of their own company, they are horrified that Israelites should be going out against Israelites. The princes show understandable distrust and command that these Hebrews should be removed from their ranks. David gives further indication of his poor spiritual state at this time for he remonstrates with the Philistine king, Achish, for not being permitted to fight against these "enemies of my lord the king" (29:8).

Returning home to Ziklag in the land of the Philistines, David and his men discover the town on fire and all their wives and children taken captive by the Amalekites. This extreme incident brings him back to his knees: "Now David was greatly distressed, for the people spoke of stoning him, because the soul of all the people was grieved,

---

[6] Three explanations have been given for the "appearance" of Samuel: (i) Samuel actually appeared to Saul; (ii) the medium at En Dor deceived Saul; and (iii) an evil spirit assumed the form of Samuel. For a discussion see Ernest W. Hengstenberg, *History of the Kingdom of God under the Old Testament*, vol. 2 (Edinburgh: T & T Clark, 1877), 104–106.

every man for his sons and his daughters. But David strengthened himself in the LORD his God" (30:6).

David no doubt felt the guilt of his behaviour in leadership. To compound his deception and lies, he had commanded the slaughter of men and women when attacking the Amalekites (27:8-9). It was no thanks to him that the Amalekites did not slaughter the families at Ziklag. It was the Lord who overruled to ensure the safety of the women and children. Guilt becomes conviction; conviction becomes confession, and "David strengthened himself in the LORD his God" (30:6).

Meanwhile, the Philistines make war against Israel, win a decisive victory and pursue Saul and his sons. Jonathan, Abinadab and Malchishua are killed and their father Saul is severely wounded. He falls upon his sword to avoid being humiliated by the Philistines.

1 SAMUEL / **CHRIST AND HIS CHURCH**

TYPES

It is in this book that we first find the expression "the LORD of hosts" (1:3). This is the first of the 281 occurrences of that name and title that signify the God of Israel as the Lord of all the multitudes in heaven and earth. That "Jehovah of Hosts" is a title sometimes applied to Christ is seen by comparing Isaiah 6:1-5 with John 12:41, and Isaiah 8:13-14 with 1 Peter 2:5-8.

1. Priest

The judgement of God upon Eli and his family includes a wonderful promise: "Then I will raise up for Myself a faithful priest who shall do according to what is in My heart and in My mind. I will build him a sure house, and he shall walk before My anointed [Messiah] forever" (2:35). This promise no doubt includes a reference to Samuel and then Zadok, but goes beyond them, and applies to the priesthood generally, and points for its final fulfilment to the Lord Jesus Christ.[7]

2. Prophet

"Dark days call for great men. Often God gives His choicest gifts to

---

[7] Edersheim, *Israel under Samuel, Saul, and David*, 12.

those who lead when times are the most difficult."⁸ Judged against the backdrop of the terrible spiritual state of Israel at this time, the prophet Samuel brought an enormous influence for good, and well deserves his place among the greatest of the Old Testament heroes. He was God's man for one of the most significant points in Israel's history. Given by God in answer to prayer, he was returned to God in adoration and praise. Raised and instructed by the high priest Eli, he was thoroughly acquainted with the ceremonies of the tabernacle. He also had easy access to the Scriptures kept there, and was well informed about the spiritual state of the nation through the regular visits of priests from all parts. Added to this were the remarkable revelations he received directly from the Lord. He was well equipped for the ministry God gave him. The testimony of Saul's servant is borne out by the whole record of Scripture: "Look now, there is in this city a man of God, and he is an honorable man; all that he says surely comes to pass" (9:6).

Samuel lived at a time when "the word of the Lord was rare...there was no widespread revelation" (3:1). He was most likely the founder/leader of a group or company of prophets (10:5–10; 19:20). With travel being difficult and time-consuming, it was important to have reliable messengers of the Word of God to dispatch it throughout the land. The tradition of training men for this kind of ministry was continued by the prophets Elijah and Elisha (2 Kings 2:3–7,15–18; 6:1).

Samuel "is the actual starting-point of the series of prophets after Moses"⁹ (cf. Acts 3:24). He preached repentance to the whole of Israel (7:2–6). "He was the forerunner of David, as John was of Christ."¹⁰ Samuel the prophet provides another strong link in the chain between the promise of a great Prophet given through Moses (Deuteronomy 18:15) and the coming of the Lord Jesus Christ.¹¹ He provides a fitting type of Christ as a prophet, priest and judge. Of young Samuel it is said that he "grew in stature, and in favour both with the Lord and men" (2:26); of the Saviour when young it is said that he "increased in wisdom and stature, and in favor with God and men" (Luke 2:52; cf. v. 40).

---

[8] Leon J. Wood, *The Distressing Days of the Judges* (Grand Rapids: Zondervan, 1975), 341.
[9] Rudolf Stier, *The Words of the Apostles* (1869; Minneapolis: Klock and Klock, 1981), 191.
[10] Stier, *The Words of the Apostles*, 191.
[11] See chapter on Deuteronomy.

3. King

In prayer, Hannah prophesied:

> The adversaries of the LORD shall be broken in pieces;
> From heaven He will thunder against them.
> The LORD will judge the ends of the earth.
>
> "He will give strength to His king,
> And exalt the horn of His anointed [Messiah]" (2:10).

The style and subject matter of her prayer are later reflected in many of the psalms.

The purpose behind 1 Samuel is to record the establishment of the monarchy and the part played by Samuel, the last of the judges and the first in a long line of great prophets. In Saul, we see a picture of a selfish autocrat, a ruler who possesses absolute and unrestricted authority. In David, the second king of Israel, we see the man after God's own heart (13:14). Yet before David comes to rule he must undergo many trials, setbacks and disappointments:

> For whom the Lord loves He chastens,
> And scourges every son whom He receives (Hebrews 12:6; cf. Proverbs 3:12).

David is one of the primary Old Testament types of the Lord Jesus Christ. Born in Bethlehem, working as a shepherd, reigning as the anointed King of Israel—in all these things he prefigures his glorious descendant in whom all the types and prophecies find wonderful and glorious fulfilment.[12] The early experiences of David tending sheep provided ample material for spiritual reflection. Psalm 23 is no doubt built upon those formative years. How many of the Lord's people, generation after generation, have found unique help and encouragement in that profound analogy! "The LORD is my shepherd; I shall not want" (Psalm 23:1) finds enriched meaning in the appearing of the "good shepherd" who lays down "His life for the sheep" (John 10:11),

---

[12] The character of David's rule as a type of Christ's reign will become more obvious as we study 2 Samuel.

the "Great Shepherd" who is brought up from the dead (Hebrews 13:20) and the "Chief Shepherd" who is now in glory (1 Peter 5:4).

1 SAMUEL / **CONCLUSION**

Four main characters appear in the 1 Samuel: Eli, Samuel, Saul and David.

Eli, the priest and judge, may be described as "a man whose weakness impaired his witness."[13] Failure at home brought dishonour and the judgement of God.

Although *Samuel*, the prophet, priest and judge, also failed in his home, he nevertheless was a man of prayer. Whether facing difficulties, confronted by hard decisions, needing guidance, or praising God for his mercy and kindness, Samuel prayed. His prayers were backed by action, for the prophet not only prayed, he obeyed (16:4).

Saul started out well, but soon fell into the snare of the autocrat. Such absolute power is not easily controlled. Disobedient to the Word of God, he violated his office, usurped that of another, burned with jealousy toward David and ended his life beset by periods of insanity.

Last of the foursome is *David* who, in spite of his many sins and failings, is nevertheless described as a man after God's own heart (13:14). Persecution, afflictions, trials and temptations shaped and fashioned this man of God as he was prepared to be the next and greatest king of Israel.

---

[13] Raymond Brown, *Let's Read the Old Testament* (London: Victory Press, 1971), 67.

1 SAMUEL / **APPLICATION AND REFLECTION**

1. Prayer and intercession

The key to the message of the book is the meaning of Samuel's name ("Heard by God") and the frequent occurrence of the words, *prayer* and *prayed*. Like Moses years before, Samuel was a great intercessor (Jeremiah 15:1). 1 Samuel is a book full of prayer. Here are examples of prayer offered in various situations:

Hannah

While the opening verses give insight into the problems of polygamy (1:2-7), they contain the moving account of Hannah's supplication to the Lord. Well does the apostle Paul exhort the Philippians: "Be anxious for nothing, but in everything by prayer and supplication, with thanksgiving, let your requests be made known to God" (Philippians 4:6).

Hannah prayed. "She was in bitterness of soul, and...wept in anguish"— but she prayed (1:10). Her song of thanksgiving (2:1-10) is close in content to the song of the Virgin Mary (Luke 1:46-55). This no doubt indicates how familiar Mary was with the prayer of Hannah recorded in the Scriptures.

It is interesting to observe the sequence of events. Hannah prays in the vicinity of the door of the tabernacle (1:9-10). Eli sees Hannah's lips moving and assumes she has been drinking far too much wine. Hannah explains her behaviour. Eli blesses her: "Go in peace, and the God of Israel grant your petition which you have asked of Him" (1:17). The following morning she rises "early in the morning and [worships] before the Lord" (1:19). What a challenge! Sadly, it seems to be the pattern that when Christians face difficulties, afflictions and disappointments, they do not pray, they do not worship. They stay at home or take a weekend break from their church in order to cheer themselves up. The solution to problems is never found in absence from the assembly of God's people (Hebrews 10:24-25).

Mizpah

The prayers of Samuel are linked with the delivery of Israel at Mizpah (7:2-13). This marks a notable turning-point in the condition of Israel in relation to her near neighbours, the Philistines. Like Joshua before him, Samuel calls a national convocation (Joshua 23:2; 24:1-2), for the confession of national sins and renewal of national obligations toward the Lord.

He desired to unite all who were like-minded in a purpose of repentance and reformation, and to rouse them to a higher pitch of intensity by contact with a great multitude animated by the same spirit. When the assembly met, it was in a most proper spirit.[14]

In humility and repentance, the Israelites acknowledge their sins. Meanwhile, the Philistines learn of the gathering together of all Israel and plan their attack. The Israelites hear of the advancement of their enemy and plead with the prophet to intercede for them. Samuel offers sacrifices and then cries out to the Lord for Israel, "and the LORD answered him" (7:9).

"Give us a king"

The people's request for a king was sinful. Israel was a theocracy, with the Lord as an invisible king. Asking for a (visible) king, like the other nations, was firstly, a symptom of unbelief, and secondly, a rejection of God's rule over them (8:7). It reflected an increasing trust in the outward and visible, in distinction from the inward and spiritual.

When the people pleaded for a king, Samuel turned to the Lord in prayer:

> Then all the elders of Israel gathered together and came to Samuel at Ramah, and said to him, "Look, you are old, and your sons do not walk in your ways. Now make us a king to judge us like all the nations."
> But the thing displeased Samuel when they said, "Give us a king to judge us." So Samuel prayed to the LORD (8:4-6).

Prayer for Israel

In his last public address, Samuel promises unceasing prayer for the people of Israel:

> For the LORD will not forsake His people, for His great name's sake, because it has pleased the LORD to make you His people. Moreover, as for me, far be it from me that I should sin against the LORD in ceasing to pray for you; but I will teach you the good and the right way. Only fear the LORD, and serve Him in truth with all your heart; for consider what great things He has done for you. But if you still do wickedly, you shall be swept away, both you and your king (12:22-25).

---

[14] Blaikie, *The First Book of Samuel*, 91.

The prophet/priest Samuel was a great intercessor. His commitment to this aspect of prayer is evident when he says, "Far be it from me that I should sin against the LORD in ceasing to pray for you." Such commitment is a worthy example to the people of God. Intercession is a vital part of prayer (1 Timothy 2:1-2; Ephesians 6:18-19; Matthew 9:38).

The vital nature of intercessory prayer is supremely evident in the work of the Godhead. The greatest prophet/priest, our Lord and Saviour Jesus Christ, "continues forever [and] has an unchangeable priesthood. Therefore He is also able to save to the uttermost those who come to God through Him, since He always lives to make intercession for them" (Hebrews 7:24-25). Furthermore, believers have the constant presence of the Holy Spirit who "helps in our weaknesses. For we do not know what we should pray for as we ought, but the Spirit Himself makes intercession for us" (Romans 8:26).

2. A father's responsibility

Eli the priest is represented as a devout man. At the same time, he seems to have lacked a sense of parental responsibility. Both his sons are described as "corrupt [literally, sons of Belial]; they did not know the LORD" (2:12). The fact that they were not spiritual cannot be laid at Eli's door. Parents have no power, and consequently no responsibility, to convert their offspring. Eli was not punished for something totally out of his control. He was punished because he did not curb the behaviour of his sons:

> Then the LORD said to Samuel: "Behold, I will do something in Israel at which both ears of everyone who hears it will tingle. In that day I will perform against Eli all that I have spoken concerning his house, from beginning to end. For I have told him that I will judge his house forever for the iniquity which he knows, because his sons made themselves vile, and he did not restrain them. And therefore I have sworn to the house of Eli that the iniquity of Eli's house shall not be atoned for by sacrifice or offering forever" (3:11-14).

The failure and neglect of Eli in relation to his two sons was all the worse in that he was a priest and a judge, and his sons were also in the priestly office. Eli had not only a domestic responsibility, but also an ecclesiastical responsibility for his sons. Leadership among the people of God not only means good and faithful oversight of the saints in the church, but also good and faithful oversight of the family in the home:

> A bishop [i.e. an overseer] then must be blameless, the husband of one wife, temperate, sober-minded, of good behavior, hospitable, able to teach; not given to wine, not violent, not greedy for money, but gentle, not quarrelsome, not covetous; one who rules his own house well, having his children in submission with all reverence (for if a man does not know how to rule his own house, how will he take care of the church of God?) (1 Timothy 3:2-5).

This domestic rule not only includes elders, for it is applied to deacons as well: "Let deacons be the husbands of one wife, ruling their children and their own houses well" (1 Timothy 3:12).

The word translated *rule* might accurately be translated into modern idiom as *exercise management skills*. Such activity involves "planning, organization, enlistment, training and deployment of personnel, administration and discipline."[15] Clearly, the modern practice of "reasoning without restraint" and "talking without training" is the error for which Eli was punished. Of course, this does not mean that *only* elders and deacons should rule their homes in this manner. *All* fathers should do so. Nevertheless, it is especially important that leaders give a right example in this matter. In our own day, there is much discredit brought upon church leaders by the unruly behaviour of their children. How many ministers, elders and deacons would be caused to resign their office if the domestic test were seriously applied?

The judgement of God against Eli for failure as a father was communicated through Samuel while the latter was still a boy (3:1). The sad sequel is that Samuel also failed in this regard. Godly as he undoubtedly was, spiritually-minded as he most certainly was, prayerful as he decidedly was, nevertheless he was a poor father:

> Now it came to pass when Samuel was old that he made his sons judges over Israel. The name of his firstborn was Joel, and the name of his second, Abijah; they were judges in Beersheba. But his sons did not walk in his ways; they turned aside after dishonest gain, took bribes, and perverted justice (8:1-3).

---

[15] Jay E. Adams, "The Pastor and his Family," *Reformation Today* 81 (1984): 29.

3. Friendship

Two extremes of friendship are illustrated—one the purest and most noble, the other sinful and worldly: the first between David and Jonathan, the second between David and Achish. Behaviour is usually affected (or sometimes infected) by the company we keep (1 Corinthians 15:33). Between David and Jonathan, there was an unusual bond. It was a pure, God-honouring relationship between two godly men with mutual respect and mutual affection, for "the soul of Jonathan was knit to the soul of David, and Jonathan loved him as his own soul" (18:1). The Lord's people can experience a deep and a rich relationship with members of their own gender. Freud is wrong in supposing that all relationships have elements of libido (sexual urge or desire). This is just another Satanic attempt to provide grounds to besmirch the good name of the righteous:

> Let the lying lips be put to silence,
> Which speak insolent things proudly and contemptuously against the righteous (Psalm 31:18—a psalm of David).

> The wicked plots against the just,
> And gnashes at him with his teeth.
> The LORD laughs at him,
> For He sees that his day is coming.
> The wicked have drawn the sword
> And have bent their bow,
> To cast down the poor and needy,
> To slay those who are of upright conduct.
> Their sword shall enter their own heart,
> And their bows shall be broken (Psalm 37:12-15—a psalm of David).

The Lord Jesus sanctified friendship in his close companionship with the twelve apostles, the three—Peter, James and John (Matthew 17:1; 26:36-37)—and with the apostle John, in particular (John 19:26-27; 20:2; 21:7,20).

Whereas the friendship between David and Jonathan indicates the *heights* to which friendship with the godly may rise, that between David and Achish shows the *depths* to which friendship with the worldly can sometimes plunge. David was wrong in seeking protection from Saul by turning to King Achish of the Philistines. He placed himself under obligation to an enemy of Israel. Trapped by his own deceit and lies, David professed allegiance to King

Achish (28:1-2), who was thoroughly taken in by David's prevarications. The man who had twice insisted that Saul should not be killed (24:6; 26:9) was now in league with the army that would destroy Saul—and Jonathan too! Friendship with the world always leads to serious problems for the Lord's people (1 John 2:15-16; Romans 12:2; 2 Corinthians 6:17-18).

Like David and Jonathan, pastors and leaders also need to cultivate Christian friendships for mutual encouragement and enrichment.

4. Obedience

The importance of obeying the Word of God is brought into sharp focus in the Lord's punishment of King Saul. His first disobedience occurred when he performed the function of a priest (a duty which, under the Mosaic covenant, only a Levite could fulfil). On the brink of a major battle against the Philistines, with his army unsettled and dispersing, and the priest Samuel not having arrived at the appointed time, Saul took matters into his own hands (13:9) with disastrous results. The second major disobedience occurred when the Lord ordered King Saul to carry out the *total* destruction of the Amalekites and all their livestock (15:2-3). In the event, Saul spared the life of Agag, the king of Amalek, and confiscated the best of the livestock as booty (15:9). Samuel confronted Saul with the Lord's judgement against him:

> Has the LORD as great delight in burnt offerings and sacrifices,
> As in obeying the voice of the LORD?
> Behold, to obey is better than sacrifice,
> And to heed than the fat of rams.
> For rebellion is as the sin of witchcraft,
> And stubbornness is as iniquity and idolatry.
> Because you have rejected the word of the LORD,
> He also has rejected you from being king (15:22-23).

The same emphasis upon obedience to the Lord is found in the New Testament. The Lord Jesus expects love to be demonstrated practically in obedience (John 14:15; 15:10,14). Also, the connection between faith and obedience is so strong that the Scripture which says, "Abraham believed God, and it was accounted to him for righteousness," is seen by one New Testament writer as a fine example of faith, and by another as an indisputable illustration of obedience (Romans 4:2-5; James 2:21-24).

5. Overruling providence

Among the many, two major incidents illustrate the overruling providence of God. The first concerns David's intended revenge upon Nabal, who would not give supplies to David's servants (25:21-22). Rebuffed by this rich farmer, David responds immediately.

> How did David now receive their report? Did he humble himself and commend his cause to God the Lord? On the contrary, we meet him now, for the first time, not master of his own spirit, but hurried along by his natural passionateness of disposition. With a flaming anger... glowing with a spirit of revenge he led his band of four hundred armed men to the little town of Carmel.... Surely he had not this time either prayed or enquired of the Lord by the "Urim and Thummim." If he had carried out what his anger suggested to him...he would have given the death-blow to his own honour and to his cause. Then he would have appeared before God and all the world as an outlaw: a man over whom not only his enemies would have triumphed, but who must also be given up by his friends as unworthy of the crown of Israel.[16]

In the providence of God there is someone there to save the day. Abigail intervenes and not only averts a tragedy for her husband and servants, but also prevents David from ruining his reputation.

The second illustration of the overruling providence of God is seen in David's foolish alliance with King Achish of the Philistines. Having placed himself under obligation to this enemy of Israel, David is determined to go to war on the side of the Philistines against Israel (29:1-2,8). The Lord uses the princes of the Philistines to block David's stupidity (29:3-4). Had David gone to battle against Israel it would have destroyed his credibility before his own people for ever.

6. Grace and gifts

When the people cried out for a king, their acceptance of Saul was probably based on his striking appearance and his natural skills which suited him as

---

[16] F. W. Krummacher, *David—the King of Israel* (1868; Grand Rapids: Baker Book House, 1982), 173. Krummacher's writings are highly recommended for their faithfulness to Scripture, devotional emphasis and clear and easy style. Other titles (also published by Baker) include *Elijah the Tishbite*, *Elisha a Prophet for Our Times*, *The Suffering Saviour* and *The Martyr Lamb*.

a military leader. However, his religious commitment and spiritual state reflected the state of the nation at the time: "that of combining zeal for the religion of Jehovah, and outward conformity to it, with utter want of real heart submission to the Lord, and of true devotedness to Him."[17] Saul was never born again and yet, following his anointing to the office of King of Israel, he was granted "signs" that God was with him (10:7). One of these signs was that the Spirit of the Lord would come upon him and he would prophesy together with a group of prophets (10:6). This raises the serious question of the relationship between the grace of God and the gifts of the Holy Spirit. Here is a man, Saul, who evidently prophesied by the power of the Holy Spirit and yet he was not a child of God and was ultimately totally rejected.

The Lord Jesus Christ draws attention to this possibility that someone might exercise spiritual gifts and yet not possess spiritual grace when he declares:

> Not everyone who says to Me, "Lord, Lord," shall enter the kingdom of heaven, but he who does the will of My Father in heaven. Many will say to Me in that day,"Lord, Lord, have we not prophesied in Your name, cast out demons in Your name, and done many wonders in Your name?" And then I will declare to them, "I never knew you; depart from Me, you who practice lawlessness!" (Matthew 7:21-23).

The apostle Paul makes the same sober assessment:

> Though I speak with the tongues of men and of angels, but have not love, I have become sounding brass or a clanging cymbal. And though I have the gift of prophecy, and understand all mysteries and all knowledge, and though I have all faith, so that I could remove mountains, but have not love, I am nothing (1 Corinthians 13:1-2).

Love for God and obedience to God are the marks of true godliness, not the exercise of gifts—natural or spiritual!

7. Religious superstition

The ark of the covenant (or "ark of the Testimony") built according to the exact specifications given by God (Exodus 25:10-21) was the place where

---

[17] Edersheim, *Israel under Samuel, Saul, and David*, 36.

God met with Moses as he had promised: "And there I will meet with you, and I will speak with you from above the mercy seat, from between the two cherubim which are on the ark of the Testimony, about everything which I will give you in commandment to the children of Israel" (Exodus 25:22).

The ark of the covenant held a prominent place in the history of Israel. The mercy seat, forming the lid of the ark and supporting the two golden cherubim, was associated with the presence of God (Psalm 80:1). When the priests carrying the ark entered the waters of the River Jordan, a pathway was miraculously opened up and the huge company of Israelites walked on the dry riverbed into the land of Canaan (Joshua 3:14-17). Shortly afterward, the ark was carried for seven days around Jericho before the walls of the city fell (Joshua 6:6-20). After Israel's settlement in Canaan, the ark remained for a while in the tabernacle at Gilgal, and then it was relocated to Shiloh, where it remained until the days of Eli.

Entering into battle with the Philistines, Israel was defeated (4:1-2). They rightly concluded that their failure to succeed was evidence that the Lord had withdrawn his support. The method they used to try to secure God's help in the next battle was entirely wrong. Instead of humbling themselves and repenting, confessing their sins and their backsliding, they decided to transport the ark of the covenant from the tabernacle at Shiloh into the camp, in the misguided notion that God's presence was inseparably linked to the mercy seat (4:4). Disastrous results followed, including the capture of the ark of the covenant.

Symbols instituted by God never possess power. The Israelites, and other people since, often made the mistake of dissociating external symbols from internal realities. The true cause of Israel's defeat was the disapproval of God upon their spiritual backsliding. *The answer was entirely spiritual.* Let Israel repent and return in true contrition to the Lord and he would once more support and defend them.

Reliance upon the outward form without the internal spiritual reality became the trademark of the Pharisees in New Testament times (Matthew 23:25-28).

The same error can be made with regard to the Christian symbols of bread and wine in the celebration of the Lord's Supper. Taking the symbols without sincere spiritual awareness can lead to a drastic outcome: "For he who eats and drinks in an unworthy manner eats and drinks judgment to himself, not discerning the Lord's body. For this reason many are weak and sick among you, and many sleep" (1 Corinthians 11:29-30).

2 SAMUEL

MEANING	AUTHOR	KEY THOUGHT
(sequel to 1 Samuel)	**Nathan and Gad** *(1 Chronicles 29:29–30)*	**Before the Lord**

THEME

Trials and triumphs for the servant of God

THEME VERSE
So let Your name be magnified forever.... And let the house of Your servant David be established before You.
2 SAMUEL 7:26

2 SAMUEL / **SUMMARY**

The reign of King David

PART 1 / **THE OPENING YEARS** 1:1–9:13

- a. Preliminary events — 1:1–27
  - (1) David's avenging of Saul's death — 1:1–16
  - (2) David's lament over Saul and Jonathan — 1:17–27
- b. David as king of Judah and Israel — 2:1–9:13
  - (1) The counter-claim of Ishbosheth and Abner — 2:1–4:12
  - (2) The capture of Jerusalem — 5:1–16
  - (3) The defeat of the Philistines — 5:17–25
  - (4) The ark brought to Jerusalem — 6:1–23
  - (5) God's covenant and David's gratitude — 7:1–29
  - (6) Summary of David's wars and lists of officials — 8:1–18
  - (7) Reinstatement of Mephibosheth — 9:1–13

PART 2 / **THE MIDDLE YEARS** 10:1–19:43

- a. Great military successes over Ammon and Syria — 10:1–11:1
- b. David's fall and punishment — 11:2–12:24
  - (1) David's adultery and subsequent marriage to Bathsheba — 11:2–27
  - (2) Nathan's denouncement of David and his repentance — 12:1–23
  - (3) The birth of Solomon — 12:24–31
- c. Amnon and Tamar; the flight of Absalom — 13:1–39
- d. Absalom's readmission to the court — 14:1–33
- e. Absalom's revolt and death — 15:1–18:32
- f. David's lamentation — 18:33–19:4
- g. Joab's rebuke and David's attempted reorganization — 19:5–43

PART 3 / **THE FINAL YEARS** 20:1-24:25

- a. The revolt of Sheba and the northern tribes 20:1-26
- b. Three years of famine: David avenges the Gibeonites 21:1-14
- c. Continuing trouble with the Philistines 21:15-22
- d. A psalm of David 22:1-51
- e. Summary of the exploits of David's heroes 23:1-39
- f. The census and its consequences 24:1-25

2 SAMUEL

In the original Hebrew Bible, 1 and 2 Samuel formed a single volume. There is an obvious cohesion between the two parts although each has characteristics of its own. The first is concerned with the history surrounding three notable figures: Samuel, the last of the judges; Saul, the first of the kings; and David, Israel's greatest king. Second Samuel is almost entirely devoted to a history of David as king. Both books emphasize the importance of prayer. In the second book the expression "enquired of the Lord" appears four times (2:1; 5:19,23; 21:1). Furthermore, there is a strong emphasis throughout almost the whole of this history that David constantly recognized the presence of God with him at all times.

2 SAMUEL / **AUTHOR**

The authors of this second book were probably Nathan and Gad, two prophets who were contemporaries of David:

> Now the acts of King David, first and last, indeed they are written in the book of Samuel the seer, in the book of Nathan the prophet, and in the book of Gad the seer, with all his reign and his might, and the events that happened to him, to Israel, and to all the kingdoms of the lands (1 Chronicles 29:29–30).

Other sources were evidently used in compilation of this history, such as "the Book of Jasher" (1:18).

2 SAMUEL / **HISTORICAL SETTING**

The book begins with David's accession to the throne (1010 B.C. over Judah, 1003 B.C. over the united kingdom of Israel and Judah) and gives an account of significant events during his reign of forty years, to his death in 970 B.C. He rises to unparalleled power and influence nationally and internationally; falls to the temptation of lust; commits adultery and murder; and reaps the consequences of his sin in his family and in the nation.

2 SAMUEL / **OUTLINE**

Second Samuel records the life of David in his triumphs and his troubles. In no other biblical character is there such a variety of spiritual experiences as in the life of David.

PART 1 / **THE OPENING YEARS (1:1-9:13)**

King Saul is dead. News reaches David and his men, in their self-imposed exile in the Philistine town of Ziklag (1 Samuel 27:5-6). The messenger is a young Amalekite who claims to have ended Saul's life. The Amalekite clearly hopes for a reward, a demonstration of gratitude, some great honour on account of his professed action (4:10). But he reckons without the noble spirit and God-fearing heart of the young heir apparent to the throne of Israel. David is overwhelmed with grief over the death of Saul and Jonathan. Though Saul had persistently sought to kill him, and almost succeeded on more than one occasion, yet he was "the LORD's anointed" (1:14; cf. 1 Samuel 24:6,10; 26:11,16,23). David would not lay a finger on him. Nor will he reward the man who does. The Amalekite is executed for his professed action.[1] "As an Amalekite, he was doomed to destruction (Deuteronomy 25:17-19), and as the elect-king, David was now required to put the sentence into execution."[2]

Amid the ruins of Ziklag, David pays tribute to the enemy who had sought his life and to the friend who had stood by him in adversity. David is just thirty (5:4) and yet shows remarkable maturity. All the years of persecution and harassment, the countless sleepless nights, the anxiety, the distress, the journeyings—all these are gone from his heart and mind. There is no recrimination over Saul's character, no note of relief at Saul's death, not the slightest sense of joy that his enemy is no more—indeed the very opposite is true. As he pours out his praise and grief, he does not distinguish between Saul and Jonathan until the penultimate verse of the song (1:26), where "comparison

---

[1] The Amalekite's account of events is untrue (see 1 Samuel 31:3-5), but David has no way of knowing this.
[2] Arthur W. Pink, *The Life of David*, 2 vol. (Grand Rapids: Baker Book House, 1981), 1:233.

to the love of women is expressive of the deepest earnestness of devoted love."[3]

"Israel lost the battle of Gilboa, but she was now standing on the threshold of undreamed-of triumphs. It was about the year 1010 B.C. and David had advanced to the foot of a throne."[4] David would know full well that speedy and decisive action often wins the day. He could lead his men, rally support in Israel and claim the crown and throne. Instead, he turns to the Lord for guidance and direction: "David enquired of the Lord, saying, 'Shall I go up to any of the cities of Judah?' And the Lord said to him, 'Go up.' David said, 'Where shall I go up?' And he said, 'To Hebron'" (2:1).

The Lord directs David to Hebron in Judah. Hebron was originally called Kirjath Arba (Joshua 14:15) and lies twenty miles east of Ziklag and eighteen miles south of Jerusalem. This move marks the first step in David's rise to supreme power. Until now, Judah has been simply a province of Israel. Now it is to become a kingdom. At Hebron, David is anointed "king over the house of Judah" (2:4). Upon hearing of the courageous deed of the men of Jabesh Gilead in retrieving the bodies of Saul and his sons, David sends a message commending them for their action. This no doubt allays any fears that they or any other old friends of King Saul might have had with the ascendancy of David. Instead of trying to punish those who have faithfully served Saul, David is inclined to show them favour, to confer distinctions and honour upon them, rather than forcing them into exile.

Five years after the defeat by the Philistines, Abner, commander-in-chief of Saul's army (and Saul's cousin, 1 Samuel 14:50), proclaims Saul's son Ishbosheth as king of Israel (2:8–9)—that is, the eleven tribes excluding Judah. It was Abner who brought young David to King Saul after he had slain Goliath (1 Samuel 17:57). In proclaiming Ishbosheth as king, Abner knows he is acting against the revealed will of God that the throne should pass from the house of Saul to David (3:9–10). This act of defiance leads to civil war between Israel and Judah.

---

[3] Carl F. Keil and Franz Delitzsch, *Biblical Commentary on the Books of Samuel* (Grand Rapids: Eerdmans, 1950), 292.

[4] Charles Gulston, *David, Shepherd and King: The Life and Heritage of David* (Grand Rapids: Zondervan, 1980), 98.

It is while living in Hebron that David shows further evidence of serious weakness, in his love of women. To the two wives he had taken with him, he adds four more (cf. Deuteronomy 17:14–17). All six bear sons to David at Hebron.

> Though polygamy was not allowed to David…this toleration of polygamy did not and could not prevent the evils to which, from its very nature, it gives rise. There could be no unity in David's family, none of that delightful feeling of oneness, which gives such a charm to the family home. On the contrary, occasions of estrangement and opposition would be perpetually apt to arise among the different branches of the household, and it would require all his gentleness and wisdom to keep these quarrels within moderate bounds.[5]

In spite of the express warning of Moses that a king must not multiply wives (Deuteronomy 17:17), David will take more wives and concubines when he eventually moves to Jerusalem (5:13) (see Table 6). But great grief is to come to David through his family: his favourite wife will turn against him (6:20–22); his daughter Tamar will be raped by her half-brother (13:14); his son Amnon will be murdered by his half-brother (13:28–29); his favourite son Absalom will take the throne from him (15:13) and be murdered (18:14); another son Adonijah will also try to take the throne (1 Kings 1:5) and he too will be murdered by his half-brother (1 Kings 2:24–25). As Moses warned all Israel, "Be sure your sin will find you out" (Numbers 32:23).

At the death of King Ishbosheth and Abner, their commander-in-chief, the demoralized Israelites turn to David and yield to his rule. The elders recognize the purposes of God in the person of David. They give three reasons for choosing him as king: first, that he is of their kin; second, that he has experience as an army captain in war; and, third, that the Lord promised the kingdom to him. The elders of Israel ought to have put the last first, for that is the most important reason of all. Had they been governed by spiritual considerations and thoughts of pleasing the Lord, then they would have been satisfied with the one

---

[5] William G. Blaikie, *David, King of Israel: The Divine Plan and Lessons of His Life* (1861; Minneapolis: Klock and Klock, 1981, 145.

Table 6. David's wives and sons

Wife	Son	Death
Michal	no children	
Ahinoam	Amnon (violated Tamar)	killed by Absalom
Abigail	Chileab (Daniel)	died in his youth
Maacah	Absalom (brother of Tamar)	killed by Joab
Haggith	Adonijah	killed by Solomon
Abital	Shephatiah	
Eglah	Ithream	
Bathsheba	**Solomon (Jedidiah)**	
	Shimea (Shammua)	
	Shobab	
	Nathan	
One of the above wives	Ibhar	
One of the above wives	Elishama (Elishua)	
One of the above wives	Eliphelet (Elpelet)	
One of the above wives	Nogah	
One of the above wives	Nepheg	
One of the above wives	Japhia	
One of the above wives	Elishama	
One of the above wives	Eliada (Beeliada)	
One of the above wives	Eliphelet	
Concubines	others (1 Chronicles 3:9)	

reason—it was God's revealed will. That they were not motivated by high spiritual principles and concerns is clear in regard to two further factors: the fact that they took so long to take this action, since seven-and-a-half years had passed since the death of Saul, and the way in which God's will was made a secondary consideration—they only began to express regard for it when no other course was possible.

After seven-and-a-half years as King of Judah, David is anointed as king over the united kingdoms of Israel and Judah. He makes "a covenant with them at Hebron before the LORD" (5:3). God's great promise is fulfilled, as David, of the tribe of Judah, becomes king over the united kingdom of Israel:

Judah, you are he whom your brothers shall praise;
Your hand shall be on the neck of your enemies;
Your father's children shall bow down before you.
Judah is a lion's whelp;
From the prey, my son, you have gone up.
He bows down, he lies down as a lion;
And as a lion, who shall rouse him?
The sceptre [the symbol of royalty] shall not depart from Judah,
Nor a lawgiver [the king's long staff] from between his feet,
Until Shiloh [the Pacifier, the Prince of Peace] comes;
And to him shall be the obedience of the people (Genesis 49:8–10).

The covenant which the elders and David made that day (5:3) would no doubt have set out the duties of king and subjects, and have included promises made on behalf of each party.

David chooses Jerusalem, the stronghold of Zion, for his royal residence. Jerusalem, with its cluster of hills, had a sacred history. Here Abraham met the mysterious Melchizedek, King of Salem (Jeru-Salem, i.e. "Place of Peace") who gave him bread and wine and blessed him with the solemn words:

Blessed be Abram of God Most High,
Possessor of heaven and earth;
And blessed be God Most High
Who has delivered your enemies into your hand.
(Genesis 14:19–20)

Here on Mount Moriah, where Jerusalem was built, Abraham had taken his son to offer him as a burnt offering to the Lord (Genesis 22:1–2) and spoken those unforgettable words: "God will provide for Himself the lamb for a burnt offering" (Genesis 22:8). The ancient name of Salem was changed to Jebus at the time of Joshua's invasion. In the days of the judges, the Jebusites (inhabitants of Jebus) were described as "a city of foreigners, who are not of the children of Israel" (Judges 19:12).

Jerusalem, otherwise virtually impenetrable, is taken by Joab, leading a band of David's courageous men up the watershaft into the city (5:7–8; 1 Chronicles 11:6).

The Philistines hear that David is now king of the united Israel and, lest he should have time to consolidate his position, they move immediately into action. They advance as far as the Valley of Rephaim. Though such danger is on his threshold, David turns to God for counsel. Under the Lord's direction, David fights against the Philistines and wins a decisive victory.[6] A further battle ensues and, once more under the direction of the Lord, David succeeds in driving the Philistines out of Israel.

The ark of the Testimony

The ark of the Testimony, or the ark of the covenant, had been constructed according to the Lord's detailed instructions to Moses on Sinai (Exodus 25:10–22). Bearing the mercy seat as its lid, and housed in the Holy of Holies inside the tabernacle tent, it was the piece of furniture at the heart of divinely ordained, God-honouring worship in Old Testament times. It was carried in front of the Israelites as they left Mount Sinai (Numbers 10:33) and the Levites became the only authorized handlers of it (Deuteronomy 10:8). A copy of the completed law of Moses was eventually placed inside (Deuteronomy 31:26). The ark led the way over the Jordan river and into the promised land (Joshua 3:6,8) and was carried around Jericho before the city wall collapsed (Joshua 6:8). The ark was captured by the Philistines (1 Samuel 4:10–11), but brought them so much distress that they returned it to Israel (1 Samuel 5:1–6:12). Eventually it was placed in the house of Abinadab (1 Samuel 7:1), where it remained until David planned to move it into Jerusalem.

About seventy years had passed since the ark of God had stood in the tabernacle.[7] With the uniting of the twelve tribes of Israel under the reign of David, it was fitting to pay careful attention to the centrality of worship, for the ark represented the presence of God. There was no place more suitable for the ark than the capital city, Jerusalem,

---

[6] David may have composed Psalm 63 at this time. While many commentators place Psalm 63 in the days when David hid from Saul in the wilderness of Judah, it is most unlikely that David would have called himself "the king" at that time (v.11). Spurgeon places it later, when David was fleeing from Absalom.

[7] Keil and Delitzsch calculate twenty years to the victory at Ebenezer, forty years under Samuel and Saul, and about ten years under David (Keil and Delitzsch, *The Books of Samuel*, 330).

which became known as the City of David. So the king prepared a tent to house the ark of the Testimony, the ark of the covenant.

Tragic thoughtlessness surrounds the first attempt to transport the ark into Jerusalem (6:2–7). Obviously more concerned to follow the example of the Philistines (1 Samuel 6:7), rather than the express commandments of God, the Israelites move the ark on a new cart. The First Chronicles provides a fuller account of the measures taken by David and the priests to make the second attempt according to the revealed Word of God: "And the children of the Levites bore the ark of God on their shoulders, by its poles, as Moses had commanded according to the word of the LORD" (1 Chronicles 15:15).

With great thanksgiving, the ark is brought into the City of David. The king, full of spiritual excitement, dances "before the LORD with all his might" (6:14). His wife Michal, daughter of King Saul, witnesses her husband's behaviour and despises him "in her heart" (6:16).[8] The relationship between the two is never the same again.

Settled in Jerusalem and given rest by the Lord from all his enemies, David feels increasingly ill at ease that his house is more substantial than the place where the ark of God is kept. He longs to build a permanent building, a temple for the Lord. The prophet Nathan at first encourages David to go ahead, but when night comes God shows Nathan his presumption and error (7:4). Nathan is charged to deliver a message to the king: David will not build a house for God—God will build a house for David (7:11). There is a play on words here. God's house is a building—David's house is his descendants. Receiving the news, King David responds with characteristic reverence and humility. He leaves the royal palace and makes his way to the humble tent which houses the sacred ark. There "King David went in and sat before the LORD" (7:18). He has just received news that would have inflated many a man, filled him with a sense of his own importance and caused him to act arrogantly toward others. But this man, "a man after [God's] own heart" (1 Samuel 13:14), is quite different. Humbled, filled with amazement at God's great kindness, David goes to the place of worship to pour out his heart in wonder, love and praise (cf. Psalm 132).

---

[8] Michal possessed an idol (1 Samuel 19:13; cf. Genesis 31:19) and evidently loved the courageous hero and majestic king. She had no sympathy with David's humility in taking the priestly ephod and behaving with such spiritual enthusiasm.

David's kingdom is strengthened and enlarged. The full conquest of the Philistines is followed by the subjugation of the Moabites and the expansion of the kingdom to the northeast as far as the River Euphrates. Syria falls, as do Ammon, Amalek and Edom. "The LORD preserved David wherever he went" (8:14).

Remembering his promise made years before to his best friend, Jonathan, David enquires to see if there is any member of his family still alive (1 Samuel 20:15,17). Discovering one remaining son of Jonathan, lame Mephibosheth, David restores to him the family land which belonged to his grandfather Saul. He then pledges that Mephibosheth will constantly sit as an honoured guest at his table.

PART 2 / **THE MIDDLE YEARS (10:1-19:43)**

David and his troops win a decisive victory against the Syrians, but the following spring he decides *not* to accompany his troops into battle. This marks a dreadful turning-point in the life of this God-fearing man. His early life, chequered as it was, is nevertheless characterized by triumphs. The remaining years will be characterized by troubles. Things begin to go horribly wrong. The spiritual downfall of David begins when he turns from the path of duty, stays in Jerusalem when his men are out fighting and passes his time in idleness. He sees a beautiful woman bathing. He "is tempted when he is drawn away by his own desires and enticed. Then, when desire has conceived, it gives birth to sin" (James 1:14–15). And one sin leads to another. From taking another man's wife, he is soon taking another man's life. He is guilty of adultery, scheming and murder. And God's wrath is kindled. David the king is rebuked by Nathan the prophet. In a most notable parable personally addressed by Nathan to David (12:1–15), the king is brought under spiritual conviction. David repents. Psalm 51 is wrung from his heart.

Although the sense of divine retribution is clearly and decisively portrayed in this book, there is also the record of the amazing grace of God. God is always ready to forgive even terrible sins (12:13). Sometimes, however, pardoned sin still has its consequences (12:14). David is no ordinary man. He is king of Israel. Position brings responsibility. The higher the position, the greater the responsibility. Failure brings requisite discipline. Those who lead, like those who teach, will "receive a stricter judgement" (James 3:1). The whole subsequent history of David is a record of the consequences resulting from his sin. The child conceived in the sinful union with Bathsheba dies. David's family life becomes chaotic. The man who is able to rule his nation wisely cannot rule his home. His son Amnon commits a dreadful sin against his half-sister Tamar, and David is simply "very angry" (13:21). No further action is taken until, two years later, Absalom (full brother to Tamar, half-brother to Amnon) takes matters into his own hands, murders Amnon and flees the country. *"The tragedy in the life of King David was no more evident than in the sorrows his own sons heaped upon his head. And it was in Absalom that he reaped the bitterest harvest of all."*[9]

David grieves for his son Absalom and longs for his return to Israel. Not a day passes in three years in which David does not miss his favourite son. Joab, commander-in-chief of Israel's army and close confidant of his uncle David, plans to resolve the difficulties and restore Absalom to his father. As with Nathan, Joab employs a scheme that will force David to pass judgement on an imaginary case which is similar to that of Absalom. Even though David learns that Joab is behind the ploy, he nevertheless accepts the point and commands that Absalom be brought home—but not brought before the king! This is an incomprehensible proviso to the agreement that he should be brought back. The father grieves for his son but refuses to see him. There is no greeting for Absalom, no opportunity for repentance and forgiveness, no restoration of relationship. The instruction is: "do not let him see my face" (14:24). In this action David may well have contributed to the later rebellion of Absalom!

Two years pass with no change in the attitude of his father, so Absalom forces the issue himself. Joab speaks to the king and Absalom is brought to his father and reconciliation takes place. But five years of estrangement have taken their toll upon this son of David. Whatever pride and ambition may lie in his heart at this point, subsequent events are to demonstrate these sins in uncontrolled profusion.

In his late twenties, and with his brothers Amnon and Chileab both dead, Absalom is the heir to the throne of Israel. Because of his past behaviour, he may doubt the support of his father and the nation. Furthermore, there is young Solomon, the second son of Bathsheba,

---

[9] Gulston, *David, Shepherd and King*, 153 (emphasis his).

who is possibly being groomed to sit upon the throne. Absalom plans a manoeuvre. In contrast to his father the king, he determines on a high-profile strategy, regularly appearing in public with an impressive entourage. He also sits at the palace gate listening to those who come with grievances, telling them what justice he would dispense if he were in power. He embraces anyone who shows him significant respect. So, by such cunning and craft, "Absalom stole the hearts of the men of Israel" (15:6). After four years, Absalom is confident of sufficient support to mount a revolt.

Psalm 41 may have been composed about this time:

> if we place this psalm into the time of the rebellion of Absalom, it would fit exceptionally well. The "bosom friend" could well be Ahithophel. The period of illness would have led to the omission of the carrying out of many duties in David's administrative work, which would explain how Absalom was able to claim that men were not getting just treatment under David's administration.[10]

On the pretext of honouring a vow made some years earlier, Absalom visits Hebron, the town of his birth (3:2–3). Two-hundred friends, who are oblivious of his intentions, go with him. He is also accompanied by one of David's most trusted counsellors, Ahithophel. So David's favourite son and his trusted friend join forces in a conspiracy to usurp the throne (15:31). Psalm 55 fits these events, though, as Spurgeon notes,

> It would be idle to fix a time, and find an occasion for this psalm with any dogmatism. It reads like a song of the time of Absalom and Ahithophel.... Altogether it seems to us to relate to that mournful era when the king was betrayed by his trusted counsellor.'[11]

When news of the rebellion reaches David, he gathers his household and servants and makes a hasty departure from Jerusalem. The man

---

[10] H.C. Leupold, *Exposition of the Psalms* (London: Evangelical Press, 1969), 329.
[11] Charles Haddon Spurgeon, *The Treasury of David*, 3 vol. (McLean: MacDonald Publishing Company, 1990), 1:445.

who had for many years been a fugitive from godless Saul is now to become a fugitive from his own godless son (cf. Psalm 3).

> How long, O you sons of men,
> Will you turn my glory to shame?
> How long will you love worthlessness
> And seek falsehood?
> But know that the LORD has set apart for Himself him
>   who is godly;
> The LORD will hear when I call to Him (Psalm 4:2–3).

During this time, David and his party are met by Ziba, the servant of Mephibosheth. Ziba lies about his master, saying *he* is a usurper. David believes Ziba and rewards him accordingly. One day David will learn the truth and discover that he has been deceived (19:24–30). His fault lies in believing Ziba without evidence; consequently Mephibosheth is judged an ungrateful traitor. In these circumstances, it is difficult for David to know whom to trust. He ought to postpone judgement until conversant with all the facts. Believers are warned not to "judge according to appearance, but [to] judge with righteous judgement" (John 7:24).

David recognizes the judgement of God on his life, as is evident in his reaction to Shimei, the son of Gera, of the house of Saul. When Abishai wants to kill Shimei for cursing David, the king replies, "What have I to do with you, you sons of Zeruiah? So let him curse, because the LORD has said to him, 'Curse David.' Who then shall say, 'Why have you done so?'" (16:10). There is very little brightness in David's life, since his sins against Uriah and Bathsheba.

David is brought very low by news of the death of Absalom. He retires to the privacy of his own room and weeps. "It was a king who heard his armies had been victorious, but it was a father who grieved."[12] "O my son Absalom—my son, my son Absalom—if only I had died in your place! O Absalom my son, my son!" (18:33).

David's grief as a father completely overshadows his responsibilities as a king. He should have been joining with his people in the praise of God for victory, and publicly acknowledging the faithfulness of his

---

[12] Gulston, *David, Shepherd and King*, 170.

loyal subjects. Joab, his commander-in-chief, rightly rebukes him. David accepts the criticism and goes out to greet the people.

With the death of Absalom and the defeat of his army, David could well have returned immediately and with military force have regained the throne in Jerusalem. He chooses rather to wait until the elders of both Israel and Judah invite him back.

As David begins his return journey to Jerusalem, the men of Judah cross the Jordan to escort him. A contingent of Benjamites, and Ziba with his sons, also accompany him. Once over the Jordan, King David is greeted by Shimei, who is full of remorse for his past offence (16:5–8). David forgives him and will not permit anyone to harm him.

The next person to greet the returning king is lame Mephibosheth. Tricked by Ziba, his servant, he was unable to join David when he left Jerusalem. As an open gesture of his grief since David's departure, Mephibosheth has neglected his appearance. His loyalty to David is now visibly evident.

The return is not without its problems. The men of Israel challenge the men of Judah for taking the honour of escorting King David over the Jordan, for it was Judah who was at first reticent to see David returned to power. Judah responds by claiming their tribal relationship as warrant for the honour. They argue fiercely and will not relent. The scene is set for a new division.

PART 3 / **THE FINAL YEARS (20:1–24:25)**

A Benjamite leads the opposition. Sheba sounds the trumpet and calls upon all Israelites to turn away from King David. He has caught the spirit of the day and the Israelites respond in totality. Judah alone escorts King David to Jerusalem.

A dark shadow is once more cast over Israel: three years of famine afflict the land. At length, David seeks an explanation from the Lord. It is revealed that the famine is punishment for a crime committed some years earlier: the breaking of a peace treaty with the Gibeonites that had been entered into in the days of Joshua (Joshua 9:3–15). King Saul had violated this covenant (21:2). Responding to their request, David hands over seven male descendants of Saul. They are executed and their bodies hung on trees or stakes. Rizpah, Saul's concubine, keeps vigil over the bodies. Her action in respect for the dead prompts

David to recover the bodies of Saul, Jonathan and the seven grandsons who were hung. He ensures their burial in the tomb of Kish, Saul's father, in the town of Zelah of the land of Benjamin (21:14; cf. 1 Samuel 9:1–2). The famine ends.

At an age when most men have settled down to a less strenuous existence, David is still leading his army into battle.[13] While fighting an old enemy, the Philistines, David collapses on the battlefield (21:15), is rescued by Abishai and requested by his men not to accompany them to war again (21:17). At sixty-eight years of age, the courageous soldier and outstanding military leader, more often than not conscious of the Lord's enabling (22:30,35,37–51), has to hang up his sword. But his work is not yet over.

> The righteous shall flourish like a palm tree,
> He shall grow like a cedar in Lebanon.
> Those who are planted in the house of the LORD
> Shall flourish in the courts of our God.
> They shall still bear fruit in old age;
> They shall be fresh and flourishing,
> To declare that the LORD is upright;
> He is my rock, and there is no unrighteousness in Him
> (Psalm 92:12–15).

Retirement from military activity gives David the opportunity to reflect upon his long and eventful life. Under the influence of the Holy Spirit, he composes a song of thanksgiving that forms an appropriate conclusion to the history of his active life (22:1–51; cf. Psalm 18). As David advances in years, he appears to grow more thankful to the Lord, "and it is delightful to see him, as it is delightful to see any old man, not turning sour, as the infirmities of age gathered upon him, but more grateful, more humble, more genial than ever."[14]

---

[13] There are differences of opinion as to when these various clashes recorded in chapter 21 actually took place. Three of the wars are recorded in 1 Chronicles 20:4–8, being included in a general survey of David's war exploits. It is fair to assume, however, that at least the first battle is correctly located here since it records how David ceased from accompanying his men to war (21:15–17).

[14] Blaikie, *David, King of Israel*, 317.

David claims divine inspiration for the psalm recorded in chapter 22 (and by implication all his other psalms), for immediately following the psalm he declares:

> The Spirit of the LORD spoke by me,
> And His word was on my tongue.
> The God of Israel said,
> The Rock of Israel spoke to me… (23:2–3).

These lines may be intentionally *trinitarian* in their reference to God the Holy Spirit ("The Spirit of the LORD spoke by me"), God the Father ("The God of Israel said") and God the Son ("The Rock of Israel spoke to me"; cf. Isaiah 32:2; 1 Corinthians 10:4: "and that Rock was Christ").[15]

Testimony is recorded of "David's heroes," the mighty men who were loyal to David, and an account given of an outstanding example of heroic devotion. In the early days of David's flight from the wrath of King Saul, three men came to David at harvest time when he was in the Cave of Adullam (1 Samuel 22:1). David was on the mountain fortress and the Philistine post was then in Bethlehem. David longed for water and said, "Oh, that someone would give me a drink of the water from the well of Bethlehem, which is by the gate!" (23:15). Bethlehem was his birthplace and he longed to be home. The three mighty men, disregarding their own safety, broke through the ranks of the enemy, by strategy or by sword, to obtain the desired water. Their deed was all the more remarkable in that David was a fugitive, had not been crowned king—nor, humanly speaking, was there any prospect of his being crowned king—was not in a position to honour these men and had issued no command. Their respect and devotion for David are unquestionable. When the water was brought to David he immediately understood the danger to which the men had exposed themselves and viewed the water as far too precious for his consumption, "but poured it out to the LORD" (23:16).

---

[15] The opening words of chapter 23 present something of a difficulty since David's life is not yet at an end; there is more to follow. Arthur Pink suggests a solution: "2 Samuel 23 refers to 'the last words of David' not so much as those merely of a man, but rather as being a mouthpiece of God, thus forming a brief appendix to his Psalms" (Pink, *The Life of David*, 2:286).

The final chapter of 2 Samuel "concerns an episode which though simple and plain in some of its features, is in other respects shrouded in deep mystery."[16] David determines to number the nation of Israel to ascertain the strength of his people. His captains resist the idea and David himself later confesses that he has "sinned greatly" (24:10). The Lord also indicates his displeasure by sending a plague that kills 70,000 men (24:15).

Years before, Moses had, under instruction from the Lord, numbered the people twice: immediately following the construction of the tabernacle in the Wilderness of Sinai (Numbers 1:1–3), and on the plains of Moab just prior to entering the land of Canaan (Numbers 26:1–2). It would seem that David had a precedent for taking a census of fighting men, so what was the nature of his great sin? Various explanations have been given. One is that David sinned in numbering the people without the express instruction to do so from the Lord; another that David was motivated by personal pride in wanting to know the extent of his military power. A third suggestion is that David failed to require the half-shekel which was to be paid by each person for the service of the sanctuary when the people were numbered (Exodus 30:12–13). When the Scriptures provide no explanation it is unwise to form any strong conclusions.

The Lord gives David a choice of punishments: seven years of famine, three months of defeat in battle or three days of plague. David's response indicates that his confession is sincere and his repentance is genuine: "Please let us fall into the hand of the LORD, for His mercies are great" (24:14). The plague hits the nation—70,000 men die. The angel is poised to strike the capital. David pleads with God. The Lord answers and an altar is to be erected "to the LORD on the threshing-floor of Araunah" (24:18). "And David built there an altar to the LORD; and offered burnt offerings and peace offerings. So the LORD heeded the prayers for the land, and the plague was withdrawn from Israel" (24:25).

---

[16] Pink, *The Life of David*, 2:309. Pink adds: "nor do we profess to be able to solve it fully"!

2 SAMUEL / **CHRIST AND HIS CHURCH**

TYPES

1. David as a type of Christ

"I will establish one shepherd over them, and he shall feed them—My servant David. He shall feed them and be their shepherd. And I, the LORD, will be their God, and My servant David a prince among them; I, the LORD, have spoken" (Ezekiel 34:23–24). "David My servant shall be king over them, and they shall all have one shepherd; they shall also walk in My judgments and observe My statutes…. and My servant David shall be their prince for ever" (Ezekiel 37:24–25; cf. Jeremiah 30:9). This posthumous use of the name "David" in reference to the promised Messiah at least permits, if not implicitly commends, the examination of the life of David as a type of Christ.

Many parallels may be drawn (see Table 7). David was three times anointed—in his father's house, over Judah and, lastly, over Israel (1 Samuel 16:13; 2 Samuel 2:4; 5:3). God has anointed Jesus of Nazareth with the oil of gladness in the Father's house, over his people the church and ultimately over all things.

Though anointed king, David experienced exile for many years while Saul reigned over Israel. In like manner, the Lord is rejected by the world and "the god of this age" (2 Corinthians 4:4) reigns in the hearts of the people. Like David, the Saviour gathers to himself a motley band of followers.

The pardoning of Shimei resembles the pardoning of such sinners as the thief on the cross, who had mocked the Saviour, and "illustrates the sufficiency of God's mercy for the greatest sinner and the vilest rebel—even for those who have poured blasphemy and reproach on His holy name."[17] We cannot form too high a view of the grace and goodness of God in Christ. No sin is too great for him to be able to forgive it.

2. David and Mephibosheth as a type of Christ and sinners

David's dealings with Mephibosheth provide a type of the Saviour's dealings with a sinner (see Table 8). The name Mephibosheth means

---

[17] Blaikie, *David, King of Israel*, 300.

Table 7. David as a type of Christ

	David	Christ
One of his brethren	"Indeed we are your bone and your flesh" (2 Samuel 5:1). "one from among your brethren you shall set as king over you" (Deuteronomy 17:15).	"Inasmuch then as the children have partaken of flesh and blood, He Himself likewise shared in the same" (Hebrews 2:14).
One by whom the Lord would deliver his people	"And I have been with you ...and have cut off all your enemies from before you" (2 Samuel 7:9; cf. 22:38-41).	"Blessed is the Lord God of Israel, For He has visited and redeemed His people, And has raised up a horn of salvation for us" (Luke 1:68-69). "For He must reign till He has put all enemies under His feet" (1 Corinthians 15:25).
Anointed	"Then Samuel took the horn of oil and anointed him in the midst of his brothers" (1 Samuel 16:13; cf. 2 Samuel 2:4; 5:3).	"Therefore God, Your God, has anointed You With the oil of gladness more than Your companions" (Hebrews 1:9; cf. Psalm 45:7).
Hated without cause	"Why then will you sin against innocent blood, to kill David without a cause?" (1 Samuel 19:5) "Let them not rejoice over me who are wrongfully my enemies; Nor let them wink with the eye who hate me without a cause" (Psalm 35:19; cf. Psalm 69:4).	"But this happened that the word might be fulfilled which is written in their law, 'They hated Me without a cause'" (John 15:25).

	David	**Christ**
Opposing kingdoms	"So Saul became David's enemy continually" (1 Samuel 18:29).	Satan is continually the enemy of Christ: "the ruler of this world" (John 12:31). "the prince of the power of the air, the spirit who now works in the sons of disobedience" (Ephesians 2:2).
Gathers a motley band of followers	"And everyone who was in distress, everyone who was in debt, and everyone who was discontented gathered to him" (1 Samuel 22:2).	"But God has chosen the foolish things...the weak things...and the things which are despised" (1 Corinthians 1:27-28).
Grants pardon for sinners	"'Shall not Shimei be put to death for this, because he cursed the Lord's anointed?' ...the king said to Shimei, 'You shall not die'" (2 Samuel 19:21-23).	"Even the robbers who were crucified with Him reviled Him" (Matthew 27:44). "And Jesus said to him, 'Assuredly, I say to you, today you will be with Me in Paradise'" (Luke 23:43).
Betrayed by a close friend	"Then Absalom sent for Ahithophel the Gilonite, David's counselor.... And the conspiracy grew strong" (2 Samuel 15:12). "Even my own familiar friend in whom I trusted, Who ate my bread, Has lifted up his heel against me" (Psalm 41:9).	"Judas, one of the twelve, went before them and drew near to Jesus to kiss Him. But Jesus said to him, 'Judas, are you betraying the Son of Man with a kiss?'" (Luke 22:47-48). "I know whom I have chosen; but that the Scripture may be fulfilled, 'He who eats bread with Me has lifted up his heel against Me'" (John 13:18).

	David	Christ
The betrayer hangs himself	"Then [Ahithophel] put his household in order, and hanged himself, and died" (2 Samuel 17:23).	"Then [Judas] threw down the pieces of silver in the temple and departed, and went and hanged himself" (Matthew 27:5).
Gentiles share the king's rejection	"But Ittai answered the king and said, 'As the Lord lives, and as my lord the king lives, surely in whatever place my lord the king shall be, whether in death or life, even there also your servant will be'" (2 Samuel 15:21).	"For to you it has been granted on behalf of Christ, not only to believe in Him, but also to suffer for His sake" (Philippians 1:29). "Yes, and all who desire to live godly in Christ Jesus will suffer persecution" (2 Timothy 3:12).
Has devoted followers	Three mighty men risked their lives to bring water for David: "'Is this not the blood of the men who went in jeopardy of their lives?' Therefore he would not drink it" (2 Samuel 23:17).	"... our beloved Barnabas and Paul, men who have risked their lives for the name of our Lord Jesus Christ" (Acts 15:25-26; cf. 2 Corinthians 11:23-27; Revelation 12:11).

"a shameful thing" and, polluted by sin, "We are all like an unclean thing" (Isaiah 64:6), following "the lusts of our flesh, fulfilling the desires of the flesh and of the mind" (Ephesians 2:3). Mephibosheth was lame in both feet; in the same way, we too are by birth and behaviour crippled as a result of a fall. Mephibosheth was a fugitive from the wrath of a king; we "were by nature children of wrath, just as the others" (Ephesians 2:3), unable to please God (Romans 8:8). Mephibosheth lived in Lo Debar, which means, "the place of no pasture"; like the prodigal son, sinners are in a far country where there is severe famine (Luke 15:13-14). Mephibosheth was brought to Jerusalem, "the place of peace." By the unmerited favour of the king, he would dine at the king's table for the rest of his life. Forgiven sinners will dine with Christ for eternity.

Table 8. David and Mephibosheth as a type of Christ and sinners

Mephibosheth	Sinners
Mephibosheth means "a shameful thing." He was unclean; he had not cared for his personal hygiene since David left (see 2 Samuel 19:24).	"But we are all like an unclean thing, And all our righteousnesses are like filthy rags" (Isaiah 64:6).
He was lame in both feet as the result of a fall (see 2 Samuel 4:4).	Sinners are crippled by birth and behaviour as a result of Adam's fall (see Romans 5:12).
He was a fugitive from the wrath of a king (see 2 Samuel 4:4).	Sinners are under the wrath of God (see Romans 1:18; Ephesians 2:3).
He lived in Lo Debar, which means "the place of no pasture" (see 2 Samuel 9:4).	Like the prodigal son, sinners are in a far country where there is a severe famine (see Luke 15:13-14).
He was reconciled to the king (2 Samuel 19:24-30)	"And you, who once were alienated and enemies in your mind by wicked works, yet now He has reconciled" (Colossians 1:21).
He was brought to Jerusalem, which means "the place of peace" (2 Samuel 9:13)	"Peace I leave with you, My peace I give to you; not as the world gives do I give to you. Let not your heart be troubled, neither let it be afraid" (John 14:27).
By the unmerited favour of the king, Mephibosheth would dine at the king's table for the rest of his life (see Samuel 9:13).	"If anyone hears My voice and opens the door, I will come in to him and dine with him, and he with Me" (Revelation 3:20; cf. 19:9).

The defection of David's close companion Ahithophel is a type of the betrayal of Jesus by Judas. It is thought that Ahithophel was one whom the king included among his closest friends, with whom he had fellowship in spiritual matters, and of whom he spoke when he said that they "took sweet counsel together, and walked to the house of God in the throng" (Psalm 55:14). David felt the betrayal deeply:

> Even my own familiar friend in whom I trusted,
> Who ate my bread,
> Has lifted up his heel against me (Psalm 41:9).

Ahithophel hanged himself, and so did Judas.

In the loyal Philistine Gittites, who fled Jerusalem with David, there is a type of Gentile believers who join the Saviour and share his dishonour in the world. The height of devotion to Christ is illustrated in the willingness and eagerness with which the three mighty men of David discounted thoughts of their own safety in order to fulfil the desire of their beloved leader (23:15–17).

PROPHECIES

1. The seed of David

After David had brought the ark of the covenant to Jerusalem and had placed it in a temporary tabernacle, he planned to build a beautiful and more permanent temple. The Lord responded to his desire by sending word through Nathan the prophet: David would not build the house of the Lord; the Lord would build the house of David (7:5,11). The Lord gave David a prophetic promise: "Your house and your kingdom shall be established forever before you. Your throne shall be established forever" (7:16).

There is an intriguing ambiguity in the promise that the Lord gives to David:

> When your days are fulfilled and you rest with your fathers, I will set up your seed after you, who will come from your body, and I will establish his kingdom. He shall build a house for My name, and I will establish the throne of his kingdom forever (7:12–13).

Solomon was not yet born. Was this promise to be fulfilled in Solomon, or in the Lord Jesus Christ, or in both? When God said, "I will be his Father, and he shall be my son" (7:14) the ultimate fulfilment is reserved for the Lord Jesus Christ (Hebrews 1:5).[18] Later generations would clearly see the thread of history: the promised seed of Eve (Genesis 3:15) is the promised seed of Abraham (Genesis 12:3, 7) who

---

[18] Charles Alexander argues that on the basis of this revelation, David wrote Psalms 2 and 110 concerning the eternal Son and Psalm 16:10 concerning the resurrection of Messiah; see Charles D. Alexander, *The Heavenly Mystery of the Song of Songs* (Liverpool: Bible Exposition Fellowship, 1965), 12–15.

is the promised seed of David (7:12–13; cf. Romans 1:3). David is in the ancestral line of the promised Messiah (Matthew 1:6). This Messiah will build the true house of God (7:13): "Christ...a Son over His own house, whose house we are if we hold fast the confidence and the rejoicing of the hope firm to the end" (Hebrews 3:6; cf. Zechariah 6:12–13; 1 Corinthians 6:19–20; Ephesians 5:30).

The continuity between the covenant with Abraham and the covenant with David is highlighted by the prophet Jeremiah:

> Thus says the LORD: "If My covenant is not with day and night, and if I have not appointed the ordinances of heaven and earth, then I will cast away the descendants of Jacob and David My servant, so that I will not take any of his descendants to be rulers over the descendants of Abraham, Isaac, and Jacob. For I will cause their captives to return, and will have mercy on them" (Jeremiah 33:25–26).

The elements of the promises made to David are strikingly similar to those in the promises made to Abraham (see Table 9). Like Abraham, David is promised that his name will be great and that the nation will have security in its own land. David is promised offspring: kings are to descend from him. God declares himself as the God of Israel and they are his very own people. The promises to Abraham and to David are eternal. The only element of the promise to Abraham that seems to be lacking in 2 Samuel 7 is the extension of the divine blessing to Gentiles.[19]

The hope of the prophets was based upon confidence in the promise of God, for, "If the promise ever came to an end, the messianic hope would die."[20] If the promise ever failed the whole purposes of God would be shattered and the kingdom of Christ could never be established.

The promise made to Abraham of a seed to come has now, through David, "attained the high stature of a triumphant and universal king

---

[19] Thomas E. McComiskey, *The Covenants of Promise: A Theology of the Old Testament* (Nottingham: Inter-Varsity Press, 1985), 21.
[20] McComiskey, *The Covenants of Promise*, 26.

Table 9. Promises to Abraham and to David

Promise	Abraham	David
A great name	Genesis 12:2	2 Samuel 7:9
A land for his descendants	Genesis 12:7	2 Samuel 7:10
A great nation	Genesis 12:2	2 Samuel 7:12
A royal line	Genesis 17:6	2 Samuel 7:16
To be their God	Genesis 17:7	2 Samuel 7:14
An everlasting promise	Genesis 17:7	2 Samuel 7:13

Abraham	David
"I will make you a great nation; I will bless you And make your name great; And you shall be a blessing. I will bless those who bless you, And I will curse him who curses you; And in you all the families of the earth shall be blessed" (Genesis 12:2-3). "To your descendants I will give this land" (Genesis 12:7). "I will make you exceedingly fruitful; and I will make nations of you, and kings shall come from you. And I will establish My covenant between Me and you and your descendants after you in their generations, for an everlasting covenant, to be God to you and your descendants after you. Also I give to you and your descendants after you the land in which you are a stranger, all the land of Canaan, as an everlasting possession; and I will be their God" (Genesis 17:6-8).	"And I have been with you wherever you have gone, and have cut off all your enemies from before you, and have made you a great name, like the name of the great men who are on the earth. Moreover I will appoint a place for My people Israel, and will plant them, that they may dwell in a place of their own and move no more; nor shall the sons of wickedness oppress them anymore, as previously, since the time that I commanded judges to be over My people Israel, and have caused you to rest from all your enemies. Also the LORD tells you that He will make you a house." "When your days are fulfilled and you rest with your fathers, I will set up your seed after you, who will come from your body, and I will establish his kingdom. He shall build a house for My name, and I will establish the throne of his kingdom forever. I will be his Father, and he shall be My son. If he commits iniquity, I will chasten him with the rod of men and with the blows of the sons of men. But My mercy shall not depart from him, as I took it from Saul, whom I removed from before you. And your house and your kingdom shall be established forever before you. Your throne shall be established forever" (2 Samuel 7:9-16).

of Judah."[21] As we are now privileged to see, Messiah is "King of Kings and Lord of Lords" (Revelation 19:16; 17:14), and "He will reign… forever, and of His kingdom there will be no end" (Luke 1:33; Hebrews 1:8).

2. The Lord's anointed

It is David who first describes a king as "the Lord's anointed" (1 Samuel 24:6), a phrase which gives a high and exalted view of kingship (1:14,16). Having witnessed his own phenomenal rise to the throne, followed by his devastating fall into the sins of lust, adultery and murder, David has seen his life closely aligned with the promised Messiah in his own rising, but separate from the promised Messiah in his own falling. By the end of his life, David in his writings clearly separates himself from the Promised One. The picture of the future in 1 Samuel 23 "is nothing else than the image of the Messiah, which now has been entirely separated from [David's] subjectivity, and which stands before him as purely objective."[22]

> The God of Israel said,
> The Rock of Israel spoke to me:
> "He who rules over men must be just,
> Ruling in the fear of God.
> And he shall be like the light of the morning when the sun rises,
> A morning without clouds,
> Like the tender grass springing out of the earth,
> By clear shining after rain" (23:3–4).

The later prophets would build upon this prophecy of the *just* or *righteous* rule of Messiah. Although the prophecies were obscure and built upon each other, we have the advantage, at this side of Calvary, of seeing the fulfilment of the detail and tracing the thread back:

> Behold, your King is coming to you;
> He is just and having salvation,

---

[21] Patrick Fairbairn, *Prophecy: Viewed in Respect to Its Distinctive Nature, Its Special Function, and Proper Interpretation* (1865; Grand Rapids: Baker, 1976), 179.

[22] Franz Delitzsch, *Messianic Prophecies* (Edinburgh: T&T Clark, 1880), 51.

Lowly and riding on a donkey,
A colt, the foal of a donkey (Zechariah 9:9; cf. Jeremiah 23:5–6; Psalm 72:2).

In Psalm 2 the phrase "the LORD's anointed" is portrayed in clear focus: God's anointed (the Messiah) is the one whom God has appointed King of Zion and is God's Son to whom all should yield unreserved submission and trust (Psalm 2:2,6,7,12).

2 SAMUEL / **CONCLUSION**

David was a man after God's own heart (1 Samuel 13:14). In a lifespan of about seventy years, he "served his own generation by the will of God" (Acts 13:36).

David was Israel's greatest king, designated by God as the kingly type of Christ the Messiah. He is the only person in Scripture with the name David. There are fifty-eight New Testament references to him. David's career, though outstanding at times, was marred by atrocious sins. His honesty and sincere repentance in acknowledging and confessing those sins brought God's forgiveness. He knew how to cry to God:

Have mercy upon me, O God,
According to Your lovingkindness;
According to the multitude of Your tender mercies,
Blot out my transgressions.
Wash me thoroughly from my iniquity,
And cleanse me from my sin (Psalm 51:1–2).

He knew also the joy of salvation and justification by faith alone:

Blessed is he whose transgression is forgiven,
Whose sin is covered.
Blessed is the man to whom the LORD does not impute iniquity,
And in whose spirit there is no deceit.

When I kept silent, my bones grew old
Through my groaning all the day long.

> For day and night Your hand was heavy upon me;
> My vitality was turned into the drought of summer.
> I acknowledged my sin to You,
> And my iniquity I have not hidden.
> I said, "I will confess my transgressions to the Lord,"
> And You forgave the iniquity of my sin (Psalm 32:1–5).

David is a key figure in the unfolding purposes of God, centring on Christ and his church.

2 SAMUEL / **APPLICATION AND REFLECTION**

1. Human plans and divine purposes

Good ideas, even ideas which are honouring to God, should be brought before the Lord for his approval (7:1-17). If we do not regard God's will as *supreme*, we are entirely at fault. Our first question ought to be: "What says the Lord?" or "What would the Lord have me to do?" There is some credit to the Israelites that the question does come second or third in line of consideration. There is some merit that it is there at all. Yet, if we would honour God, it will be our first and foremost consideration. Life is short. All plans must be made in the conscious presence of God and with due consideration to the purposes of God:

> Come now, you who say, "Today or tomorrow we will go to such and such a city, spend a year there, buy and sell, and make a profit"; whereas you do not know what will happen tomorrow. For what is your life? It is even a vapor that appears for a little time and then vanishes away. Instead you ought to say, "If the Lord wills, we shall live and do this or that" (James 4:13-15).

2. God's work in God's way

David always acknowledged that God was behind his accession to the throne of Israel and Judah: "David knew that the LORD had established him as king over Israel, and that He had exalted His kingdom for the sake of His people Israel" (5:12). Such awareness keeps a believer humble before God and others, and dependent upon God alone (Deuteronomy 8:11-18).

David was often conscious of God's presence and involvement in his life. It was not a periodic intervention into his life and circumstances; David acknowledged God's *constant* involvement—though he did not always live as we would expect of one who was continually aware of it. When he fought against the Philistines, he humbly acknowledged that his victory in war was the Lord's doing; before he fought, he prayed to know the mind of God; having received word from the Lord that he should proceed, he won a great victory. When the Philistines were defeated David declared, "The LORD has broken through my enemies before me, like water bursting a breach" (5:20).

David did, however, make some serious mistakes in this regard. In seeking to bring the ark of the covenant into Jerusalem, his intentions were good but his initial approach was bad. Rather than seeking the mind of God and consulting the Scriptures, David consulted his leaders (1 Chronicles 13:1), making democracy his guiding principle (1 Chronicles 13:2,4) with staggering and tragic results (6:6-7).

When the ark was first constructed on Mount Sinai, it was made to God's exact specifications. The Lord not only laid down the dimensions, he also stipulated the materials from which each section should be composed. The Lord was not, however, concerned simply for accuracy in the manufacture of the ark, but also for its housing and transportation. It was in the moving of the ark that the covenantal law of God was violated:

> When the camp prepares to journey, Aaron and his sons shall come, and they shall take down the covering veil and cover the ark of the Testimony with it. Then they shall put on it a covering of badger skins, and spread over that a cloth entirely of blue; and they shall insert its poles (Numbers 4:5-6).

"And when Aaron and his sons have finished covering the sanctuary and all the furnishings of the sanctuary, when the camp is set to go, then the sons of Kohath shall come to carry them; but they shall not touch any holy thing, lest they die" (Numbers 4:15). "To the sons of Kohath he gave [no carts or oxen] because theirs was the service of the holy things, which they carried on their shoulders" (Numbers 7:9).

The design of the ark provided for rings into which poles were inserted "that the ark *may be carried by them*" (Exodus 25:14, emphasis added). The Israelites failed to do this and it cost Uzzah his life. It may seem that Uzzah was unfairly treated by the Lord since he was attempting to stop the ark falling to the ground. But the whole incident was another sad case of men disregarding God's instructions and warnings. God's revelation is never to be dismissed in preference for human invention. God's work must be done in God's way. Wilful defiance does not go unpunished. Furthermore, the Israelites added insult to injury in that they followed the practice of the godless Philistines and built a new cart to transport the ark. What God permits the heathen to do in ignorance he will not allow his people to do in disobedience.

Three months after the death of Uzzah, the ark was removed from the house of Obed-Edom the Gittite (6:11-12) and brought to the city of Jerusalem. This time David followed the divine instructions on the transportation of the ark of the covenant (1 Chronicles 15:2,11-15).

3. Monogamy

From the beginning of creation, God's design for marriage was that it should be an exclusive covenant relationship between one man and one woman (Genesis 2:24; cf. Matthew 19:3-6). David's polygamy (marriage to more than one wife) brought immense grief and heartache into his home. His numerous wives with their numerous children produced enormous pressures and problems.[23]

In our own day, the widespread practices of temporary cohabitation and easy divorce not only damage the stability of society, but also bring difficult problems into the church. New converts often have complex relationships such as previous spouses and children from different partners. Pastoral wisdom, love and patience need to be exercised to ensure maximum stability for all who are in less than ideal circumstances.

4. Clouded judgement

The remarkable skill displayed by David in gathering, organizing and leading thousands of people was not so evident in the management of his own household. When his son Amnon raped his half-sister Tamar (David's daughter by another wife) the only response from King David, who was used by Amnon as an unwitting accomplice, was, "He was very angry" (13:21; cf. v.6). David's failure as a father to punish Amnon and ensure justice and honourable treatment for Tamar contributed to the actions of another son, Absalom, who eventually took matters into his own hands, murdered Amnon and fled from his father, his home and his country.

When, after three years, David permitted Absalom to return from exile, he refused to see his son for a further two years (14:24,28,33). Even when they were reconciled, the difficulties between father and son were far from over. Absalom caused untold distress in Israel and led a civil war against his father.

Despite these immense problems, David persisted in his love for Absalom, so that when his son fell in battle, King David mourned with inconsolable grief: "O my son Absalom—my son, my son Absalom—if only I had died in your place! O Absalom my son, my son!" (18:33). David's love for his son Absalom clouded his judgement; overcome with his personal grief, he disregarded those who had risked their lives for him. Joab's rebuke was well deserved:

---

[23] See "Part 1 / The opening years."

Today you have disgraced all your servants who today have saved your life, the lives of your sons and daughters, the lives of your wives and the lives of your concubines, in that you love your enemies and hate your friends. For you have declared today that you regard neither princes nor servants; for today I perceive that if Absalom had lived and all of us had died today, then it would have pleased you well (19:5-6).

Leaders among the people of God are responsible to ensure that family ties do not cloud their judgement. As well as the danger of nepotism (favouritism shown to relatives or friends in conferring offices or privileges), the leader is open to being more lenient toward members of his own family. Where elders are appointed from within the local church (a practice that is highly commended in the New Testament), there is the risk of their being influenced in their judgement by family members. It is crucial therefore that an elder must be "one who rules his own house well" (1 Timothy 3:4), and is also aware of the dangers inherent in extended family relationships within the church.

5. Relying on the promises of God

Second Samuel teaches patience and dependence on God to keep his promises (2:1; 5:1-3). There were certainly many occasions in the life of David when he had only the bare promises of God to cling on to. Trusting in the Lord to preserve him from all danger and deliver him from all harm, David would not speed up the purposes of God by any actions of his own; though God had said that he would be king of Israel (1 Samuel 16:13), David took no action to bring it to pass. Indeed, when a man came, saying that he had killed King Saul, David was horrified and had the man executed there and then. When Rechab and his brother Baanah thought to win David's favour by murdering Saul's remaining son Ishbosheth, they grossly misjudged the reaction of David. He was once more horrified and ordered the execution of these two murderers (4:12).

David had to wait years to see the unfolding of God's promises. God has often taught his people patience. Abraham had to wait twenty-five years for his son of promise. Moses had to wait forty years in obscurity before leading the children of Israel out of Egypt. "In quietness and confidence shall be your strength" (Isaiah 30:15).

6. Exposure of sin

This book also contains a serious warning which may be expressed in the words found in the book of Numbers: "Be sure your sin will find you out" (Numbers 32:23). This is illustrated in:

- the Amalekite, who claimed to have killed King Saul, "the LORD's anointed" (1:14-16)
- Abner, who ignored what he knew to be God's purpose when he made Saul's son, Ishbosheth, king (2:8-9; 3:9; cf. v. 27)
- Rechab and Baanah, who tried to win David's favour by means of murdering Ishbosheth (4:5-12)
- Amnon, and the rape of Tamar (13:1-17; cf. vv. 28-29)
- David, in his adultery with Bathsheba and the murder of Uriah (11:1-27; 12:7-14)

Whenever God shows the weakness, failing and sinfulness of his saints in the Scriptures, we must take great care. We must take note of the exhortation of Paul when he urges, Consider "yourself lest you also be tempted" (Galatians 6:1). "He who is without sin among you, let him throw a stone... first" (John 8:7).

7. Discipline

"For whom the LORD loves he corrects, just as a father the son in whom he delights" (Proverbs 3:12). Though David was a mighty leader of men, he failed to exercise discipline in his own home. When his son Amnon violated his half-sister Tamar, David was "very angry" (13:21) but took no action. Had he disciplined Amnon with appropriate disciple, David might well have averted the subsequent murder of Amnon by his brother Absalom. The tragic aftermath might have been avoided. Furthermore, David's later dealings with Absalom show a distinct lack of wisdom. The purpose of godly discipline is to bring about *repentance* and *restoration*. David made no such provision but exacerbated the situation by refusing to meet with Absalom. The consequences for the family and the nation were horrific. No wonder Absalom became so embittered and set about winning "the hearts of the men of Israel" (15:6), with the resulting rebellion and the flight of his father, David, from Jerusalem.

At times, discipline is also required in the family of God. The Lord teaches its importance but also emphasizes the manner and the "spirit of gentleness" (Galatians 6:1) in which discipline is to be undertaken. When God disciplines his children, it is an indication of his love (Hebrews 12:7-11). Though it may be quite painful at the time, "afterward it yields the peaceable fruit of righteousness to those who have been trained by it."

1 KINGS

MEANING	AUTHOR	KEY THOUGHT
(the history of the kings of Israel and Judah)	**Unknown** (maybe Jeremiah)	**"...as did his father David"**

THEME

Obedience blessed, disobedience punished, penitents forgiven

THEME VERSE
*Behold, I will tear the kingdom out of the hand of Solomon....
And to his son I will give one tribe, that My servant David may always have a lamp before Me in Jerusalem.*
1 KINGS 11:31,36

1 KINGS / **SUMMARY**

The rise and fall of the kingdom of Israel

PART 1 / **THE ESTABLISHMENT OF THE KINGDOM 1:1-2:46**

a.	The death of David and the accession of Solomon	1:1-2:12
b.	Solomon executes his enemies	2:13-46

PART 2 / **THE GLORY OF THE KINGDOM** 3:1-10:29

a.	The marriage of Solomon	3:1-2
b.	The prayer of Solomon	3:3-15
c.	The wisdom of Solomon	3:16-28
d.	The greatness of Solomon	4:1-34
e.	The building of the temple	5:1-7:51
f.	The dedication of the temple	8:1-66
g.	The Lord's second appearance to Solomon	9:1-9
h.	The fame of Solomon	9:10-28
i.	The visit of the Queen of Sheba	10:1-13
j.	The wealth of Solomon	10:14-29

PART 3 / **THE DIVISION OF THE KINGDOM** 11:1-12:24

a.	Solomon's backsliding and death	11:1-43
b.	The accession and stubbornness of Rehoboam	12:1-19
c.	Jeroboam becomes king of the ten tribes (Israel)	12:20-24

PART 4 / **THE DIVIDED KINGDOMS OF ISRAEL AND JUDAH** 12:25-22:53

JUDAH		ISRAEL	
(two southern tribes)		(ten northern tribes)	
	12:25-14:20	a.	The reign of Jeroboam (bad)
	12:25-33		(1) Jeroboam's apostasy
	13:1-34		(2) Prophecy against calf worship
	14:1-20		(3) Destruction of the dynasty predicted
b. The reign of Rehoboam (bad)	14:21-31		
c. The reign of Abijam (bad)	15:1-8		
d. The reign of Asa (good)	15:9-24		
	15:25-32	e.	The reign of Nadab (bad)
	15:33-16:7	f.	The reign of Baasha (bad)
	16:8-14	g.	The reign of Elah (bad)
	16:15-20	h.	The reign of Zimri (bad)
	16:21-28	i.	The reign of Omri (bad)
	16:29-22:40	j.	The reign of Ahab (bad)
	16:29-34		(1) Ahab introduces false worship
	17:1		(2) Elijah confronts Ahab
	17:2-24		(3) Elijah miraculously sustained
	18:1-19		(4) Elijah meets godly Obadiah
	18:20-46		(5) Elijah on Mount Carmel
	19:1-18		(6) Elijah's flight to the wilderness
	19:19-21		(7) Elijah appoints Elisha
	20:1-43		(8) Ahab defeats the Syrians
	21:1-29		(9) Ahab and Naboth's vineyard
	22:1-28		(10) Ahab and Jehoshaphat
	22:29-40		(11) Ahab's death in battle
k. The reign of Jehoshaphat (good)	22:41-50		
	22:51-53	l.	The reign of Ahaziah (bad)

1 KINGS

First Kings may be described as the rise and fall of the nation of Israel. The first half of the book recounts the notable events in the forty-year reign of King Solomon, son of David and Bathsheba. The second half presents a sketch of the history of the divided kingdom—split into Israel (the northern kingdom of the ten tribes) and Judah (the southern kingdom of the two tribes—that is, Judah and Benjamin).

The book is written to show the causes of the establishment and decline of the kingdom. When loyal to God alone ("You shall have no other gods before Me"—Exodus 20:3), Israel flourished. But when the Israelites turned from God, his covenant and his law established through Moses, their morals and their kingdom declined. Jehovah is the sovereign ruler "sitting on his throne" (22:19). He blesses the obedient; he punishes the disobedient; he forgives the penitent.

1 KINGS / **AUTHOR**

The author of the book is unknown, although Jewish tradition ascribes authorship to the prophet Jeremiah. Whoever he was, he compiled his history using a number of sources, such as "the book of the acts of Solomon" (11:41), "the book of the chronicles of the kings of Israel" (14:19; 15:31, etc.) and "the book of the chronicles of the kings of Judah" (14:29; 15:7,23, etc.). These books appear to have been public records, probably written down by various prophets through the years. "Under divine inspiration, the author of Kings made his choice from these written documents."[1] It is considered probable that the bulk of the work was completed before the exile and that 2 Kings 25 was added during the period of captivity.[2]

---

[1] Edward J. Young, *An Introduction to the Old Testament* (Grand Rapids: Eerdmans, 1949), 189.

[2] William Hendriksen, *Survey of the Bible: A Treasury of Bible Information* (Welwyn: Evangelical Press, 1976), 226.

1 KINGS / **HISTORICAL SETTING**

The two books of Kings, like the books of Samuel, were originally one book.[3] Together they cover a period of Israel's history from the accession of King Solomon (970 B.C.), to the final exile of the people of Judah to the land of Babylon (586 B.C.). The dividing point of the two books comes during the reign of Ahaziah, son of Ahab of Israel (not to be confused with Ahaziah, son of Jehoram of Judah—2 Kings 8:25–26), around 853 B.C.

The history recorded in 1 Kings follows on from that of 2 Samuel, though with a notable omission: the place where the altar was erected. The punishment of God for the sin of King David in taking a census ends when David builds "an altar to the LORD" and offers "burnt offerings and peace offerings" (2 Samuel 24:25; 1 Chronicles 21:26). From the parallel history in 1 Chronicles, it is evident that the command to "erect an altar to the LORD on the threshing-floor of Araunah the Jebusite" (2 Samuel 24:18) is quite sufficient for David to conclude that this is the Lord's designated site for the temple which his son Solomon will build.[4] Consequently, David says, "This is the house of the LORD God, and this is the altar of burnt offering for Israel" (1 Chronicles 22:1).

In appreciation of forgiveness and in anticipation of the temple to be built, David composes Psalm 30. The title given to this psalm in our English versions may be misleading, as Spurgeon notes:

> "A Psalm and Song at the Dedication of the House of David," or rather, "A Psalm; a Song of Dedication *for* the House. *By* David." A song of faith since the house of Jehovah, here intended, David never lived to see. A psalm of praise, since a sore judgement had been stayed, and a great sin forgiven.[5]

---

[3] The explanation for making one book into two is given in the introduction to the chapter on the book of 1 Samuel.
[4] Carl F. Keil and Franz Delitzsch, *Biblical Commentary on the Books of Samuel* (Grand Rapids: Eerdmans, 1950), 512.
[5] Charles Haddon Spurgeon, *The Treasury of David*, 3 vol. (McLean: MacDonald Publishing Company, 1990), 2:43; emphasis added.

David prepared for the building of the temple. He began to assemble the skilled workers and gather the materials for its construction. He also instructed Solomon about his responsibilities before God (1 Chronicles 22:2–19).

1 KINGS / **OUTLINE**

The history of the kings of Judah and Israel has been amplified by reference to the various historical and prophetic books of the Old Testament in order to present a composite account.

PART 1 / **THE ESTABLISHMENT OF THE KINGDOM (1:1–2:46)**

King David is old, and Adonijah, the next in line to the throne, determines that he will assume the throne. It is David's duty to appoint his successor. The Lord has revealed that Solomon is *his* choice (1 Chronicles 28:5). For some reason, David delays making a public announcement and in so doing gives opportunity for Adonijah to strengthen his own support.

Adonijah seems to be well aware that not only David but, more especially, the Lord, has promised the throne to his brother Solomon (2:15). David takes immediate steps to proclaim Solomon as the future king. Zadok the priest, Nathan the prophet and Benaiah the military leader are instructed to ensure that Solomon is anointed and declared the king of Israel (cf. 1 Chronicles 23:1). Once the news of the appointment breaks, the followers of Adonijah turn back from supporting his claim to the throne. In dread of his life, Adonijah flees and grasps the horns of the altar, demonstrating that he is placing himself under divine protection. Solomon assures him that he is in no danger, provided he behaves wisely and does not repeat his earlier blunders (1:52).

David calls together all the leaders of Israel to make detailed provision for the continuing worship of God, the organization of the army and the functioning of government (1 Chronicles 23–27). This he achieves in the last year of his life (1 Chronicles 26:31). This national assembly provides David with the opportunity to acknowledge Solomon publicly as the new king of Israel and to repeat—in public—some of the instructions and warnings which he had previously given to

Solomon in private (1 Chronicles 28:2–10; 22:7–19). David officially hands over to Solomon the plans, the materials, the gold and silver for the building of the temple, and the arrangements for the services of the priests and Levites (1 Chronicles 28:11–21). In a fitting conclusion to his reign, David leads the whole congregation in the worship of God:

> Blessed are You, Lord God of Israel, our Father, forever and ever.
> Yours, O Lord, is the greatness,
> The power and the glory,
> The victory and the majesty;
> For all that is in heaven and in earth is Yours;
> Yours is the kingdom, O Lord,
> And You are exalted as head over all.
> Both riches and honor come from You,
> And You reign over all.
> In Your hand is power and might;
> In Your hand it is to make great
> And to give strength to all.
>
> Now therefore, our God,
> We thank You
> And praise Your glorious name (1 Chronicles 29:10–13).

After a long and chequered life, godly David dies "in a good old age, full of days and riches and honor; and Solomon his son reigned in his place" (1 Chronicles 29:28).

The reign of Solomon

Upon his accession to the throne, Solomon sets about establishing his reign (2:12; 1 Chronicles 29:23–25). First of all, he punishes the rebels. Adonijah comes through Bathsheba with a request which Solomon immediately interprets as a further attempt to usurp his throne. Although Abishag had been only the nurse to King David, in the eyes of the people she was regarded as his concubine. Taking the harem of a deceased or conquered king was equivalent to establishing a claim to the throne (2:22; 2 Samuel 12:8). Adonijah is executed, Abiathar the priest is exiled, Joab is executed and Shimei is brought to Jerusalem and placed under house arrest. Three years later, Shimei breaks the terms of his agreement, leaves the city to recover two slaves and forfeits his life. So Solomon fulfils the dying requests of his father (2:5-6,8-9).

PART 2 / **THE GLORY OF THE KINGDOM (3:1-10:29)**

Once Solomon has secured his throne, he enters into an alliance with Egypt by marrying Pharaoh's daughter (3:1). She is not his first wife for he had married Naamah an Ammonitess before his accession (14:21; cf. 11:42-43). Marriage to an Egyptian was not forbidden, for it was only marriages contracted with women of the seven indigenous nations that were prohibited (Deuteronomy 7:1-4; Exodus 34:16). Furthermore, it seems evident that the Egyptian princess renounced all Egyptian gods and confessed faith in Jehovah as the one true God, since when he married Pharaoh's daughter it is said of him, "Solomon loved the LORD, walking in the statutes of his father David" (3:3). In addition, the daughter of Pharaoh is distinguished from the foreign "wives who turned his heart after other gods" (11:1,4).

The early years of Solomon's reign have been described as "the Golden Age of Israel."[6] These years were made famous by Solomon's character and deeds. There are seven pointers to Solomon's significance and renown during this early period: his humility, wisdom, administration, palace, temple, cities and wealth and his distinguished visitor.

1. Solomon's humility

Seeking the blessing of God upon his reign, Solomon, accompanied by representatives of the whole nation, offers 1,000 burnt offerings on the bronze altar before the tabernacle at Gibeon (the only item missing from the tabernacle is the ark of the covenant, which David had brought to the city of Jerusalem—2 Chronicles 1:4). The Lord appears to Solomon in a dream and allows him one request. Showing distinct humility, aware of his inexperience, and conscious of the daunting task to which he has been called, Solomon requests of God "an understanding heart to judge Your people, that I may discern between good and evil. For who is able to judge this great people of Yours?" (3:9). This request pleases the Lord and he not only gives him wisdom beyond all

---

[6] Thompson Chain Reference Bible.

others, but promises him riches and honour as well. Solomon is also promised a long life on the condition that he follows the example of his father David and walks faithfully before God. Returning to Jerusalem, Solomon visits the location of the ark of the covenant, offers sacrifices and holds a feast for all his servants.

2. Solomon's wisdom

Solomon's great wisdom is illustrated in his handling of two women who are arguing over a baby. Both gave birth around the same time: one child died; the other lived. Both mothers claim the living child. Solomon solves the dilemma by commanding that the child be cut in two, and one half given to each woman. One of the women immediately protests and pleads with the king to give the child to the other woman. The second woman agrees to the division of the child. Solomon thereby reveals the true mother, who "yearned with compassion for her son" and would rather that he be given to another than put to death. Solomon restores the baby to his mother: "And all Israel heard of the judgment which the king had rendered; and they feared the king, for they saw that the wisdom of God was in him to administer justice" (3:28).

The outstanding wisdom that God had given to Solomon was soon known throughout the surrounding nations:

> And God gave Solomon wisdom and exceedingly great understanding, and largeness of heart like the sand on the seashore. Thus Solomon's wisdom excelled the wisdom of all the men of the East and all the wisdom of Egypt. For he was wiser than all men—than Ethan the Ezrahite, and Heman, Chalcol, and Darda, the sons of Mahol; and his fame was in all the surrounding nations. He spoke three thousand proverbs, and his songs were one thousand and five. Also he spoke of trees, from the cedar tree of Lebanon even to the hyssop that springs out of the wall; he spoke also of animals, of birds, of creeping things, and of fish. And men of all nations, from all the kings of the earth who had heard of his wisdom, came to hear the wisdom of Solomon (4:29–34).

3. Solomon's administration

The vastness of Solomon's kingdom is described (see Map 7):

> So Solomon reigned over all kingdoms from the River [Euphrates] to the land of the Philistines, as far as the border of Egypt. They brought tribute and served Solomon all the days of his life.... For he had dominion over all the region on this side of the River from Tiphsah even to Gaza, namely over all the kings on this side of the River; and he had peace on every side all around him. And Judah and Israel dwelt safely (4:21,24–25).

4. Solomon's temple

The building of the temple described in 1 Kings 5 and 6 is the result of a king committed to the service of almighty God. Solomon's concern was to obey God. He spared no expense in building a magnificent temple for the worship of Jehovah the living God. Solomon seems to have been raised up specially for the purpose of erecting the temple. His father David had said,

> And of all my sons (for the Lord has given me many sons) He has chosen my son Solomon to sit on the throne of the kingdom of the LORD over Israel. Now He said to me, "It is your son Solomon who shall build My house and My courts; for I have chosen him to be My son, and I will be his Father. Moreover I will establish his kingdom forever, if he is steadfast to observe My commandments and My judgments, as it is this day" (1 Chronicles 28:5–7).

At that time, David also addressed his son directly:

> As for you, my son Solomon, know the God of your father, and serve Him with a loyal heart and with a willing mind; for the LORD searches all hearts and understands all the intent of the thoughts. If you seek Him, He will be found by you; but if you forsake Him, He will cast you off forever. Consider now, for the LORD has chosen you to build a house for the sanctuary; be strong, and do it (1 Chronicles 28:9–10).

Map 7. The extent of Solomon's kingdom

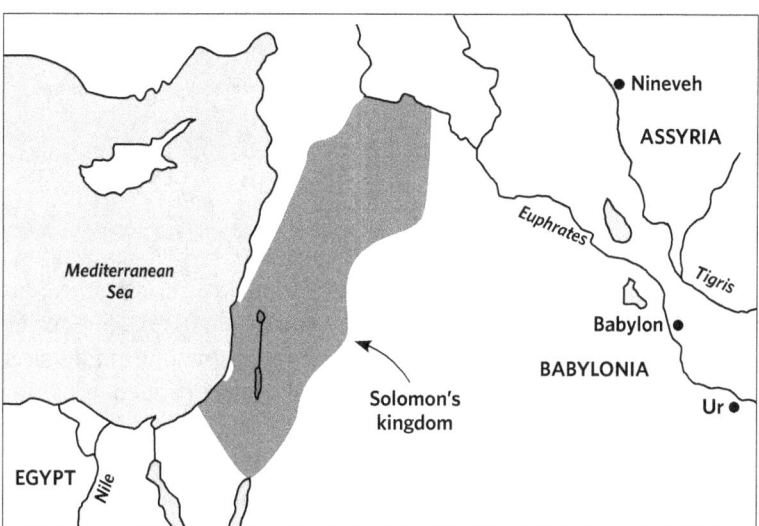

5. Solomon's palace

The building of the temple took seven years (6:38); the building of the palace took thirteen years (7:1). This detail may indicate that there were significantly more workmen involved in the building of the temple. It may also, however, indicate something quite different— that the splendour of the king's palace was greater than that of the Lord's temple!

6. Solomon's cities and wealth

> And Solomon built Gezer, Lower Beth Horon, Baalath, and Tadmor in the wilderness, in the land of Judah, all the storage cities that Solomon had, cities for his chariots and cities for his cavalry, and whatever Solomon desired to build in Jerusalem, in Lebanon, and in all the land of his dominion (9:17–19).

> The weight of gold that came to Solomon yearly was six hundred and sixty-six talents of gold, besides that from the traveling merchants, from the income of traders, from all the kings of Arabia, and from the governors of the country.... For the king had

merchant ships at sea with the fleet of Hiram. Once every three years the merchant ships came bringing gold, silver, ivory, apes, and monkeys. So King Solomon surpassed all the kings of the earth in riches and wisdom.

Now all the earth sought the presence of Solomon to hear his wisdom, which God had put in his heart (10:14–15,22–24).

7. Solomon's distinguished visitor

The Queen of Sheba, "the queen of the South…came from the ends of the earth to hear the wisdom of Solomon" (Luke 11:31). She "came to test him with hard questions" (10:1). By posing one riddle after another she intended to discover the skill and prudence of this renowned king. Nothing proved too difficult for him—either to understand or to explain to her.

PART 3 / **THE DIVISION OF THE KINGDOM (11:1-12:24)**

In the second half of Solomon's life, the consequences are evident of what happens when a servant of God turns from his first love, disregards the commandments and warnings of the Word of God and yields to nearly unbridled passion. Here are some of the most sober warnings against serious backsliding. With all his wisdom, Solomon is not able to control his lust. He begins well; he ends badly. Despite all the blessings God has showered upon him, Solomon nevertheless forgets the Lord his God:

> But King Solomon loved many foreign women, as well as the daughter of Pharaoh: women of the Moabites, Ammonites, Edomites, Sidonians, and Hittites— from the nations of whom the LORD had said to the children of Israel, "You shall not intermarry with them, nor they with you. Surely they will turn away your hearts after their gods." Solomon clung to these in love. And he had seven hundred wives, princesses, and three hundred concubines; and his wives turned away his heart. For it was so, when Solomon was old, that his wives turned his heart after other gods; and his heart was not loyal to the LORD his God, as was the heart of his father David.… Solomon did evil in the sight

of the Lord, and did not fully follow the Lord, as did his father David (11:1–4,6).

Solomon could not plead ignorance, for the warnings of God had been given in the law of Moses. Concerning any king of Israel, God had said,

> But he shall not multiply horses for himself, nor cause the people to return to Egypt to multiply horses, for the Lord has said to you, "You shall not return that way again." Neither shall he multiply wives for himself, lest his heart turn away; nor shall he greatly multiply silver and gold for himself (Deuteronomy 17:16–17).

Solomon did all three. Added to these three areas of disobedience, Solomon included a fourth by marrying many *pagan wives*. He "is an enigma, for he was both the perfecter of Israel's glory and the architect of its destruction."[7]

The decline of Solomon's kingdom is brought about by:

- his extravagant lifestyle (10:14–29)
- his notorious lust (11:1–3)
- his turning from God (11:4–10)
- his enemies who were raised up by God (11:14–25).

So, in the latter part of his life, Solomon seriously falls from his spiritual walk with God. Through external and internal means, the Lord brings punishment. Rebellion by some of the subject neighbour-states is accompanied by internal disruption within Israel. Solomon's servant Jeroboam rebels against the king (11:26). As the Lord had raised up adversaries *outside* Israel (11:14,23), so the Lord raises up this adversary *inside* Israel and, through the prophet Ahijah, predicts the devastating division of the kingdom of Israel (11:29–31). At the same time God confirms his earlier promise to David to maintain his line: "And to his son I will give one tribe, that My servant David may always have a lamp before Me in Jerusalem, the city which I have chosen for Myself,

---

[7] Graeme Goldsworthy, *Gospel and Kingdom: A Christian Interpretation of the Old Testament* (Carlisle: Paternoster, 1981), 72.

to put My name there" (11:36). Jeroboam is warned to walk in obedience to the Lord so that he may enjoy God's full blessing upon his life and reign. Hearing of the prophecy, Solomon seeks Jeroboam to take his life. Jeroboam escapes to Egypt and places himself under the protection of King Shishak.

After a reign of forty years, Solomon dies and his son Rehoboam comes to the throne. At the same time, by popular request, Jeroboam is called back from Egypt. Jeroboam champions the cause of the people, making representations to King Rehoboam for a reduction of the heavy taxation. Rehoboam proves a stubborn and foolish king. Rejecting the counsel of his father's older and wiser counsellors and listening rather to the advice of his young bosom friends, he *increases* rather than *lessens* the burden upon the people. The scene is set for open revolt. When Rehoboam sends Adoram, his minister of finance, to collect the new taxes, Adoram is stoned to death by the people (12:18). King Rehoboam makes a speedy return to Jerusalem, with all Israel in uproar. Jeroboam is made king over the ten tribes of Israel. Meanwhile King Rehoboam, once in Jerusalem, assembles the armies of Judah and Benjamin, intending to attack the other ten tribes and force their submission to his rule. The Lord intervenes through Shemaiah, the man of God, and Judah and Benjamin are forbidden to go to war with Israel. The people of the two tribes obey the word of God and return to their homes.

PART 4 / **THE DIVIDED KINGDOMS OF ISRAEL AND JUDAH (12:25-22:53)**

Solomon reigned in Israel for forty years (11:42). God's judgement upon the twelve tribes of the nation coincides with his death. The people as a whole have turned from the true and living God. They have forgotten his law, violated his covenant and disobeyed his commands. They have turned to the heathen and pagan gods of the surrounding nations. The once strong and united kingdom of Israel and Judah is now divided into two weak and squabbling nations: the larger, ten tribes under King Jeroboam; the smaller, the two tribes of Judah and Benjamin under King Rehoboam. With the division of the kingdom in 931 B.C., the serious deterioration, decline and disintegration of the twelve tribes of Israel has begun.

Map 8. The divided kingdoms of Israel and Judah

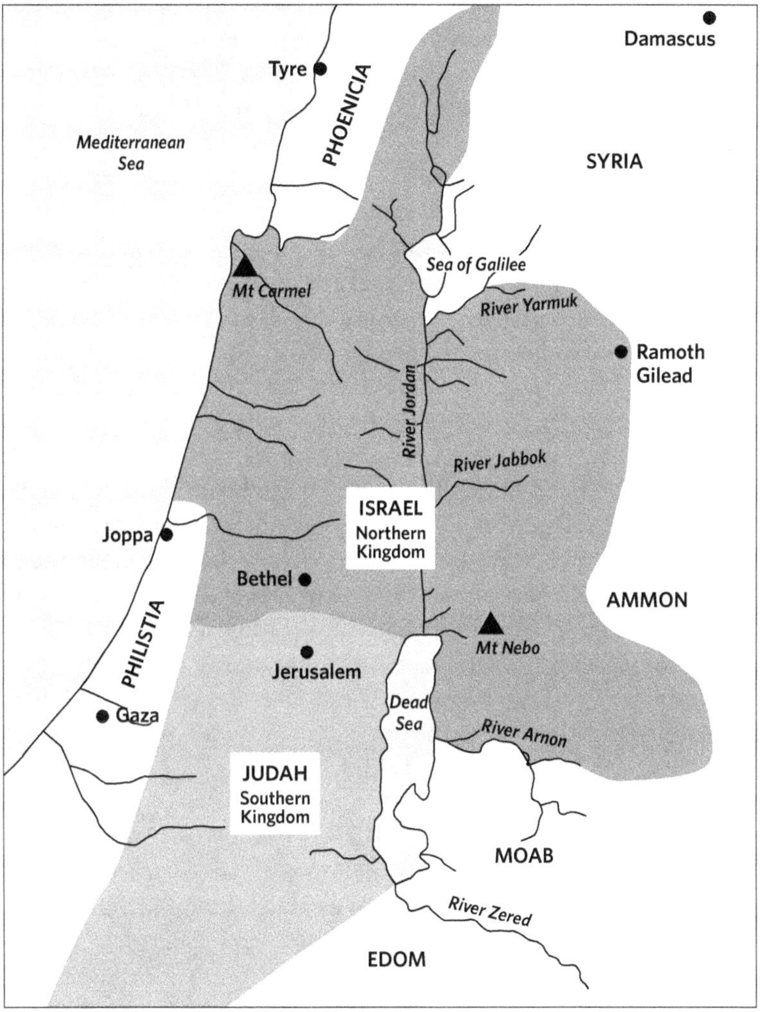

Jeroboam in Israel: 931–909 B.C. (12:20–14:20)
Although the Lord had given Jeroboam wonderful promises through the prophet Ahijah (11:37–38), the new king of Israel does not trust in God and he disregards all the warnings. Seeking to consolidate his position on the throne, and in outright rebellion against the revealed will of God, Jeroboam introduces a corrupted alternative place of

worship and a blasphemous form of idolatry. A golden calf is erected at both Bethel and Dan, and King Jeroboam says to the people, "It is too much for you to go up to Jerusalem. Here are your gods, O Israel, which brought you up from the land of Egypt!" (12:28). He makes shrines on the high places and appoints a priesthood from all the tribes of Israel, contravening the law of God that priests were to come only from the tribe of Levi. Jeroboam institutes sacrifices and feast days to match those that are celebrated at Jerusalem.

The scene is set for a succession of bad kings to sit upon the throne of the northern kingdom. Had a good and godly king arisen, he would of necessity have destroyed the shrines to false gods, sought reconciliation with Judah, directed the people to worship in the temple which God had appointed at Jerusalem, and yielded to the claims of the king of Judah as being in the line of God's promise to Judah, David and his descendants.

God gives a word of prophecy in the presence of King Jeroboam. Addressing the altar, a man of God says, "O altar, altar! Thus says the Lord: 'Behold, a child, Josiah by name, shall be born to the house of David; and on you he shall sacrifice the priests of the high places who burn incense on you, and men's bones shall be burned on you'" (13:2).[8] In spite of miracles, King Jeroboam does not amend his ways but continues in his godless path of rebellion. His offences are so serious before the Lord as to lead to the judgement being pronounced that his family line will be exterminated (13:34).

Rehoboam in Judah: 931–913 B.C. (14:21–31; cf. 2 Chronicles 11:5–12:16)

Following the division of the kingdom with the revolt of the ten northern tribes, Rehoboam seeks to establish himself in Judah. He builds strong cities for defence, with fortified strongholds storing large stores of food and weaponry. A further strategy is to disperse some of his many sons throughout the territory of Judah and Benjamin. He is supported and encouraged by the migration of a large number of priests and Levites expelled from Israel:

---

[8] This prophecy against the altar was fulfilled 300 years later (2 Kings 23:15–20).

Map 9. International superpowers after the division of the united kingdom of Israel and Judah.

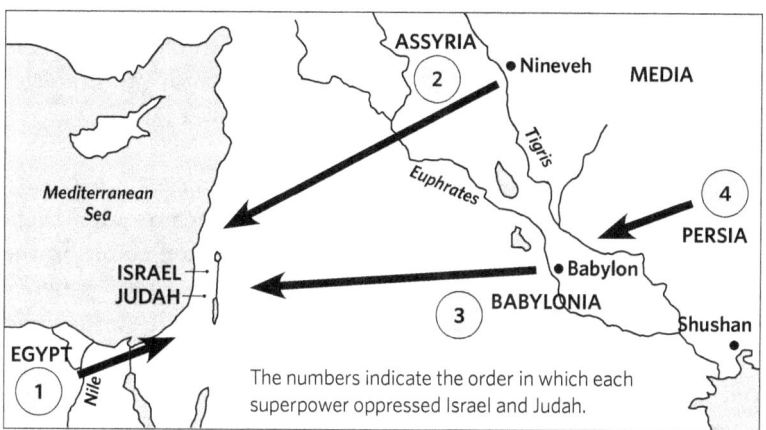

And from all their territories the priests and the Levites who were in all Israel took their stand with him. For the Levites left their common-lands and their possessions and came to Judah and Jerusalem, for Jeroboam and his sons had rejected them from serving as priests to the LORD.... And after the Levites left, those from all the tribes of Israel, such as set their heart to seek the LORD God of Israel, came to Jerusalem to sacrifice to the LORD God of their fathers. So they strengthened the kingdom of Judah, and made Rehoboam the son of Solomon strong for three years, because they walked in the way of David and Solomon for three years (2 Chronicles 11:13–14,16–17).

This is a description of people committed to a life of true worship and faithful service. They move home at considerable personal sacrifice. They are loyal to the temple, the priesthood and the king, in spite of the fact that King Rehoboam is stubborn and foolish. The presence of these godly immigrants does not, however, halt the deterioration in the spiritual and moral life of the nation, for we read, "Judah did evil in the sight of the LORD, and they provoked Him to jealousy with their sins which they committed, more than all that their fathers had done" (14:22).

Whatever his earlier sympathies concerning loyalty to the living God, once Rehoboam has established his position and strengthened his control he forsakes "the law of the LORD, and all Israel along with him" (2 Chronicles 12:1). The Lord punishes this defection through Shishak, king of Egypt. He delivers Judah from destruction but commits the people to become servants of Egypt. Shishak plunders the gold from the temple and the king's palace, and takes everything away (2 Chronicles 12:9). Rehoboam is allowed to continue his reign over Judah.

Abijam[9] in Judah: 913–910 B.C. (15:1–8; cf. 2 Chronicles 13:1–22)

Throughout the seventeen years of his father Rehoboam's reign, there had been hostility between Israel and Judah. Abijam comes to the throne when tension is high between the two kingdoms. 1 Kings merely records the animosity, whereas 2 Chronicles provides a detailed account of a great battle fought between the two nations. Severely outnumbered by two to one when the battle lines are drawn, Abijam gives every impression of being a God-fearing king as he challenges Jeroboam from Mount Zemaraim (2 Chronicles 13:4–12). As he speaks, Israelite soldiers move into position behind the army of Judah. Outflanked, the men of Judah cry out to God. The Lord responds to their prayers in spite of the fact that King Abijam is described as one who "walked in all the sins of his father [Rehoboam], which he had done before him; his heart was not loyal to the LORD his God, as was the heart of his father David" (15:3). The Lord's kindness to Judah is evidently "for David's sake" (15:4), and in the maintenance of his covenant purposes in relation to the tribe of Judah (Genesis 49:10; 2 Samuel 7:12–16).

Under King Abijam, Israel is subdued by Judah because the latter rely "on the LORD God of their fathers" (2 Chronicles 13:18). Judah captures a number of towns and cities from Israel. After a short reign Abijam dies and is succeeded by his son Asa.

Asa in Judah: 910–869 B.C. (15:9–24)[10]

As a result of the battle between Judah and Israel in the days of King Abijam, Judah experiences some years of rest. Asa comes to the throne and enjoys a peaceful reign for ten years. Unlike his father and his

---

[9] Spelled Abijah in 2 Chronicles 12:16, etc.
[10] See the fuller account, including the first religious revival since the division of the kingdom, recorded in 2 Chronicles 14:1–16:14.

grandfather, "Asa did what was right in the eyes of the LORD, as did his father David" (15:11). He removes pagan altars, demolishes heathen pillars, chops down wooden images and banishes perverted people from the land. He commands the people of Judah to seek the Lord and to obey his law and commandments. He also fortifies the cities of Judah with walls, towers and gates. Although he experiences considerable blessing from the Lord, he seriously backslides toward the end of his long reign. At his death he is succeeded to the throne by his godly son Jehoshaphat.

Ahab in Israel: 874-853 B.C. (16:29-22:40; cf. 2 Chronicles 18:1-34)
For thirty-five years, from the death of Jeroboam, Israel is ruled by six godless kings. Most of them reign for very short periods and are noted only for their wickedness. Eventually there arises the most notorious of them all, Ahab. Ahab excels in wickedness, for he "did evil in the sight of the LORD, more than all who were before him" (16:30). He shows his contempt for the Word of God and the honour of God's name by marrying Jezebel and worshipping her god, Baal. Ahab sets up an altar in a temple to Baal in the city of Samaria. In complete disregard of God's warning through Joshua, Ahab rebuilds Jericho (16:34; cf. Joshua 6:26).

The true prophets of the Lord are outlawed; the priests of the Most High are persecuted and put to the sword. The worship of the true God is banned. Baal is now the official god of Israel. The prophets and priests of Baal take over the religious life of the nation. The spiritual condition of the country is at an all-time low. From the darkness of this evil time, God raises up a man; a figure stands out as a true witness for the living God. He is to be the living proof that God is quietly working onward toward his eternal kingdom of righteousness.

Elijah the prophet in Israel[11]
It is a testimony to God's grace that he continued to send messengers to the northern kingdom of Israel. They were still his covenant people and he continued to urge them to repentance and to return to himself. This would inevitably lead to the restoration of the one nation under

---

[11] See Arthur W. Pink, *The Life of Elijah* (Edinburgh: Banner of Truth Trust, 1956); and F.W. Krummacher, *Elijah the Tishbite* (Grand Rapids: Baker, 1977).

the one king from the tribe of Judah, with one centre of worship in the temple at Jerusalem, in accordance with the law of Moses.

Elijah, the rugged prophet of the wilderness, dressed in a camel-hair tunic with a leather belt, suddenly bursts upon the scene and confronts godless King Ahab: "As the Lord God of Israel lives, before whom I stand, there shall not be dew nor rain these years, except at my word" (17:1).

The Lord had warned the people through Moses, over 500 years earlier, when the Israelites were on the threshold of the promised land:

> Take heed to yourselves, lest your heart be deceived, and you turn aside and serve other gods and worship them, lest the Lord's anger be aroused against you, and He shut up the heavens so that there be no rain, and the land yield no produce, and you perish quickly from the good land which the Lord is giving you (Deuteronomy 11:16–17).

Elijah brings the message to the wicked and godless King Ahab. During the three and a half years of drought that follow, the Lord miraculously sustains the prophet. Eventually there is a confrontation on Mount Carmel, and for a short while it appears as though the nation of Israel has turned back to the Lord. But their recognition of the true God is short-lived.

Elijah leaves Mount Carmel, is threatened by Queen Jezebel and makes his way south to Beersheba with his servant.[12] He leaves his servant under the jurisdiction of godly King Jehoshaphat in Judah (19:3) and journeys into the wilderness. Sustained by the Lord, he travels for over a month to arrive at "Horeb, the mountain of God" (19:8), also called Mount Sinai.

Though Elijah thinks his ministry has largely failed and must now be over, the Lord gives him further commissions and reassures him that there are still many faithful souls to be found in Israel. Responding with renewed enthusiasm, Elijah seeks out Elisha to appoint him as his successor.

Meanwhile King Ben-Hadad of Syria, with thirty-two allies, moves against Samaria. Even though the miracle on Mount Carmel failed to

---

[12] The claim that Elijah was gripped by cowardly fear and running for his life is examined later in the "Application and reflection" section.

influence Ahab, the Lord is determined to show mercy toward him. A prophet of God is sent to Ahab prophesying a great victory: "Thus says the LORD: "Have you seen all this great multitude? Behold, I will deliver it into your hand today, and you shall know that I am the LORD"' (20:13). Ahab wins a double victory against Syria. These victories were "a fruit of the seven thousand who had not bent their knee before Baal,"[13] because of their faithfulness to the living God (19:18; cf. Mark 13:20; Luke 18:7). Elijah would also learn that the Lord has not yet departed from the rebellious kingdom.

Following the battles with Ben-Hadad there is peace between Israel and Syria for two years. Ahab dies of wounds received in battle the following year.

Jehoshaphat in Judah: 872-848 B.C. (22:41-50)[14]

Like his father Asa before him, Jehoshaphat is a godly king, keen to live in obedience to the Lord and to encourage the people of Judah to be faithful to the true God. He

> sought the God of his father, and walked in His commandments and not according to the acts of Israel. Therefore the LORD established the kingdom in his hand; and all Judah gave presents to Jehoshaphat, and he had riches and honor in abundance. And his heart took delight in the ways of the LORD (2 Chronicles 17:4-6).

The blessings of God rested on the labours of Jehoshaphat and he responds by seeking to strengthen the nation spiritually. He sends out civil leaders and Levites throughout all Judah to teach the people the law of God.

Ahaziah in Israel: 853-852 B.C. (22:51-53)

A brief reference to the reign of Ahaziah the son of Ahab draws 1 Kings to a close. He behaves in the same manner as his father and mother (Ahab and Jezebel) who had introduced the worship of Baal into the

---

[13] Carl F. Keil, *Biblical Commentary on the Books of the Kings* (Grand Rapids: Eerdmans, 1950), 261.

[14] See the fuller account, including the second religious revival since the division of the kingdom, in 2 Chronicles 17:1-20:37.

kingdom of Israel, and after the manner of Jeroboam who had set up the golden calves (16:30–33). The brief reign of godless King Ahaziah comes to an end when he falls "through the lattice of his upper room in Samaria" (2 Kings 1:2). His injury, contact with Elijah the prophet and subsequent death form the opening chapter of 2 Kings.

1 KINGS / **CHRIST AND HIS CHURCH**

The relationship of Elijah to the unfolding purposes of God for Christ and his church are discussed in the next chapter on 2 Kings.

TYPES

King David and King Solomon both function as types of Christ as King. While both men fall far short of that sinlessness and holiness which are so perfect and complete in the Lord Jesus Christ, nevertheless God uses these human vessels to portray something of the glory and grandeur that belong to "the only begotten of the Father" (John 1:14) who is "the Christ of God" (Luke 9:20).

Both men present different perspectives upon the kingly reign of the Messiah. King David stands for the Christ engaged in battle. He is the fighting monarch. In contrast, Solomon, as his name implies, is the Prince of Peace. Solomon means "peaceful," for the name derives from the root word *shalom*, meaning peace, quiet, tranquillity, contentment, completeness, soundness, welfare, health. King Solomon's peaceful kingdom was the result of the victories King David had won.

1. David the king

David was anointed three times as king: first, in his father's house, then, over Judah and, lastly, over all Israel. God has anointed Jesus of Nazareth with the oil of gladness (Hebrews 1:9; cf. Psalm 45:7). He is King of kings and Lord of lords (Revelation 17:14; 19:16). As David—though anointed king—was in exile while Saul reigned over the people, so Christ is rejected by the world, and the "ruler of this world" (John 12:31) is reigning in the majority of human hearts.

God's promise to Israel was that he would save them from all their enemies by the hand of David. There is no indication that David was ever defeated in battle. So Christ will vanquish his (and our) enemies, including the great enemy, Satan. The Son of God has come to this earth:

> To grant us that we,
> Being delivered from the hand of our enemies,
> Might serve Him without fear,
> In holiness and righteousness before Him all the days of our life (Luke 1:74–75).

Christ "must reign till He has put all enemies under His feet" (1 Corinthians 15:25). For:

> Of the increase of His government and peace
> There will be no end,
> Upon the throne of David and over His kingdom,
> To order it and establish it with judgment and justice
> From that time forward, even forever.
> The zeal of the LORD of hosts will perform this (Isaiah 9:7).

2. Solomon the king

King Solomon symbolizes the Lord Jesus Christ reigning in peace after the battle. Our Saviour is the "Prince of Peace" (Isaiah 9:6). He is "Shiloh" the "Pacifier," the "Peacemaker" of the tribe of Judah (Genesis 49:10). As God promised David, "Behold, a son shall be born to you, who shall be a man of rest; and I will give him rest from all his enemies all around. His name shall be Solomon, for I will give peace and quietness to Israel in his days" (1 Chronicles 22:9).

The apostle Paul declares, "the kingdom of God is…righteousness *and peace* and joy in the Holy Spirit" (Romans 14:17, emphasis added), for Christ has "made peace through the blood of His cross" (Colossians 1:20).

Solomon's kingdom is a picture of the reign of Christ in his kingdom (4:21–34; 5:4; cf. Psalm 72). There are, however, notable differences: firstly, our Lord's kingdom will stretch to every corner of the globe, for he will reign over the whole earth (Revelation 11:15); secondly, it will be composed of "a great multitude which no one could number, of all nations, tribes, peoples, and tongues" (Revelation 7:9); and, thirdly, it will be an everlasting kingdom (Luke 1:33).

King Solomon was very rich; Christ is far richer and far more benevolent: "For you know the grace of our Lord Jesus Christ, that though He was rich, yet for your sakes He became poor, that you through His poverty might become rich" (2 Corinthians 8:9). "He who did not spare His own Son, but delivered Him up for us all, how shall He not with Him also freely give us all things?" (Romans 8:32). Christians have an amazing inheritance reserved in heaven (1 Peter 1:4). Even in this present life, "God shall supply all your need according to His riches in glory by Christ Jesus" (Philippians 4:19).

The wisdom of Solomon is a foreshadowing of the wisdom of Christ, "in whom are hidden all the treasures of wisdom and knowledge" (Colossians 2:3). The Lord Jesus said to the Jews of his day,

> The queen of the South will rise up in the judgment with the men of this generation and condemn them, for she came from the ends of the earth to hear the wisdom of Solomon; and indeed a greater than Solomon is here (Luke 11:31).

The queen of the South, the Queen of Sheba, "came to test him [Solomon] with hard questions" (10:1). Interesting spiritual parallels may be drawn from this visit. The Queen of Sheba may be seen to symbolize a seeker coming to Christ and finding full satisfaction in him. She came a great distance in response to "a true report" (cf. "the gospel of Christ"). So those "who once were far off have been made near by the blood of Christ" (Ephesians 2:13). She came with her "hard questions" and "spoke with him about all that was in her heart" (10:1–2). And "there was nothing so difficult for the king that he could not explain it to her" (10:3). In a greater sense, "Christ Jesus…became for us wisdom from God" (1 Corinthians 1:30).

This is the amazing testimony that the queen gave:

> It was a true report which I heard in my own land about your words and your wisdom. However I did not believe the words until I came and saw with my own eyes; and indeed the half was not told me. Your wisdom and prosperity exceed the fame of which I heard. Happy are your men and happy are these your servants, who stand continually before you and hear your wisdom! Blessed be the LORD your God, who delighted in you,

setting you on the throne of Israel! Because the LORD has loved Israel forever, therefore He made you king, to do justice and righteousness (10:6–9).

Such words are so appropriate for the Christ of God and his happy servants. Following the encounter with the Lord Jesus at the well of Sychar, the Samaritan woman returned to proclaim Christ to her fellow citizens. They responded in words similar to those of the Queen of Sheba. After having met Jesus they said to the woman, "Now we believe, not because of what you said, for we have heard for ourselves and know that this is indeed the Christ, the Saviour of the world" (John 4:42).

1 KINGS / **CONCLUSION**

First Kings relates the history of the kingdom of Israel from the death of David to the death of Ahab. Most of the first half of the book is dominated by the reign of Solomon. The historian faithfully relates the strengths and weaknesses of this wisest of men. The second half is devoted to a description of the reigns of the early kings of the divided kingdom, "a nation passing from affluence and influence, to poverty and paralysis."[15] The northern kingdom is beset by a succession of bad kings. Not one good and godly king emerges. Had such a king arisen, he would inevitably have taken action which would have disbanded the nation; he would have sought reconciliation with Judah and yielded to their king as being in the line of God's promise to Judah and a descendant of King David.

Through all the ups and downs of the people of Israel, there is demonstrated "'the historical reality of God's faithfulness to his promises to David."[16]

---

[15] G. Campbell Morgan, *Student Survey of the Bible* (Iowa Falls: World Bible Publishers, 1993), 101.

[16] Raymond B. Dillard and Tremper Longman III, *An Introduction to the Old Testament* (Leicester: Apollos, 1995), 165.

1 KINGS / **APPLICATION AND REFLECTION**

1. God-honouring prayer

At the dedication of the temple, King Solomon led the congregation in prayer (8:22-53). Kneeling on a platform (or kind of pulpit) and facing the congregation, he raised his hands toward heaven (2 Chronicles 6:12-13). The form of his prayer is that of imploring God to remember his promises and to act in accordance with his Word (cf. Leviticus 26 and Deuteronomy 28). The repeated theme is that of asking God to hear and forgive those who return to him in prayer, confessing their sins. Throughout his prayer, Solomon acknowledges the uniqueness, incomparable greatness and awesome splendour of God. Sadly, this is often lacking in modern-day worship. "LORD God of Israel, there is no God in heaven above or on earth below like You, who keep Your covenant and mercy with Your servants who walk before You with all their heart" (8:23). "Behold, heaven and the heaven of heavens cannot contain You" (8:27; cf. vv. 39,42).

Solomon had, in his father David, a special model for his prayer life. The Psalms are the divinely inspired prayerbook for the church, and Christians would do well to model their prayers upon those fine examples:

> O LORD, our Lord,
> How excellent is Your name in all the earth,
> Who have set Your glory above the heavens! (Psalm 8:1)

> LORD, You have been our dwelling place in all generations.
> Before the mountains were brought forth,
> Or ever You had formed the earth and the world,
> Even from everlasting to everlasting, You are God (Psalm 90:1-2).

> O God, You are my God;
> Early will I seek You;
> My soul thirsts for You;
> My flesh longs for You
> In a dry and thirsty land
> Where there is no water.
> So I have looked for You in the sanctuary,
> To see Your power and Your glory.

Because Your lovingkindness is better than life,
My lips shall praise You.
Thus I will bless You while I live;
I will lift up my hands in Your name.
My soul shall be satisfied as with marrow and fatness,
And my mouth shall praise You with joyful lips (Psalm 63:1-5).

I will love You, O Lord, my strength.
The Lord is my rock and my fortress and my deliverer;
My God, my strength, in whom I will trust;
My shield and the horn of my salvation, my stronghold.
I will call upon the Lord, who is worthy to be praised (Psalm 18:1-3).

I have called upon You, for You will hear me, O God;
Incline Your ear to me, and hear my speech.
Show Your marvelous lovingkindness by Your right hand,
O You who save those who trust in You
From those who rise up against them (Psalm 17:6-7).

You are the God who does wonders;
You have declared Your strength among the peoples.
You have with Your arm redeemed Your people (Psalm 77:14-15).

Prayers in a Christian assembly are often nothing more than coming to God with a shopping list—making one request after another—without addressing God in worship, praise and blessing and speaking of his wondrous works, attributes or promises.

The model for Christian prayer was provided by the Lord Jesus Christ when he said:

In this manner, therefore, pray:

Our Father in heaven,
Hallowed be Your name.
Your kingdom come.
Your will be done
On earth as it is in heaven (Matthew 6:9-10).

Before making requests of God, the priority is to show respect, honour and submission to the great God of heaven himself.

It is further to be noted that the Lord Jesus teaches to *whom* we are to speak in prayer: "Our Father in heaven." Despite the clearer revelation in the New Testament concerning the Son of God, this has not altered the person who is to be addressed in prayer.

> There has developed a trend in which prayer is almost exclusively addressed to the Lord Jesus Christ—sometimes simply to "Jesus." It is almost as if the Father did not exist.... When, however, we turn to the New Testament we find that the consistent pattern in prayer and praise is an approach to the Father.[17]

2. Marriage to the ungodly

Wisdom and the knowledge of God are no defence against falling into serious sin. The sad spiritual decline of Solomon was brought about by his unbridled passion. Loving many women—marrying 700 and having 300 more as concubines—resulted in his turning away from God (11:1-4,6). They influenced him to serve their gods. The Word of God through Moses warned of this danger (Deuteronomy 17:17).

Throughout the Old Testament, there is a consistent pattern showing the problems, dangers and disasters that arise when the people of God marry outside the faith. Esau brought great grief to his parents by his marriage to two Hittite women (Genesis 26:34-35). The law prohibited marriage with Canaanites (Deuteronomy 7:1-4). Samson distressed his parents by going outside Israel and marrying a Philistine (Judges 14:3). "Is she a fair Philistine? Why is not the deformity of the soul more powerful to dissuade us, than the beauty of the face to allure us?"[18]

> When the interests of godliness do not govern the people of God in the choice of marital partners, irreparable confusion is the result and the interests, not only of spirituality, but also of morality, are destroyed. ...marital life is to be guided, not by impulse or fancy, but by consider-

---

[17] Herbert M. Carson, *Hallelujah!: Christian Worship* (Welwyn: Evangelical Press, 1980), 36.

[18] Cited by Charles Bridges, *A Commentary on Proverbs* (1846; London: Banner of Truth Trust, 1968), 300.

ations which conserve and promote the interests of godliness. It is the Old Testament counterpart of the New Testament principle that Christians should marry only "in the Lord."[19]

Under the New Covenant, as under the Old Covenant, believers are forbidden to marry those who are not God's people. Such marriages violate the fundamental principle that believers should not be unequally yoked together[20] with unbelievers: "For what fellowship has righteousness with lawlessness? And what communion has light with darkness?" (2 Corinthians 6:14).

3. Backsliding and apostasy

There are sober warnings in the Scriptures about *apostasy*—falling away from the faith. Of Hebrews 6:4-8, John Calvin remarks:

> The apostle is not talking here about theft, or perjury, or murder, or drunkenness or adultery. He is referring to a complete falling away from the Gospel, not one in which the sinner has offended God in some one part only, but in which he has utterly renounced His grace.[21]

Backsliding, however, means turning away from God and returning to the former way of life. It is a pardonable offence against God. As a true believer in the Lord, David was guilty of serious backsliding in his adultery with Bathsheba and the murder of Uriah (2 Samuel 11:2-17), and he repented (Psalm 51; cf. Galatians 6:1; James 5:19-20).

Did Solomon apostatize (fall away and seriously deny the faith) or just seriously backslide? The idolatry into which Solomon fell in his old age seems incomprehensible for one so wise and God-fearing as he was in earlier days. "But great wisdom and a refined knowledge of God are not a defence against the folly of idolatry, since this has its roots in the heart, and springs from sensual desires and the lust of the flesh."[22]

Solomon's spiritual state is more complex than that of his father, in that

---

[19] John Murray, *Principles of Conduct: Aspects of Biblical Ethics* (London: Tyndale Press, 1957), 46.

[20] A clear allusion to the forbidden practice of yoking different kinds of animal together (Deuteronomy 22:10).

[21] John Calvin, *The Epistle of Paul the Apostle to the Hebrews and the First and Second Epistles of St Peter* (1549; Edinburgh: St. Andrew Press, 1963), 74-75.

[22] Keil, *The Books of the Kings*, 166.

there is no record of repentance and a wholehearted return to the Lord. Hengstenberg makes a point which is difficult to refute when he argues: "The first fruit of his conversion would have been to destroy the scandals which he had established."[23] The contrary view that Solomon was eventually restored to a right relationship with God is not based upon any record of repentance (though Ecclesiastes 12:13-14 might be seen to indicate this) but upon the grace, mercy and power of God. The Lord had a special love for Solomon:

> Then David comforted Bathsheba his wife, and went in to her and lay with her. So she bore a son, and he called his name Solomon. *Now the LORD loved him*, and He sent word by the hand of Nathan the prophet: So he called his name *Jedidiah* [i.e. "Beloved of the LORD"], because of the LORD (2 Samuel 12:24-25, emphasis added).

There is, further, the prophecy of Nathan to David:

> When your days are fulfilled and you rest with your fathers, I will set up your seed after you, who will come from your body, and I will establish his kingdom. He shall build a house for My name, and I will establish the throne of his kingdom forever. I will be his Father, and he shall be My son. *If he commits iniquity*, I will chasten him with the rod of men and with the blows of the sons of men. *But My mercy shall not depart from him*, as I took it from Saul, whom I removed from before you. And your house and your kingdom shall be established forever before you. Your throne shall be established forever" (2 Samuel 7:12-16, emphasis added).

Clearly, there is in this prophecy an intermingling of two promises, one relating to Solomon, the other relating to Christ. The establishment of David's kingdom and his throne "forever" has reference to "the everlasting kingdom of our Lord and Saviour Jesus Christ" (2 Peter 1:11). No mere man can rule for ever and ever—only God can do that. On the other hand, there is reference to iniquity, to wickedness, to sin, and the warning that God would certainly punish sin; yet there is the promise that God would not take

---

[23] Ernest W. Hengstenberg, *History of the Kingdom of God under the Old Testament*, vol. 2 (Edinburgh: T & T Clark, 1877), 134.

away his mercy from that one. This surely is not a reference to Christ but to Solomon. Solomon was punished with "the rod of men and with the blows of the sons of men." While he was still on the throne, Edom began to throw off its allegiance, under the guidance of Hadad; Rezon took Damascus and the surrounding area from Solomon, and founded a kingdom which would afterward prove very destructive to the Israelites; a still heavier punishment came through his own family, for the greater part of his kingdom would be taken from his son. Preparation was made for the fulfilment of this threat even in Solomon's lifetime.

Is any Christian immune from relapse into sin when for a season he relaxes his vigilance and ceases to watch and pray lest he enter into temptation? ...It is because few of us have any claim to fame that our individual failures are known only to God.... Those failures might be magnified a thousand times if we were exalted to positions of absolute power. Let him who is without sin cast the first stone at Solomon.[24]

4. God's power and provision

No circumstances are too difficult for the Lord. This is vividly illustrated in this book by the fire descending onto the water-soaked altar and by other wonderful miracles experienced by the prophet Elijah. During a three-and-a-half-year famine, he was first fed by ravens bringing bread and meat each morning and evening (17:6) and then sustained by a supernatural supply of oil and flour (17:16).

David confidently declared:

I have been young, and now am old;
Yet I have not seen the righteous forsaken,
Nor his descendants begging bread (Psalm 37:25).

The apostle Paul thanks the Christians at Philippi for their kind support and generous gift and then reassures them of the provision of God: "And my God shall supply all your need according to His riches in glory by Christ Jesus" (Philippians 4:19).

---

[24] Charles D. Alexander, *The Heavenly Mystery of the Song of Songs* (Liverpool: Bible Exposition Fellowship, 1965), 3.

However, the Lord's *ordinary* providences are no less wonderful than the more spectacular display of power: "Now to Him who is able to do exceedingly abundantly above all that we ask or think, according to the power that works in us, to Him be glory in the church by Christ Jesus to all generations, forever and ever. Amen" (Ephesians 3:20-21).

5. Fleeing persecution

Elijah has been much maligned. His experiences following the events on Mount Carmel are often used to illustrate the way in which the godly may become cowardly and depressed:

> God's heroes are never supermen. "Elijah," wrote James, "was a man just like us" (James 5:17). So from attaining heights of courage and seeming fearlessness, he suddenly plumbs the depths of fear and runs for his life. His flight, however, did not lead to freedom, but rather into a cul-de-sac of self-pity and abject depression. Indeed we find him teetering on the brink of despair. That is why he is such a help to us in facing depression.[25]

> Alas, instead of spreading his case before God, he takes matters into his own hands; instead of waiting patiently for Him, he acts on hasty impulse, deserts the post of duty, and flees from the one who sought his destruction.... His eyes were fixed on the wicked and furious queen: his mind was occupied with her power and fury, and therefore his heart was filled with terror.... Elijah's mind was no longer stayed upon Jehovah, and therefore fear took possession of him...he lost sight of the Lord.[26]

Charles Alexander has challenged this interpretation of Elijah as a depressed coward in the strongest possible terms: "In the case of Elijah's flight from Jezebel, no shadow of guilt is attributed to Elijah anywhere in Holy Scripture, but rather, as we shall see, his flight was divinely ordained to prepare the way prophetically for the Coming of the Saviour."[27] No New

---

[25] Herbert M. Carson, *Depression in the Christian Family* (Darlington: Evangelical Press, 1994), 28-29.
[26] Pink, *The Life of Elijah*, 196-197.
[27] Charles D. Alexander, *Elijah: 'Crouching Coward' or Hero of the Faith?* (Liverpool: Bible Exposition Fellowship, n.d.), 4.

Testament writer attributes any depression to the prophet Elijah. Alexander further points out that Elijah was the only source of information of these events, that there was neither rebuke from the Lord nor repentance from the prophet for the sin of cowardice, and that Elijah is never once criticized as though deserting the nation in its hour of need.

Flight from persecution is not only acceptable before God, but also recommended by him. Jacob fled from his brother Esau (Genesis 27:43); David fled from Saul (1 Samuel 19:10; 20:1); Joseph and Mary fled from Herod (Matthew 2:13-15); the apostle Paul fled from irate Jews (Acts 9:23-25). Are these then to be regarded as the actions of depressed cowards? The Lord Jesus Christ advised his disciples: "when they persecute you in this city, flee to another" (Matthew 10:23).

Furthermore, the Lord does not translate cowards. Moses was not permitted to enter the promised land because of one momentary lapse, yet God translated Elijah into heaven that he might not experience death.

The Hebrew of 19:3 is translated in a variety of ways. The RAV and AV read: "And when he saw that, he arose and went for his life." The NIV reads: "Elijah was afraid and ran for his life."[28] Some Hebrew manuscripts have the word for "saw," others have the alternative "[was] afraid." Apart from the more complex issue of which group of manuscripts is more reliable, the straightforward issue to determine which word is correct in 19:3 can be resolved by the context:

> For it is obvious that Elijah did not flee from any fear of the vain threat of Jezebel, from the fact that he did not merely withdraw into the kingdom of Judah, where he would have been safe under Jehoshaphat from all the persecutions of Jezebel, but went to Beersheba, and thence onwards into the desert, there to pour out before the Lord God his weariness of life (v. 4)...he went upon his soul...i.e. not to save his life (as I once thought, with many other commentators), for his wish to die (v. 4) is opposed to this; but to care for his soul in the manner indicated in v. 4, i.e. to commit his soul or his life to the Lord his God in the solitude of the desert, and see what He would determine concerning him.[29]

---

[28] The NIV has a footnote: "Or Elijah saw."
[29] Keil, *The Books of the Kings*, 253.

6. Called to service

At the commandment of the Lord, Elijah called Elisha to the prophetic office (19:16). When Elijah found Elisha, the latter was busy ploughing. Elisha's reaction was to leave his work. Many men, called by God to the ministry of the Word, have also responded by leaving their work. When called by the Lord Jesus Christ to accompany him, Simon Peter and Andrew his brother were fishing in the Sea of Galilee. Jesus said to them, "'Come after Me, and I will make you become fishers of men.' And immediately *they left their nets* and followed him" (Mark 1:17-18, emphasis added). In the same manner, when called to follow the Lord Jesus Christ and join the close company of the apostles, Matthew was busy at his work: "And *he left all*, rose up, and followed Him" (Luke 5:28, emphasis added). Today, the cost is the same for some Christians in serving the Lord Jesus Christ: "Sell all that you have and distribute to the poor, and you will have treasure in heaven; and come, follow Me" (Luke 18:22).

Elisha cooked a yoke of oxen and gave them to his family and neighbours. In using the wooden yoke as fuel, he forcefully demonstrated that he would not be returning to his former work. From here on, he was looking to the Lord to provide for him by some other means: "Even so the Lord has commanded that those who preach the gospel should live from the gospel" (1 Corinthians 9:14), for "the labourer is worthy of his wages" (Luke 10:7; cf. 1 Timothy 5:17-18; 1 Corinthians 9:7-11; Galatians 6:6).

2 KINGS

MEANING	AUTHOR	KEY THOUGHT
(continuation of 1 Kings)	**Unknown** (maybe Jeremiah)	**According to the word of the Lord**

THEME

The word of the Lord is sure and certain to saint and sinner

THEME VERSE

Know now that nothing shall fall to the earth of the word of the LORD... for the LORD has done what He spoke by His servant Elijah.
2 KINGS 10:10

2 KINGS / **SUMMARY**

JUDAH		ISRAEL	
(two southern tribes)		(ten northern tribes)	
Reigning king:	1:1–2:25	a.	The reign of Ahaziah (bad)
Jehoshaphat (good)	1:1–18		(1) Elijah calls down fire
	2:1–11		(2) Elijah's translation to heaven
	2:12–18		(3) Elisha divides the Jordan
	2:19–22		(4) Elisha heals the waters
	2:23–25		(5) Elisha taunted by youths
	3:1–8:15	b.	The reign of Joram (bad)
	3:1–4:7		(1) Elisha and the miracles of water and oil
	4:8–37		(2) Elisha raises the Shunammite's son
	4:38–41		(3) Elisha heals the deadly stew
	4:42–44		(4) Elisha feeds 100 men
	5:1–19		(5) Elisha heals Naaman the leper
	5:20–27		(6) Elisha's servant smitten with leprosy
	6:1–7		(7) Elisha floats the iron axehead
	6:8–12		(8) Elisha discloses Syria's plans
	6:13–33		(9) Elisha and the Syrians' blindness
	7:1–20		(10) Prophecy: ending of a famine
	8:1–6		(11) Restoration of the Shunammite's land
	8:7–15		(12) Prophecy: Hazael to be king of Syria
c. The reign of Jehoram (bad)	8:16–24		
d. The reign of Ahaziah (bad)	8:25–29		
	9:1–10:36	e.	The reign of Jehu (bad)
f. The reign of Queen Athaliah (bad)	11:1–3		
g. The reign of Joash (good when under the influence of Jehoida the priest)	11:4–12:21		

JUDAH		ISRAEL	
(two southern tribes)		(ten northern tribes)	
	13:1-9	h.	The reign of Jehoahaz (bad)
	13:10-13	i.	The reign of Jehoash (bad)
	13:14-19		(1) Elisha prophecies on his deathbed
	13:20-25		(2) Elisha's bones revive dead man
j. The reign of Amaziah (began well, ended in idolatry)	14:1-22		
	14:23-29	k.	The reign of Jeroboam (bad)
l. The reign of Uzziah (began well, ended badly)	15:1-7		
	15:8-31	m.	The reigns of five idolatrous kings: Zechariah, Shallum, Menahem, Pekahiah, Pekah
n. The reign of Jotham (good)	15:32-38		
o. The reign of Ahaz (bad)	16:1-20		
	17:1-41	p.	The reign of Hoshea (bad) **Captivity of Israel by Assyria**
q. The reign of Hezekiah (good)	18:1-20:21		
r. The reign of Manasseh (bad)	21:1-18		
s. The reign of Amon (bad)	21:19-26		
t. The reign of Josiah (good)	22:1-23:30		
u. The reign of Jehoahaz (bad)	23:31-34		
v. The reign of Jehoiakim (bad)	23:35-24:7		
w. The reign of Jehoiachin (bad)	24:8-16		

2 KINGS / **SUMMARY**

JUDAH		ISRAEL
(two southern tribes)		(ten northern tribes)

x. The reign of Zedekiah (bad)	24:17–20	
Captivity of Judah by Babylon	25:1–21	
Gedaliah: governor of the land of Judah	25:22–26	
Jehoiachin's last days	25:27–30	

2 KINGS

In the original format there was only one book of Kings which "begins with King David and ends with the King of Babylon; opens with the Temple built and closes with the Temple burnt; begins with David's first successor on the throne of his kingdom, and ends with David's last successor released from the house of his captivity."[1] For practical reasons the original book was divided into two. Consequently what has been written concerning the author under the introduction to 1 Kings applies also to this second book.

2 KINGS / **HISTORICAL SETTING**

Following the death of Solomon it was not long before the twelve tribes which composed the nation of Israel experienced civil war. Jeroboam, one of Solomon's key leaders, a mighty man of valour and also highly industrious (1 Kings 11:28), rebelled against Solomon and fled to Egypt. When he heard of King Solomon's death and the coronation of his son Rehoboam, he returned to Israel and became a significant leader among the people. Jeroboam led a delegation of Israelites who visited the new king and asked for a lifting of the heavy burdens which King Solomon had imposed on the people. They assured King Rehoboam that, if he would just slacken the demands, they would willingly serve him (1 Kings 12:4). But Solomon's son, Rehoboam, was an arrogant young man. He listened more to the young men who had grown up with him than to the elders who had been in close consultation with his father Solomon (1 Kings 12:6–8). The result was that Rehoboam made even heavier demands and, consequently, stirred up a rebellion among the general populace.

The division of the kingdom

In 931 B.C., the division of the nation of Israel took place. There were now two distinct nations—Israel and Judah. Jeroboam was proclaimed king of Israel, the large northern kingdom composed of ten of the

---

[1] Dr. Bullinger, cited by Robert Lee, *The Outlined Bible: An Outline and Analysis of Every Book in the Bible* (London: Pickering and Inglis, 1930), analysis no. 12.

twelve tribes. Rehoboam was left with Judah, the southern kingdom composed of the two remaining tribes of Judah and Benjamin, based at Jerusalem. Israel extended from Bethel to Dan, from the Mediterranean to Syria and Ammon. The new centre for Israel became the city of Samaria.

Second Kings covers the history of the kingdoms of Israel and Judah from the reign of Ahaziah in Israel, and that of Jehoshaphat in Judah, to the time of the Assyrian and Babylonian exiles respectively. As far as the history of Israel is concerned, it is a dark picture of degenerate rulers and sinful people, ending in slavery. The only slight upturn occurs under the rule of Jehu when he enacts the punishment of God, but he cannot be described as godly. Jehu executed Joram, Ahaziah, Jezebel, seventy of Ahab's children and the worshippers of Baal (9:1–10:36).

The kingdom of Judah was also on the downgrade, but judgement was not visited upon her so speedily because of the influence of a number of godly kings who reigned during this period.

2 KINGS / **OUTLINE**

The history of the kings of Judah and Israel has been amplified by reference to the various historical and prophetic books of the Old Testament in order to present a composite account.

The first eight chapters are dominated by the final days of the prophet Elijah followed by the outstanding ministry of his successor, the prophet Elisha. The remaining chapters outline the decline of Israel and Judah—spiritually and morally. The majority of the kings of the divided kingdom are godless and wicked. The historian highlights the notable exceptions.

At the opening of 2 Kings, Ahaziah rules Israel and Jehoshaphat rules Judah. There is a marked contrast between these two. Of King Ahaziah of Israel it is written:

> He did evil in the sight of the Lord, and walked in the way of his father and in the way of his mother and in the way of Jeroboam the son of Nebat, who had made Israel sin; for he served Baal and worshiped him, and provoked the LORD God of Israel to anger, according to all that his father had done (1 Kings 22:52–53).

By contrast, of King Jehoshaphat of Judah it is written: "And he walked in all the ways of his father Asa. He did not turn aside from them, doing what was right in the eyes of the LORD" (1 Kings 22:43). So while Israel is ruled by a bad king, Judah is experiencing the benefits of the leadership of a good and godly king.

Ahaziah in Israel: 853–852 B.C. (1:1-18)
The Moabites had been under subjection to Israel since the days of David (2 Samuel 8:2). Following the defeat of Israel by the Syrians at Ramoth Gilead (1 Kings 22:29–38), Moab takes advantage of the weakened power of Israel on the east of the River Jordan, and rebels (1:1).

The brief reign of godless King Ahaziah comes to an end when he falls "through the lattice of his upper room in Samaria" (1:2). Since he had no son, his brother Joram (also spelt Jehoram) reigns in his place.

Meanwhile the prophet Elijah is about to be translated to heaven. Having appointed Elisha as his successor, Elijah—moved no doubt by modesty at the great honour to be conferred upon him—attempts to leave Elisha, first at Gilgal, then at Bethel and finally at Jericho. Each time Elisha is insistent on accompanying his mentor—for he knows as well as Elijah what is about to take place on the other side of the River Jordan. The Lord is to put his seal of approval on the ministry of Elijah by translating the prophet to heaven so that he does not experience death. The Lord has also revealed the departure of Elijah to the sons of the prophets at Bethel and at Jericho (2:3,5).

Elisha the prophet in Israel[2]
Elijah performs his last miracle in dividing the waters of the River Jordan and the two prophets cross over on dry ground, in full sight of fifty of the sons of the prophets. There is a strong resemblance to the crossing of the Red Sea by the Israelites years before. There Moses, the leader of the people, performed his miracle with his rod (Exodus 14:16,21); here Elijah the prophet divides the river with his prophet's cloak (2:8). Once over the river, Elijah invites Elisha to make one final

---

[2] See Arthur W. Pink, *Gleanings from Elisha: His Life and Miracles* (Chicago: Moody Press, 1972); F.W. Krummacher, *Elisha: A Prophet for Our Times* (Grand Rapids: Baker, 1976); and F.W. Krummacher, *The Last Days of Elisha* (Grand Rapids: Baker, 1981).

request. Probably basing his response upon the law of Moses regarding the firstborn (Deuteronomy 21:16–17), Elisha asks for a double portion of Elijah's spirit. If he is to take up the prophetic office where Elijah lays it down, then he will need the authority and power of the Holy Spirit. This is not in Elijah's power to grant. Leaving the matter in the Lord's hands, Elijah promises that if Elisha sees his departure, that will be the sign that God has granted his request. The chariot and horses of fire appear and transport Elijah away into heaven. Elisha witnesses the whole event. The Lord has granted his request. Returning to the River Jordan, Elisha takes Elijah's cloak, strikes the water and walks across the dry bed of the river. The sons of the prophets see the evidence that the spirit of Elijah now rests on Elisha. His call to office has been publicly confirmed.

The second and third miracles performed by Elisha are intended to establish before the people of Israel his appointment to the prophetic office. The healing of the water at Jericho has similarities to the miracle carried out by Moses when he cast a tree into the bitter waters of Marah (Exodus 15:23–25) and re-emphasizes the revelation: "I am the LORD who heals you" (Exodus 15:26; cf. 2 Kings 2:21). Here at Jericho, a blessing falls at the place of a curse (Joshua 6:26; 1 Kings 16:34). Shortly afterward, a curse falls at Bethel, which had been the place of a blessing (Genesis 28:16–17,19); a large gang of boys, over forty of them, taunt the prophet and hurl abuse at him. They sin on at least three counts: (1) they deride Elisha for a natural condition—premature baldness (he lived another fifty years); (2) they show marked disrespect and contempt for an adult; and (3) they show their hostility toward a man of God in shouting, "Go up, you baldhead!" (2:23), which is evidently a reference to the translation of Elijah. An insult to a man of God, because he is a man of God, is an insult against God himself. The behaviour of these youths is symptomatic of the moral and spiritual disorder in the community, which is anti-God!

Joram in Israel: 852–841 B.C. (3:1–8:15)
Following the death of Ahaziah, his brother Joram accedes to the throne of Israel. He is not as evil as his parents, since he tries to remove the worship of Baal from the land. He does, however, perpetuate the sin of Jeroboam in encouraging the worship of the true God through the image of the calf.

Chapters 4 to 8 record a series of miracles performed by Elisha. These confirm that he is continuing the work that Elijah had begun in seeking to turn the people of Israel from the worship of Baal to the worship of the true and living God. One of the significant contributions which Elisha makes in this connection is to continue the training and the encouragement of the sons of the prophets, who labour as itinerant preachers throughout the land. Elijah had established schools for disciples at Gilgal, Bethel and Jericho (2:3,5; 4:38). Under Elisha's tutelage, the number of students at Jericho increases to such an extent that new premises are required. It is while they are engaged in this enterprise that the head falls from the shaft of a borrowed axe and Elisha recovers it in a most unusual manner (6:6).

Since Elisha died during the reign of Jehoash of Israel (13:14), his ministry must have extended some fifty-five years or more—over the combined reigns of Joram, Jehu, Jehoahaz and Jehoash. His long ministry is not characterized by demonstrations of the power and might of Jehovah, but by "the tender care, the sufficient provision, and the ever-present help which the Lord extends to His own servants and people."[3] This is strikingly illustrated in many ways: the miraculous provision for a widow and her sons; the ending of the Shunammite's barrenness and the subsequent restoration of her dead son; the rendering harmless of a poisonous stew by the addition of a quantity of flour; and the miraculous increase of twenty small loaves so that there is more than sufficient to feed 100 men.

Jehoram in Judah: 853-841 B.C. (8:16-24; cf. 2 Chronicles 21:1-20)

Jehoram becomes king while his father Jehoshaphat is still king. They exercise a co-regency for a few years until Jehoshaphat hands over sole government to his son. Jehoram's wife is Athaliah, the daughter of Ahab and Jezebel of Israel (2 Chronicles 21:6). No doubt through her evil influence, Jehoram introduces Baal worship into Judah. Immediately following his father's death, Jehoram murders all his brothers, to whom Jehoshaphat had given great treasures and who had been strategically placed in fortified cities around Judah (2 Chronicles 21:1-4). This wickedness would have resulted in the destruction of Judah had

---

[3] A.R. Buckland and A.L. Williams, ed., *Universal Bible Dictionary* (London: The Religious Tract Society, 1914), 146.

it not been for the covenant which the Lord had made with David. Jehoram will not, however, escape punishment. The Lord inspires Elijah the prophet to send a letter to Jehoram in which his sins and his subsequent punishment are clearly spelt out (2 Chronicles 21:12-15). The prophecy is fulfilled and Jehoram dies of a terrible disease after a protracted illness of two years.

Ahaziah (Azariah)[4] *in Judah: 841* B.C. *(8:25-29; cf. 2 Chronicles 22:1-9)*

His mother Athaliah, daughter of the idolatrous Queen Jezebel and wicked King Ahab of Israel, exercises a powerful and evil influence over him, so that as king of Judah, Ahaziah follows in the evil ways of Ahab of Israel.

Ahaziah joins with Joram of Israel, his mother's brother, in a war against the Syrians at Ramoth Gilead. Fighting over this city had previously cost Ahab his life (1 Kings 22:3-4,34-35).

Jehu in Israel: 841-814 B.C. *(9:1-10:36)*

Meanwhile, Elisha the prophet continues to fulfil the ministry of his master Elijah. He sends one of the sons of the prophets to anoint Jehu as king of Israel in the place of Joram (9:1-3; cf. 1 Kings 19:16), with a commission to avenge the death of the executed prophets and faithful servants of the Lord (1 Kings 18:4; 19:10). Jehu is to kill the male descendants of Ahab, and Jezebel is to die. With the full support of his fellow-captains, Jehu sets about planning the downfall of King Joram. He leads his troops to Jezreel and kills Joram, king of Israel, and his nephew, Ahaziah, king of Judah (9:16,24,27; 2 Chronicles 22:7-9). Queen Jezebel hears of the deaths of Joram and Ahaziah, and prepares to meet Jehu. She uses make-up, not to allure Jehu by her charm but to present an imposing appearance and die as a queen.[5]

Jehu, king of Israel, continues to exterminate the family of Ahab. He uses trickery and deceit to massacre not only the descendants of Ahab but also the priests, prophets and servants of Baal. Yet, in spite of this apparent zeal for the Lord and the word spoken through the

---

[4] 2 Chronicles 22:6, etc.
[5] Carl F. Keil, *Biblical Commentary on the Books of the Kings* (Grand Rapids: Eerdmans, 1950), 345.

prophet Elijah, Jehu seems to have been motivated more by personal ambition than by concern for the honour of the living God. "Jehu took no heed to walk in the law of the LORD God of Israel with all his heart, for he did not depart from the sins of Jeroboam, who had made Israel sin" (10:31).

Queen Athaliah in Judah: 841-835 B.C. (11:1-3; cf. 2 Chronicles 22:10-23:21)

After the death of King Ahaziah, Athaliah his mother, daughter of Ahab and Jezebel (8:18,26), seizes the throne. When Jehu of Israel murders the forty-two brothers of Ahaziah of Judah, Athaliah puts to death all the remaining members of the royal family of Judah (her grandchildren).[6] Only one son of Ahaziah, the young child Joash, escapes. As a one-year-old, he is rescued by his aunt Jehosheba, daughter of Jehoram (probably by a wife other than Athaliah[7]) whose husband is the godly high priest Jehoiada (2 Chronicles 22:11). Joash and his nurse are moved into hiding in the home of the high priest in one of the buildings in the court of the temple.

Joash in Judah: 835-796 B.C. (11:4-12:21)[8]

Hidden and protected for six years, the seven-year-old Joash is revealed as the rightful king of Judah. After he is anointed king, and Queen Athaliah has been put to death, Jehoiada the high priest renews the covenant between Jehovah and the king and people (cf. Exodus 24:3-8; Deuteronomy 27:9-10). Religious reformation continues, but only while the king is under the godly eye and influence of Jehoiada the high priest. Upon the priest's death, Joash changes his ways—for the worse. He restores Baal worship and the building of groves to Ashtoreth.

Hazael, king of Syria, marches along the coast after defeating Israel (13:3), takes the city of Gath which Rehoboam had built for the defence of Judah (2 Chronicles 11:5,8) and moves against Jerusalem. Although his forces are small, he conquers a much larger army because

---

[6] Another devilish plot to try to destroy the covenant promises that the Lord made to David (2 Samuel 7:12-13,16).

[7] It is most unlikely that Athaliah would have permitted her daughter to marry a godly high priest of Jehovah.

[8] See the fuller account, including the third religious revival since the division of the kingdom, recorded in 2 Chronicles 24:1-25.

the Lord is using him to punish Judah and King Joash (2 Chronicles 24:24). Having emptied the treasuries of the temple and the palace, Hazael withdraws from Jerusalem leaving King Joash seriously wounded. While Joash is recovering in bed, his servants, seeking revenge for the death of a prophet named Zechariah, end his life.

Jehoahaz in Israel: 814–798 B.C. (13:1–9)

Upon the death of Jehu, his son Jehoahaz becomes king of Israel. Jehoahaz follows the sinful practices of Jeroboam by perpetuating the worship of the golden calf. The Lord punishes him, for throughout the whole of his reign Israel is under the domination of the Syrian king Hazael and his son Ben-Hadad, who force Jehoahaz to drastically reduce his military forces. The Syrian oppression is so severe that King Jehoahaz eventually turns in desperation to the Lord. The Lord hears his cry and sends a deliverer who frees them from the Syrian yoke.[9] After reigning for seventeen years, Jehoahaz dies and is succeeded by his son Jehoash (also spelt Joash).

Jehoash in Israel: 798–782 B.C. (13:10–25)

During his sixteen-year reign over Israel, King Jehoash visits the prophet Elisha on his deathbed. At that meeting, Jehoash is promised three victories over his enemies the Syrians. Consequently, King Ben-Hadad is defeated three times and Israel regains possession of a number of cities. Jehoash is also successful in the battle with Judah. Challenged to a war he did not wish to fight, Jehoash wins a decisive victory, takes King Amaziah prisoner, sacks the city of Jerusalem, plunders the temple and the palace, and takes many prisoners back to Samaria.

Amaziah in Judah: 796–767 B.C. (14:1–22; cf. 2 Chronicles 25:1–28)

Upon the murder of his father Joash, Amaziah becomes king of Judah. His twenty-nine-year reign begins reasonably well. He seems to have been somewhat responsive to the Word of God (14:3,6), though a serious departure results in severe punishment from the Lord for, like

---

[9] The deliverer may have been either of the successors of Jehoahaz to the throne of Israel, Jehoash (13:25) or Jeroboam II (14:25); or it may have been Adad-Nirari III of Assyria, who blockaded Damascus about 803 B.C.

his father Joash before him, Amaziah falls into idolatry in the closing years of his life. The chronicler sums up Amaziah's behaviour: "And he did what was right in the sight of the LORD, but not with a loyal heart" (2 Chronicles 25:2).

Jeroboam II in Israel: 793-753 B.C. (14:23-29)

Jeroboam II, son of Jehoash of Israel, reigns forty-one years. The prophets Jonah, Amos and Hosea exercise their ministry during his long reign (14:25; Amos 1:1; Hosea 1:1).

The only prophecy of Jonah to Israel which has been included in Scripture is in keeping with his name. Jonah ("the dove") brings a message of comfort and encouragement to the nation.[10] The Lord has seen the terrible distress of his people Israel, and he has determined to deliver them by the hand of King Jeroboam:

> He restored the territory of Israel from the entrance of Hamath to the Sea of the Arabah, according to the word of the LORD God of Israel, which He had spoken through His servant Jonah the son of Amittai, the prophet who was from Gath Hepher. For the LORD saw that the affliction of Israel was very bitter; and whether bond or free, there was no helper for Israel. And the LORD did not say that He would blot out the name of Israel from under heaven; but He saved them by the hand of Jeroboam the son of Joash (14:25-27).

Israel regains the territory lost through the invasions of the Syrians, restoring the ancient boundaries of the kingdom as in the days of Solomon (cf. 1 Kings 8:65). Jeroboam not only drives out the Syrians (cf. 13:4-5), but pursues them and takes their capital city, Damascus, in fulfilment of the prophecy of Amos (Amos 1:3,5). Jeroboam's conquest of Damascus is, however, to prove a rash move as it destabilizes the international scene. By weakening Syria, Israel leaves herself wide open to attack from another enemy—the Assyrians.

Other problems arise for the Israelites during this period of international peace and economic prosperity: the worship of the true God

---

[10] Keil maintains that this prophecy was given to King Jeroboam II by Jonah in person. See Carl F. Keil, *The Twelve Minor Prophets* (Grand Rapids: Eerdmans, 1949), 379.

is corrupted by idolatry (Hosea 4:12–14; 13:6; Amos 2:8); materialism, greed, immorality and injustice are rife throughout the land (Amos 2:6–7; 4:1; 6:6).

Uzziah in Judah: 792–740 B.C. (15:1-7; cf. 2 Chronicles 26:1-23)

Uzziah[11] becomes king of Judah at the age of sixteen. He begins his reign well, for "he did what was right in the sight of the LORD, according to all that his father Amaziah had done" (15:3). "He sought God in the days of Zechariah, who had understanding in the visions of God; and as long as he sought the LORD, God made him prosper" (2 Chronicles 26:5). He wins great victories over his enemies: the Philistines, the Arabians who live in Gur Baal and against the Meunites, for "God helped him" (2 Chronicles 26:7). He strengthens the fortification of the city of Jerusalem, builds towers in strategic desert locations, amasses a great army equipped with the finest weaponry and becomes exceedingly powerful and famous.

These many successes, however, are to prove to be Uzziah's downfall. He becomes proud and self-confident. Entering the temple, he violates the declared will of God by burning incense on the altar when he is not of the priestly tribe. Azariah the high priest and eighty of his colleagues rebuke Uzziah, who reacts with rage. God strikes Uzziah that very moment, as a direct consequence of his serious and wilful sin. Uzziah is afflicted with leprosy to the day of his death. For the next ten years, Uzziah is king in name only for his son Jotham is the effective monarch.

Uzziah reigns for a total of fifty-two years, during which time the southern kingdom of Judah experiences a period of well-being and affluence. As with the northern kingdom of Israel at this time, the people of Judah respond to days of prosperity by increasing self-indulgence, paganism and godlessness, as the prophet Isaiah records (Isaiah 2:1–3:26).

The reigns of five idolatrous kings in Israel: 753–732 B.C. (15:8-31)

Zechariah assumes the throne and is the fourth-generation king in Jehu's family (10:30), but his reign is terminated after only six months. *Shallum* reigns over Israel for only one month, when he is murdered

---

[11] Called Azariah in 14:21; 15:1–7, and Uzziah in 2 Chronicles 26:1; Isaiah 6:1, etc.

by Menahem. After a ten-year reign, Menahem dies and is succeeded by his son Pekahiah who reigns for two years. The next king, Pekah, follows in the godless and evil tradition of the Israelite kings.

Jotham in Judah: 750-732 B.C. (15:32-38; cf. 2 Chronicles 27:1-9)

Jotham is the effective ruler, though his father Uzziah (Azariah) is the official king for the last ten years of his life (15:5). On Uzziah's death, Jotham spends about five years as sole monarch after which he is joined by his son Ahaz. For a few years, the two reign together over Judah, until Jotham's death.

King Jotham "did what was right in the sight of the LORD, according to all that his father Uzziah had done (although he did not enter the temple of the LORD)"[12] (2 Chronicles 27:2). His success is attributed to his commitment to honour and obey the living God, for he "became mighty, because he prepared his ways before the LORD his God" (2 Chronicles 27:6). In spite of the king's godly example, the nation as a whole still acted corruptly (2 Chronicles 27:2).[13]

King Jotham must, however, bear some of the responsibility for the people's poor spiritual state since idolatry is permitted in the land (15:35). While Jotham extends the building of the Lord's temple, he does not remove the many pagan temples scattered throughout Judah. Consequently, toward the end of Jotham's reign, the Lord's displeasure is expressed against the king and nation because they are not being entirely true to the living God. Syria and Israel form an alliance against Judah: "In those days the LORD began to send Rezin king of Syria and Pekah the son of Remaliah against Judah" (15:37).

Ahaz in Judah: 735-715 B.C. (16:1-20; cf. 2 Chronicles 28:1-27)

King Ahaz is unlike his father Jotham, for he has no regard for the worship and honour of the true and living God. He is an active and passionate idolater who goes further than his godless ancestors in that he sacrifices some of his own children by fire to the Baal god Moloch in the Valley of Ben Hinnom (16:3; cf. 23:10; Jeremiah 7:30-31; Ezekiel 16:20-21).

---

[12] A reference to Uzziah's arrogance in burning incense in the temple in direct disobedience to the law of God (2 Chronicles 26:16).

[13] The prophets Isaiah and Micah specifically address this sinfulness (Isaiah 2:5-9; 5:7-30; Micah 1:5; 2:1-2).

Upon King Ahaz's refusal to join them against Assyria, Syria and Israel attack Judah (16:5; Isaiah 7:1). They intend, not only to overthrow Judah, but also to remove the descendants of David from the throne in Jerusalem (Isaiah 7:6).[14]

The prophet Isaiah is commissioned by the Lord to inform King Ahaz that he must not yield to the attack from Syria and Israel. King Ahaz is urged to trust in Jehovah, for the Lord is well able to defend the king and the nation. Ahaz is invited to ask a sign from the Lord in the assurance of the Lord's protection, but he refuses on the hypocritical pretext that he would not presume to test the Lord in such a way (Isaiah 7:1–12). The prophecy is nevertheless given: "Behold, the virgin shall conceive and bear a Son, and shall call His name Immanuel [which means, *God with us*]" (Isaiah 7:14).[15] But Ahaz refuses to trust in the Lord, and the kingdom of Judah suffers heavy casualties and losses under the combined forces of Syria and Israel.

Syria takes many captives back to Damascus; Israel kills 120,000 soldiers in one day, and takes 200,000 women and children captive (2 Chronicles 28:5–8).[16] As the army returns to Samaria with the captives, Oded, the prophet of the Lord, confronts and rebukes them for their extreme hostility, and orders them to return the captives to their own land of Judah. The women and children are treated kindly, fed and clothed and returned home.

Judah is brought low. The cause is not military but moral, not a matter of strategy but of spirituality:

> For the LORD brought Judah low because of Ahaz king of Israel, for he had encouraged moral decline in Judah and had been continually unfaithful to the LORD. Also Tiglath-Pileser king of Assyria came to him and distressed him, and did not assist him. For Ahaz took part of the treasures from the house of the LORD,

---

[14] Yet another satanic plot to try to destroy the covenant promises the Lord made to David (2 Samuel 7:12–13,16).

[15] This amazing prediction is a wonderful prophecy concerning Christ (Matthew 1:23).

[16] The precise relationship between the accounts in Kings and Chronicles is not easy to determine with the information available; see Edward J. Young, *The Book of Isaiah*, vol. 1 (Grand Rapids, Michigan: Eerdmans, 1965), 267–268.

from the house of the king, and from the leaders, and he gave it to the king of Assyria; but he did not help him.

Now in the time of his distress King Ahaz became increasingly unfaithful to the LORD. This is that King Ahaz. For he sacrificed to the gods of Damascus which had defeated him, saying, "Because the gods of the kings of Syria help them, I will sacrifice to them that they may help me." But they were the ruin of him and of all Israel (2 Chronicles 28:19–23).

And so, toward the close of his sixteen-year reign, the idolatrous and immoral King Ahaz adds a further insult against Jehovah when he suspends public worship by closing down the temple (2 Chronicles 28:24), having first desecrated it by the introduction of a pagan altar and a corrupt sacrificial system.

Hoshea in Israel: 732–721 B.C. (17:1–41)

Hoshea assumes the throne of Israel after murdering King Pekah (15:30). He follows in the godless and evil tradition of so many of the kings of Israel. His reign lasts nine years and comes to an end when an attempted conspiracy with Egypt against Assyria is exposed. Shalmaneser[17] has succeeded Tiglath-Pileser as king of Assyria. He moves against Israel, and in 721 B.C., following a three-year siege, the capital of Samaria is destroyed and numerous Israelites are deported to Assyria. From that time, the nation of the northern kingdom, the ten tribes of Israel, ceases to exist. The judgement of God has fallen upon a godless and wicked people. Their demise comes as a direct consequence of unfaithfulness and wickedness.

The Assyrians repopulate Samaria by bringing people from the five nations of Babylon, Cuthah, Ava, Hamath and Sepharvaim. The immigrants bring their own pagan religious rituals, and these are practised alongside the worship of Jehovah (17:41).

---

[17] Some Bible scholars suggest Shalmaneser is to be identified with Shalman (Hosea 10:14) and Sargon (Isaiah 20:1), while others suggest a co-regency for Shalmaneser and Sargon, and still others take Sargon to be the same as Sennacherib (18:13). There seems to be no way to form a conclusion based upon the evidence supplied in Scripture.

Hezekiah in Judah: 715–686 B.C. (18:1–20:21)[18]

King Hezekiah, son of wicked Ahaz, is generally regarded as one of the wisest and best of the kings of Judah (18:5–7; 2 Chronicles 31:20–21). At the commencement of his reign, he entirely reverses the wicked policy of his father Ahaz, and with true zeal destroys the idols and heathen temples that had been set up in the land, restoring and purifying the worship of Jehovah. Having taken extensive steps to restore God-honouring temple worship, King Hezekiah calls the nation to unite in the celebration of a great Passover (2 Chronicles 30:5).

Some years later, when attacked by Sennacherib, king of Assyria, Hezekiah places his entire confidence in Jehovah. With a heaven-sent miracle, Judah is delivered from the enemy.

Shortly after these events, Hezekiah becomes seriously ill and is dying. Isaiah the prophet visits him and says, "Set your house in order, for you shall die, and not live" (20:1). The reaction of King Hezekiah once more indicates his godliness. He prays and weeps before the Lord. The Lord responds by giving a message through Isaiah:

> Return and tell Hezekiah the leader of My people, "Thus says the LORD, the God of David your father: 'I have heard your prayer, I have seen your tears; surely I will heal you. On the third day you shall go up to the house of the LORD. And I will add to your days fifteen years'" (20:5–6).

A miraculous sign is given to King Hezekiah in confirmation of the promise of God (20:11). In response to his illness and remarkable recovery, Hezekiah composes a beautiful psalm of praise to the Lord (Isaiah 38:10–20).

Manasseh in Judah: 697–642 B.C. (21:1–18; cf. 2 Chronicles 33:1–20)

Manasseh is twelve when he becomes king, and he reigns in Jerusalem for fifty-five years. He is a complete contrast to his father Hezekiah. No doubt under the influence of the corrupt priests and false prophets who unsuccessfully tried to influence his father, Manasseh succumbs and follows the pagan practices of the neighbouring nations

---

[18] See the fuller account, including the fourth religious revival since the division of the kingdom, recorded in 2 Chronicles 29:1–32:33.

surrounding Judah, and even exceeds their evil and corruption (21:9,11; cf. Isaiah 28:7,14–15; 30:9–11). He rebuilds the pagan places of worship that his father Hezekiah had destroyed. He builds altars to the Baals, makes wooden idols and worships the gods of the Assyrians. He builds two altars to the Assyrian gods and places them in the temple of the living God. He sacrifices some of his sons as burnt offerings to the god Moloch in the Valley of the Son of Hinnom.[19] This vile practice of sacrificing children to Moloch was introduced into Judah by Manasseh's godless grandfather, King Ahaz (2 Chronicles 28:3). King Manasseh has a devastating influence upon the nation and brings Judah very low spiritually and morally.

"And the LORD spoke to Manasseh and his people, but they would not listen" (2 Chronicles 33:10). As a result of this disobedience and refusal to listen, the Lord brings severe punishment upon Manasseh through the hands of the Assyrians. He is captured by Assyrian generals and taken with nose-hooks and chains back to Babylon.

Then a wonderful change takes place in the mind and heart of King Manasseh:

> Now when he was in affliction, he implored the LORD his God, and humbled himself greatly before the God of his fathers, and prayed to Him; and He received his entreaty, heard his supplication, and brought him back to Jerusalem into his kingdom. Then Manasseh knew that the LORD was God (2 Chronicles 33:12–13).

Manasseh sincerely repents and turns in true faith to God. On his return to Jerusalem, he begins to undo all the harm he had perpetrated. He takes away the foreign gods and the idols from the temple; he tears down all the altars that he had built in Jerusalem; he repairs the altar of the Lord and sacrifices peace offerings and thank offerings on it, and he commands the people of Judah "to serve the LORD God of Israel" (2 Chronicles 33:15–16).

---

[19] In the New Testament, the word *hell* is used nine times to translate the Greek word *Gehenna* (e.g. Luke 12:5), which derives from "the Valley of Hinnom," south of Jerusalem, where, in New Testament times, rubbish and dead animals from the city were burned.

Amon in Judah: 642-640 B.C. (21:19-26; cf. 2 Chronicles 33:21-25)

Amon reigns only two years. Evidently unaffected by his father's repentance, Amon follows in the practice of idolatry.

Josiah in Judah: 640-609 B.C. (22:1-23:30)[20]

Josiah succeeds to the throne at the age of eight and by his mid-teens shows signs of true conversion (2 Chronicles 34:3). At the age of twenty, he begins a thorough reformation of religion throughout the whole nation. Rediscovery of the Book of the Law (22:8)[21] has a profound effect upon the king. He becomes even more concerned for himself and the people in relation to the living God.

Josiah responds with a sincere commitment to follow the Lord and obey the law of Moses. He calls upon the people to join him in making a solemn covenant with the Lord. A great Passover to the Lord is celebrated at his command. This Passover is particularly distinguished by two things: first, the inclusion of the remnant of the ten tribes of Israel together with the nation of Judah—including Benjamin (2 Chronicles 35:18); and, secondly, the fact that the celebration was conducted strictly in accordance with the law of Moses (the Passover in the days of Hezekiah was held on a day other than that stipulated in God's law because there were not enough priests already consecrated for the service; neither did all the people fulfil the purification requirements—2 Chronicles 30:2-3,17-20).

The calibre and uniqueness of King Josiah are summed up as follows: "Now before him there was no king like him, who turned to the LORD with all his heart, with all his soul, and with all his might, according to all the Law of Moses; nor after him did any arise like him" (23:25). There is an obvious allusion here to the law of Moses, where it is written: "You shall love the LORD your God with all your heart, with all your soul, and with all your strength. And these words which I command you today shall be in your heart" (Deuteronomy 6:5-6).

Josiah is killed in battle. For his burial in Jerusalem, the prophet Jeremiah composes a funeral hymn that continued to be sung for many

---

[20] See the fuller account, including the fifth religious revival since the division of the kingdom, recorded in 2 Chronicles 34:1-35:27.

[21] This may have been the original copy of the law of Moses (2 Chronicles 34:14).

years afterward (2 Chronicles 35:25). A copy of that manuscript is no longer in existence.

Jehoahaz in Judah: 609 B.C. (23:31-34; cf. 2 Chronicles 36:1-4)
Upon the death of godly Josiah, the people proclaim Jehoahaz, his younger son, king. Jehoahaz reigns only three months yet earns the reputation of doing "evil in the sight of the LORD, according to all that his fathers had done" (23:32). Jehoahaz is appropriately nicknamed "Shallum" (meaning, "retribution") by the prophet Jeremiah as he relays the judgement of God upon him (Jeremiah 22:11-17). The prophet Ezekiel compares Jehoahaz to a young lion that learned to catch prey and devour men who, when the nations hear, is captured in a pit and led to the land of Egypt (Ezekiel 19:3-4).

Jehoiakim in Judah: 609-598 B.C. (23:35-24:7; cf. 2 Chronicles 36:5-8)
King Jehoiakim proves no better a king than his younger brother Jehoahaz. He follows in the tradition of his ungodly ancestors. Jeremiah speaks of him as a bad king who will be "buried with the burial of a donkey, dragged and cast out beyond the gates of Jerusalem" (Jeremiah 22:19), and not missed by anyone (Jeremiah 22:18).

In the third year of Jehoiakim's reign, Nebuchadnezzar, king of Babylon, invades Judah and lays siege to the city of Jerusalem (Daniel 1:1-2). He fastens the king in chains in preparation for his deportation to Babylon (2 Chronicles 36:6). It would seem that Jehoiakim assures Nebuchadnezzar of his willing allegiance and therefore he is released and allowed to stay on the throne of Judah paying tribute to Babylon. Some of the king's descendants and some of the nobles are taken into captivity. Among those Jewish exiles is a young man named Daniel who is destined by God to become a great prophet (Daniel 1:3-6).

King Jehoiakim is responsible for many atrocities during his reign: "he had filled Jerusalem with innocent blood, which the LORD would not pardon" (24:4), even if great intercessors like Moses and Samuel were to stand before him (Jeremiah 15:1). One such victim of Jehoiakim is the prophet Urijah who prophesies against Jerusalem and Judah, is pursued into Egypt, brought back and killed in Jerusalem (Jeremiah 26:20-23). The evil reign of Jehoiakim spans eleven years and terminates with his unceremonious death (Jeremiah 36:30).

Jehoiachin in Judah: 598–597 B.C.. (24:8–16; cf. 2 Chronicles 36:9–10)
Upon the death of his father Jehoiakim, eighteen-year-old Jehoiachin succeeds to the throne. He reigns only three months and ten days (2 Chronicles 36:9) and follows in the evil practices of his godless ancestors. Jeremiah the prophet speaks words of warning to the king whom he refers to as Coniah (Jeremiah 22:24–30), but King Jehoiachin shows no sorrow, no repentance. Like Jehoahaz, he is as a lion devouring men, until he is trapped and deported in chains to Babylon (Ezekiel 19:5–7).

Zedekiah in Judah: 597–586 B.C.. (24:17–20; cf. 2 Chronicles 36:11–13)
Upon the deportation of Jehoiachin to Babylon, Nebuchadnezzar places Jehoiachin's uncle Mattaniah (whose name he changes to Zedekiah) on the throne of Judah. He is under the influence and control of the powerful nobles in the land (Jeremiah 38:1–6,24–26). Like them he does not listen to the Word of God through the prophet Jeremiah (Jeremiah 37:2; 2 Chronicles 36:12).

Nebuchadnezzar marches against Judah. When Jerusalem is taken, Zedekiah tries to escape. He is captured on the plains of Jericho, and blinded (25:7). Two seemingly contradictory prophecies come true: "Zedekiah king of Judah shall not escape from the hand of the Chaldeans, but shall surely be delivered into the hand of the king of Babylon, and shall speak with him face to face, and see him eye to eye" (Jeremiah 32:4); and, "'I will bring him to Babylon, to the land of the Chaldeans; yet he shall not see it, though he shall die there" (Ezekiel 12:13).

The Babylonians sack Jerusalem; they destroy the temple, the palace, all substantial houses and the city wall. They take all civil and religious leaders back to Babylon where they are executed (Jeremiah 52:24–27). The remaining people of Jerusalem are taken captive to Babylon, with the exception of poor vine-dressers and farmers who are left to tend the land (25:12) with Gedaliah as governor. In three invasions, Nebuchadnezzar has taken a total of 4,600 captives (Jeremiah 52:30). The remaining inhabitants experience internal strife and flee to Egypt, against the word of Jeremiah the prophet (Jeremiah 43:5–7).

The kingdom of Judah is at an end.

2 KINGS / **CHRIST AND HIS CHURCH**

In many ways the spiritual encouragement of the 2 Kings is principally to be found in the early section recounting the lives of the two prophets Elijah and Elisha. They both play an important role in the purposes of God that centre in his Son, the Lord Jesus Christ.

TYPES AND PROPHECIES

1. Elijah, John and Jesus Christ

Elijah is a type of John the Baptist, the forerunner of Jesus Christ. Like Enoch (Genesis 5:24), Elijah did not experience death. He was privileged to be translated to heaven.

The return of Elijah is predicted at the close of the Old Testament period (c. 400 B.C.): "Behold, I will send you Elijah the prophet before the coming of the great and dreadful day of the LORD" (Malachi 4:5). John the Baptist is the fulfilment of this remarkable prophecy.

John knew of his special connection with the prophet Elijah. An angel of the Lord visited his father Zacharias while he was burning incense in the temple (Luke 1:9,11). The angel informed Zacharias that he and his wife Elizabeth were to have a son in their old age, one who would be special:

> For he will be great in the sight of the Lord, and shall drink neither wine nor strong drink. He will also be filled with the Holy Spirit, even from his mother's womb. And he will turn many of the children of Israel to the Lord their God. He will also go before Him in the spirit and power of Elijah, "to turn the hearts of the fathers to the children," and the disobedient to the wisdom of the just, to make ready a people prepared for the Lord (Luke 1:15–17).

A further confirmation that John understood his connection with the prophet Elijah is indicated by the way he dressed "in camel's hair, with a leather belt around his waist" (Matthew 3:4; cf. 2 Kings 1:8; see also Zechariah 13:4, where the "robe of coarse hair" is the uniform of the true prophet, used occasionally by false prophets in order to deceive).

Years later, when challenged by priests and Levites from Jerusalem who asked who he was, John denied being Elijah and claimed to be nothing other than the forerunner of the Lord (John 1:21–23; cf. Isaiah 40:3). The Lord Jesus indicates how this apparent contradiction is resolved. Speaking of John the Baptist, the Saviour says,

> Assuredly, I say to you, among those born of women there has not risen one greater than John the Baptist; but he who is least in the kingdom of heaven is greater than he…. *And if you are willing to receive it, he is Elijah who is to come.* He who has ears to hear, let him hear! (Matthew 11:11,14–15, emphasis added).

John was not literally Elijah (John 1:21), but he came "in the spirit and power of Elijah" (Luke 1:17).

Later the Lord informs his disciples,

> Jesus answered and said to them, "Indeed, Elijah is coming first and will restore all things. But I say to you that *Elijah has come already*, and they did not know him but did to him whatever they wished. Likewise the Son of Man is also about to suffer at their hands." *Then the disciples understood that He spoke to them of John the Baptist* (Matthew 17:11–13, emphasis added).

2. Elijah, Moses and Jesus Christ

Elijah and Moses are linked in the final promise of the Old Testament:

> Remember the Law of Moses, My servant,
> Which I commanded him in Horeb for all Israel,
> With the statutes and judgments.
> Behold, I will send you Elijah the prophet
> Before the coming of the great and dreadful day of the Lord
> (Malachi 4:4–5).

In the New Testament, the strongest connection is confirmed between Elijah, Moses and the Lord Jesus Christ. When the Lord Jesus took Peter, James and John to the Mount of Transfiguration, they were to witness an amazing sight. Not only did they see the remarkable splendour of deity shining from the person of the Lord Jesus Christ when the Saviour's "face shone like the sun, and His clothes became as white as the light" (Matthew 17:2; cf. Hebrews 1:3), they also heard the voice which came "from the Excellent Glory: 'This is My beloved Son, in whom I am well pleased'" (2 Peter 1:17). Involved in the whole episode were two men from the past—Moses and Elijah, standing with the Lord Jesus. These two "appeared in glory and spoke of His decease [Greek: *exodos*]" (Luke 9:31). Fourteen hundred years had passed since Moses had died and been secretly buried by the Lord (Deuteronomy 34:5-6). Eight hundred and fifty years had passed since Elijah had been translated "by a whirlwind into heaven" (2:11). These two great champions of the faith represent the law and the prophets respectively.

> Moses and Elijah were great men in their day; but Peter and his companions were to remember that in nature, dignity, and office, they were far below Christ. He was the true sun: they were the stars depending daily on His light. He was the root: they were the branches. He was the Master: they were the servants. Their goodness was all derived: His was original and His own. Let them honour Moses and the prophets, as holy men; but if they would be saved they must take Christ alone for their Master, and glory only in Him. "Hear ye Him."[22]

Jesus said, "Do not think that I came to destroy the Law or the Prophets. I did not come to destroy but to fulfill. For assuredly, I say to you, till heaven and earth pass away, one jot or one tittle will by no means pass from the law till all is fulfilled" (Matthew 5:17-18).

3. Elijah, Elisha and Jesus Christ

Shortly after the amazing incident on Mount Carmel, Elijah journeyed far south, out of the land of Israel, through the land of Judah, into the wilderness region, arriving at his destination at Horeb, the mountain of the Lord (1 Kings 19:8). It was here on Mount Sinai in Horeb that the Lord had called Moses to be leader of the children of Israel (Exodus 3:1-4:17). Here too, the law was given, the priesthood instituted and the tabernacle constructed. It is to this mountain that the Lord directs the prophet Elijah. Here Elijah is given a further commission from

---

[22] J.C. Ryle. *Expository Thoughts on the Gospels: St. Matthew* (Cambridge: James Clarke, 1973), 208-209.

God. His work is not yet over. One of the tasks he is to perform is to anoint Elisha the son of Shaphat of Abel Meholah as prophet in his place (1 Kings 19:16). Mount Sinai is very much associated with the law, but God's glory is not fully expressed in the law. His true glory is revealed in grace. Elijah is the forerunner of Elisha, as John the Baptist is the forerunner of Christ. Both Elijah and John the Baptist anoint their successors at the Jordan River. In the contrast of their characters and of their missions, Elijah is a type of John the Baptist and Elisha a type of our Saviour:

> The coming of Elisha was prophetic of Christ. Of all the prophets Elisha was the most remarkable type of Christ. His name means "The Salvation of God" and the name of his father Shaphat means "Justice" or "Judgement." Abel-Meholah where he dwelt signifies the place of mourning and weakness, for Christ was the Man of Sorrows, crucified through weakness—the weakness of human nature and patient submission to the holy will of the Father.[23]

All the miracles of Elisha were miracles of mercy and link with the Lord Jesus Christ.[24] Elisha fed the hungry, cured the leper, healed the sick, raised the dead, and thereby provides a wonderful illustration of "the Coming One" (Matthew 11:3–5). The cursing of the children at Bethel was not a miracle but a judgement. Christ came for judgement as well as for mercy (John 9:39). Even in death, Elisha is a type of Christ, for when a dead man's corpse touched the bones of the prophet, the dead man revived; in the same way, there is life through the death of Christ. He has died that we might live.

2 KINGS / **CONCLUSION**

The reign of Solomon had a profound effect upon the nation of Israel. His rise meant prosperity and power for the nation; his fall into a terrible spiritual state opened the way for a major deterioration in the

---

[23] Charles D. Alexander, *Elijah: 'Crouching Coward' or Hero of the Faith?* (Liverpool: Bible Exposition Fellowship, n.d.), 17.

[24] Miracles are only associated with three sets of men: Moses and Joshua, Elijah and Elisha, Jesus and his apostles.

religious and moral life of the people. It can be seen how far the nation had fallen under the reign of Solomon from the fact that, only a short time after his death, Jeroboam could introduce the worship of golden calves without creating a public outcry.

The separate nation of Israel existed for just a little over 200 years, from 931 to 721 B.C. Its entire history is an almost unbroken chain of wickedness, with each successive king coming to the throne through the murder of his predecessor. The much smaller nation, Judah, existed longer—almost 350 years, until 586 B.C.

> The kings of Judah are judged in accordance with the promise given to David in 2 Samuel 7:12–16, whereas those of the northern kingdom, all of whom are condemned, are condemned because they have continued in the sin of Jeroboam the son of Nebat who made Israel to sin.[25]

At the close of 2 Kings the ten tribes of Israel are in exile in Assyria and the two tribes of Judah are in exile throughout Babylon. "It lay in the plan of the divine providence to abandon them to oppression, to lead them to repentance through the school of misery."[26] The temple, palace and city of Jerusalem lie in ruins. David's kingdom appears to have been destroyed. Disobedience to the law of God through Moses and the breaking of the covenant have resulted in God's punishment.

But the Lord will not forget his ancient promises. The nation will rise again—as from the dead!

---

[25] Edward J. Young, *An Introduction to the Old Testament* (Grand Rapids: Eerdmans, 1949), 189.
[26] Ernest W. Hengstenberg, *History of the Kingdom of God under the Old Testament*, vol. 2 (Edinburgh: T & T Clark, 1877), 139

2 KINGS / **APPLICATION AND REFLECTION**

1. Wicked youths

The incident at Bethel is a sober reminder that "God is not mocked" (Galatians 6:7); that children must be brought up "in the training and admonition of the Lord" (Ephesians 6:4); and that those who trouble the godly will be punished (2 Thessalonians 1:6). The wisest of men said, "Even a child is known by his deeds, by whether what he does is pure and right" (Proverbs 20:11). God's restraints on children operate "largely through parental control—moral training in the home, wholesome instruction and discipline in the school, and adequate punishment of young offenders by the state"[27] (cf. Proverbs 22:6,15; 13:24; 19:18).

2. Pure worship

Some time after the majority of the people of the northern kingdom of Israel had been taken into captivity to Assyria, Esarhaddon, king of Assyria, brought in replacements (Ezra 4:2). He brought people from the five nations of Babylon, Cuthah, Ava, Hamath and Sepharvaim (17:24), who brought their own pagan religious practices with them and amalgamated them with a corrupted form of the worship of Jehovah (17:41). These are the ancestors of the Samaritans of New Testament times who were much detested by the Jews (John 4:9).

In a remarkable way, the Samaritan woman who met the Lord Jesus at the well of Sychar is a representative of her race. She had been married five times, and the man she was currently living with was not her husband (John 4:18).

> She had had five husbands; and he whom she now had was not her husband, not having deigned to connect himself with her in marriage. So with the nation. It had previously been in fivefold spiritual marriage with its idols, and this marriage had been dissolved as frivolously as it had been concluded. The people sued for marriage with Jehovah; but this was denied them, because they did not belong to Israel.[28]

---

[27] Pink, *Gleanings from Elisha*, 47.
[28] Ernest W. Hengstenberg, *Commentary on the Gospel of St John*, vol. 1 (1865; Minneapolis, Minnesota: Klock and Klock, 1980), 230.

The Samaritan woman, as, indeed, her whole nation, needed to turn in faith to Christ before God could be worshipped "in spirit and truth" (John 4:24; cf. vv. 41-42). It is "through Jesus Christ" only and exclusively that the penitent believer is able "to offer up spiritual sacrifices acceptable to God" (1 Peter 2:5).

3. Rulers and nations

Throughout the history of Judah and Israel there is more often than not a clear correlation between the spiritual state of the king and that of the nation. Usually when a godly king governs Judah, the people fear the living God. The result is that the nation prospers. When a godless, evil king rules Judah, then the people tend to become more idolatrous and immoral. The result is that the nation suffers defeat in battles and domestic disasters. Occasionally there is an exception to the maxim: "Like king, like nation." One such exception is to be found during the reign of Jotham. King Jotham is described as a man who "did what was right in the sight of the LORD" (2 Chronicles 27:2). He "became mighty, because he prepared his ways before the LORD his God" (2 Chronicles 27:6). In spite of this godly example in the king, the nation as a whole still acted corruptly (2 Chronicles 27:2; Isaiah 2:5-9; 5:7-30; Micah 1:5; 2:1-2).

The spiritual message of the book as a whole is that rulers have a powerful influence for good or bad upon a nation. This should give cause for concern in our own day and our own land. While modern states are not monarchies like Israel and Judah, it is still true that "Righteousness exalts a nation, but sin is a reproach to any people" (Proverbs 14:34). It is imperative that the people of God pray for those who have the rule over them:

> Therefore I exhort first of all that supplications, prayers, intercessions, and giving of thanks be made for all men, for kings and all who are in authority, that we may lead a quiet and peaceable life in all godliness and reverence. For this is good and acceptable in the sight of God our Savior, who desires all men to be saved and to come to the knowledge of the truth (1 Timothy 2:1-4).

The first object of such prayer is to enable the people of God to "lead a quiet and peaceable life in all godliness and reverence." The second object of such prayer is to enable the work of the gospel to have free course in the land. Our prayer might be:

Oh, that You would rend the heavens!
That You would come down!
That the mountains might shake at Your presence—
As fire burns brushwood,
As fire causes water to boil—
To make Your name known to Your adversaries,
That the nations may tremble at Your presence! (Isaiah 64:1-2)

1 CHRONICLES

MEANING	AUTHOR	KEY THOUGHT
"events of the days"	**Unknown** *(possibly Ezra)*	**God reigns over all**

THEME

The sovereignty of God: blessing obedience, punishing disobedience

THEME VERSE

Yours is the kingdom, O Lord,
And You are exalted as head over all.
Both riches and honor come from You,
And You reign over all.
1 CHRONICLES 29:11–12

1 CHRONICLES / **SUMMARY**

PART 1 / **GENEALOGIES** — 1:1–9:44

1. **Patriarchal period** — 1:1–54
   a. Adam to Abraham — 1:1–27
   b. Descendants of Abraham — 1:28–54

2. **National period** — 2:1–9:44
   a. Sons of Israel — 2:1–2
   b. Judah to David — 2:3–17
   c. The families of Hezron, Jerahmeel and Caleb — 2:18–55
   d. The familes of David, Solomon and Jeconiah — 3:1–24
   e. The families of Judah and Simeon — 4:1–43
   f. The families of Reuben, Gad and Manasseh (east) — 5:1–26
   g. The families of Levi and Aaron — 6:1–81
   h. Other families — 7:1–40
   i. The families of Benjamin (including King Saul) — 8:1–40
   j. Inhabitants of Jerusalem, etc. — 9:1–44

PART 2 / **DAVID'S REIGN** — 10:1–29:30   *Compare with*

1. **The overthrow and death of Saul** — 10:1–14   1 Samuel 31:1–13

2. **David's coronation and reign** — 11:1–22:19
   a. David, king over all Israel, moves to Jerusalem — 11:1–9   2 Samuel 5:1–12
   b. David's mighty men — 11:10–12:40   2 Samuel 23:8–39
   c. David's mistake in transporting the ark — 13:1–14   2 Samuel 6:1–11
   d. David's victory over the Philistines — 14:1–17   2 Samuel 5:17–25
   e. The ark brought to Jerusalem — 15:1–29   2 Samuel 6:12–23
   f. A great festival of thanksgiving — 16:1–43

				Compare with
g.	David's desire to build a temple is not permitted		17:1–27	2 Samuel 7
h.	Great military victories		18:1–17	2 Samuel 8:1–18
i.	Trouble from Ammon and Syria		19:1–19	2 Samuel 10:1–19
j.	Ammon subdued and Philistine giants destroyed		20:1–8	2 Samuel 11: 1
k.	The sinful census of Israel and Judah		21:1–30	2 Samuel 24:1–25
l.	Preparation for building the temple by Solomon		22:1–19	

3. **David's final years** — 23:1–29:30
   a. The organization of Levites, priests, musicians, gatekeepers, treasurers, military leaders and officials — 23:1–27:34
   b. David's instructions to the leaders and to Solomon concerning the building of the temple — 28:1–21
   c. Offerings for building the temple — 29:1–9
   d. David praises God in the presence of the people — 29:10–20
   e. Solomon anointed king of Israel — 29:21–25
   f. The death of David — 29:26–30 — 1 Kings 2:10–11

1 CHRONICLES

Every historian writes from a particular viewpoint. Each event is selected on a predetermined basis (cf. John 20:30–31; 21:25). Everything cannot be included. The historian of Chronicles (1 and 2 Chronicles were one book in the original version) is making his selection on the basis of a clear goal and purpose. He is tracing the history of the chosen people of Israel, and in particular, the tribe of Judah from which the Messiah will rise (Genesis 49:10). The content "is solid history, but the selective character of that content reveals a thoroughgoing theological and spiritual purpose."[1]

Some of the historical descriptions found in 1 and 2 Chronicles are almost identical with those of the earlier books: 1 Chronicles contains material found in 2 Samuel; and 2 Chronicles contains material found in 1 and 2 Kings. Whereas in 2 Samuel the main concern is with the political aspects of David's kingdom, 1 Chronicles views David's kingdom from the religious perspective, the spiritual welfare of the nation and the continuity of the covenant promise. In a similar manner, 1 and 2 Kings contain prophetic judgements and historical records of Israel and Judah, whereas 1 and 2 Chronicles contain priestly hopes and spiritual outlook on blessings and punishments of Judah only.

The books of Chronicles form, however, much more than a mere supplement to the other historical books. They are an independent work in which the history of the chosen people is related in a new manner, and from a new vantage-point. While often the same events are recorded, they are nevertheless viewed from a different perspective. "In Samuel and Kings we have the facts of history; here we have the Divine words and thoughts about these facts."[2] In the former books these facts are related from a human standpoint; in Chronicles they are viewed from a divine standpoint. Chronicles provides us, therefore, with a more heavenly perspective.

---

[1] Irving L. Jensen, *Jensen's Survey of the Old Testament: Search and Discover* (Chicago: Moody, 1978), 207.

[2] Jensen, *Jensen's Survey of the Old Testament*, 207.

Table 10. The source material for the author of Chronicles

Source material	Citation
The book of the kings of Israel	1 Chronicles 9:1; 2 Chronicles 20:34
The chronicles of King David	1 Chronicles 27:24
The book of Samuel the seer*	1 Chronicles 29:29
The book of Nathan the prophet*	1 Chronicles 29:29; cf. 2 Chronicles 9:29
The book of Gad the seer*	1 Chronicles 29:29
The prophecy of Ahijah the Shilonite	2 Chronicles 9:29
The visions of Iddo the seer	2 Chronicles 9:29
The book of Shemaiah the prophet	2 Chronicles 12:15
The book of Iddo the seer concerning genealogies	2 Chronicles 12:15
The annals of the prophet Iddo	2 Chronicles 13:22
The book of the kings of Judah and Israel	2 Chronicles 16:11; 25:26
The book of Jehu the son of Hanani	2 Chronicles 20:34
The many oracles in the annals of the book of the kings	2 Chronicles 24:27
The writings of the prophet Isaiah the son of Amoz	2 Chronicles 26:22
Probably the actual letters of Sennacherib king of Assyria	2 Chronicles 32:17
The vision of Isaiah the prophet, the son of Amoz	2 Chronicles 32:32
The sayings of Hozai	2 Chronicles 33:19
The written instruction of David†	2 Chronicles 35:4
The written instruction of Solomon†	2 Chronicles 35:4

* These may be references to parts of what we now know as 1 and 2 Samuel.
† The last two may have had joint authorship

1 CHRONICLES / **AUTHOR**

There is a very clear resemblance in style and language between the two books of Chronicles and those of Ezra and Nehemiah. The contents suggest a priestly authorship: emphasis on genealogies, the temple, the priesthood, obedience to the law of God, and the Davidic line from Judah. Consequently, 1 and 2 Chronicles are generally credited to Ezra the priest, who was a skilled scholar and teacher of the Jewish law

(Ezra 7:6). The author functioned like a research historian drawing on a considerable range of material (see Table 10).[3] While a number of these books, records, genealogies and letters may refer to the same source under a different title, it is still evident that a wide range of material was available to the author.

The books of Chronicles were probably written shortly after the Babylonian captivity in 536 B.C. If this were the case, it would explain why, having been written for the Jews (contraction of "Judahs") who were returning from the Babylonian exile, it contains a more positive emphasis than either the books of Samuel or Kings. Its purpose is *to encourage the returning exiles* to rebuild the temple at Jerusalem, for God has not forgotten his covenant promises to his people: "All is not lost; though the glory has departed and they are under the control of Gentile powers, God still has a future for them. The throne of David was gone but the line of David still stood."[4]

This book teaches the strong lessons of Israel's history: apostasy, idolatry, intermarriage with Gentiles and lack of unity were the reasons for their recent ruin. The Babylonian captivity had a profound effect upon the returning Jews and their descendants: "It is significant that after the exile, Israel never again worshipped foreign gods."[5]

1 CHRONICLES / **HISTORICAL SETTING**

The two books of Chronicles cover the history of the chosen people of God over a period of thirty-five centuries, from creation to the proclamation of Cyrus, king of the Medes and Persians, encouraging the Jews to return to Jerusalem (539 B.C.).

1 Chronicles divides into two periods: the genealogies from Adam to David (1:1–9:44), and the reign of David over the united kingdom of Israel and Judah from 1003–970 B.C. (10:1–29:30).

---

[3] According to the non-inspired historical record of 2 Maccabees 2:13–15, Nehemiah collected an extensive library which would have been available to Ezra for his research.
[4] Bruce Wilkinson and Kenneth Boa, *Talk Thru the Old Testament* (Nashville: Nelson, 1983), 101.
[5] Wilkinson and Boa, *Talk Thru the Old Testament*, 101.

1 CHRONICLES / **OUTLINE**

PART 1 / **GENEALOGIES (1:1-9:44)**

Of the Old Testament it is declared: "All Scripture is given by inspiration of God, and is profitable for doctrine, for reproof, for correction, for instruction in righteousness, that the man of God may be complete, thoroughly equipped for every good work" (2 Timothy 3:16–17).

The early genealogies might seem dry and uninspiring. The underlying purpose in presenting these ancestral lines is to show the fulfilment of the covenant promises. History is selectively reported to demonstrate that God is at work choosing and preserving a people for himself from the beginning. The line of God's covenant promise is traced from Adam through Abraham to David. The Lord is constantly selecting, constantly choosing: rejecting the unfaithful and disobedient; blessing the faithful and obedient. The one thing that counts is obedience, and the character that grows out of it:

> The purpose of selection, as revealed in these genealogies, is that from the beginning the ultimate is in view…the apparently crooked way is yet the straight way to the goal. The straight way would have followed the inheritance through the firstborn, and that would often have been the straight way to failure and defeat. Whenever God made a new selection, setting aside rights and privileges…choosing men who were not in the line of ordinary human expectation, He did so because His mind was set upon the ultimate goal.[6]

Genealogies were very important to the Jews because of the promises associated with their tribes. The genealogies link the returning exiles with their forefathers and reassure them that they are still God's chosen people. The earliest prophecy of the Messiah simply promised a saviour from the human race (Genesis 3:15). Over time, the specific race and then the particular family from which the Messiah would

---

[6] G. Campbell Morgan, *Student Survey of the Bible* (Iowa Falls: World Bible Publishers, 1993), 123.

emerge were identified: of Abraham (Genesis 12:3); of Judah (Genesis 49:10); of David (2 Samuel 7:12–16).

The genealogies were not only important in relation to the coming of Messiah; they were also necessary for the faithful administration of the temple, its worship and all priestly functions. Carelessness in the past had brought punishment from God (1 Samuel 13:12–14). Only legitimate men of the tribe of Levi were to minister as priests of the living God.

PART 2 / **DAVID'S REIGN (10:1-29:30; cf. 2 SAMUEL 5:1-24:25)**

Following a brief account of the death and dishonour of King Saul at the hands of the Philistines (the Lord's executioners, 10:13–14), and the courageous intervention of the men of Jabesh Gilead, the main theme is introduced: David, king over all Israel.

In 1 Chronicles, King David is presented in all his strength. In consequence there are significant omissions: David's agonizing years with King Saul; his seven-year reign over Judah prior to becoming king of all Israel; his many wives; his sin with Bathsheba and treachery toward Uriah; and the rebellion of his sons Absalom and Adonijah. In this book, with the exception of the census (21:1–30),[7] the king is presented in his best light, for he personifies the hopes of the nation. He is the one to whom the Israelites look for a type of the messiah/deliverer.

Though David is the central character, it is God's dealings with and through David which form the true heart of 1 Chronicles. This is expressed in the covenant and the temple.

God's covenant

The prominent feature, indeed the pivotal point, of this book is the covenant that God made with King David:

> And it shall be, when your days are fulfilled, when you must go to be with your fathers, that I will set up your seed after you, who will be of your sons; and I will establish his kingdom. He shall

---

[7] Included only to explain what led up to the purchase of the threshing-floor of Ornan the Jebusite for the erection of an altar to the Lord, and later to be used as the site for the temple.

build Me a house, and I will establish his throne forever. I will be his Father, and he shall be My son; and I will not take My mercy away from him, as I took it from him who was before you. And I will establish him in My house and in My kingdom forever; and his throne shall be established forever (17:11–14; cf. 2 Samuel 7:12–16; 1 Kings 11:36).

God promises David that a descendant will reign on the throne of Israel forever. All covenant promises of land, blessing, honour and prosperity are tied to this Coming One. Though Solomon will fulfil something of the promises, a greater than Solomon is envisaged (cf. Matthew 12:42).

In 1 Chronicles, the central nation is Judah; the central personality is David; the central issue is the covenant with David; the central objective is the temple. Nation, king, covenant and temple belong together in the unfolding purposes of God.

God's temple

This book provides information not recorded in the history of 2 Samuel: the extensive plans and preparation that David made for the temple and its services of worship. The importance of this project for David, for the Israelites, and for the cause of true religion throughout the world, gradually emerges. The temple is to be the permanent structure to replace the tabernacle in the wilderness as the symbol of the visible presence of God among his people. David was passionate about the cause of God; that is why he cared about the ark of the covenant; that is why he desired to build the temple. But God had determined that David's part in the project would only be *preparatory*. While he is not permitted to build the temple (28:3), David nevertheless prepares the site (21:18,22,28; 2 Chronicles 3:1; cf. Genesis 22:2), draws up the plans, collects the building materials (22:1–5) and structures the duties of the Levites, priests, musicians, singers, gatekeepers and treasurers (23:1–26:32). (See Figure 10.)

The book draws to a close with David's remarkable and beautiful public prayer of praise to God at Solomon's coronation (29:10–25).

Figure 10. Structure of worship in the temple (25:1-31)

	Three prophets	
	David	
Nathan	(Acts 2:29-30)	Gad
(2 Chronicles 29:25)		(2 Chronicles 29:25)
	Four leaders			
	Chenaniah			
Asaph	(15:22)	Heman	Jeduthun	
(25:6)		(25:6)	(25:6)	Total
4 sons		14 sons	6 sons	24
Each son supervised 11 singers				264
Choir:	So the number of them, with their brethren who were instructed in the songs of the Lord, all who were skillful, was two hundred and eighty-eight (25:7)			288
Orchestra:	"four thousand praised the Lord with musical instruments" (23:5)			

1 CHRONICLES / **CHRIST AND HIS CHURCH**

TYPES AND PROPHECIES

1. Son of David

The importance of David in the ancestry of the Messiah is paramount. Announcing the birth of the Lord Jesus Christ, the angel specifically referred to his stepfather as "Joseph, son of David" (Matthew 1:20). Later, when the Lord began his ministry of preaching and healing, the sick frequently pleaded for his help calling, "Son of David, have mercy on us!" (Matthew 9:27; cf. 20:30).

As his ministry progressed, the question arose among the people: "Could this be the son of David?" (Matthew 12:23). Even a Gentile woman addressed him with the cry: "O Lord, son of David!" (Matthew 15:22). The Messianic hopes connected with a descendant of King David reached their zenith with the adulation of the crowd at the Lord's triumphal entry into Jerusalem:

Hosanna to the Son of David!
"Blessed is He who comes in the name of the LORD!"
Hosanna in the highest! (Matthew 21:9)

Not many days before his death, the Lord Jesus posed a question to a group of Pharisees:

"What do you think about the Christ? Whose Son is He?"
They said to Him, "The Son of David."
He said to them, "How then does David in the Spirit call Him 'Lord,' saying:

'The Lord said to my Lord,
"Sit at My right hand,
Till I make Your enemies Your footstool"'?

If David then calls Him 'Lord,' how is He his Son?" And no one was able to answer Him a word (Matthew 22:42–46; cf. Psalm 110:1).

This is not a trick question. It is designed to provoke profound thought. The Lord Jesus is leading them from the known to the unknown, from the clear to the mysterious. Though the Messiah will descend from David, he will be *greater* than David. David's words in Psalm 110 indicate his insight into the person of the Messiah: Jehovah (the LORD) addresses the promised Seed as "Lord." In Psalm 110, God is promising the "Lord," that is, the Messiah, "such pre-eminence, power, authority, and majesty as would be proper only for One who, as to his person, from all eternity was, is now, and forever will be God"[8] (Acts 2:33–36; Ephesians 1:20–23; Philippians 2:5–11; Hebrews 2:9; Revelation 5:1–10).

The deity of the Lord Jesus Christ is not a doubtful or dubious doctrine, as present-day heretics would teach. It is clear from the New Testament that the early Christians were thoroughly convinced from the Old Testament Scriptures and from the words of Jesus. Though

---

[8] William Hendriksen, *The Gospel of Matthew* (Edinburgh: Banner of Truth Trust, 1973), 812.

they never used the term "Trinity," their teaching on the respective persons of Father, Son and Holy Spirit necessitates such a conclusion.[9] The Messiah is not only "of the seed of David according to the flesh," but he is also "declared to be the Son of God with power, according to the Spirit of holiness, by the resurrection from the dead" (Romans 1:3–4).

2. King Messiah

David understood something of the profound relationship that exists between the Lord and his Messiah (Anointed One). He declared God's decree concerning the position of honour ascribed to the Messiah:

> I will declare the decree:
> The Lord has said to Me,
> "You are My Son,
> Today I have begotten You" (Psalm 2:7; cf. Acts 13:33).

In the same psalm, David reveals that Messiah is not only the Son of God but is also the one whom God has set as King over his "holy hill of Zion" (Psalm 2:6). This is the Son of David, Son of God, whose throne will be established forever (17:11–14). David and his kingdom become a type of Christ and his kingdom. The prophets provide deep insight into this connection, with its comparisons and contrasts (Isaiah 9:6–7; 55:3–4; Ezekiel 37:24; 34:23; Amos 9:11).

In Psalm 45, the King is declared to be "the God whose throne is forever and ever.... This is no mere mortal and his everlasting dominion is not bounded by Lebanon and Egypt's river."[10] "Some here see Solomon and Pharaoh's daughter only—they are short-sighted; others see both Solomon and Christ—they are cross-eyed; well-focused spiritual eyes see here Jesus only."[11]

---

[9] See Stuart Olyott's highly readable and convincing books: *Jesus Is Both God and Man—What the Bible Teaches About the Person of Christ* (Darlington: Evangelical Press, 2000); and *The Three are One: What the Bible Teaches About the Trinity* (Welwyn: Evangelical Press, 1979).

[10] Charles Haddon Spurgeon, *The Treasury of David*, 3 vol. (McLean: MacDonald Publishing Company, 1990), 1:315.

[11] Spurgeon, *The Treasury of David*, 1:315.

1 CHRONICLES / **CONCLUSION**

Together, the books of 1 and 2 Chronicles summarize not only the history, but also the theology of the Old Testament: the revelation that God gave of himself at creation, to the patriarchs, through Moses, during the monarchy, exile and restoration.[12]

First Chronicles is concerned from beginning to end to magnify God and give him his rightful place in the worship and service of Israel. King David typifies the godly person who wants his whole life to be devoted to the Lord. The apostle Paul summed up the life of David when he said, "David…served his own generation by the will of God" (Acts 13:36). As shepherd, king, psalmist and prophet, he lived with an eye almost continually set upon the glory and honour of God, and thus he prayed:

> Blessed are You, Lord God of Israel, our Father, forever and ever.
> Yours, O Lord, is the greatness,
> The power and the glory,
> The victory and the majesty;
> For all that is in heaven and in earth is Yours;
> Yours is the kingdom, O Lord,
> And You are exalted as head over all.
> Both riches and honor come from You,
> And You reign over all.
> In Your hand is power and might;
> In Your hand it is to make great
> And to give strength to all.
>
> Now therefore, our God,
> We thank You
> And praise Your glorious name (29:10–13).

---

[12] Andrew Stewart, *A Family Tree: 1 Chronicles simply explained* (Darlington: Evangelical Press, 1997), 11.

1 CHRONICLES / **APPLICATION AND REFLECTION**

1. Obedience

In 1 Samuel 31 it is simply recorded that King Saul met his death in battle with the Philistines. In 1 Chronicles 10:14 it is reported that *the Lord* killed him. The Philistines were merely executioners acting out Jehovah's justice, for King "Saul died for his unfaithfulness which he had committed against the Lord, because he did not keep the word of the Lord" (10:13). An earlier reference to Achan also highlights the same rebellious heart (2:7). Achan knew that all the spoil had to be devoted to the Lord (Joshua 6:17-19; 7:15-25) but he did not choose to obey God's Word. These two both knew what God required and chose to disobey.

A further powerful lesson on obedience is presented in the account of the return of the ark of the covenant to Israel and its eventual transportation to Jerusalem. The historical record in 1 Chronicles (13:1-14; 15:1-16:43) is much longer than that in 2 Samuel (2 Samuel 6:1-23). In the present book, an explanation is given as to why the Lord slew Uzzah and how David admitted Israel's serious error in not consulting the Lord "about the proper order" (13:7,9-11; 15:2,13).

It is evident from these incidents how important obedience is in God's sight. Today, obedience is still a crucial aspect in the life of faith:

> Now by this we know that we know Him, if we keep His commandments. He who says, "I know Him," and does not keep His commandments, is a liar, and the truth is not in him. But whoever keeps His word, truly the love of God is perfected in him. By this we know that we are in Him (1 John 2:3-5).

2. Prayer

Two fine examples of powerful prayer are presented in the early genealogies. These may be easily overlooked, and yet they provide a great incentive to resist fatalism and to plead with God. This is illustrated in the life of an individual and in a group.

Jabez is an example to all believers. He was not content to accept his name and pessimistically wait for it to be fulfilled. He sought God. He pleaded with the Lord. And God answered:

Now Jabez was more honorable than his brothers, and his mother called his name Jabez [*lit.* "He will cause pain"], saying, "Because I bore him in pain." And Jabez called on the God of Israel saying, "Oh, that You would bless me indeed, and enlarge my territory, that Your hand would be with me, and that You would keep me from evil, that I may not cause pain!" So God granted him what he requested (4:9-10).

The second example of prayer is given in the events surrounding a large group of unnamed warriors from the tribes of Reuben, Gad and Manasseh:

The sons of Reuben, the Gadites, and half the tribe of Manasseh had forty-four thousand seven hundred and sixty valiant men, men able to bear shield and sword, to shoot with the bow, and skillful in war, who went to war. They made war with the Hagrites, Jetur, Naphish, and Nodab. And they were helped against them, and the Hagrites were delivered into their hand, and all who were with them, for they cried out to God in the battle. He heeded their prayer, because they put their trust in Him (5:18-20).

In the Scriptures there are many instructions, illustrations and incentives in regard to prayer, whether private or public (e.g. Matthew 6:5-13; Luke 18:1-14; Acts 2:42; Ephesians 6:18; Philippians 4:6-7).

The reason so many people do not pray is because of its cost. The cost is not so much in the sweat of agonizing supplication, as in the daily fidelity to the life of prayer. It is the acid test of devotion. Nothing in the life of Faith is so difficult to maintain. There are those who resent the association of discipline and intensity with prayer.[13]

"True praying is a strenuous spiritual exercise which demands the utmost mental discipline and concentration."[14]

---

[13] Samuel Chadwick, *The Path of Prayer* (London: Hodder and Stoughton, 1931), 16, 13.

[14] Oswald Sanders, *Spiritual Leadership* (Basingstoke: Marshal Morgan and Scott, 1967), 78.

3. Service

Details are given about the Levites and their appointment "to every kind of service of the tabernacle of the house of God" (6:48). They seem to have responded enthusiastically to their duties and responsibilities. Later, some of the priests are described as "very able men for the work of the service of the house of God" (9:13). When the historian calls them "very able men," he is highlighting the importance that only the best is good enough for the service of God.

There is also an emphasis on the considerable *variety* of gifts that were employed in God's service. Years later, the apostle Paul would remind the Christians at Corinth that there is great variation in the spiritual gifts which God the Holy Spirit gives to the children of God:

> There are diversities of gifts, but the same Spirit. There are differences of ministries, but the same Lord. And there are diversities of activities, but it is the same God who works all in all. But the manifestation of the Spirit is given to each one for the profit of all (1 Corinthians 12:4-7).

The efficiency and effectiveness of the local church depends upon each member making his or her individual contribution for the good of the whole. It is only when "every part does its share" that the result is the "growth of the body for the edifying of itself in love" (Ephesians 4:16).

4. No redundancy!

With the prospect of a permanent building, the duties of the Levites relating to the dismantling, transportation and erection of the tabernacle were no longer required (23:26). They were not, however, declared redundant! David wisely designated new duties: maintaining the fabric of the temple, preparing the offerings and utensils, leading daily worship and generally assisting the priests in their religious duties (23:27-32).

> Redundancy is a word that many people in the modern world have come to dread. A person who has been made redundant has lost more than his employment and income, for he has lost his dignity. He feels like someone who has been dismissed as a superfluous human being—surplus to requirements. However, we may be thankful that in the service of God there is no such thing as a redundant person. All God's

people are needed, because when one avenue of service is closed another is opened to them.[15]

5. Leadership skills

In the mighty men surrounding David (11:10-12:38), there is clear evidence of David's ability to train and to inspire others. At Adullam, he had attracted a motley band—men in distress, in debt and everyone who was discontented—and he had become captain over them (1 Samuel 22:2). Under his leadership, these men became a disciplined, highly competent fighting unit.

Eventually, David's army was composed of men who could use "both the right hand and the left" (12:2), indicating not only their competence but also the level of training they had received. There were also men "who could handle shield and spear" (12:8); in other words, they were experts in offensive and defensive warfare.

Of all the mighty men, there was one mightier—David the king. He won their loyalty; he won their hearts (11:15-19). In this, too, he is a type of the Lord Jesus Christ. Christians are inspired by the Saviour's leadership.

Under the New Covenant, the importance of spiritual leadership is emphasized. Besides the regular training given through the weekly exposition of the Word of God (Ephesians 4:11-16), there is also the specific training of future leaders (2 Timothy 2:2). Church leaders are responsible for the training of new leaders. That training should be accompanied by a worthy example: "Imitate me, just as I also imitate Christ" (1 Corinthians 11:1; cf. Philippians 4:9). A godly example inspires others (1 Timothy 4:12).

6. Orderly worship

Though the Lord had never commanded it, or indicated that he required it, David longed to build a temple for the worship of God (17:1). Though not permitted to construct the temple, he did undertake meticulous preparation for it. David was not concerned with a beautiful building for its own sake, nor for any kudos it might bring to his kingdom or city—he was concerned for the pure worship of God. As a prophet, he wrote many beautiful psalms under the inspiration of God. Most were composed for public worship. As already noted, he also made elaborate preparations for training orchestras and choirs so that a high standard of music and song would lead the people in adoration and praise to God.

---

[15] Stewart, *A Family Tree*, 187.

The New Covenant gives great freedom to worship anywhere and at any time, but it does not give licence for shoddy, careless, ill-prepared worship under the guise of spontaneity. "God is not the author of confusion," and he requires that worship in his church "be done decently and in order" (1 Corinthians 14:33,40). The worship of God is still of major importance to God, and to God's people. "True worshipers will worship the Father in spirit and truth; for the Father is seeking such to worship Him" (John 4:23).

> The LORD loves the gates of Zion
> More than all the dwellings of Jacob.
> Glorious things are spoken of you,
> O city of God! (Psalm 87:2-3)

God loves his people individually ("the dwellings of Jacob"), but he delights more in the assembly of the saints at worship ("the gates of Zion"). As Spurgeon comments, "God delights in the prayers and praises of Christian families and individuals, but he has a special eye to the assemblies of the faithful, and he has a special delight in their devotions in their church capacity."[16]

The psalmist makes reference to the new birth that makes a person a member of Zion (Psalm 87:5-6).

---

[16] Spurgeon, *The Treasury of David*, 2:478.

2 CHRONICLES

MEANING	AUTHOR	KEY THOUGHT
"events of the days" *(continued)*	**Unknown** *(possibly Ezra)*	**Preparing the heart to seek God**

THEME

The slippery slope to ruin

THEME VERSE

The Lord is with you while you are with Him. If you seek Him, He will be found by you; but if you forsake Him, He will forsake you.
2 CHRONICLES 15:2

2 CHRONICLES / **SUMMARY**

PART 1 / **THE REIGN OF SOLOMON**	1:1–9:31	*Compare with*
a. Solomon establishes his reign	1:1–17	1 Kings 2:13–4:34
b. The temple	2:1–7:11	
(1) Preparation for the temple	2:1–18	1 Kings 5:1–18
(2) The construction of the temple	3:1–5:1	1 Kings 6:1–7:51
(3) The glory of the Lord fills the temple	5:2–6:11	1 Kings 8:1–13
(4) The dedication of the temple	6:12–7:11	1 Kings 8:22–66
c. The Lord's second appearance to Solomon	7:12–22	1 Kings 9:1–9
d. Solomon's additional achievements	8:1–18	1 Kings 9:15–28
e. Visit of the Queen of Sheba	9:1–12	1 Kings 10:1–13
f. The wealth of Solomon	9:13–28	1 Kings 10:14–29
g. Solomon's death	9:29–31	1 Kings 11:1–43

PART 2 / **CIVIL WAR**	10:1–11:23	
a. The ten tribes of Israel rebel	10:1–19	1 Kings 12:1–19
b. Rehoboam consolidates Judah	11:1–23	1 Kings 12:21–24

PART 3 / **KINGS OF JUDAH**	12:1–36:13	
a. Rehoboam (bad)	12:1–16	1 Kings 14:21–31
b. Abijah/Abijam (bad)	13:1–22	1 Kings 15:1–8
c. Asa (good)	14:1–16:14	1 Kings 15:9–24
d. Jehoshaphat (good)	17:1–20:37	1 Kings 22:41–50
e. Jehoram (bad)	21:1–20	2 Kings 8:16–24
f. Ahaziah (bad)	22:1–9	2 Kings 8:25–29
g. Queen Athaliah (bad)	22:10–23:21	2 Kings 11:1–3
h. Joash (good when under the influence of Johoiada the high priest)	24:1–27	2 Kings 11:4–12:21

			Compare with
i.	Amaziah (began well, ended in idolatry)	25:1-28	2 Kings 14:1-22
j.	Uzziah/Azariah (began well ended badly)	26:1-23	2 Kings 15:1-7
k.	Jotham (good)	27:1-9	2 Kings 15:32-38
l.	Ahaz (bad)	28:1-27	2 Kings 16:1-20
m.	Hezekiah (good)	29:1-32:33	2 Kings 18:1-20:21
n.	Manasseh (bad but repented)	33:1-20	2 Kings 21:1-18
o.	Amon (bad)	33:21-25	2 Kings 21:19-26
p.	Josiah (good)	34:1-35:27	2 Kings 22:1-23:30
q.	Jehoahaz (bad)	36:1-4	2 Kings 23:31-34
r.	Jehoiakim/Eliakim (bad)	36:5-8	2 Kings 23:35-24:7
s.	Jehoiachin (bad)	36:9-10	2 Kings 24:8-16
t.	Zedekiah (bad)	36:11-13	2 Kings 24:17-20

PART 4 / **BABYLONIAN CAPTIVITY** 36:14-21   2 Kings 25:1-21

PART 5 / **THE BEGINNING OF THE RESTORATION OF JUDAH**
    36:22-23

2 CHRONICLES

As noted in the chapter on 1 Samuel, the division into what are now the First and Second Chronicles occurred for purely practical reasons. In the original form, there was only one book of Chronicles. Consequently, what has been written concerning the author and his source material under the introduction to 1 Chronicles equally applies to this second book.

It is still the spiritual aspect of the nation's history that receives the emphasis: the promises of God and his constant faithfulness; the vital importance of God-centred and God-honouring worship; and the power of his Word to transform an individual or a nation.

The historian is dedicated to the encouragement of the Israelites in their Babylonian captivity. In Chronicles, David and Solomon are portrayed as glorious, obedient, all-conquering figures who enjoy not only divine blessing but also the support of the nation. The chronicler does not mention that David only saves the kingdom for Solomon at the last minute due to the intervention of his wife Bathsheba and the prophet Nathan (1 Kings 1).

God's covenant promises, as they centre on King David, Solomon and their descendants, are the overriding concern. Consequently, whereas in the book of Kings, Solomon's wisdom is expressed in terms of wisdom to rule, in 2 Chronicles it is seen primarily as wisdom for building the temple.

2 CHRONICLES / **HISTORICAL SETTING**

First Chronicles closes with the death of King David. Second Chronicles opens with the reign of his son King Solomon and traces the distinction, division and destruction of the kingdom (970–586 B.C.). Focusing on the history of Judah, a bleak picture is presented of a nation in decline and apostasy. Nevertheless, there are striking periods of spiritual revival and religious reformation.

Much of the history recorded in 2 Chronicles is found in 1 and 2 Kings.

2 CHRONICLES / **OUTLINE**

PART 1 / **THE REIGN OF SOLOMON (1:1-9:31)**

Solomon's reign is Israel's golden age of peace and prosperity. The glory and grandeur of Solomon's kingdom span from the border of Egypt to the west and south, to the River Euphrates to the east and north (1 Kings 4:21). The area has been roughly calculated as covering 50,000 square miles[1] (about half the size of the British Isles). But in the vast kingdom of Solomon, it is the temple that dominates. Plans for the temple which dominated the latter part of 1 Chronicles find realization under the leadership of Solomon. The building is to be "exceedingly magnificent, famous and glorious throughout all countries" (1 Chronicles 22:5).

Commenced in the fourth year of Solomon's reign (3:2), 480 years after the delivery of Israel from Egypt (1 Kings 6:1), the temple was the first large single structure to be built by any ruler of Israel. Solomon realized the temple's significance as the house of God, "since heaven and the heaven of heavens cannot contain Him," and at the same time he was aware of his own inadequacy for the task (2:4–6).

The Lord appears to Solomon a second time at the dedication of the completed temple. God clearly states the basis upon which the nation will know his blessing or his punishment:

> If My people who are called by My name will humble themselves, and pray and seek My face, and turn from their wicked ways, then I will hear from heaven, and will forgive their sin and heal their land. Now My eyes will be open and My ears attentive to prayer made in this place (7:14–15).

The worship of God is central to the nation's future; seeking God is the crucial factor in its survival. This theme provides the thread throughout the remaining chapters, for even as the nation deteriorates in its spiritual and moral life there are outstanding periods of spiritual awakening and renewed faithfulness to the Lord.

---

[1] Irving L. Jensen, *Jensen's Survey of the Old Testament: Search and Discover* (Chicago: Moody, 1978), 212.

God gave Solomon outstanding wisdom: he was skilled in pithy and wise sayings, a musician and poet; he was an expert botanist and zoologist; he was a prudent counsellor and king (1 Kings 4:29–34). Solomon wrote the books of Proverbs, Ecclesiastes, Song of Solomon and at least two psalms: Psalm 72 and Psalm 127.

PART 2 / **CIVIL WAR (10:1–11:23)**

As in 1 Chronicles, David's sins in relation to Bathsheba and Uriah are omitted (although the chronicler does refer the reader to the books of Samuel, Nathan and Gad for a fuller account of the reign of David, 1 Chronicles 29:29–30), so in 2 Chronicles there is no mention of Solomon's taking revenge on David's enemies (1 Kings 2). Nor are the sins of Solomon recounted, which in 1 Kings 11 are presented as the reason for the division of the kingdom. The emphasis here falls upon the agents of the division, Jeroboam's rebellion and the inexperience of Solomon's son Rehoboam (13:6–7).

PART 3 / **KINGS OF JUDAH (12:1–36:13)**

The record of the kings of the northern kingdom (Israel) is omitted from 2 Chronicles since the concern of the chronicler is to trace the line of Judah, with special reference to the Lord's covenant promise to David (1 Chronicles 17:11–14) and commitment to the true worship of God in the temple at Jerusalem. These two central concerns were abandoned by the ten tribes of the northern kingdom. There could be no restoration, no true reformation among the people called "Israel" without repentance toward God and a return in submission to the God-ordained ruler out of Judah (Genesis 49:10), descendant of David (2 Samuel 7:12–16), and to the priesthood that God had instituted and the true temple at Jerusalem. The temple symbolizes God's presence with his people and provides a visible link for the Jews uniting their past and their future.

Although there were more bad kings ruling Judah, the sum total of their years on the throne amounts to considerably less than that of the combined reigns of the good kings.

The author is tracing the *spiritual line of promise* and the *preserving power of God*. For this reason, prominence is given to Judah's kings who were noted for leading significant reformations of religion: Asa, Jehoshaphat, Joash (credited entirely to the godly influence exerted upon him by Jehoiada the priest), Hezekiah and Josiah. Five distinct waves of revival and reformation emphasize the connection between seeking God and the well-being of the kingdom.

1. Religious reformation under King Asa (14:1-16:14; cf. 1 Kings 15:9-24)

Unlike his father and his grandfather, Asa does "what was good and right in the eyes of the LORD his God" (14:2). He removes pagan altars, demolishes heathen pillars, chops down wooden images and banishes perverted people from the land. He commands the people of Judah to seek the Lord and to obey his law and commandments.

When the Ethiopians attack with an army twice the size of Judah's, King Asa turns in total reliance upon the Lord and experiences a great and overwhelming victory. The Lord gives a promise with a condition:

> Hear me, Asa, and all Judah and Benjamin. The LORD is with you while you are with Him. If you seek Him, He will be found by you; but if you forsake Him, He will forsake you.... But you, be strong and do not let your hands be weak, for your work shall be rewarded! (15:2,7)

King Asa responds wholeheartedly to the prophecy: we read that he "took courage, and removed the abominable idols from all the land of Judah and Benjamin...and he restored the altar of the LORD" (15:8). He gathers all Judah and Benjamin together with all the God-fearing people who have migrated from the tribal lands of Ephraim, Manasseh and Simeon. All these "entered into a covenant to seek the LORD God of their fathers with all their heart and with all their soul.... And the LORD gave them rest all around" (15:12,15).

Toward the end of his long reign, King Asa seems to lose his earlier confidence in the Lord. Maybe the absence of war for some fifteen years or so has resulted in the king and nation becoming spiritually lethargic. Easy times rarely promote spiritual growth. When Baasha, king of Israel invades Judah (cf. 1 Kings 15:33–16:7), Asa makes a terrible mistake. Relying upon the "arm of the flesh" (32:8), he does not seek the help of God. He gathers together the gold and silver from the temple and from the palace and sends them as a gift to King Ben-Hadad of Syria. With the gift is the request that Ben-Hadad would break his treaty with Israel and make a treaty with Judah, resulting in his withdrawal from Judah. The plan works but the Lord disapproves. Asa ends his days in a spiritually backslidden state and in severe physical pain.

2. Religious reformation under King Jehoshaphat (17:1–20:37; cf. 1 Kings 22:41–50)

Like his father Asa in his earlier days, Jehoshaphat is a godly king, keen to live in obedience to the Lord and to encourage the people of Judah to be faithful to the true God. The blessings of God rest upon his labours, and Jehoshaphat responds by seeking to strengthen the nation spiritually. He sends out civil leaders and Levites throughout all Judah to teach the people the law of God from "the Book of the Law of the LORD"[2] (17:9). This strategy has such an effect that the nations around Judah are gripped by "the terror of Jehovah" and none of them attempts to make war with Judah. Indeed, some of the Philistines and some of the Arabians bring presents to Jehoshaphat to ensure his goodwill toward them.

As a result of a marriage alliance with Israel, followed by a state visit to King Ahab, Judah becomes involved in assisting Israel against the Syrians. The battle that follows leads to Ahab's death. The Lord disapproves of Jehoshaphat's involvement with Israel: "Should you help the wicked and love those who hate the LORD? Therefore the wrath of the LORD is upon you. Nevertheless good things are found in you" (19:2–3). The godly king responds to the rebuke—and the encouragement—by continuing his work of civil and spiritual reformation. The administration of justice is improved throughout the whole land of Judah.

Some years later the Ammonites, with the Moabites and the inhabitants of Mount Seir, come up against Judah. When news of this mighty invasion reaches the king of Judah, he reacts as only the godly can do:

> And Jehoshaphat feared, and set himself to seek the LORD, and proclaimed a fast throughout all Judah. So Judah gathered

---

[2] That is, the Pentateuch, the five books of Moses: Genesis to Deuteronomy.

together to ask help from the LORD; and from all the cities of Judah they came to seek the LORD (20:3–4).

King Jehoshaphat leads the vast congregation in prayer and worship (20:6–12). The Lord responds:

> Then the Spirit of the Lord came upon Jahaziel.... And he said, "Listen, all you of Judah and you inhabitants of Jerusalem, and you, King Jehoshaphat! Thus says the LORD to you: 'Do not be afraid nor dismayed because of this great multitude, for the battle is not yours, but God's.... You will not need to fight in this battle. Position yourselves, stand still and see the salvation of the LORD, who is with you, O Judah and Jerusalem!' Do not fear or be dismayed; tomorrow go out against them, for the LORD is with you" (20:14–15,17).

The king humbles himself before the Lord. He and the whole congregation continue to worship. The following day they experience a remarkable delivery—without wielding a single sword. The battle is indeed the Lord's!

3. Religious reformation under King Joash (24:1–27; cf. 2 Kings 11:4–12:21)

Wicked Queen Athaliah, daughter of Ahab and Jezebel of Israel, seizes the throne of Judah upon the death of her son King Ahaziah. She ushers in one of the bleakest episodes in the history of the Hebrews. Athaliah puts to death all the remaining members of the royal family of Judah (her grandchildren). Only one son of Ahaziah, the young child Joash, escapes. As a one-year-old, he is rescued by his aunt Jehoshabeath, daughter of Jehoram (probably by a wife other than Athaliah) whose husband is the godly high priest Jehoiada (22:11). Joash and his nurse are moved into hiding in the home of the high priest adjoining the court of the temple.

For some years, the God-fearing people among the tribe of Judah must have thought that all their hope was lost. It must have seemed as though the Lord had failed to keep his covenant promise to David. As far as the people of Judah were concerned, there was no remaining male descendant of David (2 Samuel 7:16).

After six years with the wicked Athaliah as queen of Judah, Jehoiada the high priest reveals the rightful heir to the throne, the seven-year-old boy Joash. The temple of Baal is pulled down, its priest killed and its images and altars destroyed. A period of prosperity follows and the worship of the true God is re-established. Joash instigates major repairs of the temple at Jerusalem.

The behaviour of Joash changes at the death of Jehoiada the high priest. He is no longer resolute in following the Lord. Without the presence of the godly priest, Joash comes under the influence of bad counsellors and restores Baal-worship and the building of groves to Ashtoreth. God sends prophets to the people, but they will not listen. Eventually, the Spirit of the Lord directs Zechariah, the son of Jehoiada the priest, with a message for the people. But his message incenses the king—and he orders the assassination of Zechariah! His murder is carried out "in the court of the house of the LORD" (24:21). This atrocity is even more obnoxious because it is performed between the sanctuary (the Holy Place and the Holy of Holies) and the altar of burnt sacrifice (Matthew 23:35). In effect, it is done in the very presence of God.[3] In commanding the death of Zechariah, Joash disregards the years of immense kindness shown to him by Zechariah's father Jehoiada.

4. Religious reformation under King Hezekiah (29:1-32:33; cf. 2 Kings 18:1-20:21)

King Hezekiah is generally regarded as one of the wisest and best of the kings of Judah:

> Thus Hezekiah...did what was good and right and true before the LORD his God. And in every work that he began in the service of the house of God, in the law and in the commandment, to seek his God, he did it with all his heart. So he prospered (31:20-21).

> He trusted in the LORD God of Israel, so that after him was none like him among all the kings of Judah, nor who were before him.

---

[3] The Talmud (a collection of ancient writings on Jewish civil and ceremonial law and tradition) deplores it as one of the most atrocious of Jewish crimes against God's servants. See R.C.H. Lenski, *The Interpretation of St. Matthew's Gospel* (1943; Minneapolis: Augsburg Publishing House, 1961), 919.

For he held fast to the LORD; he did not depart from following Him, but kept His commandments, which the LORD had commanded Moses. The LORD was with him; he prospered wherever he went (2 Kings 18:5–7).

At the commencement of his reign, Hezekiah entirely reverses the wicked policy of his father Ahaz and, with true zeal, destroys the idols and heathen temples that had been set up in the land, restoring and purifying the worship of Jehovah. Having taken extensive steps to restore God-honouring temple worship, King Hezekiah calls the nation to unite in the celebration of a great Passover (30:5). On the day set for the observance of the Passover, there is an atmosphere of genuine repentance, of turning from idolatry and returning to the living God.

Some years later, when Sennacherib becomes king of Assyria (705 B.C.) and marches on Jerusalem, Hezekiah follows good military procedure by creating an aqueduct to reroute the water supply, fortifying the city and ensuring a good supply of weapons (32:1–5). But it is Hezekiah's encouragement to the people which truly demonstrates his godliness. He calls the people to trust in the Lord:

> "Be strong and courageous; do not be afraid nor dismayed before the king of Assyria, nor before all the multitude that is with him; for there are more with us than with him. With him is an arm of flesh; but with us is the LORD our God, to help us and to fight our battles." And the people were strengthened by the words of Hezekiah king of Judah (32:7–8).

Hezekiah places his entire confidence in Jehovah. When the king of Assyria blasphemes God and publishes libellous letters against the king of Judah, Hezekiah takes the letters into the temple and spreads them before the Lord and prays:

> O LORD of hosts, God of Israel, the One who dwells between the cherubim, You are God, You alone, of all the kingdoms of the earth. You have made heaven and earth. Incline Your ear, O LORD, and hear; open Your eyes, O LORD, and see; and hear all the words of Sennacherib, which he has sent to reproach the

living God. Truly, Lord, the kings of Assyria have laid waste all the nations and their lands, and have cast their gods into the fire; for they were not gods, but the work of men's hands—wood and stone. Therefore they destroyed them. Now therefore, O Lord our God, save us from his hand, that all the kingdoms of the earth may know that You are the Lord, You alone (Isaiah 37:16–20).

The future for Jerusalem looks bleak, utterly impossible. The Lord sends Isaiah the prophet to reassure King Hezekiah that his prayers have been heard and his confidence in the living God will be rewarded (2 Kings 19:20–34).

The miraculous delivery is described: "Then the angel of the Lord went out, and killed in the camp of the Assyrians one hundred and eighty-five thousand; and when people arose early in the morning, there were the corpses—all dead" (Isaiah 37:36). The people of God can always rely upon the Lord, even when facing seemingly insurmountable opposition.

5. Religious reformation under King Josiah (34:1–35:27; cf. 2 Kings 22:1–23:30)

Josiah came to the throne of Judah at the age of eight years. When he was sixteen years old, the young king "began to seek the God of his father David" (34:3). At the age of twenty, he began the destruction of the pagan places of worship and the numerous images that littered the country. He travelled extensively throughout the land and personally supervised the destruction of all the paraphernalia of paganism.

At twenty-six years of age, in the eighteenth year of his reign, he began to repair the temple. It was during this work of renovation that Hilkiah the high priest found the lost Book of the Law.[4] This may have been the original copy of the law of Moses (34:14). It is likely that the reading of the law had been prohibited during the evil reigns of Manasseh and Amon.

When passages of this book were read to King Josiah, they had a remarkable effect upon him (34:19). It would seem that Josiah had never before heard these words, though many copies of the law had

---

[4] It was 250 years earlier that Jehoshaphat had instructed the Levites to go throughout Judah to teach from "the Book of the Law of the Lord" (17:9).

been made years earlier under the direction of godly King Hezekiah. It is likely that, with the passage of time and the influence of two godless kings, the people now followed only an outward form of ritual, and had little or no interest in the Word of God.

Josiah responded with great concern for himself and his people. He commanded that the Lord should be consulted. Steps were taken to understand the implications of the law of God and, although Judah was to be punished for her many sins, King Josiah was singularly favoured by the Lord. God said to him,

> …because your heart was tender, and you humbled yourself before God when you heard His words against this place and against its inhabitants, and you humbled yourself before Me, and you tore your clothes and wept before Me, I also have heard you…. Surely I will gather you to your fathers, and you shall be gathered to your grave in peace; and your eyes shall not see all the calamity which I will bring on this place and its inhabitants (34:27-28).

Josiah responded with a sincere commitment to follow the Lord and obey the law given through Moses. He called the people to join him in making a solemn covenant with the Lord (34:30-33).

Out of twenty rulers over Judah, from the division of the kingdom to the captivity, five led spiritual reformations, two others also sought to follow the Lord, another repented in the latter years of his reign, but the remainder were godless and immoral.

PART 4 / **BABYLONIAN CAPTIVITY (36:14-21)**

After godly Josiah, four godless kings follow in quick succession. Over a period of twenty years, three invasions by the Babylonians bring the nation of Judah to her knees. Nobles (including the prophet Daniel), priests (including the prophet Ezekiel) and people are taken captive to Babylon. But the Lord has not yet fulfilled his covenant promise to Judah and to his servant David. The promised Messiah has not yet appeared.

PART 5 / **THE BEGINNING OF THE RESTORATION OF JUDAH (36:22-23)**

Jeremiah's prediction of a seventy-year captivity in Babylon (36:21; Jeremiah 29:10) is fulfilled in two ways: firstly, a *political captivity* in which Jerusalem is controlled by Babylon from 605 B.C. to 539 B.C. with its inhabitants taken into exile in three phases; and, secondly, a *religious captivity* from the destruction of the temple in 586 B.C. to the completion of the new temple in 516 B.C.[5]

Seventy years pass and Babylon is conquered by the Medes and Persians. The king of that vast empire is King Cyrus, of whom the prophet Isaiah had spoken around 200 years before. Cyrus will instigate the return of the Jews to Jerusalem with the object of rebuilding the temple:

> Thus says the LORD, your Redeemer...
> Who says to Jerusalem, "You shall be inhabited,"
> To the cities of Judah, "You shall be built"...
> Who says of Cyrus, "He is My shepherd,
> And he shall perform all My pleasure,
> Saying to Jerusalem, 'You shall be built,'
> And to the temple, 'Your foundation shall be laid'"
> (Isaiah 44:24,26,28).

2 CHRONICLES / **CHRIST AND HIS CHURCH**

TYPES AND PROPHECIES

1. David's line

Satan is constantly trying to thwart the purposes of God. If he can instigate a massacre of the royal family, then the Son of God cannot fulfil the prophecies of the Old Testament. The line of promise was clear: seed of Eve (Genesis 3:15), seed of Abraham (Genesis 12:1-3) and seed of King David. The Lord made a promise to David through Nathan the prophet:

---

[5] Bruce Wilkinson and Kenneth Boa, *Talk Thru the Old Testament* (Nashville: Nelson, 1983), 109.

When your days are fulfilled and you rest with your fathers, I will set up your seed after you, who will come from your body, and I will establish his kingdom. He shall build a house for My name, and I will establish the throne of his kingdom forever (2 Samuel 7:12-13).

Satan was constantly looking for ways to destroy the line of David so that he could discredit God and thwart the coming of his Son as the Messiah, the Promised One. Under the evil Queen Athaliah, the devil almost achieved his objective. When she sought to execute all the members of the royal family of Judah (22:10) she was probably only concerned about protecting her claim to the throne. Behind her was Satan who was seeking the failure of the covenant promises concerning Christ and his church. Athaliah annihilated all her grandchildren. Unbeknown to her, however—and in the wonderful providence of almighty God—one grandson, baby Joash, was rescued from slaughter.

When Syria and Israel attacked Judah they planned the removal of the royal line and the installation of a complete outsider on the throne of Judah (Isaiah 7:1,6). Had they succeeded, what would have become of the promised Seed? The ruler out of Israel must be a descendant not only of Judah (Genesis 49:10), but especially of David. "Yet the LORD would not destroy the house of David, because of the covenant that He had made with David" (21:7).

Wars, assassinations, scheming, persecution and exile threaten the Messianic line, but it remains unbroken from Adam to Jeconiah. The throne was destroyed, but the line continues. The prophecy to David that his throne would be forever is only fulfilled in Christ. The genealogies recorded in Chronicles, which demonstrate the unbroken prophetic line for the Messiah, are continued in the genealogies of Luke 3:23-38 and Matthew 1:1-17.[6] Jesus of Nazareth is demonstrated to fulfil the prophetic criteria, for truly he was "born of the seed of David according to the flesh" (Romans 1:3). The prophecies of the Old Testament *must* be fulfilled. This is God's safeguard to false claims.

---

[6] The differences between the two lists may be explained in that Matthew presents the legal line through Joseph whereas Luke presents the natural line through Mary. See William Hendriksen, *The Gospel of Luke* (Edinburgh: Banner of Truth Trust, 1979), 220-225.

This is God's proof that Jesus of Nazareth is "the Christ, the Son of God" (John 20:31). The Old Testament Scriptures, together with his miracles, ministry, suffering and death, and the declarations of John the Baptist, accredit Jesus of Nazareth as the Son of God (John 5:31–47; Acts 2:22,36; 1 Corinthians 15:3–4).

2. Solomon's temple

Central to 1 Chronicles is God's *covenant* made with David. Central to 2 Chronicles is God's *temple* constructed by Solomon. The history and significance of the temple are central to the biblical teaching concerning Christ and his church.

The temple which David designed and for which he prepared materials and labourers, and which Solomon his son actually constructed, was built "at Jerusalem on Mount Moriah" (3:1). This is the mountain range to which the Lord directed Abraham when he commanded him to sacrifice his son Isaac (Genesis 22:2). That command was never enacted. The Lord intervened. Isaac was spared. Profound connections may be seen between Abraham offering his *son*, his *only son* Isaac, *whom he loved*, and the later action of God himself offering his *Son*, his *only begotten Son*, his *beloved Son*, as the sacrifice for sin—there on that very spot! And no one intervened (Romans 8:32).

The significance of the temple is indicated by the name which it bore in its most ancient form, *Ohel Moed*, which means, "the tabernacle of congregation," the place where God met with his people (cf. Exodus 25:22, 29:43; Numbers 17:4).[7]

The temple that Solomon constructed was only to have a temporary life. Solomon began construction in 966 B.C. and concluded seven years later (1 Kings 6:1,38). The building was destroyed by the invading forces of King Nebuchadnezzar of Babylon in 586 B.C., 380 years after its foundations were laid.

After seventy years of captivity, the Jews were allowed to return home. Under the leadership of Zerubbabel, a new temple was constructed. It was not as impressive in appearance as the first, yet through the prophet Haggai, speaking at the dedication of this second temple, God gave a wonderful promise:

---

[7] Ernest W. Hengstenberg, *Commentary on the Gospel of St John*, vol. 1 (1865; Minneapolis, Minnesota: Klock and Klock, 1980), 146.

"I will fill this temple with glory," says the LORD of hosts..... "The glory of this latter temple shall be greater than the former," says the LORD of hosts. "And in this place I will give peace," says the LORD of hosts (Haggai 2:7,9).

Something was going to occur in this temple that would have drastic and far-reaching effects.

After many years, at the time of our Lord's life on earth, this second temple was enlarged. King Herod financed the extensive alterations that took a total of eighty-three years (19 B.C. to A.D. 64). This temple was destroyed by the invading Romans in A.D. 70. The question then remains: Did the Lord fulfil his promise that the glory of the second temple would exceed the glory of the first? To those who know the living God the question is not, *did* he fulfil his promise but rather, *how* did he fulfil his promise?

The prophet Malachi also gave a prophecy about the second temple:

"Behold, I send My messenger,
And he will prepare the way before Me.
And the LORD, whom you seek,
Will suddenly come to His temple,
Even the Messenger of the covenant,
In whom you delight.
Behold, He is coming,"
Says the LORD of hosts (Malachi 3:1).

John the Baptist is that messenger preparing the way for the Messenger who is Christ (Mark 1:2,4). Jesus Christ is "the LORD, whom you seek... Even the Messenger of the covenant." This is *how* the glory of the second temple exceeded the first because the incarnate Son of God, the very embodiment of the true tabernacle and true temple, personally visited this temple (Matthew 12:6).

There is a further prophecy concerning the temple which was given through Zechariah:

Thus says the LORD of hosts, saying:
"Behold, the Man whose name is the BRANCH!
From His place He shall branch out,

> And He shall build the temple of the LORD;
> Yes, He shall build the temple of the LORD.
> He shall bear the glory,
> And shall sit and *rule on His throne*;
> So He shall be a *priest on His throne*,
> And the counsel of peace shall be between them both"
> (Zechariah 6:12–13, emphasis added).

God promises that the man spoken of here as the Branch, the Messiah (cf. Isaiah 4:2; Jeremiah 23:5–6), will build, not a temple *to* the Lord, but rather *the* temple *of* the Lord. Furthermore, the Messiah would himself be the *glory* of the new temple, and he would rule in a dual capacity as *king and priest*. Such a double function, bearing the two offices of king and priest, was impossible under the terms of the Old Covenant since priests were to descend from Levi and kings were to descend from Judah. Consequently, the Lord had prepared a priestly order *above that* of Aaron and Levi—the order of Melchizedek, the king-priest (Genesis 14:18–20; Hebrews 7:1–10).[8] Messiah comes in this order of priesthood (Psalm 110:4). Christ rules the new temple, *the temple of God*, as King and Priest. He is king over his body the church (Ephesians 1:22–23), ruling, controlling, guarding. He is priest for his church having presented the one supreme sacrifice for sin (Hebrews 10:10) and since he ever lives to make intercession for us (Hebrews 7:24–25).

> He who was predicted as the seed of the woman, as the seed of Abraham, the Son of David, the Branch, the Servant of the Lord, the Prince of Peace, is our Lord, Jesus Christ, the Son of God, God manifest in the flesh. He, therefore, from the beginning has been held up as the hope of the world, the *Salvator hominum*. He was set forth in all his offices, as Prophet, Priest, and King. His work was described as a sacrifice as well as a redemption.[9]

---

[8] See the section "Christ and his church" in the chapter on Genesis.
[9] Charles Hodge, *Systematic Theology*, 3 vol. (Grand Rapids: Eerdmans, 1977), 2:370.

Messiah will personally build the temple of the Lord, the greater temple. That temple is currently under construction. It is the spiritual temple—Christ is the foundation (1 Corinthians 3:11,16), its cornerstone (Ephesians 2:20), its centre and heart (John 2:21). Believers are living stones who come to Christ to be "built up as a spiritual house" (1 Peter 2:5) and with him and in him to form the true temple (1 Corinthians 3:16; 6:19-20). The true temple, the spiritual temple, is Christ and his church.[10]

2 CHRONICLES / **CONCLUSION**

While the number of bad kings is roughly twice the number of good kings, this may lead to the wrong conclusion—that life in Israel during this period was dominated by wicked rulers. In fact, the sum total of years under bad rulers is no greater than the total of years under good rulers. Even though the judgement of God is upon the nation, there are still notable periods of spiritual awakening and revival of true religion. When the ceremonial law is breached, the Lord responds favourably to fervent prayer for cleansing and pardon. When an exceedingly wicked king truly repents there is forgiveness and restoration: "for the LORD your God is gracious and merciful, and will not turn His face from you if you return to Him" (30:9). A teenager is able to govern a nation wisely because he sought the Lord with a tender heart.

The overriding message of 2 Chronicles to the returning exiles is clear: David's line, the temple and the priesthood have *not* been eradicated. The line of descent is unbroken, the temple can be rebuilt and the priesthood is still in existence. God is the God of the covenant!

The Israelites will return to the land of promise:

> Thus says Cyrus king of Persia: "All the kingdoms of the earth the LORD God of heaven has given me. And He has commanded me to build Him a house at Jerusalem which is in Judah. Who is among you of all His people? May the LORD his God be with him, and let him go up!" (36:23)

---

[10] The Epistle to the Hebrews teaches the spiritual significance of the Old Covenant temple and its spiritual fulfilment in Christ and his church. The temple furniture, ceremonies and sacrifices all point to the person and work of the Saviour—see the section "Christ and his church" in the chapters on Exodus and Leviticus.

2 CHRONICLES / **APPLICATION AND REFLECTION**

1. Seeking God

> If My people who are called by My name will humble themselves, and pray and seek My face, and turn from their wicked ways, then I will hear from heaven, and will forgive their sin and heal their land. Now My eyes will be open and My ears attentive to prayer made in this place (7:14-15).

Striking examples are given of those who "set their heart to seek the LORD God of Israel" (11:16).

Following the division of the kingdom, there was a migration of Levites from the northern kingdom of the ten tribes. These godly people remained true to the God of Israel and, at great personal cost, moved to the southern kingdom of the two tribes (11:13-14,16). They were a people committed to a life of worship and service, loyal to the priesthood and the king, in spite of the fact that King Rehoboam was stubborn and foolish.

The second illustration of seeking God occurred in connection with a battle against the ten tribes of Israel (13:13-16). God responded to the prayers of the people in spite of the fact that King Abijam is described as one who "walked in all the sins of his father [Rehoboam], which he had done before him; his heart was not loyal to the LORD his God, as was the heart of his father David" (1 Kings 15:3).

Some years later, an invasion by an overwhelming force of Ethiopians was averted when King Asa "cried out to the LORD his God" (14:11).

His son Jehoshaphat followed him to the throne and enjoyed the blessing of God upon his reign because he "sought the God of his father, and walked in His commandments" (17:4; cf. 20:3-4).

Years later, King Uzziah (called Azariah in 2 Kings 14:21; 15:1-7) "sought God...and as long as he sought the LORD, God made him prosper" (26:5).

King Jotham became mighty, "because he prepared his ways before the LORD his God" (27:6).

His grandson King Hezekiah "did what was good and right and true before the LORD his God. And in every work that he began in the service of the house of God, in the law and in the commandment, to seek his God, he did it with all his heart. So he prospered" (31:20-21).

Where the monarch and/or the people seek God in worship and prayer,

God always responds. The spiritual message of 2 Chronicles is the sovereignty of God and the power of prayer.

2. Repentance

Manasseh was twelve when he followed his godly father Hezekiah to the throne. But he did not share his father's faith in God. Manasseh "did evil in the sight of the LORD" (33:2). He followed the practices of the heathen nations. He rebuilt the pagan places of worship that his father Hezekiah had destroyed. He built altars to the Baals, made wooden idols and worshipped the gods of the Assyrians. He went so far as to build two altars to the Assyrian gods—right in the temple of God. He sacrificed some of his sons as burnt offerings to the god Moloch in the Valley of the Son of Hinnom (known in New Testament times as *Gehenna*). This vile practice of sacrificing children to Moloch was introduced into Judah by Manasseh's godless grandfather King Ahaz (28:3). Manasseh had a devastating influence upon the nation and brought Judah very low spiritually and morally. "And the LORD spoke to Manasseh and his people, but they would not listen" (33:10). As a result of this disobedience and refusal to listen, the Lord brought severe punishment upon Manasseh through the hands of the Assyrians.

Then a wonderful change took place in the mind and heart of King Manasseh:

> Now when he was in affliction, he implored the LORD his God, and humbled himself greatly before the God of his fathers, and prayed to Him; and He received his entreaty, heard his supplication, and brought him back to Jerusalem into his kingdom. Then Manasseh knew that the LORD was God (33:12-13).

That Manasseh had sincerely repented and truly turned to God, there can be no doubt. On his return to Jerusalem:

> He took away the foreign gods and the idol from the house of the LORD, and all the altars that he had built in the mount of the house of the LORD and in Jerusalem; and he cast them out of the city. He also repaired the altar of the LORD, sacrificed peace offerings and thank offerings on it, and commanded Judah to serve the LORD God of Israel (33:15-16).

"For godly sorrow produces repentance leading to salvation, not to be regretted; but the sorrow of the world produces death" (2 Corinthians 7:10). "Bear fruits worthy of repentance" (Matthew 3:8).

Regardless of our sin, genuine repentance ensures our forgiveness, followed by glorious reconciliation.

3. Genealogies

Maintaining accurate records of the line of descent was very important in the purposes of God in preparation for the coming of the Messiah. Godly Israelites looked for the fulfilment of the promise to David and awaited, from among his descendants, "the Coming One" (Matthew 11:3).

Another reason for maintaining the genealogies was that responsibilities had been uniquely designated to certain tribes: ruling to Judah; priestly functions to Levi. The God-fearing Jews were concerned to know their ancestry and that their names were recorded, because to be part of Israel meant to be part of the people of the true and living God. This theme continues to have an important place in the New Testament church (1 Peter 2:9; Ephesians 2:19).

The prophets make mention of a record that the Lord keeps of those who are his people:

> At that time Michael shall stand up,
> The great prince who stands watch over the sons of your people;
> And there shall be a time of trouble,
> Such as never was since there was a nation,
> Even to that time.
> And at that time your people shall be delivered,
> Every one who is found written in the book (Daniel 12:1).

> Then those who feared the LORD spoke to one another,
> And the LORD listened and heard them;
> So a book of remembrance was written before Him
> For those who fear the LORD
> And who meditate on His name (Malachi 3:16).

The apostle Paul writes of those "whose names are in the book of life" (Philippians 4:3). In Revelation, frequent reference is made to names that appear in "the book of life" (Revelation 3:5; 13:8; 17:8; 20:12,15; 21:27; 22:19). Here is a clear indication that "the Lord knows those who are His" (2 Timothy 2:19) and who will enjoy eternal life with him.

EZRA

MEANING	AUTHOR	KEY THOUGHT
"help"	**Ezra** *(probably)*	**The Word of the Lord**

THEME

The place and power of the Word of God in the life of his people

THEME VERSE
For Ezra had prepared his heart to seek the Law of the Lord, and to do it, and to teach statutes and ordinances in Israel.
EZRA 7:10

EZRA / **SUMMARY**

PART 1 / **ZERUBBABEL LEADS THE FIRST RETURN OF EXILES** 1:1-6:22

a. King Cyrus authorizes the return of the captives — 1:1-4
b. Gifts from the Israelites and Cyrus — 1:5-11
c. The names of the returning remnant of Israel — 2:1-70
d. Rebuilding the altar — 3:1-7
e. Laying the foundations for the temple — 3:8-13
f. Samaritans desire to help with rebuilding — 4:1-3
g. Samaritans oppose the building work — 4:4-5
h. Opposition continues for many years — 4:6-24
i. Rebuilding the temple resumes — 5:1-6:14
j. The temple completed and worship restored — 6:15-22

PART 2 / **EZRA LEADS THE SECOND RETURN OF EXILES** 7:1-10:44

a. The arrival of Ezra — 7:1-10
b. The letter given by King Artaxerxes to Ezra — 7:11-28
c. The captives who returned — 8:1-14
d. Servants for the service of the temple — 8:15-20
e. Fasting and prayer for protection — 8:21-23
f. Gifts for the temple — 8:24-30
g. Return to Jerusalem — 8:31-36
h. Grief over the sin of intermarriage — 9:1-15
i. Repentance and reparation — 10:1-44

EZRA

The nation of Israel has been sacked. With the Israelites in exile in Assyria and the Jews (a contraction of "Judahs") banished to Babylon, the land of Israel and Judah lies desolate, farmed by a handful of poor and powerless people. The Lord's promise to Abraham lies unfulfilled:

> And the Lord said to Abram, after Lot had separated from him: "Lift your eyes now and look from the place where you are—northward, southward, eastward, and westward; for all the land which you see *I give to you and your descendants forever* (Genesis 13:14–15, emphasis added).

The duration of the exile, before a return to Judah would be made possible, is contained in a prophecy of Jeremiah to which the closing words of 2 Chronicles and the opening words of Ezra refer. In a letter, which the prophet sent to the captives in Babylon, it is stated:

> For thus says the LORD: After seventy years are completed at Babylon, I will visit you and perform My good word toward you, and cause you to return to this place. For I know the thoughts that I think toward you, says the LORD, thoughts of peace and not of evil, to give you a future and a hope. Then you will call upon Me and go and pray to Me, and I will listen to you. And you will seek Me and find Me, when you search for Me with all your heart. I will be found by you, says the LORD, and I will bring you back from your captivity; I will gather you from all the nations and from all the places where I have driven you, says the LORD, and I will bring you to the place from which I cause you to be carried away captive (Jeremiah 29:10–14).

The Lord makes promises: the Lord *keeps* all his promises!

EZRA / **AUTHOR**

The books of Chronicles, Ezra and Nehemiah form a unit. They tell one story. The language of these books is similar. There are also various references, such as the names included in the genealogies of 1 Chronicles 3 and Nehemiah 12:10–11,22, which would seem to indicate that they were brought to completion around the same time, that is, roughly 200 years after the return of the Jews to Jerusalem under Ezra (c. 458 B.C.). They may have been compiled from a number of original sources and produced by one writer: Ezra, Nehemiah or an unknown editor. These sources might include historic records compiled by Ezra (8:1–9:15) and Nehemiah (Nehemiah 1:1–7:5; 12:31–43; 13:1–31) and official decrees of Persian kings (2 Chronicles 36:23; Ezra 1:1–4; 6:1–12; 7:11–26), all interspersed with information culled from earlier books of the Old Testament.[1]

It is likely that Ezra and Nehemiah originally formed one book. Ezra and Nehemiah acknowledge Jehovah as the God who always fulfils his prophecies, who always keeps his promises. Ezra views the return from exile from the *ceremonial* standpoint, Nehemiah from the *civil*. Ezra is the book of the *rebuilding of the altar and the temple*; Nehemiah is the book of the *rebuilding of the walls* of the city. With the dawning of the days of Ezra and Nehemiah, the nation of Israel enters a bright new era. This is the time of restoration: returning from captivity and rebuilding the shattered nation.

EZRA / **HISTORICAL SETTING**

The English Old Testament is divided into three sections: history (Genesis to Esther), poetry (Job to Song of Solomon) and prophecy (Isaiah to Malachi). The seventeen books from Genesis to Esther present a panoramic view of the history of Israel in preparation for the coming of the Messiah. Beginning with the history of creation, followed by events leading up to the great Flood and the gracious delivery of Noah and his family, attention gradually becomes focused upon one man, Abraham, and his descendants through Isaac and then Jacob (Israel). Abraham is traced from Ur to Haran, and on to Canaan; the story unfolds. Eventually moved from Canaan by famine, the seventy-strong family of Jacob settles in Egypt and prospers. Four-hundred years pass and their numbers have increased to such an extent that the

---

[1] William Hendriksen, *Survey of the Bible: A Treasury of Bible Information* (Welwyn: Evangelical Press, 1976), 310.

Egyptians believe they constitute a threat to their national security. The Israelites are forced into slavery. But God has not forgotten his covenant with Abraham. He wonderfully delivers his people.

Once out of Egypt and after repeated rebellions, obstinacy and disobedience, the Israelites are led into the promised land. At last, the nation is established in its own country. Eventually, after many years, Israel becomes strong and secure under godly King David. During his son's reign, however, the united kingdom of Israel reaches its peak and then begins to plummet. The kingdom is split in two by civil war. The spiritual decline of the two nations, Israel and Judah, is manifested in repeated periods of immorality, idolatry and godlessness. Two hundred and fifty years after David's death, the peoples of the northern kingdom of the ten tribes of Israel are taken into exile in Assyria. One hundred and thirty six years later the two tribes of Judah and Benjamin, the southern kingdom, are taken in captivity to Babylon. God has punished his people.

The books of Kings and Chronicles record the successes and failures of the divided kingdom of God's chosen people—Israel and Judah. They record their eventual fall and captivity by foreign powers in foreign lands, as a divine punishment for their spiritual rebellion and sin. While the books of Kings are written from the *political* point of view, Chronicles, Ezra and Nehemiah are written from the *spiritual* perspective.

The book of Ezra covers a period of just over eighty years, from the decree of Cyrus (539 B.C.). As the people of Judah were taken captive in three successive groups (605, 597, 586 B.C.) so, coincidentally, they return in three groups. The first company returns under the leadership of Zerubbabel (2:2; 536 B.C.) and, inspired by prophets Haggai and Zechariah, they eventually rebuild the temple (520–516 B.C.). Sixty years later, the second wave returns from Babylon under the leadership of Ezra the priest (458 B.C.). This is the period covered by the book of Ezra. Fourteen years later Nehemiah leads the third group (445 B.C.),[2] and the book bearing his name records the essential features. The book

---

[2] This may have been a very small group. As well as soldiers sent to escort and protect him while in Judah, Nehemiah mentions "my brethren and my servants" in a context which distinguishes them from those already resident in Judah (Nehemiah 5:10; cf. 4:10).

Figure 11. Judah and its prophets and kings: before, during and after the exile*

	Assyrian captivity 721	Babylonian captivity 586	Kingdom of the Medes and Persians
The end of the northern kingdom of Israel			
Prophets	Ezekiel Daniel Nahum Zephaniah Habakkuk Jeremiah	Decree of Cyrus 539 First return of exiles Haggai Zechariah	Second return of exiles · Third return of exiles Malachi
Kings of the southern kingdom of Judah	Josiah 640-609 Jehoahaz 609 Jehoiakim 609-598 Jehoiachin 598-597 Zedekiah 597-586	Zerubbabel 536	Ezra 458 Nehemiah 445
		Leaders in Judah	

*Years are in B.C.

of Esther covers momentous events that took place in Babylon from 483 to 473 B.C., that is, between the first and second return.

EZRA / **OUTLINE**

There is a slight overlap forming a natural continuity between the end of 2 Chronicles (36:22–23) and the opening of the book of Ezra (1:1–3). The clear theme throughout the whole book is the place and power of the Word of God in the religious, social and civil life of his people. The key phrase is "the Word of God" expressed in a variety of words. Scripture is referred to as "the word of the LORD" (1:1); "the Law of Moses the man of God" (3:2); "the commandment of the God of Israel" (6:14); "the Book of Moses" (6:18); "the Law of your God which is in your hand" (7:14); "the words of the God of Israel" (9:4); and "the commandment of our God" (10:3).

The book of Ezra falls into two distinct sections: the first six chapters deal with the first return under Zerubbabel; the remaining four chapters record the second return eighty years later under Ezra (see Figure 11).

PART 1 / **ZERUBBABEL LEADS THE FIRST RETURN OF EXILES (1:1-6:22)**

Cyrus King of Persia conquered Babylon in 539 B.C. The prophecy of Isaiah is in the process of fulfilment:

Thus says the LORD, your Redeemer…

Who says of Cyrus, "He is My shepherd,
And he shall perform all My pleasure,
Saying to Jerusalem, 'You shall be built,'
And to the temple, 'Your foundation shall be laid.'"

Thus says the LORD to His anointed,
To Cyrus, whose right hand I have held—
To subdue nations before him
And loose the armor of kings,
To open before him the double doors,
So that the gates will not be shut:
"I will go before you
And make the crooked places straight;
I will break in pieces the gates of bronze
And cut the bars of iron.
I will give you the treasures of darkness
And hidden riches of secret places,
That you may know that I, the LORD,
Who call you by your name,
Am the God of Israel.
For Jacob My servant's sake,
And Israel My elect,
I have even called you by your name;

I have named you, though you have not known Me.
I am the LORD, and there is no other;
There is no God besides Me.
I will gird you, though you have not known Me"
(Isaiah 44:24,28; 45:1–5).

The prophet Daniel, who was exiled to Babylon as a teenager (and never returned to Israel), "prospered...in the reign of Cyrus the Persian" (Daniel 6:28; cf. 10:1). Daniel probably had an influence upon King Cyrus and the proclamation which he issued in the first year of his reign in Babylon. This decree encouraged the Israelites to return and rebuild the temple in Jerusalem (1:1–4). The people of Babylon gave gifts toward the rebuilding program (1:6). King Cyrus also restored the treasures captured from the temple (1:7). Almost 50,000 Jews (49,897 to be exact) chose to return to the land of Israel (2:64–65). Many Jews chose to remain in Babylon. Those who stayed behind did not wish to leave their secure homes or influential positions, or to face the upheaval of moving the long distance from one country to the other. According to archaeological discoveries, some of the Jews who remained succeeded reasonably well in business.[3]

When the Hebrews returned to Israel, they did not begin work with the reconstruction of the city walls, but thought first of the temple, the house of God. Even then, they did not commence with the foundations and walls of the temple itself. They began with the rebuilding of the altar (3:2). Appropriately the first feast they celebrated together was the Feast of Tabernacles. This would be significant for them since it had been instituted hundreds of years earlier to remind the Israelites of their long journey from Egypt, through the wilderness, and into the promised land (Leviticus 23:34–43). These exiles returning from Babylon had travelled over 700 miles across another difficult wilderness. They too wanted to express their gratitude to the Lord.

After a short while, the Samaritans (people brought into Israel after the Assyrian captivity to repopulate the land of Canaan—2 Kings 17:24) offered to work with the Jews in the construction of the temple. They had been introduced to a corrupted form of worship of the one true God. Their own words highlight the problem. They say, "Let us

---

[3] Raymond Brown, *Let's Read the Old Testament* (London: Victory Press, 1971), 91.

build with you, for we seek your God as you do; and we have sacrificed to Him since the days of Esarhaddon king of Assyria, who brought us here" (4:2). To be told that the Samaritans have continued to offer sacrifices to the Lord would not have pleased a godly Jew. Sacrifices not offered in Jerusalem were regarded as equivalent to sacrifices offered to idols (Leviticus 17:1–9)! Their offer of help is flatly refused. Zerubbabel and his colleagues in leadership refer to the decree of King Cyrus of Persia that only Israelites are to rebuild the temple. Consequently, the leaders of the new community are legally justified in rejecting the proposal of the colonists brought in by Esarhaddon. These people are neither members of the chosen people of God, nor Israelites, nor genuine worshippers of the true God. They are non-Israelites and, indeed, they describe themselves as those whom the king of Assyria had brought into the land.[4]

In consequence of this refusal to allow them to participate in the reconstruction of the temple, the Samaritans begin to hinder the building work. They try hard to discourage and dishearten the Israelites in their task. This opposition serves to confirm the rightness of the decision of the Hebrew leadership. Had the Samaritans been sincere in their desire to help in the construction of the temple, they would hardly have turned nasty and hindered the work. The main procedure they adopt to make life difficult for the Israelites is to hire "counsellors against them to frustrate their purpose" (4:5). They write to successive kings of Persia accusing the Jews of insurrection. The opposition successfully frustrates the temple reconstruction. Following the laying of the foundation, work is hindered for fourteen years.[5]

While the historian is recounting the opposition to the rebuilding of the temple, he skips from the days of Cyrus and Darius to show how opposition continued against the rebuilding of the city for another sixty years into the reigns of Ahasuerus (Xerxes) and Artaxerxes I (4:6–23).

The fifth chapter of Ezra returns to the events that occurred during the reign of Darius the Great of Persia. It is at this point that the

---

[4] C.F. Keil, *The Books of Ezra, Nehemiah, and Esther* (Grand Rapids: Eerdmans, 1949), 58–59.

[5] That is, the remaining five years of the reign of Cyrus (4:5), seven-and-half years of Cambyses, seven months of Smerdis and one year of Darius, until the second year of his reign (4:24).

prophets Haggai and Zechariah encourage progress on the building project (5:1–2). The temple is completed and full worship is restored.

PART 2 / **EZRA LEADS THE SECOND RETURN OF EXILES (7:1–10:44)**

Whereas about 50,000 Jews returned under the leadership of Zerubbabel, only about 2,000 returned eighty years later under the leadership of Ezra. Ezra was the great-grandson of Hilkiah (7:1), high priest during the reign of godly Josiah (640–609 B.C.). Hilkiah was the priest who found the copy of "the Book of the Law of the LORD given by Moses" (2 Chronicles 34:14). Alhough Ezra was a priest by birth, he was not able to function as a priest because he was in captivity in Babylon. Instead, he spent a considerable amount of time studying Scripture: "this Ezra came up from Babylon; and he was a skilled scribe in the Law of Moses, which the LORD God of Israel had given" (7:6). "For Ezra had prepared his heart to seek the Law of the LORD, and to do it, and to teach statutes and ordinances in Israel" (7:10).

On reading 2 Chronicles, Ezra and Nehemiah, it is evident that the people of Israel, in general, had little knowledge of the Scriptures that God had inspired. It was mainly through Ezra's ministry that the Word of God gained its rightful position for the first time in the history of Israel and Judah.

Ezra was a willing and eager Bible student. God's law was burning in his own heart and lived out in his own life before he taught it to others. This enabled him to speak with the intensity of real conviction.[6] The quality and consistency of Ezra's godly life were noted by King Artaxerxes of Persia, who gave him a letter authorizing all the people of Israel who were willing to go with him to Jerusalem (7:12–13). The letter also commanded that Ezra should be supplied with all that was necessary for the building of the house of God (7:20). Although still under the rule of Persia, Ezra was granted power to appoint magistrates and judges to rule the people in Israel. He was also instructed to teach the people the law of God (7:25).

Only about 2,000 Jews gathered at the River Ahava, and there, with

---

[6] A.M. Hodgkin, *Christ in All the Scriptures* (London: Pickering and Inglis, 1907), 93.

fasting and prayer, they committed their way to the Lord, no doubt remembering God's remarkable delivery of the Israelites under Queen Esther, which had occurred in the eighty-year interval between the first wave of returning exiles under Zerubbabel and this second wave. Ezra "was ashamed" to ask for a guard of soldiers, as it might reflect upon the Lord's power to deliver. Ezra attributes all his success, the kindness and benevolence of the king, the willingness of the people and safety in travelling to the good hand of his God upon him (8:22).

Arrival in Jerusalem

When Ezra arrived in Israel, he found the situation to be even worse than he had expected. Since the days of Zerubbabel, the Jews in Jerusalem had once more backslidden in their devotion to the one true God. Some of the descendants of those who had returned eighty years earlier had blatantly disregarded the law of God with respect to intermarriage with non-Israelites. Ezra's response shows a characteristic depth of spiritual sensitivity:

> So when I heard this thing, I tore my garment and my robe, and plucked out some of the hair of my head and beard, and sat down astonished. Then everyone who trembled at the words of the God of Israel assembled to me, because of the transgression of those who had been carried away captive, and I sat astonished until the evening sacrifice.
>
> At the evening sacrifice I arose from my fasting; and having torn my garment and my robe, I fell on my knees and spread out my hands to the LORD my God. And I said: "O my God, I am too ashamed and humiliated to lift up my face to You, my God; for our iniquities have risen higher than our heads, and our guilt has grown up to the heavens" (9:3–6).

The revival of true religion

> And now for a little while grace has been shown from the LORD our God, to leave us a remnant to escape, and to give us a peg in His holy place, that our God may enlighten our eyes and give us a measure of revival in our bondage (9:8).

The revival under Ezra takes the form of a revival of Bible study and obedience to the revealed will of God (cf. Nehemiah 8). The Word of the Lord, read and expounded by Ezra the priest, has a profound effect upon the people. Before the Babylonian exile God had spoken through Isaiah saying:

> Seek the LORD while He may be found,
> Call upon Him while He is near.
> Let the wicked forsake his way,
> And the unrighteous man his thoughts;
> Let him return to the LORD,
> And He will have mercy on him;
> And to our God,
> For He will abundantly pardon (Isaiah 55:6–7).

In returning to the Lord with all their hearts, the Israelites take steps to turn also from their disobedient lifestyle. The law of Moses has been transgressed in that many Israelites had intermarried with Gentile women. All the people of Judah are gathered together and a resolution is made to separate all foreign wives from their community. For three months, Ezra and the appointed magistrates hear and resolve individual cases. One hundred and thirteen cases of mixed marriage are identified and a strict separation enacted.

EZRA / **CHRIST AND HIS CHURCH**

But for the grace of God there would have been no restoration of Israel. Not one of the tribes of Israel deserved such kind and benevolent treatment at the hands of the Lord:

> If we are faithless,
> He remains faithful;
> He cannot deny Himself (2 Timothy 2:13).

PROPHECIES

The restoration of a remnant of Israel to their land was vitally important in the purposes of God. So many promises and prophecies were associated with the land of Judah—promises to Abraham, Isaac and Jacob and prophecies through Isaiah, Micah and Jeremiah—that restoration to the promised land was essential. Nevertheless, there is the greater goal always in the background. The return from exile in Babylon and the re-establishment of the Jews in their own land paved the way for the coming of the promised Messiah, the Christ of God. God's Son was to be "born of the seed of David according to the flesh" (Romans 1:3; cf. 2 Samuel 7:12–13). Yet it was not sufficient for him to have the right *ancestry*. He must also be born in the right *place*. God had specified that place. Two hundred years earlier, the Lord had promised through the prophet Micah:

> But you, Bethlehem Ephrathah,
> Though you are little among the thousands of Judah,
> Yet out of you shall come forth to Me
> The One to be Ruler in Israel,
> Whose goings forth are from of old,
> From everlasting (Micah 5:2).

The Son of God was to be born in Bethlehem, not Babylon; in the holy land of promise, not in the land of captivity. A remnant of the Jews was to return to the promised land.

Bethlehem, Nazareth and Jerusalem were some of the geographic locations woven into the promises concerning our Lord's advent. In just over 400 years after the days of Ezra, "when the fullness of the time had come, God sent forth His Son, born of a woman" (Galatians 4:4). It is to those

> who are Israelites, to whom pertain the adoption, the glory, the covenants, the giving of the law, the service of God, and the promises; of whom are the fathers and from whom, according to the flesh, Christ came, who is over all, the eternally blessed God (Romans 9:4–5).

EZRA / **CONCLUSION**

The book of Ezra reveals the power and grace of God in protecting his people, leading his people, teaching his people and restoring his people.

Central throughout is the importance of the revealed Word of God. Ezra himself is shown to be a man of the Word, a man of faith, a man of prayer and a man of courage. He loved the Word of God, believed in its message, taught its truths, lived by its principles, and by proclaiming it, he influenced the lives of the restored children of captivity. Such men of the Word are needed in every generation and in every nation.

The church of Jesus Christ is only spiritually strong when Christians read, study, teach and obey the Scriptures.

EZRA / **APPLICATION AND REFLECTION**

1. Right priorities
It is interesting to note the order of priority when the Hebrews returned to Israel. They did not begin with the rebuilding of the city walls. Even before they thought of building homes for themselves, the returning Jews thought first of the temple, the house of God. Nor did they commence with the foundations and walls of the temple itself. They began with the rebuilding of the altar (3:2). This is a beautiful illustration of the timeless truth that atoning work must come first and be at the heart of all of our life's concerns—in the church, in the home and in society at large. "Jesus Christ and Him crucified" (1 Corinthians 2:2) is to be the centre of concern, and the controlling principle, in all areas of life.

2. True repentance
When the Holy Spirit illuminates the Word of God, wonderful results follow, one of which is genuine heartfelt repentance. So Israel responded to the teaching of Scripture, for "a very large congregation of men, women, and children assembled to [Ezra] from Israel; for the people wept very bitterly" (10:1). There is, however, "a sorrow of the world" and a "godly sorrow" (2 Corinthians 7:10). The first kind of grief is pain experienced through remorse or regret at the resulting consequences. This does not lead to repentance or to salvation. The second kind of grief brings a sinner to God in confession of sin and seeking forgiveness and mercy.

A further mark of "godly sorrow [which] produces repentance to salvation, not to be regretted" is a turning away from sin, or a desperate cry to God for the grace and strength to turn away from sin (Isaiah 55:7; Hebrews 4:16; Galatians 5:16). Christians are motivated and empowered by the love of Christ (2 Corinthians 5:14-15) to produce "fruits worthy of repentance" (Matthew 3:8), and "to lead a life worthy of the calling with which [they] were called" (Ephesians 4:1).

3. Separation
There is a thread of separation in the book of Ezra: first, separation from Babylon (1:1-3); secondly, separation from worldly help in building the house of God (4:1-3); thirdly, separation from dependence upon human protection (8:21-23); and, fourthly, separation from sinful partnerships (10:11-12).

Drawing from the prophecies of Isaiah 52:11 and 2 Samuel 7:14, the apostle Paul pleads for spiritual separation when he urges Christians not to be "unequally yoked together with unbelievers" (2 Corinthians 6:14) with these words:

> Come out from among them
> And be separate, says the Lord.
> Do not touch what is unclean,
> And I will receive you.
> I will be a Father to you,
> And you shall be My sons and daughters,
> Says the Lord Almighty (2 Corinthians 6:17-18).

Zerubbabel and the Jewish leadership rightly refused the Samaritans' offer of help in rebuilding the temple. Alhough the Samaritans claimed to worship the true God (4:2), they actually practised a corrupted form of Jehovah-worship. They followed the practices of the early immigrants to Samaria who "feared the LORD, yet served their own gods—according to the rituals of the nations from among whom they were carried away" (2 Kings 17:33). Zerubbabel knew that the worship of God had become corrupt and degraded.

A clear distinction is to be made between those who worship the true God and those who do not. It is inappropriate for non-Christians to be confused with genuine members of the church of Jesus Christ or to work on behalf of the church.

NEHEMIAH

MEANING	AUTHOR	KEY THOUGHT
"whom Jehovah comforts"	**Nehemiah** *(probably)*	**Prayer and hard work**

THEME

Building the kingdom of God by prayer, hard work and perseverance

THEME VERSE

Nevertheless we made our prayer to our God, and...set a watch against them day and night.... So we labored in the work.
NEHEMIAH 4:9,21

NEHEMIAH / **SUMMARY**

PART 1 / **NEHEMIAH BECOMES GOVERNOR OF JUDAH**   1:1–2:10

    a.   News reaches Nehemiah of the sad state of Jerusalem   1:1–3
    b.   Nehemiah responds in earnest and prolonged prayer   1:4–11
    c.   After four months of prayer, God opens the way   2:1–10

PART 2 / **REBUILDING THE WALLS OF JERUSALEM**   2:11–6:19

    a.   Nehemiah arrives in Jerusalem and inspects the ruins   2:11–16
    b.   Nehemiah inspires the people to work   2:17–20
    c.   The workers and their work   3:1–32
    d.   Hostility and contempt overcome by prayer and hard work   4:1–23
    e.   Nehemiah confronts internal injustice and oppression   5:1–13
    f.   Nehemiah's example of generosity   5:14–19
    g.   Nehemiah resists attempts to interfere with the work   6:1–14
    h.   The city wall is completed in fifty-two days   6:15–19

PART 3 / **ORGANIZATION, WORSHIP AND APPOINTMENTS**   7:1–12:47

    a.   Instructions concerning the city guard   7:1–3
    b.   The register of returned exiles, servants and animals   7:4–73
    c.   The great assembly   8:1–10:39
         (1) Reading and exposition of the Word   8:1–12
         (2) Celebrating the Feast of Tabernacles   8:13–18
         (3) Confessing sin and signing the covenant   9:1–10:27

	d. Contents of the covenant	10:28-39
d.	People who came to live in the city	11:1-24
e.	People who lived outside the city	11:25-28
f.	Register of priests and Levites	12:1-26
g.	Nehemiah dedicates the walls of Jerusalem	12:27-43
h.	Appointments to temple duties	12:44-47

PART 4 / **ANOTHER REFORMATION NEEDED** 13:1-31

a.	Social and religious reforms	13:1-3
b.	The sin of Eliashib the priest	13:4-5
c.	Nehemiah returns to Jerusalem after an absence of twelve years	13:6-7
d.	Social and religious reforms	13:8-31

NEHEMIAH

When Ezra the priest arrived in Judah, he found the morale of the community in Judah very low. Disappointment had led to disillusionment, and disillusionment to religious and moral laxity. This is evident from the words of the prophet Malachi (a contemporary of Nehemiah) and those of Nehemiah. Priests, bored with their duties, offered sick and injured animals to the Lord (Malachi 1:6–14). They earned the derision and disgust of the people by showing partiality in the administration of justice (Malachi 2:7–9). God's law concerning the Sabbath was ignored: it was just another day for business and trade (Nehemiah 13:15–18). The non-payment of tithes forced Levites to neglect their duties in order to earn a living (Malachi 3:7–10; Nehemiah 13:10–13). The high incidence of divorce was a public scandal (Malachi 2:13–16). The people were totally spiritually disheartened and had lost confidence in their religious leaders (Malachi 2:17; 3:13–15). There was a prevalence of witchcraft, adultery, bearing false witness and exploitation of workers and the underprivileged (Malachi 3:5). The poor, having mortgaged their fields in time of drought, or to pay taxes, found themselves and their children reduced to slavery (Nehemiah 5:1–5). Intermarriage with heathens was common (Malachi 2:11). As the children of those mixed marriages became more numerous, there were serious implications for the future of the nation (13:23–27).

With no sense of direction and a distinct lack of morale, there was a real danger that the Jewish community in Judah would disintegrate. Drastic measures were needed. Thoroughgoing reform of the nation's life—spiritual, social and civil—was desperately needed.

In the providence of God, two men implemented the reforms that would save the nation and provide the necessary stability for the remaining four centuries until the coming of the Messiah. These men, Ezra and Nehemiah, were to have a profound effect upon the nation. Ezra reorganized and reformed the nation's spiritual life. Nehemiah reconstituted its civil government.

NEHEMIAH / **AUTHOR**

Since the books of Ezra and Nehemiah display similarities in style and perspective, and because they were originally one book in the Hebrew Bible, they may have been produced by one writer. Ezra, Nehemiah or an unknown editor may have drawn together a number of original sources including historic records compiled by Ezra (Ezra 7:27–9:15), and by Nehemiah (1:1–7:5; 12:31–43; 13:1–31), with official decrees of Persian kings (2 Chronicles 36:23; Ezra 1:1–4; 6:1–12; 7:11–26), all interspersed with information culled from earlier books of the Old Testament.[1]

NEHEMIAH / **HISTORICAL SETTING**

In 550 B.C., Cyrus became king of Persia. Eleven years later, he conquered Babylon. In the first year as ruler of Babylon, Cyrus issued a proclamation encouraging the Jews to return to Judah and rebuild the temple of the Lord in Jerusalem. Consequently, in 536 B.C., 50,000 Jews returned to the land of Israel (Ezra 2:64–65) under the leadership of Zerubbabel (Ezra 2:2). Eventually, after considerable opposition from the Samaritans and great encouragement from the prophets Haggai and Zechariah, the temple was completed and dedicated in 516 B.C. All seemed set for a period of stability and growth.

Little is known about the next period in Jewish history. The early enthusiasm evidently began to wane: the mass of Jews dispersed throughout the Persian empire lost interest in the restoration program in Israel and settled down, content to remain where they were. The future of the Jewish community in Judah became uncertain and discouraging. Babylon remained the centre of Jewish life for centuries. A number of the Israelite exiles and their descendants prospered. Some of them, like Nehemiah, rose to high positions in the Persian government.

Thirteen years after the second return of exiles under the leadership of Ezra, Nehemiah hears news of the sad state of affairs in Jerusalem and is troubled. He turns from the comfort, luxury and status of Persia to join the suffering people of God in Jerusalem.

---

[1] William Hendriksen, *Survey of the Bible: A Treasury of Bible Information* (Welwyn: Evangelical Press, 1976), 310.

NEHEMIAH / **OUTLINE**

The book of Nehemiah is mostly autobiographical. Nehemiah's recorded activity takes place during the reign of King Artaxerxes I of Persia, from the twentieth year until some time after the thirty-second year of his reign (2:1; 13:6)—that is, from 445 B.C. and beyond 433 B.C. The prophet Malachi was also in Jerusalem, actively engaged in the work to which God had appointed him, during this period.[2]

This book contains a striking description of a man who works for God. As Ezra is an example of a minister of the Word, diligent to present himself "approved to God, a worker who does not need to be ashamed, rightly dividing the word of truth" (2 Timothy 2:15), so Nehemiah is a worker for God, combining hard work with the essential ingredient of regular and persistent prayer.

PART 1 / **NEHEMIAH BECOMES GOVERNOR OF JUDAH (1:1–2:10)**

Nehemiah was born into the community of Jewish exiles living in Babylon. He rose to the high position of cupbearer to Artaxerxes I, the great king of the vast Persian empire. While serving the king in Shushan the capital, Nehemiah receives news from Hanani, one of his brothers, that the city of Jerusalem is in a sad condition and the people of Judah are generally distressed and disheartened (1:1–3). Nehemiah prays. He prays persistently and earnestly.[3] He is a godly man. He is a righteous man. He is a man who fears God, obeys the law of God and is deeply concerned for the honour and glory of God. He is also a man of prayer. He prays privately; he prays among fellow believers. That is suggested by his words: "O Lord, I pray, please let Your ear be attentive to the prayer of Your servant, and to the prayer of Your servants who desire to fear Your name" (1:11).

After four months of prayer, an opportunity arises, by the providence of God, for Nehemiah to share his concern with the king. With remarkable courage Nehemiah responds to the king's enquiry and clearly presents his requests to travel to Judah to rebuild Jerusalem.

---

[2] It is beneficial to read the book of Malachi alongside that of Nehemiah.
[3] Cf. Elijah (1 Kings 18:41–44), of whom James writes, "The effective, fervent prayer of a righteous man avails much" (James 5:16).

King Artaxerxes, indicating something of the esteem in which Nehemiah is held, grants him everything he requires and provides him with a substantial army escort. Nehemiah knows, however, that the provision of the king is due to a higher authority. The man of God records, "And the king granted them to me according to the good hand of my God upon me" (2:8).

PART 2 / **REBUILDING THE WALLS OF JERUSALEM (2:11–6:19)**

Once in Jerusalem, Nehemiah rests for three days, no doubt recovering from the long and arduous journey. He then slips out alone by night to make a personal assessment of the damage to the city wall and its gates (2:12–16). Both Ezra and Nehemiah bring distinctive godliness to Jerusalem. They are each men of great faith, persistent prayer and ready obedience. Whereas Ezra also brings years of learning in the Scriptures, skill in exposition and application of the Word of God, Nehemiah brings keen organizational and administrative skills.[4] Moving around the city walls he would have been formulating his strategy for the rebuilding programme.

Having made his assessment and decided upon a strategy, Nehemiah's next task is to inform the civic leaders and enthuse them for the work. He credits the Lord's goodness as the driving force behind the whole proceedings (2:18). Once informed, men with a variety of skills come forward and receive their assignments (3:1–32). But there is no lack of opposition.

External opposition

Jerusalem comes under the jurisdiction of Sanballat and Tobiah, Gentiles living over in Samaria. They are not at all pleased with the arrival of Nehemiah. Indeed, "they were deeply disturbed that a man had come to seek the well-being of the children of Israel" (2:10). When plans for rebuilding the city wall leak out to Sanballat and his colleagues, they respond with mockery and derision (2:19). They charge the Jews with planning insurrection. They would not be slow to get that message relayed back to the Persian royal palace. Nehemiah, however, has

---

[4] See the later section "Application and reflection."

the full approval and cooperation of King Artaxerxes so he has nothing to fear from that quarter.

Governor Sanballat's displeasure only increases as the rebuilding work commences. He "was furious and very indignant, and mocked the Jews" (4:1). As the work proceeds, Sanballat's hostility intensifies. He and Tobiah conspire with the Arabs, the Ammonites and the Ashdodites to make a secret attack against Jerusalem and generally to cause as much confusion as possible among the Israelites (4:8). Nehemiah's response is classic: "Nevertheless we made our prayer to our God, and because of them we set a watch against them day and night" (4:9). Seeing that the Israelites are not deterred, their enemies begin to stir up fear. They instigate rumours among the Jews that their enemies are all around them, that they will all be destroyed, that they will not even see their attackers. Nehemiah counters these rumours by reminding the people of the protection of their "great and awesome"- God (4:14). He urges them to fight in God's name and in the defence of their people, their families and their homes. They continue building: "With one hand they worked at construction, and with the other held a weapon" (4:17).

The rebuilding of the wall of the city of Jerusalem is completed in just fifty-two days (6:15). This remarkable achievement comes about because the men work hard and for long periods. Nehemiah is himself fully occupied in the rebuilding program. He and his coworkers sleep in their work clothes and only remove them for washing (4:23).

Once the walls are rebuilt, Sanballat resorts to a more subtle approach in his opposition. He and his allies send an official invitation to Nehemiah to join them for discussions. The subject for debate is the purpose behind the rebuilding of the city walls of Jerusalem. Nehemiah knows that they intend to remove him from the scene by any means they can (6:2). He therefore refuses to accept the invitation, though it is made to him on five different occasions.

PART 3 / **ORGANIZATION, WORSHIP AND APPOINTMENTS (7:1-12:47)**

When the wall is built Nehemiah is aware that the nations around are "very disheartened in their own eyes," since they recognize "that this work was done by our God" (6:16). He spends a considerable period of time, maybe as long as twelve years, organizing the small nation of Judah, and the affairs of the city of Jerusalem, in preparation for his return to the Persian capital.

One of the highlights of this period is the holding of a great assembly or conference. Nehemiah and Ezra call all the Israelites together: men, women and children old enough to understand what is being said and done (8:1,3). Ezra and the trained Levites teach the people the Word of God. The Scriptures are read, translated for the benefit of those who do not know Hebrew and explained (8:8). The people worship God and celebrate the Feast of Tabernacles. There is mourning over sin (9:1-3), rejoicing in God's mercy and kindness (9:5-38) and a sense of deep spiritual exercise among the people. They seal their devotion to God with a solemn covenant (10:28-39).

A public register is set up to record the number of people living within the city walls, the number living outside and the number who are priests and Levites. Then, following the dedication of the walls of Jerusalem and the appointment of Levites to certain temple duties, Nehemiah leaves for Babylon.

PART 4 / **ANOTHER REFORMATION NEEDED (13:1-31)**

After a period of absence at the Persian court, Nehemiah returns to Jerusalem and finds that another reformation is needed. Eliashib the high priest has given up a large room in the forecourt of the temple (13:5,7) to Tobiah the Ammonite (cf. 2:10), probably for use as a private dwelling when he was in the city. This man was a good friend of Sanballat and neither of them had shown themselves friendly toward Israel. Nehemiah roundly condemns this worldly alliance between Eliashib and Tobiah. He throws out all Tobiah's furniture, reconsecrates the rooms and restores them to their divinely appointed use (13:8-9). Nehemiah also tackles the age-old problem of mixed marriages. The issue was not racial or cultural, but religious. Israelites must not marry Gentiles unless they become Israelites. The people of God must not marry pagans and unbelievers. The ungodly, through marriage, will lead the people of God into idolatry and sin. The example of King Solomon is cited to show how even that one who was "beloved of his God" fell into sin through the influence of his ungodly wives (13:26). The reformation is strictly enforced with solemn warnings.

NEHEMIAH / **CHRIST AND HIS CHURCH**

PROPHECIES

By this time in the history of Israel, a great many wonderful prophecies had been given concerning the promised Messiah. The full revelation of God's purposes in sending his Son into the world was almost complete; only the prophecies of Malachi remained to be disclosed. Hindering the return of exiles from Babylon was the devil's vital strategy in seeking to thwart the promises of God. Once the Jews were settled back in Israel, then the devil concentrated on instigating all manner of hindrances and obstacles to the rebuilding work. If the city walls remained in ruins, the Israelites would be vulnerable to their many enemies. The reconstruction work undertaken under the leadership of Nehemiah, both in buildings and civil government, and the spiritual reformation undertaken by Ezra form a partnership essential to the restoration of the nation of Israel.

The settlement of the Hebrews in their own land was of paramount importance to the covenant promises of God. What Nehemiah achieved with God's enabling served a vital role in the unfolding and eventual fulfilling of God's purpose for Christ and his church.

NEHEMIAH / **CONCLUSION**

Nehemiah was a remarkable man of God. With great sacrifice he devoted himself to the work of God. He exercised strategy in planning for the people of Israel. He inspired others to work for the cause of God. He used his God-given talents for the service of the Lord and the Lord's people. He was a man of deep faith, ardent prayer and willing obedience. He is a fitting example for any Christian in combining the essential ingredients of godliness, hard work and prayer for the building up of the church of God.

Nehemiah brings a fitting conclusion to Old Testament history. Everything that appears in the Bible after this book has been collated under poetry or prophecy. With the exception of Malachi, who was a contemporary of Nehemiah, all the other books precede Nehemiah in terms of chronology. Throughout three and a half millennia, an amazing number of wonderful prophecies have been given to Israel: "God

…at various times and in various ways spoke in time past to the fathers by the prophets" (Hebrews 1:1). The book of Nehemiah closes that Old Testament history. The Lord had determined to leave the nation with a sense of hope and expectancy. Israel, reduced to a remnant composed mainly of those of the tribe of Judah, is restored to its own land to await the Messiah. Now they are known more as Jews than Israelites.

Four hundred years are to pass in prophetic silence until the coming of the forerunner of the Lord Jesus Christ. The silence will be broken by the messenger heralding the coming of "the Messenger of the covenant" (Malachi 3:1). John the Baptist will break the silence by bursting upon the scene of history as "the voice of one crying in the wilderness: 'Prepare the way of the LORD'" (Isaiah 40:3; cf. Mark 1:2–3).

NEHEMIAH / **APPLICATION AND REFLECTION**

1. Personal sacrifice
Nehemiah was not simply a court butler responsible for serving wine; he was evidently one of the most trusted men in the kingdom. The cupbearer to the king was responsible to taste the wine in the king's chalice just before the king drank from it, to establish that the wine was not poisoned; as was often the case, such a trusted position also meant that the cupbearer acted in an advisory capacity to the king. That Nehemiah held such a privileged and respected role is evident in the king's appointment of him as governor of Judah. Nehemiah must also have had considerable administrative skills.

The spiritual stature of Nehemiah is blatantly obvious: he is deeply distressed on hearing news of the sad situation in far-away Jerusalem; he prays hard and long for wisdom and guidance to know how he should personally respond; he willingly leaves the comfort, position and prestige of the Persian court to travel nearly 1,000 miles over rough terrain to the ruins of a once famous city—for the honour and glory of God. Nehemiah is a fine example of a man who puts God first, whose career is subservient to the needs of the kingdom of God, who willingly leaves everything when the Lord requires it.

2. Fasting and prayer
Nehemiah shows where a believer begins a significant work for God—in fasting and persistent prayer (1:4; cf. Acts 13:3; 14:23). This is also the way to deal with any major crisis or problem (Daniel 9:3-19). Fasting is an important part of a Christian's devotional life (Matthew 9:14-15; 1 Corinthians 7:5). It is a secret activity intimately related to prayer (Matthew 6:16-18). As far as possible, no one should know. Upon our knees we cry, "Lord, what do You want me to do?" (Acts 9:6).

A further lesson from the prayers of Nehemiah is the way in which he addresses God, reminding him of his covenant, his character and his promises (1:5,8-10). The appeal to God is based upon all that God has revealed about himself and his purposes and will: "Now this is the confidence that we have in Him, that if we ask anything according to His will, He hears us" (1 John 5:14).

3. Strategy for the church
Nehemiah's nighttime inspection of the city walls illustrates the place of strategy and planning in the Lord's work (2:12-16). God had put the thought

in his mind, but it was his job to work out the best way of achieving the goal. All our natural talents, innate skills, learned techniques and spiritual maturity and insights are to be brought into the service of God, from whom they came. "Every good gift and every perfect gift is from above, and comes down from the Father" (James 1:17). To present the whole of ourselves—body, mind, spirit, with all our accumulated knowledge, education and wisdom— "a living sacrifice, holy, acceptable to God, which is your reasonable service" (Romans 12:1).

Nehemiah's second step was to inspire the leadership to work hard in God's service (2:17-18). Years later in the New Testament period, Joses earned the nickname "Barnabas," meaning, "Son of encouragement" (Acts 4:36). He had the skill of stimulating others in their work for the Lord (Acts 11:22-24).

The third part of Nehemiah's strategy was to utilize and arrange the skills and expertise of a whole variety of people (3:1-32). In this there is an illustration of the truth that *all* believers have a contribution to make to the well-being and progress of the church of Christ (1 Corinthians 12:12-27). The task of church leaders is "the equipping of the saints for the work of ministry, for the edifying of the body of Christ" (Ephesians 4:12). This includes instructing, organizing, facilitating and inspiring members of the local church, so that the work of God is strengthened and developed.

ESTHER

MEANING	AUTHOR	KEY THOUGHT
"star"	**Unknown** *(maybe Mordecai)*	**For such a time as this**

THEME

The hidden, though certain, providence of God

THEME VERSE

Yet who knows whether you have come to the kingdom for such a time as this?

ESTHER 4:14

ESTHER / **SUMMARY**

PART 1 / **THE FEAST OF AHASUERUS AND ITS SEQUEL** 1:1-2:23

a.	A six-month feast for the nobility	1:1-4
b.	A seven-day feast for all the citizens of the capital	1:5-8
c.	Queen Vashti is ordered to appear but refuses	1:9-12
d.	The angry king dethrones the queen	1:13-22

(Between chapters 1 and 2, King Ahasuerus leads five million soldiers in a historic attack on Greece. At the battle of Thermophylae, the Medes and Persians suffer a severe defeat.)

e.	The search for a new queen: Esther chosen	2:1-20
f.	Mordecai saves the life of King Ahasuerus	2:21-23

PART 2 / **EVENTS LEADING UP TO ESTHER'S BANQUET AND ITS SEQUEL** 3:1-7:10

a.	Mordecai refuses to pay homage to Haman	3:1-4
b.	Haman's scheme to destroy the Jews	3:5-15
c.	Mordecai and the Jews mourn over the decree	4:1-4
d.	Mordecai's message to Queen Esther	4:5-14
e.	Esther's fast	4:15-17
f.	Esther's courageous approach to the king	5:1-8
g.	Haman constructs gallows on which to hang Mordecai	5:9-14
h.	Sleepless King Ahasuerus reads history	6:1-3
i.	Haman's vanity leads to great honour for Mordecai	6:4-14
j.	Esther's feast; Haman exposed	7:1-6
k.	Haman hung on gallows erected for Mordecai	7:7-10

PART 3 / **THE INSTITUTION OF THE FEAST OF PURIM AND ITS SEQUEL**   **8:1-10:3**

a. Queen Esther pleads for the life of her people — 8:1-6
b. King Ahasuerus authorizes the Jews to organize self-defence — 8:7-17
c. The day of self-defence for the Jews — 9:1-19
d. The institution of the Feast of Purim — 9:20-32
e. The advancement of Mordecai — 10:1-3

ESTHER

Throughout history God has raised up a series of heathen kingdoms to punish his people for their rebellion and sin. Five great empires afflicted Israel during the Old Testament period and right into the era of the New. The first great empire was Assyria, with its capital at Nineveh on the River Tigris. This was ultimately overthrown by Babylon, whose capital of that name was on the River Euphrates. Then came Cyrus the Great (c. 600–530 B.C.) from Persia (present-day Iran). He conquered the Medes, establishing the kingdom of the Medes and Persians, and then he extended his vast kingdom by defeating Nebuchadnezzar (c. 630–c. 562 B.C.) of Babylon. The Greeks built the next great empire under Alexander the Great (356–323 B.C.) and finally, bringing us into New Testament times, the Roman empire emerged as the world power.

The book of Esther speaks of God's faithful dealings with his people Israel during the era of the great Persian empire.

ESTHER / **AUTHOR**

The author of the book of Esther is unknown, although there may be a hint that Mordecai was the historian (9:20). He was, after all, not only an eyewitness of the events that took place but also played the principal role in them. If it was not written by Mordecai, then the author no doubt used Mordecai's records and may also have had access to the chronicles of the kings of Media and Persia (2:23; 10:2). Augustine credited Ezra with being the journalist. Yet, as we have repeatedly noted, the human author is not important to Bible-believing people. The book's divine authorship is certain.

Does the book of Esther qualify to be included in the divinely inspired Scriptures? There has not always been agreement among Jews or Christians as to whether Esther should be included in the Old Testament canon. Luther is reputed to have disliked the book and wished that it did not exist![1] There are also those of our own day who

---

[1] Robert Lee, *The Outlined Bible: An Outline and Analysis of Every Book in the Bible* (London: Pickering and Inglis, 1930), analysis no. 17.

question the right of this little book to be included in the canon of Scripture. The arguments against its inclusion in Scripture are based upon its lack of spiritual content: firstly, the name of God does not appear in its pages, while a heathen king is referred to 187 times; secondly, there is no mention of prayer, no reference to the law of Moses, nor to any kind of service for God, with the possible exception of fasting; thirdly, the only reference to the supernatural is in the superstitious habit of heathens in observing lucky days (3:7); fourthly, it is never quoted in the New Testament; and, fifthly, the Feast of Purim has no connection with New Testament doctrine.

While these are strong arguments against the canonicity of the book of Esther, a simple explanation counters all the objections: the book was written for Jews living in an alien social environment. The book of Revelation was written in a similar context of persecution; hence its use of symbolism and dramatic word-pictures which only Christians would be able to interpret and understand.

In the first place, the book was written in Persia and could not be overtly God-honouring. Any use of a Persian name for God would have greatly dishonoured the Lord.

Secondly, the name of God (YHWH) does appear in acrostic form four times in the Hebrew text (1:20: 5:4,13; 7:7). The initial letters of four consecutive words in the Hebrew form the name YHWH in four different verses.

Thirdly, the absence of God's name serves the purpose of illustrating the hidden but providential care of God, in spite of outward appearances (Deuteronomy 31:18; cf. v. 8). Finally, the omission of God's name and of any direct spiritual references may be a mark of God's disapproval upon those Jews who preferred the comfort of Persia and were unwilling to emigrate and rebuild the temple and the nation in Judah.[2]

The Jews assign to this piece of ancient history a place second only to the five books of Moses. They also annually observe the Feast of Purim according to the instruction of Mordecai.

The book of Esther makes a unique contribution in highlighting the power of God to preserve his people and fulfil his covenant promises.

The crisis in Babylon recorded in the book of Esther had implications not only for the future of the Jews in Babylon itself but throughout the

---

[2] Bruce Wilkinson and Kenneth Boa, *Talk Thru the Old Testament* (Nashville: Nelson, 1983), 133.

whole Persian empire, including Judah. The success of the enemies of God's people would have led to the extermination of the Jews from the face of the earth.

But God's Word *will* be fulfilled. His Son will come to earth "born of a woman" (Galatians 4:4). The covenants with Abraham and David will be honoured. The prophecy of Micah will be fulfilled and Messiah will be born in Bethlehem Ephrathah (Micah 5:2). The book of Esther holds a worthy place in the Scriptures "given by inspiration of God" (2 Timothy 3:16).

ESTHER / **HISTORICAL SETTING**

The greatest days of the Israelite nation were undoubtedly those enjoyed under the reign of King David. When his son Solomon became king there was an initial period of tranquillity, but although Solomon had outstanding and unmatched wisdom he was not able to curb his sinful tendencies and excesses. The king's weaknesses and sins contributed to the decline that was to result eventually in the division of the kingdom. Ten tribes formed the nation bearing the name "Israel," while two tribes formed the nation bearing the name "Judah." Although the ten tribes had the name "Israel," it was the two tribes who maintained much more of the spiritual calibre of the true Israel. Repeated sin and godlessness resulted in the Assyrians attacking Israel and eventually taking the people of the northern kingdom into exile. The two tribes of Judah and Benjamin, based at Jerusalem, lasted longer as a nation. It was almost 350 years after the death of Solomon that these remaining members of the tribes of Israel were removed into exile. In 586 B.C., Nebuchadnezzar of Babylon took them into exile 700 miles from home. Seventy years were to pass in exile in the land of Babylon before the Lord would begin the process of restoring them to the promised land and of rebuilding the nation.

Ezra, Nehemiah and Esther fit into the latter days of the Babylonian exile. The first return from Babylonian exile took place in 536 B.C. under the leadership of Zerubbabel (Ezra 2:2) and the second took place eighty years later under the leadership of Ezra (Ezra 7:1–8). Fourteen years later, Nehemiah was to leave the Babylonian court to join Ezra in Jerusalem (Nehemiah 2:1,11).

The book of Esther belongs within the eighty-year period between the first and second return of exiles to Jerusalem (536–458 B.C.). This is the period between the first six chapters of the book of Ezra and the remaining four chapters. It provides the only biblical account of the events faced by the vast majority of Jews who had chosen to remain in Persia rather than to return to Israel from exile. It is possible to fix precisely the dates covered by the book of Esther by the name of the king. Ahasuerus is the Hebrew name, and Xerxes the Greek name, of King Khshayarsh of Persia (486–464 B.C.). The feast of Ahasuerus took place in the third year of his reign (1:3) hence the year 483 B.C. The historian Herodotus refers to this banquet as the occasion when Ahasuerus planned his war with Greece. Three years later (480 B.C.) he was defeated by the Greeks at Salamis, and Herodotus records that Ahasuerus sought consolation in his harem. This corresponds to the time when young women were brought before him and Esther was chosen and crowned queen of Persia (2:16–17). Since the events of the rest of the book occurred in 473 B.C. (3:7–12), the time span is a ten-year period from 483–473 B.C.[3]

ESTHER / **OUTLINE**

Three feasts dominate the book of Esther: the feast of Ahasuerus (1:1–2:23), Esther's banquet (3:1–7:10) and the Feast of Purim (8:1–10:3).

PART 1 / **THE FEAST OF AHASUERUS AND ITS SEQUEL (1:1-2:23)**

King Ahasuerus reigned over the vast empire of the Medes and Persians from 486 to 464 B.C. His kingdom included the land of Babylon; in fact he "reigned from India to Ethiopia, over one hundred and twenty-seven provinces" (1:1). He was the son of Darius, who is mentioned in the books of Ezra and Daniel, and the grandson, on his mother's side, of King Cyrus who issued the decree for the return of the Jews to Jerusalem to rebuild the temple (2 Chronicles 36:22–23; Ezra 1:1–4; Isaiah 45:1).

In the third year of his reign, Ahasuerus gives a banquet for the princes, governors and civil servants who rule over his 127 provinces

---

[3] Wilkinson and Boa, *Talk Thru the Old Testament*, 131.

(1:3). After six months of uninterrupted feasting with the nobility, he invites all the citizens of his capital to join him in festivities lasting seven days (1:5). On the last day, he commands his queen, Queen Vashti, to attend the final night, but she adamantly refuses to parade herself before her husband's male guests. Ahasuerus is furious and on the advice of counsellors he divorces and dethrones Queen Vashti.

The most beautiful women in the empire are brought to the capital so that the king might choose a new wife at his pleasure. Among these virgins is a young Jewess named Hadassah, known by her Persian name Esther. Born a Jewish exile in the land of Persia, and having lost her parents when very young, she had been adopted by her cousin Mordecai, an Israelite of the tribe of Benjamin.

After the customary preparation, Esther is brought before the king and he chooses her to be his queen. And so, four years after divorcing Queen Vashti, Ahasuerus marries Esther and she becomes queen of all Persia. At this time Esther does not disclose her race.

After her marriage, Esther continues to closely communicate with Mordecai, her beloved guardian and trusted mentor. During one of his daily visits to the palace grounds, Mordecai overhears a plot to assassinate the king. He informs Esther, who in turn recounts the news to her husband, King Ahasuerus. The conspiracy is exposed; the would-be assassins hanged. Mordecai's action in protecting the king's life is "written in the book of the chronicles in the presence of the king" (2:23)—and then seemingly forgotten.

Some time after the marriage of Ahasuerus and Esther, Haman the Agagite is appointed to the post of prime minister. The king commands that Haman be given the highest respect. In his presence, the people are to bow and pay homage. But Mordecai refuses to comply (3:2). When asked for an explanation of his refusal to bow before Haman, Mordecai tells his questioners "that he was a Jew" (3:4). Now in their long history there had been thousands upon thousands of Israelites who would not hesitate to bow down to anyone, or anything, if it was to their advantage. The mere fact of bowing to a dignitary was not a contravention of any law of God. The Israelites were in the habit of falling down to the earth before an exalted person, especially before a king (2 Samuel 14:4; 18:28; 1 Kings 1:16). Mordecai's refusal to show this honour to Haman must indicate that something else was involved here. It is likely that the Persians attached divine significance to dignitaries, especially to the king. This homage, which was probably regarded as an act of reverence and worship to a god, was, by the command of the king, to be paid to Haman as his representative. This Mordecai could not do without a denial of his faith. The man who had counselled his young charge not to reveal her people and race (2:10,20) will not now remain silent himself. In this simple statement, "He told them that he was a Jew," there is a declaration that he was a God-fearing Jew, a man of keen principle, a man of deep devotion to God.

Haman is incensed. The discovery that Mordecai is a Jew only serves to increase his feelings of enmity, for he is an Amalekite, a descendant of King Agag (3:1; cf. 1 Samuel 15:1–33). The age-old hostility between Amalek and Israel is reignited: Haman plans the annihilation of the whole race of Israel on one specific day. By subtle strategy and careful concealing of the truth, Haman obtains a decree from King Ahasuerus for the extermination of the Jews throughout the *whole* of the empire (this would include those who had returned to Jerusalem).

Hearing the news, Mordecai sends word to Queen Esther, who is oblivious of the decree. Her cousin strongly urges her to use her influence with the king. His words form the key words to the whole book:

> Do not think in your heart that you will escape in the king's palace any more than all the other Jews. For if you remain completely silent at this time, relief and deliverance will arise for the Jews from another place, but you and your father's house will perish. Yet who knows whether you have come to the kingdom for such a time as this? (4:13–14)

Here again there is evidence that Mordecai is a man of God in his unspoken, though clearly implied, confidence in the providence of the God of Israel.

PART 2 / **EVENTS LEADING UP TO ESTHER'S BANQUET AND ITS SEQUEL (3:1-7:10)**

Esther responds. After calling upon her people in the city to join her in a full fast for seventy-two hours, Esther resolves to risk her life in approaching the king uninvited. The king grants her an audience and, before she has revealed her purpose, he promises to grant her whatever she requests, even to the half of his kingdom. Meanwhile, Haman plans the public execution of Mordecai the Jew.

That night while Haman stews in his hatred for Mordecai, King Ahasuerus suffers insomnia. Another mark of the presence of "the finger of God" is seen in the simple words: "That night the king could not sleep" (6:1). Ahasuerus sends for the history books and during the reading of the recent records he stumbles across the account of Mordecai's loyalty to the king in disclosing the plot against his life. Ahasuerus enquires whether any reward or public acknowledgement has been given to Mordecai. The king is informed that nothing has been done for him (6:3). Immediately the king hears footsteps in the outer court. Haman has come to gain permission to execute Mordecai.

What follows displays superb dramatic irony! The king has Mordecai in mind, to honour him. Haman has Mordecai in mind, to hang him. Without mentioning Mordecai by name, the king asks Haman to suggest ways of honouring a man with whom the king is well pleased. The arrogant, conceited Haman thinks the king must be referring to himself, and so piles on the honours thick and fast (6:7–9). Suddenly, the truth dawns. The king is to honour Mordecai. Haman is to lead him through the streets. What humiliation for Haman!

When the king and Haman attend the second banquet, Esther pleads for her life and the life of her people (7:3–4). She reveals Haman as the would-be perpetrator of this genocide of the Jews. Full of anger and fury, the king walks out into the garden. Haman pleads for his life. The king returns to find Haman at the feet of his wife and supposes that he is about to do violence to her. Ahasuerus passes the sentence of death upon him instantly. The king gives all Haman's property to Queen Esther (8:1). She pleads for a reversal of the decree issued against the Jews, but the law of the Medes and Persians once decreed cannot be altered or rescinded. Mordecai is authorized to prepare another decree to the effect that the Jews throughout the empire may defend themselves, and retaliate against their enemies.

On the appointed day, nine months after the promulgation of the second decree, 500 enemies of the Jews are slain in Shushan the capital, and in the provinces 75,000 enemies are killed. The following day, a further 300 are killed in the capital. It is estimated that the Persian empire, from India to Ethiopia, consisted of a population of at least 100 million. The number of Jews was somewhere between two and three million, of which number at least 500,000 to 700,000 would be capable of bearing arms.[4] "And no one could withstand them because fear of them fell upon all people" (9:2).

PART 3 / **THE INSTITUTION OF THE FEAST OF PURIM AND ITS SEQUEL (8:1-10:3)**

In consequence of this remarkable turn of events, the Feast of Purim was instituted as a perpetual memorial among the Jews (9:26-27). It is called the Feast of Purim after the name Pur, the lot, because Haman had cast lots concerning the destruction of the Jews (3:7).

ESTHER / **CHRIST AND HIS CHURCH**

PROPHECIES

The influence and driving force behind Haman's attempted genocide of the Jews is the devil, the great enemy of God. This portion of history recounts a classic attempt by Satan to thwart the purposes of God for Messiah's birth. The annihilation of the Israelites, especially of the tribe of Judah, would remove all possibility of God fulfilling his promises (Genesis 49:10; 2 Samuel 7:12-16; 1 Kings 11:36). Haman acted as the agent of the devil in seeking the extermination of the Jews. Ahasuerus was king over all the Jews in Judah, as well as over those in Persia and Babylon. The devil knew that the Deliverer who was to arise from the descendants of David would destroy his power. He instigated Saul's attempt at David's life in twice throwing a javelin and tracking him relentlessly across the land. He inspired Queen Athaliah in her effort to annihilate the royal line. He stirred Haman to rush from a supposed insult from one man to the proposed extermination of his whole race. The same malevolent spirit prompted Herod years later to try to kill the Christ-child by the slaughter of "all the male children who were in Bethlehem and in all its districts, from two years old and under" (Matthew 2:16).

---

[4] C.F. Keil, *The Books of Ezra, Nehemiah, and Esther* (Grand Rapids: Eerdmans, 1949), 308-309.

On each occasion of satanic attack, the Lord delivered his people and safeguarded his gracious plan to send his Son into the world. Scripture predicted hostility (Genesis 3:15; cf. Romans 16:20). Satan truly inflicted pain upon the Saviour, but the Son of God triumphed over all adversity and opposition. As David predicted and the early Christian church realized,

> For truly against Your holy Servant Jesus, whom You anointed, both Herod and Pontius Pilate, with the Gentiles and the people of Israel, were gathered together to do whatever Your hand and Your purpose determined before to be done (Acts 4:27–28; cf. vv. 25–26).

TYPES

Whereas Haman illustrates the forces of evil, Esther exemplifies the powers of good. Like the Saviour, Esther put herself in danger of death for her people, but whereas she was wonderfully delivered, he was not. His death was necessary to "save his people from their sins" (Matthew 1:21).

Another point of comparison between Esther and the Lord Jesus is seen in her interceding on behalf of her people. The Saviour intercedes for his church: "Who is he who condemns? It is Christ who died, and furthermore is also risen, who is even at the right hand of God, who also makes intercession for us" (Romans 8:34). "Therefore He is also able to save to the uttermost those who come to God through Him, since He always lives to make intercession for them" (Hebrews 7:25).

ESTHER / **CONCLUSION**

Haman's attack upon the Jews was not a localized assault. Had he succeeded in his evil design, this would have led to the annihilation of the whole Israelite race. The consequences would have been catastrophic. The covenants, the prophecies and the promises given by God would all have failed. There could have been no Messiah, no Saviour for sinners, no hope, no heaven, no glory. Haman's attack was obviously instigated, motivated and maintained by the Evil One, Satan, the devil.

Mordecai's confidence that the Jews would be preserved surely indicates his confidence in a higher power and authority than that of Haman, or indeed King Ahasuerus (4:14).

Blessed be the God and Father of our Lord Jesus Christ, who according to His abundant mercy has begotten us again to a living hope through the resurrection of Jesus Christ from the dead, to an inheritance incorruptible and undefiled and that does not fade away, reserved in heaven for you, *who are kept by the power of God* through faith for salvation ready to be revealed in the last time (1 Peter 1:3–5, emphasis added).

ESTHER / **APPLICATION AND REFLECTION**

1. Inner beauty

Esther was "lovely and beautiful" (2:7) and no doubt her appearance was a crucial factor in Ahasuerus' choice of her for his wife. The historical record, however, also indicates that her character was a strong factor in her attractiveness. She was humble and submissive and yet not lacking in outstanding courage and determination.

The Word of God warns against concern for outward beauty:

Charm is deceitful and beauty is passing,
But a woman who fears the LORD, she shall be praised (Proverbs 31:30).

Do not let your adornment be merely outward—arranging the hair, wearing gold, or putting on fine apparel—rather let it be the hidden person of the heart, with the incorruptible beauty of a gentle and quiet spirit, which is very precious in the sight of God (1 Peter 3:3-4).

In a day when the beautiful body has become an idol, when obsession about physical appearance is rife throughout society, a Christian needs to take care "not be conformed to this world, but be transformed by the renewing of your mind" (Romans 12:2). Dieting and weight-training may have their benefits but they may easily become a fixation and result in a serious psychological disorder. The gentle and quiet spirit commended in Scripture "is imperishable; it is the true beauty, not one that is put on, but one that is inherent; it is not an earthly, bodily, outward thing but is inherent in the soul."[5]

The character appropriate for godly women is also appropriate for godly men. It is "'the inner person of the heart" that matters. It was foretold of the Saviour:

He has no form or comeliness;
And when we see Him,
There is no beauty that we should desire Him (Isaiah 53:2).

---

[5] R.C.H. Lenski, *The Interpretation of the Epistles of St Peter, St John and St Jude* (Minneapolis: Augsburg, 1966), 132.

The beauty from within Christ expressed itself in "love, joy, peace, longsuffering, kindness, goodness, faithfulness, gentleness, self-control" (Galatians 5:22-23).

2. Submission to the state

Mordecai and Esther provide an example of how the godly function under an ungodly government. In the New Testament, considerable emphasis is placed on the duty of Christians to be model citizens:

> Let every soul be subject to the governing authorities. For there is no authority except from God, and the authorities that exist are appointed by God. Therefore whoever resists the authority resists the ordinance of God, and those who resist will bring judgment on themselves (Romans 13:1-2; cf. 1 Peter 2:13-17).

God commands "every God-fearing, believing Christian person to respect the properly constituted government of any nation in which he dwells, whatever its morality and whatever its standards of ethics."[6] When a conflict occurs between obeying God and obeying the state, as it did with the apostles Peter and John (Acts 4:19), obedience to the Lord always takes priority.

There is nothing inappropriate about a godly person being elevated to a position of responsibility and trust by an ungodly government or by a pagan king. The Jews had a fine heritage in this regard: Joseph and the Pharaoh of Egypt; Obadiah and King Ahab of Israel; Daniel and Nebuchadnezzar of Babylon; Nehemiah and Artaxerxes of Persia. In being loyal to their king, none of these men compromised their faithfulness to God. They could not prevent every evil in government, but in keeping themselves from sin they may well have influenced the course of nations.

Nor did these men sacrifice loyalty to their own people. Of Mordecai it is testified: "For Mordecai the Jew was second to King Ahasuerus, and was great among the Jews and well-received by the multitude of his brethren, seeking the good of his people and speaking peace to all his kindred" (10:3). Patriotism is not inconsistent with religion in its purest form. Mordecai spent his time seeking the welfare of his people,

---

[6] William Still, *Eight Sermons on the Book of Esther* (Aberdeen: Didasko Press, 1973), 22.

but it was the welfare of his people, not of a particular class, or a few favourites.... His love was without partiality; and he who could not bow to a wicked minister, was not the man to pervert judgement by respect of persons.[7]

3. God-given opportunities

In the service of God opportunities may arise only once in a lifetime. As Mordecai said to Esther, "Who knows whether you have come to the kingdom for such a time as this?" (4:14). There are situations that are unique to each Christian. Opportunities for honouring God and testifying to his grace in Christ Jesus may suddenly transpire. Christians should be alert and prepared for such eventualities: "But sanctify the Lord God in your hearts, and always be ready to give a defense to everyone who asks you a reason for the hope that is in you, with meekness and fear" (1 Peter 3:15).

There may be times when, like Esther, we must be ready to take our life in our hands and risk everything for the cause of God.

4. Sovereign protection

Matthew Henry declared, "Though the name of God be not in it, His finger is."[8] The book of Esther occupies its place in Scripture because of its profound message: *God is always at work protecting his people, even in the darkest times.* It is the supreme book of providence: "And we know that all things work together for good to those who love God, to those who are the called according to His purpose" (Romans 8:28).

God is involved in all that transpires on the earth. He is no absentee landlord. God sees all, hears all, knows all and controls all (Psalm 139:1-12; Ephesians 1:11). The Lord Jesus Christ reigns over a kingdom of power and a kingdom of grace. His kingdom of power stretches over all the earth. His kingdom of grace extends over all the church. His reign over the one is for the benefit of the other. He rules the world for the good of his people (Ephesians 1:20-23).

As William Cowper (1731-1800) writes:

---

[7] Thomas McCrie, *Lectures on the Book of Esther* (Lynchburg: James Family Christian Publishing Co., [n.d.]), 306-307.

[8] Matthew Henry, *Commentary On the Holy Bible* (Nashville: Thomas Nelson Publishers, 1975), 517.

His purposes will ripen fast,
  Unfolding every hour;
The bud may have a bitter taste,
  But sweet will be the flower.

Blind unbelief is sure to err,
  And scan his work in vain;
God is his own interpreter,
  And he will make it plain.

The book of Esther demonstrates the loving care and protection that God exercises over his people. The Lord can easily disturb a king and not permit him to sleep on one crucial night. Our God can easily turn the tables on a wicked man like Haman.

God is wise in heart and mighty in strength.
Who has hardened himself against Him and prospered? (Job 9:4)

Though the name of God does not appear throughout the entire book of Esther, nevertheless his presence is abundantly evident. What a mass of "coincidences" are contained in these pages—the singular attractiveness of Esther the Jew; the king choosing her from hundreds of candidates; Mordecai overhearing the plot against the king; a record being made of Mordecai's loyalty and faithfulness; the insomnia of the king on that particular night; the fact that he called for the chronicles to be read, that his servant read that particular piece of forgotten history and that the king asked whether Mordecai had been rewarded! All these incidents combine to form an overwhelming proof of divine control.

The doctrine of divine sovereignty is a basic feature of this book, "but it is not a kind of fatalism. For where God's actions and purposes are not transparent, the importance of human obedience and faithfulness becomes the more apparent."[9] Though God is sovereign, he chooses to use ordinary people to overcome impossible circumstances and fulfil his gracious purposes.

---

[9] Raymond B. Dillard and Tremper Longman III, *An Introduction to the Old Testament* (Leicester: Apollos, 1995), 196.

Select bibliography

Alexander, Charles D. *Elijah: 'Crouching Coward' or Hero of the Faith?* Liverpool: Bible Exposition Fellowship, n.d.

───── . *The Heavenly Mystery of the Song of Songs.* Liverpool: Bible Exposition Fellowship, 1965.

Atkinson, David. *The Message of Ruth: The Wings of Refuge.* Leicester: Inter-Varsity Press, 1983.

Benton, John. *Losing Touch with the Living God.* Welwyn: Evangelical Press, 1985.

Blaikie, William G. *The Book of Joshua.* 1908; Minneapolis: Klock and Klock, 1978.

───── . *David, King of Israel: The Divine Plan and Lessons of His Life.* 1861; Minneapolis: Klock and Kloc, 1981.

───── . *The First Book of Samuel.* 1887; Minneapolis: Klock and Klock, 1978.

Bonar, Andrew A. *Christ and His Church in the Book of Psalms*. 1861; Grand Rapids: Kregel, 1978.

──────. *A Commentary on Leviticus*. 1846; Edinburgh: Banner of Truth Trust, 1966.

Borland, James A. *Christ in the Old Testament: A Comprehensive Study of Old Testament Appearances of Christ in Human Form*. Chicago: Moody, 1978.

Bridges, Charles. *A Commentary on Proverbs*. 1846; London: Banner of Truth Trust, 1968.

Brown, Raymond. *Let's Read the Old Testament*. London: Victory Press, 1971.

Buckland, A.R. and A.L. Williams, ed. *Universal Bible Dictionary*. London: The Religious Tract Society, 1914.

Calvin, John. *A Commentary on Genesis*. 1554; London: Banner of Truth Trust, 1965.

Candlish, Robert. *Studies in Genesis*. 1868; Grand Rapids: Kregel Publications, 1979.

Carson, Herbert M. *Hallelujah!: Christian Worship*. Welwyn: Evangelical Press, 1980.

Clowney, Edmund P. *The Unfolding Mystery: Discovering Christ in the Old Testament*. Leicester: Inter-Varsity Press, 1988.

──────. "Preaching Christ from All the Scriptures," in Samuel T. Logan, Jr., ed. *The Preacher and Preaching: Reviving the Art in the Twentieth Century*. Phillipsburg: Presbyterian and Reformed, 1986.

Delitzsch, Franz. *Messianic Prophecies*. Edinburgh: T & T Clark, 1880.

Dillard, Raymond B. and Tremper Longman III. *An Introduction to the Old Testament*. Leicester: Apollos IVP, 1995.

Edersheim, Alfred. *Israel under Samuel, Saul, and David, to the Birth of Solomon*. London: The Religious Tract Society, [1877?].

Fairbairn, Patrick. *Prophecy: Viewed in Respect to Its Distinctive Nature, Its Special Function, and Proper Interpretation*. 1865; Grand Rapids: Baker, 1976.

──────. *The Typology of Scripture: Viewed in Connection with the Whole Series of the Divine Dispensations*. 1900; Grand Rapids: Baker, 1975.

Fausset, Andrew R. *A Critical and Expository Commentary on the Book of Judges*. 1885; Minneapolis: James and Klock, 1977.

Goldsworthy, Graeme. *Gospel and Kingdom: A Christian Interpretation of the Old Testament*. Carlisle: Paternoster, 1981.

Gulston, Charles. *David, Shepherd and King: The Life and Heritage of David*. Grand Rapids: Zondervan, 1980.
Hendriksen, William. *Survey of the Bible: A Treasury of Bible Information*. Welwyn: Evangelical Press, 1976.
Hengstenberg, Ernest W. *Christology of the Old Testament and A Commentary on the Messianic Predictions*. 1847; Grand Rapids: Kregel Publications, 1970.
———. *History of the Kingdom of God under the Old Testament*, 2 vol. Edinburgh: T & T Clark, 1877.
Hodge, Charles. *Systematic Theology*, 3 vol. Grand Rapids: Eerdmans, 1977.
Hodgkin, A.M. *Christ in All the Scriptures*. London: Pickering and Inglis, 1907.
Hoeksema, Homer C. *'In the Beginning God...'* Grand Rapids: Reformed Free Publishing Association, 1966.
Jensen, Irving L. *Jensen's Survey of the Old Testament: Search and Discover*. Chicago: Moody, 1978.
Jukes, Andrew. *The Law of the Offerings*. 1854; Grand Rapids: Kregel Publications, 1976.
Keddie, Gordon J. *Even in Darkness: Judges and Ruth Simply Explained*. Welwyn: Evangelical Press, 1985.
Keil, Carl F. *Biblical Commentary on the Books of the Kings*. Grand Rapids: Eerdmans, 1950.
———. *The Books of Ezra, Nehemiah, and Esther*. Grand Rapids: Eerdmans, 1949.
———. *The Books of Joshua, Judges and Ruth*. Grand Rapids: Eerdmans, 1950.
Keil, Carl F. and Franz Delitzsch. *Biblical Commentary on the Books of Samuel*. Grand Rapids: Eerdmans, 1950.
———. *Commentary on the Old Testament: The Pentateuch*, 3 vol. Grand Rapids: Eerdmans, 1980.
Kellogg, Samuel H. *The Book of Leviticus*. 1899; Minneapolis: Klock and Klock, 1978.
Kiene, Paul F. *The Tabernacle of God in the Wilderness of Sinai*. Grand Rapids: Zondervan, 1977.
Krummacher, F.W. *David—The King of Israel*. 1868; Grand Rapids: Baker, 1982.
———. *Elijah the Tishbite*. Grand Rapids: Baker, 1977.

———. *Elisha: A Prophet for Our Times*. Grand Rapids: Baker, 1976.

———. *The Last Days of Elisha*. Grand Rapids: Baker, 1981.

Law, Henry. *The Gospel in Exodus*. 1855; London: Banner of Truth Trust, 1967.

Lawson, George. *Lectures on the History of Joseph*. 1807; London: Banner of Truth Trust, 1972.

Lee, Robert. *The Outlined Bible: An Outline and Analysis of Every Book in the Bible*. London: Pickering and Inglis, 1930.

Leupold, H.C. *Exposition of Genesis*, 2 vol. Grand Rapids: Baker, 1942.

Martens, E.A. *Plot and Purpose in the Old Testament*. Leicester: Inter-Varsity Press, 1981.

McComiskey, Thomas E. *The Covenants of Promise: A Theology of the Old Testament Covenants*. Nottingham: Inter-Varsity Press, 1985.

McCrie, Thomas. *Lectures on the Book of Esther*. Lynchburg: James Family Christian Publishing Co., [n.d.].

McMillen, S.I. *None of These Diseases*. London: Marshall Morgan and Scott, 1966.

Meyer, F.B. *Devotional Commentary on Exodus*. Grand Rapids: Kregel Publications, 1978.

Morgan, G. Campbell. *Student Survey of the Bible*. Iowa Falls: World Bible Publishers, 1993.

Murphy, James G. *A Critical and Exegetical Commentary on the Book of Exodus*. 1866; Minneapolis: Klock and Klock, 1979.

Nelson's Complete Book of Bible Maps and Charts. Nashville: Thomas Nelson, 1996.

Olyott, Stuart. *Jesus Is Both God and Man—What the Bible Teaches About the Person of Christ*. Darlington: Evangelical Press, 2000.

———. *The Three are One: What the Bible Teaches About the Trinity*. Welwyn: Evangelical Press, 1979.

Pink, Arthur W. *Gleanings in Exodus*. Chicago: Moody Press, 1972.

———. *Gleanings in Genesis*. Chicago: Moody Press, 1922.

———. *Gleanings in Joshua*. Chicago: Moody Press, 1964.

———. *Gleanings from Elisha: His Life and Miracles*. Chicago: Moody Press, 1972.

———. *The Life of David*. Grand Rapids: Baker Book House, 1981.

———. *The Life of Elijah*. Edinburgh: Banner of Truth Trust, 1956.

Spurgeon, Charles Haddon. *The Treasury of David*, 3 vol. McLean: MacDonald Publishing Company, 1990.

Stewart, Andrew. *A Family Tree: 1 Chronicles Simply Explained*. Darlington: Evangelical Press, 1997.

Stier, Rudolf. *The Words of the Apostles*. 1869; Minneapolis: Klock and Klock, 1981.

——. *The Words of the Lord Jesus*. 1874; Edinburgh: T & T Clark, 1985.

Thiele, Edwin R. *A Chronology of Hebrew Kings*. Grand Rapids: Zondervan, 1977.

Vos, Geerhardus. *Biblical Theology: Old and New Testaments*. 1948; Edinburgh: Banner of Truth Trust, 1975.

Watson, Thomas. *The Ten Commandments*. 1692; London: Banner of Truth Trust, 1959.

Wilkinson, Bruce and Kenneth Boa. *Talk Thru the Old Testament*. Nashville: Nelson, 1983.

Wiseman, Luke H. *Practical Truths from Judges*. 1874; Grand Rapids: Kregel, 1985.

Wood, Leon J. *Distressing Days of the Judges*. Grand Rapids: Zondervan, 1975.

Young, Edward J. *An Introduction to the Old Testament*. Grand Rapids: Eerdmans, 1949.

Appendix:
A study guide

By Paul Hudson

GENESIS / **REVIEW**

Some key verses from Genesis:
1. **Genesis 1:26-28**
   Then God said, "Let Us make man in Our image, according to Our likeness; let them have dominion over the fish of the sea, over the birds of the air, and over the cattle, over all the earth and over every creeping thing that creeps on the earth." So God created man in His own image; in the image of God He created him; male and female He created them. Then God blessed them, and God said to them, "Be fruitful and multiply; fill the earth and subdue it; have dominion over the fish of the sea, over the birds of

the air, and over every living thing that moves on the earth."
2. **Genesis 3:15**
   And I will put enmity
   Between you and the woman,
   And between your seed and her Seed;
   He shall bruise your head,
   And you shall bruise His heel."
3. **Genesis 12:1-3**
   Now the LORD had said to Abram:
   "Get out of your country,
   From your family
   And from your father's house,
   To a land that I will show you.
   I will make you a great nation;
   I will bless you
   And make your name great;
   And you shall be a blessing.
   I will bless those who bless you,
   And I will curse him who curses you;
   And in you all the families of the earth shall be blessed."
4. **Genesis 22:8**
   And Abraham said, "My son, God will provide for Himself the lamb for a burnt offering." So the two of them went together.

GENESIS / **REFLECT**

1. **Sovereign free choice:** Dr. Crossley discusses "election—God's free and sovereign choice," as the key doctrine revealed to us in the book of Genesis. He notes several instances where, contrary to human expectations, God chooses the one through whom he will work to fulfill the promise of Genesis 3:15, a coming seed of the woman who will crush the serpent's head. One example not mentioned is God's free choice of Judah as the one son of Jacob/Israel through whom the Messiah will come. Discuss God's choice of Judah (Genesis 49:8-12) in light of Judah's life to that point and in comparison with his brother Joseph.
2. **Only by grace:** With all of the tremendous examples of the free grace of God ("love and favour toward the undeserving") cited from Genesis, write about what *motivates* God's grace. Write of his amazing, steadfast love

for humankind whom he has created, and of the glory that returns to God as his amazing grace is revealed.
3. **Justification by faith:** Dr. Crossley writes, "In Genesis the truth of justification by faith is first made known." The faith of Abraham concerning God's promise of a son by Sarah (chosen instead of Ishmael, son of Hagar), who would be the one who would inherit the promises of God, was severely tested in Genesis 22. Discuss the significant foreshadowing of the work of Christ on the cross, in the location, activity and faith of Abraham, as demonstrated in his response to Isaac's question (Genesis 22:8) and the reflection of the author of Hebrews in Hebrews 11:17-19.
4. **Prevailing prayer:** Dr. Crossley writes, "The importance and value of prayer are indicated in Genesis." Reflecting on the examples he cites from Genesis, recount a time in your own life or in the life of someone close to you, where you have seen God's miraculous response to "prevailing prayer."

GENESIS / **REJOICE**

Psalm 8:1-4
To the Chief Musician. On the instrument of Gath. A Psalm of David.

O LORD, our Lord,
How excellent *is* Your name in all the earth,
Who have set Your glory above the heavens!

Out of the mouth of babes and nursing infants
You have ordained strength,
Because of Your enemies,
That You may silence the enemy and the avenger.

When I consider Your heavens, the work of Your fingers,
The moon and the stars, which You have ordained,
What is man that You are mindful of him,
And the son of man that You visit him?

EXODUS / **REVIEW**

Some key verses from Exodus:
1. **Exodus 2:23-25**
   Now it happened in the process of time that the king of Egypt died. Then the children of Israel groaned because of the bondage, and they cried out; and their cry came up to God because of the bondage. So God heard their groaning, and God remembered His covenant with Abraham, with Isaac, and with Jacob. And God looked upon the children of Israel, and God acknowledged them.
2. **Exodus 12:13**
   Now the blood shall be a sign for you on the houses where you are. And when I see the blood, I will pass over you; and the plague shall not be on you to destroy you when I strike the land of Egypt.
3. **Exodus 20:1-6**
   And God spoke all these words, saying:
   "I *am* the Lord your God, who brought you out of the land of Egypt, out of the house of bondage.
   "You shall have no other gods before Me.
   "You shall not make for yourself a carved image—any likeness *of anything* that *is* in heaven above, or that *is* in the earth beneath, or that *is* in the water under the earth; you shall not bow down to them nor serve them. For I, the Lord your God, *am* a jealous God, visiting the iniquity of the fathers upon the children to the third and fourth *generations* of those who hate Me, but showing mercy to thousands, to those who love Me and keep My commandments."

EXODUS / **REFLECT**

1. **Redemption:** Dr. Crossley identifies the doctrinal emphasis of the book of Exodus as redemption. He writes that Exodus "teaches *how* God saves: by redemption—that is, by costly deliverance." Discuss how the Passover (Exodus 12) foreshadows the redemption of God's people through the sacrifice of the Lamb of God, Christ Jesus our Saviour.
2. **Faith and obedience:** Dr. Crossley writes that "faith and obedience, belong together," and reflects on the objective and subjective uses of the word *faith*. Objectively, *the faith* is "the body of truth, the doctrines given

by God," and subjectively, *faith* is "the impulse of a regenerate soul." In the crossing of the Red Sea (Exodus 14), is the *obedience* of Moses and the people to the command to cross through the waters an obedience *to the* faith, or an obedience *of* faith? Can we really identify a distinction? Is the motivation for obedience different for Moses and the people (or some of the people)? Or, as Dr. Crossley writes, is it "much the same thing… God-given faith obeys the doctrines of God's Word"?

3. **Prevailing prayer:** From his first encounter with God in the burning bush (Exodus 3–4) until the end of his life, Moses was a "man of God" (Deuteronomy 33:1) who spoke with God "face to face" (Exodus 33:11). Read Exodus 33 and 34 and reflect on Moses' intimate, personal, direct communication with God in comparison with our own, often dry and remote, prayer life. On what attributes and actions of God revealed in Exodus can we trust in order to "come boldly to the throne of grace, that we may obtain mercy and find grace to help in time of need" (Hebrews 4:16)?

4. **The law:** Dr. Crossley writes about the different *purposes of* and *perspectives about* the law in the Old and New Covenants. It is clear that salvation is not to be earned by perfect obedience to the law, which is impossible for men and women, but by grace through faith in the Lord Jesus Christ. But what place does the law have in guiding and shaping the lives of believers? Two great prophecies concerning the New Covenant and the law are given in Jeremiah 31:31–43 and Ezekiel 36:26–27. According to these prophecies the law is not abolished. Rather, it is internalized.

> "But this *is* the covenant that I will make with the house of Israel after those days, says the Lord: I will put My law in their minds, and write it on their hearts; and I will be their God, and they shall be My people" (Jeremiah 31:33).

> "I will give you a new heart and put a new spirit within you; I will take the heart of stone out of your flesh and give you a heart of flesh. I will put My Spirit within you and cause you to walk in My statutes, and you will keep My judgments and do *them*" (Ezekiel 36:26–27).

What are your thoughts on this? Is a Christian to live by the Mosaic law or by some part of it? What is the motivation for obedience to the law—is it the desire to earn God's approval, or the desire to please our heavenly Father, to delight his heart and bring praise and honour and glory to Him?

EXODUS / **REJOICE**

Exodus 15:1-3
The Song of Moses

Then Moses and the children of Israel sang this song to the Lord, and spoke, saying:
 "I will sing to the Lord,
 For He has triumphed gloriously!
 The horse and its rider
 He has thrown into the sea!
 The Lord *is* my strength and song,
 And He has become my salvation;
 He *is* my God, and I will praise Him;
 My father's God, and I will exalt Him.
 The Lord *is* a man of war;
 The Lord *is* His name.

LEVITICUS / **REVIEW**

Some key verses from Leviticus:
1. **Leviticus 16:21**
   Aaron shall lay both his hands on the head of the live goat, confess over it all the iniquities of the children of Israel, and all their transgressions, concerning all their sins, putting them on the head of the goat, and shall send *it* away into the wilderness by the hand of a suitable man.
2. **Leviticus 19:1-2**
   And the Lord spoke to Moses, saying, "Speak to all the congregation of the children of Israel, and say to them: 'You shall be holy, for I the Lord your God *am* holy.'"
3. **Leviticus 20:24**
   "But I have said to you, 'You shall inherit their land, and I will give it to you to possess, a land flowing with milk and honey.' I *am* the Lord your God, who has separated you from the peoples."

LEVITICUS / **REFLECT**

1. **Holiness:** As Dr. Crossley points out, the book of Leviticus details sacrifices and punishments for sin that shock even many Christians. However, as he continues, "The severity of the penalties which were attached to the Levitical laws are consistent with the impeccable holy character of God." Reflect on the "holy, holy, holy" nature of God as it is demonstrated in penal substitutionary atonement, in the shedding of Christ's blood on the cross in our place and for our sin. Consider, in particular, the foreshadowing of Christ's death for us in God's commands concerning the Day of Atonement in Leviticus 16.
2. **Worship:** Although in Leviticus God commands many sacrifices to atone for sin, several passages in Scripture remind us that the *heart attitude* of the sinner is more important than the sacrifice itself. Read 1 Samuel 15:22; Proverbs 15:8; Isaiah 66:3; Jeremiah 6:20 and Malachi 1:10, and then reflect on Paul's contrast of "godly sorrow" and "the sorrow of the world" in 2 Corinthians 7:8–11. Can one truly be saved if their "repentance" for sin is in reality only "the sorrow of the world," a sorrow at being caught in sin or a dread of the wrath of God, without true brokenheartedness for having offended the holy, holy, holy God?
3. **Separation:** Dr. Crossley reminds us that Peter quotes from Leviticus 11:44; 45; 19:2, when "he urges Christians to live as obedient and transformed children of God: 'As He who called you is holy, you also be holy in all your conduct, because it is written, "Be holy, for I am holy."'" What does it mean for you to live a holy, separated life, a sanctified life, dedicated to God, in the culture in which you live?

LEVITICUS / **REJOICE**

Psalm 19:7–11
A Psalm of David.

The law of the Lord *is* perfect, converting the soul;
The testimony of the Lord *is* sure, making wise the simple;
The statutes of the Lord *are* right, rejoicing the heart;
The commandment of the Lord *is* pure, enlightening the eyes;
The fear of the Lord *is* clean, enduring forever;

The judgments of the LORD *are* true *and* righteous altogether.
More to be desired *are they* than gold,
Yea, than much fine gold;
Sweeter also than honey and the honeycomb.
Moreover by them Your servant is warned,
And in keeping them *there is* great reward.

NUMBERS / **REVIEW**

Some key verses from Numbers:
1. **Numbers 6:22-26**
   And the LORD spoke to Moses, saying: "Speak to Aaron and his sons, saying, 'This is the way you shall bless the children of Israel. Say to them:
   "The LORD bless you and keep you;
   The LORD make His face shine upon you,
   And be gracious to you;
   The LORD lift up His countenance upon you,
   And give you peace."'"
2. **Numbers 14:20-23**
   Then the LORD said: "I have pardoned, according to your word; but truly, as I live, all the earth shall be filled with the glory of the LORD—because all these men who have seen My glory and the signs which I did in Egypt and in the wilderness, and have put Me to the test now these ten times, and have not heeded My voice, they certainly shall not see the land of which I swore to their fathers, nor shall any of those who rejected Me see it."
3. **Numbers 20:12**
   Then the LORD spoke to Moses and Aaron, "Because you did not believe Me, to hallow Me in the eyes of the children of Israel, therefore you shall not bring this assembly into the land which I have given them."
4. **Numbers 27:18-20**
   And the LORD said to Moses: "Take Joshua the son of Nun with you, a man in whom is the Spirit, and lay your hand on him; set him before Eleazar the priest and before all the congregation, and inaugurate him in their sight. And you shall give some of your authority to him, that all the congregation of the children of Israel may be obedient."

NUMBERS / **REFLECT**

1. **Prepared for service:** Dr. Crossley writes, "The 'numbering' which takes place is, in reality, a registration for service...every believer is a soldier... every soldier has something to do.... Every believer has his or her special task to perform in the kingdom of God." Reflect on Paul's beautiful passage in Ephesians 2:1–10 (and all the way to verse 10!). Were you saved by God primarily for yourself, or for the glory of God in the "good works, which God prepared beforehand that we should walk in them" (Ephesians 2:10)?
2. **Gifts for the work of God:** Dr. Crossley quotes A.M. Hodgkin writing, "God delights to honour the gifts of His children," and continues, discussing the principle of the tithe, "If the principles of giving outlined in the New Testament were observed by the church, there would be no shortage of funds for ministry, evangelism or church-planting at home or abroad." Consider, not only the financial resources the Lord provides, but everything with which he has blessed you (time, talent and money). Are we not challenged, in both Old and New Testaments, to be good stewards of *all* that he gives, for his glory?
3. **Grumbling:** Dr. Crossley writes, "The book of Numbers might well be named 'the book of murmurings,' for it contains several major incidents of despondency and gloom," and "From the many references to grumbling, murmuring and complaining which appear in Scripture, it might well be concluded that this is one of our major failings in the spiritual life." We grumble and complain, even when we are abounding in God's good gifts, because we want more or different gifts or the gifts someone else has. Consider what Paul writes in Philippians 4:12–13:

   > I know how to be abased, and I know how to abound. Everywhere and in all things I have learned both to be full and to be hungry, both to abound and to suffer need. I can do all things through Christ who strengthens me.

   Do you find it more difficult *not* to grumble when you are abased or when you abound?
4. **Unbelief:** Dr. Crossley writes about God's condemnation of all who did not trust that he could lead them into the promised land. All of the generation who were twenty years old or older at the time the twelve spies

were sent into the land of Canaan were to die in the wilderness, with the exception of Caleb and Joshua (Numbers 13-14). Dr. Crossley goes on to point out that in both Old and New Testaments, "Illness and death are sometimes *directly* related to individual sin." This is a difficult truth from which we often shy away, because of distortions that have been put forward by preachers of the "prosperity gospel." Nevertheless, it is a biblical truth that we must confront: illness and death are *sometimes* directly related to individual sin. Consider what James writes in James 5:14-16:

> Is anyone among you sick? Let him call for the elders of the church, and let them pray over him, anointing him with oil in the name of the Lord. And the prayer of faith will save the sick, and the Lord will raise him up. And if he has committed sins, he will be forgiven. Confess *your* trespasses to one another, and pray for one another, that you may be healed. The effective, fervent prayer of a righteous man avails much.

The language James uses in this passage can be applied equally to salvation and to physical healing. Ultimately, we are perfectly healed when we pass from this life into the presence of the Lord our God. How would you use these thoughts to counsel and encourage both those who are sick and those who fall into sin from which they refuse to repent?

5. **Pressing forward:** Dr. Crossley suggests that the challenge of the book of Numbers is echoed in Paul's words in Philippians 3:13-14, "Forgetting those things which are behind and reaching forward to those things which are ahead, I press toward the goal for the prize of the upward call of God in Christ Jesus." How do you maintain your sights on the *prize* which lies ahead, particularly when you encounter many hardships, when suffering comes upon you for faithfulness to Christ?

NUMBERS / **REJOICE**

I'm Pressing on the Upward Way
Johnson Oatman Jr. (1898)

I'm pressing on the upward way,
New heights I'm gaining every day;
Still praying as I onward bound,

"Lord, plant my feet on higher ground."

Lord, lift me up, and let me stand
By faith on Canaan's tableland;
A higher plane than I have found,
Lord, plant my feet on higher ground.

DEUTERONOMY / **REVIEW**

Some key verses from Deuteronomy:
1. **Deuteronomy 6:4-5**
   "Hear, O Israel: The LORD our God, the LORD *is* one! You shall love the LORD your God with all your heart, with all your soul, and with all your strength."
2. **Deuteronomy 10:12-13**
   "And now, Israel, what does the LORD your God require of you, but to fear the LORD your God, to walk in all His ways and to love Him, to serve the LORD your God with all your heart and with all your soul, *and* to keep the commandments of the LORD and His statutes which I command you today for your good?"
3. **Deuteronomy 18:18**
   "I will raise up for them a Prophet like you from among their brethren, and will put My words in His mouth, and He shall speak to them all that I command Him."
4. **Deuteronomy 29:29**
   "The secret *things belong* to the LORD our God, but those *things which* are revealed *belong* to us and to our children forever, that *we* may do all the words of this law."

DEUTERONOMY / **REFLECT**

1. **Moses and Christ:** Dr. Crossley writes about the "comparisons and contrasts between Moses and the Lord Jesus." Moses, one of the greatest Old Testament characters, was used by God to lead his chosen people out of slavery in Egypt into the promised land. But, citing A.M. Hodgkin, he notes, "as the representative of the law, [Moses] could not lead the children of Israel into the promised land." As Paul writes in Romans 8:3, "What the law could not do in that it was weak through the flesh, God *did*

by sending His own Son in the likeness of sinful flesh." Reflect on how your salvation from sin through faith in Christ Jesus is by the *grace* of God and not by obedience to the *law*.
2. **Instructing the young:** Dr. Crossley reflects on the responsibility of parents to teach their children, to point their hearts to the Lord. Quoting from Deuteronomy 6:7, Dr. Crossley reminds us, "The Christian home is to be a loving centre of education—training children up in the things of God." In much of twentieth- and twenty-first-century Christian culture, parents seem to have neglected this responsibility, expecting that the church will teach their children. While we know that faith in Christ cannot be inherited and parents are not ultimately responsible for their children's salvation, why is it vitally important for children to be taught by their own parents?
3. **Things to remember:** As Dr. Crossley writes, "The key word in Deuteronomy is *remember* (occurring fourteen times)." He also points out that it is a key theme both the Psalms and the New Testament. We are to remember God's faithfulness to us, the mighty providential works whereby he has brought us to this place and time, his great love for us in Christ Jesus, saving us from our sin and welcoming us into loving relationship with him for eternity. Why is it so important for us to *remember*? Make a list of specific things in your own life and in the life of the church in your country that you *remember*, that you can recall in the presence of the next generation, that you *remember* to the glory of God.
4. **Obedience:** What is the motivation for our obedience? Dr. Crossley writes,

> Obedience from the Israelites does not *earn* the favour of God, but is required because they already enjoy his favour. They are not expected to purchase their redemption by obedience, but to obey *because* they are already redeemed.

This is a challenging aspect of both Old and New Covenant teaching. God's great, unmerited love for us (his grace) prompts him to reach out to restore people into covenant relationship with himself. Our response to God's love should be obedience to his commandments—out of love (Deuteronomy 7:7-9).

Jesus also linked love for him with keeping his commandments (obedience), three times in the Upper Room Discourse:

"If you love Me, keep My commandments" (John 14:15).
"He who has My commandments and keeps them, it is he who loves Me" (John 14:21).
"If you keep My commandments, you will abide in My love, just as I have kept My Father's commandments and abide in His love" (John 15:10).

Consider your own heart. To what extent is your obedience to the commands of Christ a result of your desire to love and please God, and to what extent is your obedience motivated by a desire to *earn* his love? Has the balance changed over time? Does it change daily? Does greater obedience come with greater understanding of the tremendous extent of God's grace, of the price that had to be paid for your salvation?

DEUTERONOMY / **REJOICE**

Psalm 103:1-5
A Psalm of David.

Bless the LORD, O my soul;
And all that is within me, *bless* His holy name!
Bless the LORD, O my soul,
And forget not all His benefits:
Who forgives all your iniquities,
Who heals all your diseases,
Who redeems your life from destruction,
Who crowns you with lovingkindness and tender mercies,
Who satisfies your mouth with good *things*,
So that your youth is renewed like the eagle's.

JOSHUA / **REVIEW**

Some key verses from Joshua:
1. **Joshua 1:7**
   "Only be strong and very courageous, that you may observe to do according to all the law which Moses My servant commanded you; do not turn from it to the right hand or to the left, that you may prosper wherever you go."

2. **Joshua 5:13-14**

    And it came to pass, when Joshua was by Jericho, that he lifted his eyes and looked, and behold, a Man stood opposite him with His sword drawn in His hand. And Joshua went to Him and said to Him, "*Are* You for us or for our adversaries?"

    So He said, "No, but *as* Commander of the army of the LORD I have now come."

3. **Joshua 24:14-15**

    "Now therefore, fear the LORD, serve Him in sincerity and in truth, and put away the gods which your fathers served on the other side of the River and in Egypt. Serve the LORD! And if it seems evil to you to serve the LORD, choose for yourselves this day whom you will serve, whether the gods which your fathers served that were on the other side of the River, or the gods of the Amorites, in whose land you dwell. But as for me and my house, we will serve the LORD."

JOSHUA / **REFLECT**

1. **Revelation:** Dr. Crossley reflects on God's primary means of communication in the book of Joshua, by means of the Word, the "Book of the Law written by Moses." "In our day," Dr. Crossley writes, "he communicates through the written Word, the Bible, and the Spirit of God opens our minds and hearts to the meaning and message of the Scriptures (John 16:13)." Dr. Crossley also quotes Joshua 1:6-9, where God commands Joshua, "Be strong and of good courage." Note that in those verses there is a cause and effect, or a *means* by which we can "be strong and courageous." We can "be strong and of good courage," it is possible for us to "not be afraid, nor be dismayed," because we have *assurance* in the Word that "the LORD your God is with you wherever you go." Write down some personal reflections on this passage, remembering times when you have and have not focused on the Word of God, and how that has affected your ability to face trials and temptations in this world.

2. **Models of faith:** Dr. Crossley's discussion of Caleb's ancestry is of great importance to every believer whose ancestry is not of the children of Israel, and this was an issue of tremendous significance and misunderstanding in the first century church. The Judaizers against whom Paul wrestled (see Galatians in particular) insisted that a Gentile must become a Jew (follow the Mosaic law—including adhering to the dietary laws and

being circumcised) in order to be a Christian. Paul's response in Galatians is very strong, but his reasoning is to be found in Romans 8-9 and Ephesians 1-3. Read Ephesians 3:1-13 and Galatians 3:3:1-29 and write down some thoughts about the *mystery* of the gospel and your own adoption by faith. Who are "Abraham's seed" and "heirs according to the promise" today (Galatians 3:29)?

3. **Separation:** Dr. Crossley cites the incident with the Gibeonites in Joshua 9 as a warning of "the possibility of deception by unbelievers, and the consequences of unholy alliances." We know that throughout Scripture there are warnings against entanglements with the world, and yet we are called to be witnesses of the gospel of Jesus Christ and ambassadors of the kingdom of God in this world. When writing to the church in Corinth about disciplining the man caught in sexual immorality, Paul urges them to put him out of the church, addressing the issue of being "in the world but not of the world" (cf. 1 John 4:3-6). He writes in 1 Corinthians 5:9-11:

> I wrote to you in my epistle not to keep company with sexually immoral people. Yet *I* certainly *did not* mean with the sexually immoral people of this world, or with the covetous, or extortioners, or idolaters, since then you would need to go out of the world. But now I have written to you not to keep company with anyone named a brother, who is sexually immoral, or covetous, or an idolater, or a reviler, or a drunkard, or an extortioner—not even to eat with such a person.

How would you counsel a member of your church who is in a business relationship with an unbeliever, or who desires to marry an unbeliever (see 2 Corinthians 6:14; Matthew 5:11-16)?

4. **Ministry support:** Dr. Crossley writes about the issue of believers supporting ministers of the gospel in the same way that Levites were allocated cities and lands and "a generous portion of the heave and wave offerings as their food, as well as the best of the oil, the wine and the firstfruits, with the tithes of the children of Israel." He notes Paul's extended discussion of this issue in 1 Corinthians 9, concluding with verses 13-14,

> Do you not know that those who minister the holy things eat *of the things* of the temple, and those who serve at the altar partake of *the*

offerings of the altar? Even so the Lord has commanded that those who preach the gospel should live from the gospel.

At the end of that passage, however, Paul discusses the fact that he accepted no support from the church in Corinth as he ministered among them (vv. 18-19).

Is the comparison of the support provided to Levites to that provided to ministers of the gospel in the Christian age legitimate? Can a pastor or ministry worker *insist* upon support from the church? What does the church lose if they cannot afford (or do not believe they can afford) to support a pastor? What struggles and what benefits are there to the church and the pastor when he must also engage in secular employment to support himself and his family?

JOSHUA / **REJOICE**

On Jordan's Stormy Banks I Stand
Samuel Stennet (1787)

On Jordan's stormy banks I stand,
And cast a wishful eye
To Canaan's fair and happy land,
Where my possessions lie.

> I am bound for the promised land,
> I am bound for the promised land;
> Oh who will come and go with me?
> I am bound for the promised land.

JUDGES / **REVIEW**

Some key verses from Judges:
1. Judges 2:10-16
When all that generation had been gathered to their fathers, another generation arose after them who did not know the Lord nor the work which He had done for Israel.

Then the children of Israel did evil in the sight of the Lord, and served the Baals; and they forsook the LORD God of their fathers, who had brought them out of the land of Egypt; and they followed other gods from *among* the gods of the people who *were* all around them, and they bowed down to them; and they provoked the LORD to anger. They forsook the LORD and served Baal and the Ashtoreths. And the anger of the LORD was hot against Israel. So He delivered them into the hands of plunderers who despoiled them; and He sold them into the hands of their enemies all around, so that they could no longer stand before their enemies. Wherever they went out, the hand of the LORD was against them for calamity, as the LORD had said, and as the LORD had sworn to them. And they were greatly distressed.

Nevertheless, the LORD raised up judges who delivered them out of the hand of those who plundered them.

2. **Judges 8:22-23**

Then the men of Israel said to Gideon, "Rule over us, both you and your son, and your grandson also; for you have delivered us from the hand of Midian."

But Gideon said to them, "I will not rule over you, nor shall my son rule over you; the LORD shall rule over you."

3. **Judges 21:25**

In those days *there was* no king in Israel; everyone did *what was* right in his own eyes.

JUDGES / **REFLECT**

1. **The human heart is prone to wander away from God:** Dr. Crossley reflects on the truth that "there is a potential prodigal in the heart of every believer" and that "it is evident that our greatest enemy is *within*." Write a personal reflection on the tendency of your own heart to wander away from God, and what spiritual disciplines (reading and meditating on the Word of God, prayer, etc.) are most helpful to keep you walking close to the Lord.
2. **God pursues and restores his backslidden people:** As Dr. Crossley writes, "God calls his people to faithful obedience. Nevertheless, if they wander from him, or wilfully turn from him, there is a way back." The book of Judges is often described as having seven ever-worsening spirals, where the people of God backslide (or turn away from God to worship idols), God brings persecution upon his people, but they cry out to him,

God raises up judges who deliver his people (see Judges 2:10-16). Reflect on the parallels between the book of Judges and Jesus' parable of the prodigal son (Luke 15:11-32), including some thoughts on how complacent, judgemental Christians might be represented by the elder son in Jesus' parable.

3. **Vows to the Lord:** Jephthah's rash vow in Judges 11:30-31 and its consequences, when his own daughter was the first to come out of the doors of his house to meet him, is quite troubling. Is it an example of the ever-worsening spiritual and moral descent of the people of Israel in the spirals of Judges, or is the interpretation offered by the commentators (Andrew Fausset, Carl Friedrich Keil, E.J. Young) cited in Dr. Crossley's meditation to be accepted? The arguments presented seem strong, but they speak from silence. The conclusion in verse 39 is simply, "And it was so at the end of two months that she returned to her father, and he carried out his vow with her which he had vowed."

4. **Strength and weakness:** Dr. Crossley points to scenes in Judges (the drastic reduction of Gideon's army, and the amazing strength given to Samson: one man against the Philistines) as examples of God working through "the weak things of the world" (1 Corinthians 1:27) "so that all glory for achievements will be given to the Lord." He quotes the apostle Paul in 1 Corinthians 1:27-31 and 2 Corinthians 12:9-10, making the same point: God has chosen to work in amazing and unexpected ways through people whom the world would normally ignore, to accomplish his purposes. Consider your "heroes in the faith" from Scripture, from church history or from your own experience. How has God worked through humble people to accomplish great things, in ways that bring praise and honour and glory to him?

5. **The weakness of the law:** "Throughout the book of Judges," Dr. Crossley writes, "the weakness of the law of Sinai is all too apparent." Very quickly after the passing of Joshua, the Israelites "proved to be constantly attracted to, and influenced by, the idolatry and sexual perversion of the Canaanite fertility religions." Without "drastic action by an intermediary" (Jesus Christ) "and drastic transformation within believers" accomplished by the indwelling of the Spirit of God, we cannot live to please God. "Those who are in Christ Jesus...do not walk according to the flesh, but according to the Spirit...that the righteous requirement of the law might be fulfilled in us" (Romans 8:1,4). How do you counsel a new believer about the transformation of life—attitudes, words and behaviours—that should

accompany faith in Christ Jesus? Does that transformation come about through hard work on the part of the believer, or by the transforming power of the indwelling Holy Spirit?

JUDGES / **REJOICE**

Come, Thou Fount of Every Blessing
Robert Robinson (1735–1790), John Wyeth (1770–1858)

Come, Thou Fount of every blessing,
   Tune my heart to sing Thy grace;
Streams of mercy, never ceasing,
   Call for songs of loudest praise.
Jesus sought me when a stranger,
   Wand'ring from the fold of God;
He, to save my soul from danger,
   Interposed His precious blood.

RUTH / **REVIEW**

Some key verses from Ruth:
1. **Ruth 1:16–17**
    But Ruth said:
       "Entreat me not to leave you,
       Or to turn back from following after you;
       For wherever you go, I will go;
       And wherever you lodge, I will lodge;
       Your people *shall be* my people,
       And your God, my God.
       Where you die, I will die,
       And there will I be buried.
       The Lord do so to me, and more also,
       If *anything but* death parts you and me."
2. **Ruth 2:20**
    Then Naomi said to her daughter-in-law, "Blessed *be* he of the Lord, who has not forsaken His kindness to the living and the dead!" And Naomi said to her, "This man *is* a relation of ours, one of our close relatives."

3. Ruth 4:17

Also the neighbor women gave him a name, saying, "There is a son born to Naomi." And they called his name Obed. He *is* the father of Jesse, the father of David.

RUTH / **REFLECT**

1. **Providence:** As Dr. Crossley writes, "The ordinary outworking of *providence* is the underlying thread of this book." Louis Berkhof defined divine providence as "that work of God in which He preserves all His creatures, is active in all that happens in the world, and directs all things to their appointed end."[1] We should remember that God's providence is seen not only in bringing Ruth and Boaz together, but with their son Obed continuing the line that would produce King David and ultimately, Christ Jesus. How and when have you recognized God's providential ordering of things in your own life and in the lives of people around you?

2. **True conversion:** Dr. Crossley reflects on Ruth's conversion, which can be contrasted with Naomi's backsliding. He writes that Ruth "has not sought God. She has been sought *by* God." Ruth's true conversion is evident by her humble obedience, stated directly in the opening chapter, when she leaves behind all that she has known in Moab. Her commitment to God demonstrates her true conversion. Jesus said,

   > "He who loves father or mother more than Me is not worthy of Me. And he who loves son or daughter more than Me is not worthy of Me. And he who does not take his cross and follow after Me is not worthy of Me" (Matthew 10:37-38).

   In past decades in the West, the *cost* of following Christ has been very low, contributing to a false sense of security among many who have not experienced *true* conversion. That cost is rising, as Western culture celebrates more and more those things that are contrary to God's Word, and tolerates less and less those who are trying to be faithful to his Word. What is your experience of the *cost* of discipleship? How can you recognize true conversion in your own life and in the lives of Christians around you?

---

[1] Louis Berkhof, *Summary of Christian Doctrine* (Grand Rapids: Eerdmans, 1938), 59.

3. **Love for God's people:** Dr. Crossley writes: "Ruth's conversion from paganism to faith in the living and true God is evidenced by her love for the people of God." He points out the "connection between love for God and love for those who are God's," and, through quotes from the apostle John in 1 John 3 and 5, notes that "this love for God's people is evidence of conversion." Jesus Christ also pointed out that the love of Christians for one another should be a powerful testimony of God's love for us, and of our true conversion: "A new commandment I give to you, that you love one another; as I have loved you, that you also love one another. By this all will know that you are My disciples, if you have love for one another" (John 13:34-35).

   What deliberate actions do you take in your personal life, and in the life of your church, to express love to one another? Is the love of Christians for one another a defining mark of Christianity in your culture? Are people amazed and convicted by the love between and among Christians where you live?

4. **Signs of backsliding:** The contrast between the humble faith and willing service of Ruth and the bitterness of Naomi and her "unacceptable," perhaps even immoral, instruction to Ruth concerning Boaz (3:1-4), is a powerful feature of the book. Dr. Crossley identifies three strong indicators of Naomi's "poor spiritual state." Where Ruth is a model of true conversion and love for God's people, Naomi may well be a model of a backsliding Christian. Do you make regular self-assessments (2 Corinthians 13:5)? Do you have a brother or sister in Christ with whom you sharpen one another (Proverbs 27:17)? Why or why not?

5. **Women in the Bible:** Dr. Crossley quite rightly points out, "No impartial reader could ever conclude that the Bible has a low view of women." He notes that though there are "occasional illustrations" of male chauvinism, even "horrible and inexplicable" incidents, "there is no word of approval." Radical feminism is also contrary to the picture of the appropriate relationship between men and women in God's Word, requiring radical feminists to "overlook or twist the clear implications" of Scripture, to "ignore, or to interpret in a distorted manner, the beautiful illustrations of godly women found" in the book of Ruth. Identify three other women whose godly character is praised in Scripture, giving a brief summary of how she is identified as being praiseworthy.

RUTH / **REJOICE**

God Moves in a Mysterious Way
William Cowper (1731-1800)

God moves in a mysterious way
    His wonders to perform
He plants His footsteps in the sea
    And rides upon the storm.

1 SAMUEL / **REVIEW**

Some key verses from 1 Samuel:
1. **1 Samuel 8:7**
   And the LORD said to Samuel, "Heed the voice of the people in all that they say to you; for they have not rejected you, but they have rejected Me, that I should not reign over them."
2. **1 Samuel 12:14-15**
   "If you fear the LORD and serve Him and obey His voice, and do not rebel against the commandment of the LORD, then both you and the king who reigns over you will continue following the LORD your God. However, if you do not obey the voice of the LORD, but rebel against the commandment of the LORD, then the hand of the LORD will be against you, as *it was* against your fathers."
3. **1 Samuel 15:22-23**
   So Samuel said:
       "Has the LORD *as great* delight in burnt offerings and sacrifices,
       As in obeying the voice of the LORD?
       Behold, to obey is better than sacrifice,
       And to heed than the fat of rams.
       For rebellion *is as* the sin of witchcraft,
       And stubbornness is as iniquity and idolatry.
       Because you have rejected the word of the LORD,
       He also has rejected you from *being* king."

1 SAMUEL / **REFLECT**

1. **Prayer and intercession:** Dr. Crossley points to prayer as a central feature of 1 Samuel, describing it as "a book full of prayer." There is Hannah's prayer at the beginning of the book and those of Samuel—at Mizpah, in response to the demand of the people for a king and in his final prayer for Israel. Many different aspects of prayer are highlighted in 1 Samuel, including supplication, worship, confession, repentance, renewal and intercession. Dr. Crossley laments our prayerlessness, writing,

   > Sadly it seems to be the pattern that when Christians face difficulties, afflictions and disappointments, they do not pray, they do not worship. They stay at home or take a weekend break from their church in order to cheer themselves up.

   Is this your experience, or do you find that when troubles afflict you, you suddenly find the time and the need to pray? At both extremes, are we not treating God with contempt? How can we encourage ourselves and those around us to be more faithful in prayer, in good times and in times of sorrow or difficulty? Is there a special responsibility for leaders (pastors, elders, teachers, parents) to pray for those whom they lead?

2. **A father's responsibility:** Dr. Crossley points out that Eli, and then Samuel, failed to oversee, curb, control and discipline their adult sons in their responsibilities as priests and judges. As both fathers and leaders, Eli and Samuel bore double responsibility. Dr. Crossley cites the qualifications for elders and deacons which Paul outlined in 1 Timothy 3, including that a leader of the church be "one who rules his own house well, having his children in submission with all reverence" (1 Timothy 3:4). He concludes, "Leadership among the people of God not only means good and faithful oversight of the saints in the church, but also good and faithful oversight of the family in the home." Dr. Crossley acknowledges that parents "have no power, and consequently no responsibility, to convert their offspring," but these examples (and others in Scripture) point out that leaders must not abandon their responsibility to "rule" over their subordinates because of familial ties. Given that both Eli and Samuel's sons were adults, rather than children, is there an age limit on the responsibility of a leader to "rule his children well"? Is there a particular

leadership challenge for fathers whose sons follow them in leadership positions in the church? What is the expectation in your culture and in your church for a leader to rule "his own house well, having his children in submission with all reverence"?

3. **Friendship:** Dr. Crossley contrasts two friendships which feature in 1 Samuel, that between David and Jonathan, and that between David and King Achish of the Philistines. The first was an "unusual bond...between two godly men with mutual respect and mutual affection," whereas the second was a relationship based on deception, with David "seeking protection from Saul" from an enemy of the nation of Israel, to the point of being willing to go to war against Israel with the Philistine army. King Achish cannot be faulted for his openness to David: Dr. Crossley describes it as an example of "the *depths* to which friendship with the worldly can sometimes plunge."

   "Friendship with the world always leads to serious problems for the Lord's people." Read the verses quoted by Dr. Crossley (1 John 2:15-16; Romans 12:2; 2 Corinthians 6:17-18) and describe your plan and practice to be "in the world, but not of the world," to be a witness for Christ in the world, but not to be attached to the world—its wisdom, passions, priorities or wickedness.

4. **Obedience:** As Dr. Crossley writes, King Saul's tragic end illustrates "the importance of obeying the Word of God." Though Dr. Crossley focuses on two major instances of disobedience on the part of King Saul, in performing "the function of a priest" when Samuel did not arrive "at the appointed time," and his failure to "carry out the *total* destruction of the Amalekites and all their livestock," there are many other incidents in 1 Samuel which illustrate Saul's disobedience, destructiveness and final descent into dependence on a medium (1 Samuel 28). Dr. Crossley points to the very strong connection, in both Old and New Testaments, between faith and obedience (Romans 4:3; Galatians 3:6; James 2:23).

   Turn to the verses quoted by Dr. Crossley in the Gospel of John (John 14:15; 15:10,14). In their context, discuss Jesus' clear declaration that true faith is demonstrated by keeping his commandments. *Must* true saving faith be accompanied by obedience?

5. **Overruling providence:** Dr. Crossley discussed the providence of God in his reflections on the book of Ruth. In that book, the evidence of God's providence is seen everywhere, as God leads and provides. Here, Dr. Crossley highlights two incidents in 1 Samuel where God exercised his

providence in a preventative, blocking or overruling fashion. First, when David was dissuaded from destroying Nabal, and second, when the Philistine princes would not permit David and his men to accompany them into battle against Israel.

Have you recognized times in your life when God has overruled your plans and intentions—later seeing how foolish you were and the consequences that would have ensued had God not providentially intervened?

6. **Grace and gifts:** Reflecting on the fact that Saul was endowed with great spiritual gifts (he "prophesied by the power of the Holy Spirit") and yet "was never born again," Dr. Crossley raises "the serious question of the relationship between the grace of God and the gifts of the Holy Spirit." He cites Jesus' words in Matthew 7:21-23, in the Sermon on the Mount, where "the Lord Jesus Christ draws attention to this possibility that someone might exercise spiritual *gifts* and yet not possess spiritual *grace*." The apostle Paul also addresses this possibility with the church in Corinth, remarking in 1 Corinthians 1:7 that they "come short in no gift" (or "are not lacking in any spiritual gift" ESV), warning in 1 Corinthians 13 that though one "speak in tongues of men and angels," or "have the gift of prophecy" or "have all faith," and yet "have not love, I am nothing;" urging them in 2 Corinthians 13:5, "Examine yourselves, to see whether you are in the faith." Dr. Crossley concludes, "Love for God and obedience to God are the marks of true godliness, not the exercise of gifts —natural or spiritual!" And yet, God has given spiritual gifts for the "edification" of the church (1 Corinthians 12-14).

How are spiritual gifts and love balanced in the church in your culture? Is there an undue emphasis of one over the other? Are certain gifts valued more highly than others (1 Corinthians 12)? Is the exercise of gifts moderated by love, by what builds rather than what tears down, by what is in keeping with orderly, respectful worship of the Lord (1 Corinthians 14:19-33)?

7. **Religious superstition:** Dr. Crossley discusses the Israelites' confusion concerning the meaning and significance of the ark of the covenant. When they suffered a setback in battle with the Philistines, they transported "the ark of the covenant from the tabernacle at Shiloh into the camp, in the misguided notion that God's presence was inseparably linked to the mercy seat" (1 Samuel 4). "Symbols instituted by God never possess power," he writes. So we quite rightly do not construct idols or worship them, or parade icons, statues, pictures, relics or any other things,

as if God's presence or favour would be invoked by so doing. And yet, we do value beautiful works of art, whether visual (paintings, sculpture) or audible (music) that bring to mind and encourage us to worship God, as the "living creatures" and the "twenty-four elders" worship God in Revelation 4:11, saying:

> You are worthy, O Lord,
> To receive glory and honor and power;
> For You created all things,
> And by Your will they exist and were created."

Is this a question of balance, of heart attitude, of correct understanding of who God is—or is it all three? How are visual representations of the glory of God treated in the culture around you and in your Christian community?

1 SAMUEL / **REJOICE**

Psalm 27:1,14
A Psalm of David.

The Lord is my light and my salvation;
Whom shall I fear?
The Lord is the strength of my life;
Of whom shall I be afraid?

Wait on the Lord;
Be of good courage,
And He shall strengthen your heart;
Wait, I say, on the Lord!

2 SAMUEL / **REVIEW**

Some key verses from 2 Samuel:
1. **2 Samuel 5:3-4**
   Therefore all the elders of Israel came to the king at Hebron, and King David made a covenant with them at Hebron before the Lord. And they

anointed David king over Israel. David was thirty years old when he began to reign, *and* he reigned forty years.
2. **2 Samuel 7:12,16**
"When your days are fulfilled and you rest with your fathers, I will set up your seed after you, who will come from your body, and I will establish his kingdom.... And your house and your kingdom shall be established forever before you. Your throne shall be established forever."
3. **2 Samuel 22:2-4**
And he said:
> "The Lord *is* my rock and my fortress and my deliverer;
> The God of my strength, in whom I will trust;
> My shield and the horn of my salvation,
> My stronghold and my refuge;
> My Savior, You save me from violence.
> I will call upon the Lord, *who is worthy* to be praised;
> So shall I be saved from my enemies."

2 SAMUEL / **REFLECT**

1. **Human plans and divine purposes:** Dr. Crossley, reflecting on David's plan to build a house for the Lord in 2 Samuel 7, writes, "All plans must be made in the conscious presence of God and with due consideration to the purposes of God." He then quotes James 4:13-15, which concludes with, "Instead you ought to say, 'If the Lord wills, we shall live and do this or that.'" Describe a time in your life when you made a plan or struck off in a particular direction, only to discover that the plan was faulty, and/or was not pleasing to God or resulted in confusion and difficulty. Had you committed the purpose or the plan to the Lord? What did you learn?
2. **God's work in God's way:** Dr. Crossley reflects on the very sad incident in 2 Samuel 6:7, when "the anger of the Lord was aroused against Uzzah" for reaching out and touching the ark of the Lord, "and God struck him there for *his* error; and he died there by the ark of God." While David's desire to move the ark of the covenant to Jerusalem was honourable, the way God had instructed this to be done was not followed. Dr. Crossley writes, "the whole incident was another sad case of men disregarding God's instructions and warnings. God's revelation is never to be dismissed in preference for human invention." This raises the difficult issue of pragmatism, where some churches and ministries turn to worldly ways and

worldly wisdom to attract and retain people, often leaving the gospel, or hard but essential elements of the gospel (such as true repentance for sin) under-stated or even unstated. In the minds of some, what appears to work, or what builds numbers, *must* be pleasing to God. Describe the danger of pragmatic approaches where elements of the gospel are hidden or ignored, or preaching and teaching is shaped to suit the "itching ears" of our generation (2 Timothy 4:1-4).

3. **Monogamy:** Reflecting on the many family problems David faced because of "his numerous wives with their numerous children," Dr. Crossley reminds us, "From the beginning of creation, God's design for marriage was that it should be an exclusive covenant relationship between one man and one woman." Today, just as in Corinth in the first century, people are coming to faith in Christ with "complex relationships such as previous spouses and children from different partners," or out of homosexual relationships or with very confused ideas of human sexuality and marriage. Are there lessons for us in 1 Corinthians 5-6 concerning how to lovingly, compassionately, consistently and firmly navigate these complex issues?

4. **Clouded judgement:** King David's judgement was so deeply clouded by his love for his family that he risked losing the kingdom on several occasions, including when Absalom led a rebellion against him. When Absalom died in the ensuing battle, David's mourning for Absalom was itself a threat, as Joab rightly pointed out. As Dr. Crossley writes,

> Leaders among the people of God are responsible to ensure that family ties do not cloud their judgement. As well as the danger of nepotism (favouritism shown to relatives or friends in conferring offices or privileges), the leader is open to being more lenient toward members of his own family.

Sin can be covered over to protect family members or friends, and unwise decisions made about appointments to positions of responsibility. In addition to the qualification that an elder be "one who rules his own house well" (1 Timothy 3:4), in what ways should a local church guard against the possibility of a leader's judgement being clouded?

5. **Relying on the promises of God:** As Dr. Crossley reminds us, David trusted God's promises even though he had to wait years to see them unfold, a point both Paul and Peter call to our attention (2 Corinthians 1:20; 2 Peter 3:3-10). It can be difficult to remain faithful to God when

things are not going well, when perhaps there is persecution and suffering. What key truths about your salvation in Christ Jesus do you cling to, in order to remind yourself that the Lord is with you, even though you "walk through the valley of the shadow of death" (Psalm 23:4)?
6. **Exposure of sin:** In Numbers 32:23, Moses warns in a specific situation, "Be sure your sin will find you out," but we know that warning has universal application, as is demonstrated many times in Scripture, even in 2 Samuel. How do you guard yourself against indulging in "secret" sins, which are not at all hidden from God?
7. **Discipline:** Dr. Crossley points to the results of David's neglect of discipline in his dealings with Amnon and Absalom, illustrating the importance of discipline, lovingly administered, with the goal of "*repentance* and *restoration.*" Failure to discipline, in the home and in the church, is not loving. Rather, it could be considered cowardly; a refusal to exercise the responsibilities of parenthood or church leadership. The neglect of discipline doesn't increase love, it deepens and widens the effects of sin. How do we lovingly and consistently exercise discipline in our families and in the church?

2 SAMUEL / **REJOICE**

Psalm 5:1-6
To the Chief Musician. With flutes. A Psalm of David.

Give ear to my words, O Lord,
    Consider my meditation.
Give heed to the voice of my cry,
    My King and my God,
For to You I will pray.
    My voice You shall hear in the morning, O Lord;
In the morning I will direct *it* to You,
    And I will look up.
For You *are* not a God who takes pleasure in wickedness,
    Nor shall evil dwell with You.
The boastful shall not stand in Your sight;
    You hate all workers of iniquity.
You shall destroy those who speak falsehood;
    The Lord abhors the bloodthirsty and deceitful man.

1 KINGS / **REVIEW**

Some key verses from 1 Kings:
1. **1 Kings 2:1-3**
   Now the days of David drew near that he should die, and he charged Solomon his son, saying: "I go the way of all the earth; be strong, therefore, and prove yourself a man. And keep the charge of the Lord your God: to walk in His ways, to keep His statutes, His commandments, His judgments, and His testimonies, as it is written in the Law of Moses, that you may prosper in all that you do and wherever you turn."
2. **1 Kings 3:7-9**
   "Now, O Lord my God, You have made Your servant king instead of my father David, but I *am* a little child; I do not know *how* to go out or come in. And Your servant *is* in the midst of Your people whom You have chosen, a great people, too numerous to be numbered or counted. Therefore give to Your servant an understanding heart to judge Your people, that I may discern between good and evil. For who is able to judge this great people of Yours?"
3. **1 Kings 8:22-23**
   Then Solomon stood before the altar of the Lord in the presence of all the assembly of Israel, and spread out his hands toward heaven; and he said: "Lord God of Israel, *there is* no God in heaven above or on earth below like You, who keep *Your* covenant and mercy with Your servants who walk before You with all their hearts."
4. **1 Kings 12:12-15**
   So Jeroboam and all the people came to Rehoboam the third day, as the king had directed, saying, "Come back to me the third day." Then the king answered the people roughly, and rejected the advice which the elders had given him; and he spoke to them according to the advice of the young men, saying, "My father made your yoke heavy, but I will add to your yoke; my father chastised you with whips, but I will chastise you with scourges!" So the king did not listen to the people; for the turn of *events* was from the Lord, that He might fulfill His word, which the Lord had spoken by Ahijah the Shilonite to Jeroboam the son of Nebat.

1 KINGS / **REFLECT**

1. **God-honouring prayer:** Dr. Crossley addresses two issues concerning prayer in the modern church. First, that "prayers in a Christian assembly are often nothing more than coming to God with a shopping list...without addressing God in worship, praise and blessing and speaking of his wondrous works, attributes or promises." Second, that our prayers are often "almost exclusively addressed to the Lord Jesus Christ—sometimes simply to 'Jesus,'" rather than to God the Father, which is "the consistent pattern in prayer and praise" in the New Testament.

    Discuss how King Solomon's prayer at the dedication of the temple in 1 Kings 8:22-53, Daniel's prayer in Daniel 9 and Jesus' model for Christian prayer in Matthew 6:9-10, guide our thinking about how we should approach our great, holy and glorious God in prayer.

2. **Marriage to the ungodly:** Dr. Crossley quotes from John Murray, *Principles of Conduct: Aspects of Biblical Ethics* as follows, "When the interests of godliness do not govern the people of God in the choice of marital partners, irreparable confusion is the result and the interests, not only of spirituality, but also of morality, are destroyed."[2] Outline how you would counsel a member of your church, male or female, who comes to you seeking approval of their intention to marry: (a) an unbeliever, or (b) someone from a different Christian background.

3. **Backsliding and apostasy:** Dr. Crossley writes about Solomon and the different theories as to whether or not he repented of his sin and returned to the Lord. Dr. Crossley quotes Charles D. Alexander in *The Heavenly Mystery of the Song of Songs* where he asks, "Is any Christian immune from relapse into sin when for a season he relaxes his vigilance and ceases to watch and pray lest he enter into temptation?" Consider Jesus' parable of the prodigal son in Luke 15:11-32 and the Reformed doctrine of the perseverance of the saints. Compare the two sons in this parable. Does one represent a true believer who has backslidden but repented, and the other someone who never had true saving faith?

4. **God's power and provision:** Dr. Crossley reminds us of God's power and provision in the lives of the prophet Elijah, David and Paul. In some cases,

---

[2] John Murray, *Principles of Conduct: Aspects of Biblical Ethics* (London: Tyndale Press, 1957), 46.

we recognize the hand of God in his miraculous provision of needs, but we should also recognize, as Dr. Crossley writes, "the Lord's *ordinary* providences are no less wonderful." Write about your personal experience of God's power and providence. Have you learned, like Paul, to trust God for his provision (Philippians 4:11–12)?

5. **Fleeing persecution:** After the triumph of God over the 450 prophets of Baal and the 400 prophets of Asherah (1 Kings 18:19), threats came from Jezebel and Elijah fled into the wilderness (1 Kings 19). Dr. Crossley writes about two perspectives on Elijah's actions: one, that he was cowardly and depressed, or two, as Charles Alexander espouses, "his flight was divinely ordained to prepare the way prophetically for the coming of the Saviour."[3] Was Elijah's flight a reasonable response to the threats of Jezebel and wholly within the will of God? Was it precipitated by a dramatic disconnect between Elijah's hope and expectation that God would bring repentance and a general revival in Israel, and the continuing wickedness of this most evil queen? Have you experienced a time when flight from evil and rest in the care and protection of the Lord was your best course of action?

6. **Called to service:** "At the commandment of the Lord, Elijah called Elisha to the prophetic office (19:16)." Dr. Crossley writes about that *call* to service, noting many in Scripture *left all* to serve the Lord full time in one ministry or another (prophet, apostle, preacher). While some are fully supported by those to whom they preach, Paul is an example of one who worked with his hands as a tentmaker, in order to support himself and others in ministry with him. What is your experience of the call to service? Have you *left all* to serve the Lord? Are you working in a secular vocation in order to support yourself and your family? Paul writes,

> Be anxious for nothing, but in everything by prayer and supplication, with thanksgiving, let your requests be made known to God; and the peace of God, which surpasses all understanding, will guard your hearts and minds through Christ Jesus (Philippians 4:6–7).

Are you able to trust in the Lord for his provision of all that *you* need?

---

[3] Alexander, *Elijah*, 4.

1 KINGS / **REJOICE**

Psalm 2

Why do the nations rage,
And the people plot a vain thing?
The kings of the earth set themselves,
And the rulers take counsel together,
Against the Lord and against His Anointed, *saying*,
"Let us break Their bonds in pieces
And cast away Their cords from us."

He who sits in the heavens shall laugh;
The Lord shall hold them in derision.
Then He shall speak to them in His wrath,
And distress them in His deep displeasure:
"Yet I have set My King
On My holy hill of Zion."

"I will declare the decree:
The Lord has said to Me,
'You *are* My Son,
Today I have begotten You.
Ask of Me, and I will give You
The nations *for* Your inheritance,
And the ends of the earth *for* Your possession.
You shall break them with a rod of iron;
You shall dash them to pieces like a potter's vessel.'"

Now therefore, be wise, O kings;
Be instructed, you judges of the earth.
Serve the Lord with fear,
And rejoice with trembling.
Kiss the Son, lest He be angry,
And you perish *in* the way,
When His wrath is kindled but a little.
Blessed *are* all those who put their trust in Him.

2 KINGS / **REVIEW**

Some key verses from 2 Kings:
1. **2 Kings 1:3**
   But the angel of the Lord said to Elijah the Tishbite, "Arise, go up to meet the messengers of the king of Samaria, and say to them, '*Is it* because *there is* no God in Israel *that* you are going to inquire of Baal-Zebub, the god of Ekron?'"
2. **2 Kings 6:17**
   And Elisha prayed, and said, "Lord, I pray, open his eyes that he may see." Then the Lord opened the eyes of the young man, and he saw. And behold, the mountain *was* full of horses and chariots of fire all around Elisha.
3. **2 Kings 17:6-8**
   In the ninth year of Hoshea, the king of Assyria took Samaria and carried Israel away to Assyria, and placed them in Halah and by the Habor, the River of Gozan, and in the cities of the Medes.
   For so it was that the children of Israel had sinned against the Lord their God, who had brought them up out of the land of Egypt, from under the hand of Pharaoh king of Egypt; and they had feared other gods, and had walked in the statutes of the nations whom the Lord had cast out from before the children of Israel, and of the kings of Israel, which they had made.
4. **2 Kings 25:8-10**
   And in the fifth month, on the seventh *day* of the month (which *was* the nineteenth year of King Nebuchadnezzar king of Babylon), Nebuzaradan the captain of the guard, a servant of the king of Babylon, came to Jerusalem. He burned the house of the Lord and the king's house; all the houses of Jerusalem, that is, all the houses of the great, he burned with fire. And all the army of the Chaldeans who *were* with the captain of the guard broke down the walls of Jerusalem all around.

2 KINGS / **REFLECT**

1. **Wicked youths:** Dr. Crossley writes about the incident at Bethel in 2 Kings 2:23-25 where a group of youths mock Elisha. When Elisha "pronounced a curse on them in the name of the Lord.... two female bears came out of the woods and mauled forty-two of the youths" (verse 24). He quotes Arthur Pink in his commentary, *Gleanings from Elisha*, God's restraints on

children operate "largely through parental control—moral training in the home, wholesome instruction and discipline in the school, and adequate punishment of young offenders by the state."[4]

Parents, and fathers in particular, bear much responsibility for raising children. As Paul writes in Ephesians 6:4, "And you, fathers, do not provoke your children to wrath, but bring them up in the training and admonition of the Lord." On the other hand, parents cannot forever impose their will upon their children, and there are many examples in Scripture of sons who have disobeyed and dishonoured their parents (e.g. Cain, Samson, Absalom). What is your experience as a child and, if applicable, as a parent? Have you seen examples of prodigal children (Luke 15) who have repented of their sin and returned to their earthly parents, to their heavenly Father?

2. **Pure worship:** Dr. Crossley writes about the syncretistic worship of the people whom the Assyrians placed in Samaria following their conquest and about their descendant, the Samaritan woman whom Jesus met at the well of Sychar in John 4. Jesus emphasized that "true worshipers will worship the Father in spirit and truth; for the Father is seeking such to worship Him" (John 4:23). Do people in your community or culture bring "their own pagan religious practices with them and amalgamate them with a corrupted form of the worship of Jehovah"? What aspects of culture infiltrate your church? What false gods or ungodly expectations corrupt your worship of the one true God?

3. **Rulers and nations:** "The spiritual message of [2 Kings] as a whole is that rulers have a powerful influence for good or bad upon a nation," Dr. Crossley asserts, reminding us of Paul's encouragement to Timothy (and the Holy Spirit's instruction to us) that "supplications, prayers, intercessions, and giving of thanks be made for all men, for kings and all who are in authority" (1 Timothy 2:1-2). While our expectation cannot be that our nations or our political leaders will make wholesale changes to worship, honour and obey the Lord, we can and *must* pray for our leaders "that we may lead a quiet and peaceable life" and that we might make the gospel of Jesus Christ known. In what ways can Christians in your country pray for those who have been put in authority over them and show respect and appropriate submission, in order to "enable the work of the gospel to have free course in the land"?

---

[4] Pink, *Gleanings from Elisha*.

2 KINGS / **REJOICE**

Psalm 96:9-12

Oh, worship the Lord in the beauty of holiness!
Tremble before Him, all the earth.
Say among the nations, "The Lord reigns;
The world also is firmly established,
It shall not be moved;
He shall judge the peoples righteously."

Let the heavens rejoice, and let the earth be glad;
Let the sea roar, and all its fullness;
Let the field be joyful, and all that is in it.
Then all the trees of the woods will rejoice before the Lord.

1 CHRONICLES / **REVIEW**

Some key verses from 1 Chronicles:
1. **1 Chronicles 17:11-14**
   "And it shall be, when your days are fulfilled, when you must go *to be* with your fathers, that I will set up your seed after you, who will be of your sons; and I will establish his kingdom. He shall build Me a house, and I will establish his throne forever. I will be his Father, and he shall be My son; and I will not take My mercy away from him, as I took *it* from *him* who was before you. And I will establish him in My house and in My kingdom forever; and his throne shall be established forever."
2. **1 Chronicles 29:11-12**
   Yours, O Lord, *is* the greatness,
   The power and the glory,
   The victory and the majesty;
   For all *that is in* heaven and in earth *is Yours;*
   Yours *is* the kingdom, O Lord,
   And You are exalted as head over all.
   Both riches and honor *come* from You,
   And You reign over all.

In Your hand *is* power and might;
In Your hand *it is* to make great
And to give strength to all.

1 CHRONICLES / **REFLECT**

1. **Obedience:** Dr. Crossley reminds us of the seriousness of obedience to God. God slew Achan (1 Chronicles 2:7) and Saul (1 Chronicles 10:13-14) for their rebellious hearts. God slew Uzzah for his violation in touching the ark (1 Chronicles 13:7-11). Even the warrior-poet-king David is disciplined by not being permitted to build God's temple, due to all the blood on his hands (1 Chronicles 22:8). Jesus said: "If you love Me, keep My commandments" (John 14:15). Obedience reveals our true measure of love and devotion to God. We cannot say we love God, and act in a disobedient manner. Are there areas or issues in your life that test your obedience to God? Make a list and ask God for his strength and courage to obey.
2. **Prayer:** This book of the Bible contains "two fine examples of powerful prayer," that of Jabez (1 Chronicles 4:9-10) and of "a large group of unnamed warriors from the tribes of Reuben, Gad and Manasseh" who "cried out to God in the battle" (1 Chronicles 5:18-20). Dr. Crossley cites Samuel Chadwick, who wrote in *The Path of Prayer* that prayer "is the acid test of devotion."[5] Reflect on this statement and write about the importance and practice of prayer in your life, and what you might do to be more faithful and expectant in prayer.
3. **Service:** Dr. Crossley points out that the Levites were skilled in their duties and responsibilities (1 Chronicles 9:13). He later shows that David's mighty men were also skilled and trained in the art of war (1 Chronicles 12:2,8). Each one of us has gifts and abilities. We ought not to compare ourselves with others but to utilize whatever God-given gift we have for the glory of our God. What gifts and abilities do you have? Make a list and prayerfully seek out opportunities to utilize them (Romans 12:4-8).
4. **No redundancy!** David re-tasked the Levites on the completion of the temple. Their previous "duties...relating to the dismantling, transportation and erection of the tabernacle were no longer required" (1 Chronicles 23:26). They were not declared redundant, but were given "new duties: maintaining the fabric of the temple, preparing the offerings and utensils,

---

[5] Chadwick, *The Path of Prayer*, 16.

leading daily worship and generally assisting the priests in their religious duties" (1 Chronicles 23:27-32). Dr. Crossley quotes from Stewart's *A Family Tree*: "A person who has been made redundant has lost more than his employment and income, for he has lost his dignity.... However, we may be thankful that in the service of God there is no such thing as a redundant person."[6] How does your culture treat people whose previous work is no longer required, or who are no longer able to continue in their work because of age or infirmity? How are they treated within their families? How are Christians to treat, encourage and honour such brothers and sisters?

5. **Leadership skills:** Dr. Crossley reminds us of David's leadership skills, turning "a motley band" of men into "a disciplined, highly competent fighting unit" at Adullam. "Under the New Covenant," Dr. Crossley writes, "the importance of spiritual leadership is emphasized," and "church leaders are responsible for the training of new leaders," pointing to such passages as Ephesians 4:11-16 and 2 Timothy 2:2. What has been your experience? Were you mentored by a more mature Christian? Were your leadership skills or potential for leadership recognized by your church leaders? Were you challenged, encouraged and nurtured in the use of the gifts with which God has blessed you? What about your future plans and purposes: do you now, or will you soon, pour yourself into "faithful men who will be able to teach others also" (2 Timothy 2:2)?

6. **Orderly worship:** Beginning with David's desire to build a temple for the worship of God, Dr. Crossley writes about beauty, high standards in worship and about worshiping the Lord "in spirit and truth" (John 4:23). What are worship gatherings of brothers in sisters in Christ like in your culture? As Dr. Crossley writes, "The New Covenant gives great freedom to worship anywhere and at any time," but has that become an excuse to approach the holy, holy, holy God with less than our very best?

---

[6] Stewart, *A Family Tree*, 187.

1 CHRONICLES / **REJOICE**

When We Walk with the Lord
John H. Sammis (1887)

When we walk with the Lord
   in the light of his Word,
   what a glory he sheds on our way!
While we do his good will,
   he abides with us still,
   and with all who will trust and obey.

> Trust and obey, for there's no other way
> to be happy in Jesus, but to trust and obey.

Then in fellowship sweet
   we will sit at his feet,
   or we'll walk by his side in the way;
what he says we will do,
   where he sends we will go;
   never fear, only trust and obey.

2 CHRONICLES / **REVIEW**

Some key verses from 2 Chronicles:
1. **2 Chronicles 7:14-15**
   "If My people who are called by My name will humble themselves, and pray and seek My face, and turn from their wicked ways, then I will hear from heaven, and will forgive their sin and heal their land. Now My eyes will be open and My ears attentive to prayer *made* in this place."
2. **2 Chronicles 15:2**
   And [Azariah] went out to meet Asa, and said to him: "Hear me, Asa, and all Judah and Benjamin. The Lord *is* with you while you are with Him. If you seek Him, He will be found by you; but if you forsake Him, He will forsake you."

2 CHRONICLES / **REFLECT**

1. **Seeking God:** The reformer kings of Judah were considered great because they set their hearts to seek the Lord God. The Lord looked kindly on them and blessed them as they turned from idols to God and then desired to turn the people back to God. They pulled down idols from their own hearts and then from the hearts of the people. Reformation is not only a spiritual awakening but propels us into *action*. What are your heart idols—fame, money, power, beauty, pride? May God's enabling grace help us to pull down our idols as we embrace godly desires and habits. Make a list of your heart idols. Ask God to help you identify them and ask God to help you turn from them. Reflect on Paul's assertion that new godly desires can replace our heart idols (Romans 12:1-2).

2. **Repentance:** One of the greatest stories of God's amazing grace in the Old Testament is the life of Manasseh. Even though Manasseh had a godly father in Hezekiah, he rebelled and wilfully turned away from the Lord God to idols—an abomination to God. Dr. Crossley points out that Manasseh built altars to the Baals and worshipped the Assyrian gods. With extreme audacity, he even went so far as to construct Assyrian idols inside the temple of God! Not only did Manasseh dishonour the Lord and defile God's temple, he even sacrificed some of his own sons to Molech! His ungodly example to Judah brought destructive and devastating results that reverberated throughout the land. However, God, rich in mercy, afflicted Manasseh—not to destroy, but to restore. This personal affliction drove Manasseh to his knees as he finally turned and cried out to the Lord God (2 Chronicles 33:12-13). He truly repented—he was transformed! His repentance is evident when he pulled down idols throughout the land, repaired God's altar and commanded Judah to serve the Lord God. Amazing grace! When we fall, when we backslide, it is not "game over." Rather, like the prodigal son parable or perhaps a better title "the gracious father," our heavenly Father is ever ready to receive, forgive and restore us—regardless of the depth of our sin! God is amazing in his grace. Make a list of God's grace in *your* life and turn that to praise!

3. **Genealogies:** Dr. Crossley writes: "Maintaining records of the line of descent was very important in the purposes of God in preparation for the coming of the Messiah." We read many genealogies from Genesis through to 2 Chronicles, and these records continue into the New Testament. We

should note, however, scriptural genealogies end in Matthew 1 and Luke 4—with the birth of Jesus, who is the Christ, "the Coming One" (Matthew 11:3). Dr. Crossley writes about the "book of life" spoken of in Daniel 12, Malachi 3, Philippians 4 and in many passages in Revelation. Why do the genealogies end with Christ? What relation do the genealogies have to Genesis 3:15? Does the "book of life" represent the true way for humankind to be reconciled to God and welcomed into the kingdom (Romans 5; 1 Corinthians 15)?

2 CHRONICLES / **REJOICE**

Amazing Grace
John Newton (1772)

Amazing grace! How sweet the sound
    That saved a wretch like me!
I once was lost, but now am found;
    Was blind, but now I see.

Through many dangers, toils and snares,
    I have already come;
'Tis grace hath brought me safe thus far,
    And grace will lead me home.

The Lord has promised good to me,
    His Word my hope secures;
He will my Shield and Portion be,
    As long as life endures.

EZRA / **REVIEW**

Some key verses from Ezra:
1. **Ezra 1:1-3**
   Now in the first year of Cyrus king of Persia, that the word of the Lord by the mouth of Jeremiah might be fulfilled, the Lord stirred up the spirit of Cyrus king of Persia, so that he made a proclamation throughout all his kingdom, and also *put it* in writing, saying,

> Thus says Cyrus king of Persia:
>> All the kingdoms of the earth the LORD God of heaven has given me. And He has commanded me to build Him a house at Jerusalem which *is* in Judah. Who *is* among you of all His people? May his God be with him, and let him go up to Jerusalem which *is* in Judah, and build the house of the LORD God of Israel (He is God), which *is* in Jerusalem.

2. Ezra 7:10
> For Ezra had prepared his heart to seek the Law of the LORD, and to do *it*, and to teach statutes and ordinances in Israel.

3. Ezra 10:2
> And Shechaniah the son of Jehiel, *one* of the sons of Elam, spoke up and said to Ezra, "We have trespassed against our God, and have taken pagan wives from the peoples of the land; yet now there is hope in Israel in spite of this."

EZRA / **REFLECT**

1. **Right priorities:** Dr. Crossley reflects on God's priorities for his people. God moved in the heart of Cyrus, the Persian king, to send Zerubbabel and God's people back to Jerusalem. The priority? To rebuild the sacred temple which had been destroyed by Nebuchadnezzar in 586 B.C. God's priority for worship remains the same for us today: we are to worship God with all our heart, in the beauty of holiness (Psalm 96:9). May the altar of our hearts burn with the sacred flame of devotion! Is that your priority in life? Make a list of your activities today and see how each can be used to worship our glorious God. Worship is God's priority—is it yours?

2. **True repentance:** Dr. Crossley cites true repentance as necessary to restore broken fellowship with God. In the second wave of restoration led by Ezra, he returned to Jerusalem and observed Israel had embraced mixed marriages with unbelieving women. This sin of disobedience led the Israelites to turn away from God and fall into a backslidden state. Ezra responded by tearing his clothes and crying out to the Lord (Ezra 9:3-6). God sees and hears. He graciously revived and restored his people, leading them into true, heartfelt repentance and dramatic change in their lifestyle. Are there pockets of sin in your life that need confession and repentance? Make a list, confess these sins to God, know that he forgives, and seek God's enabling grace to change your attitudes and, where necessary, even your lifestyle (1 John 1:9).

3. Separation: Dr. Crossley notes, "There is a thread of separation in the book of Ezra: firstly, separation from Babylon (1:1-3); secondly, separation from worldly help in building the house of God (4:1-3); thirdly, separation from dependence upon human protection (8:21-23); and fourthly, separation from sinful partnerships (10:11-12)." He concludes with this statement, "A clear distinction is to be made between those who worship the true God and those who do not. It is inappropriate for non-Christians to be confused with genuine members of the church of Jesus Christ or to work on behalf of the church."

Until Christ comes again to call his church unto himself, Christians continue to live *in* the world and are called to be a witness *to* the world. How do you balance these two imperatives? Is it founded on identification with Christ, with professed salvation, with the work of the church, in contrast to activities undertaken with the intent of representing Christ and his bride in the world? For example, is it appropriate to engage professional, non-Christian musicians in mixed events, but not in the church's worship?

EZRA / **REJOICE**

To God be the Glory
Fanny Crosby (1875)

To God be the glory, great things he hath done,
    So loved he the world that he gave us his Son,
Who yielded his life an atonement for sin,
    And opened the life-gate that we may go in.

    Praise the Lord, praise the Lord,
        Let the earth hear his voice!
    Praise the Lord, praise the Lord,
        Let the people rejoice!
    O, come to the Father, through Jesus the Son,
        And give him the glory, great things he hath done!

O, perfect redemption, the purchase of blood!
    To ev'ry believer the promise of God;
The vilest offender who truly believes,
    That moment from Jesus a pardon receives.

NEHEMIAH / **REVIEW**

Some key verses from Nehemiah:
1. **Nehemiah 1:1-4**
   The words of Nehemiah the son of Hachaliah.
   It came to pass in the month of Chislev, *in* the twentieth year, as I was in Shushan the citadel, that Hanani one of my brethren came with men from Judah; and I asked them concerning the Jews who had escaped, who had survived the captivity, and concerning Jerusalem. And they said to me, "The survivors who are left from the captivity in the province *are* there in great distress and reproach. The wall of Jerusalem *is* also broken down, and its gates are burned with fire."
   So it was, when I heard these words, that I sat down and wept, and mourned *for many* days; I was fasting and praying before the God of heaven.
2. **Nehemiah 2:7-8**
   Furthermore I said to the king, "If it pleases the king, let letters be given to me for the governors *of the region* beyond the River, that they must permit me to pass through till I come to Judah, and a letter to Asaph the keeper of the king's forest, that he must give me timber to make beams for the gates of the citadel which *pertains* to the temple, for the city wall, and for the house that I will occupy." And the king granted *them* to me according to the good hand of my God upon me.
3. **Nehemiah 4:7-9**
   Now it happened, when Sanballat, Tobiah, the Arabs, the Ammonites, and the Ashdodites heard that the walls of Jerusalem were being restored and the gaps were beginning to be closed, that they became very angry, and all of them conspired together to come *and* attack Jerusalem and create confusion. Nevertheless we made our prayer to our God, and because of them we set a watch against them day and night.

NEHEMIAH / **REFLECT**

1. **Personal sacrifice:** As Dr. Crossley notes, Nehemiah sacrificed much to make himself available to God for the work to which he called him. As the king's cupbearer, he held a position of great responsibility, even acting "in an advisory capacity to the king." He was held in such esteem that the king appointed him governor of Judah. Dr. Crossley concludes, "Nehemiah

is a fine example of a man who puts God first, whose career is subservient to the needs of the kingdom of God, who willingly leaves everything when the Lord requires it." Have you, or has a mentor or example to you, surrendered worldly riches, worldly enterprises, worldly ambitions and dreams, in order to serve the Lord? Is there anything in your life that you would *not* be willing to surrender to serve the King of kings?
2. **Fasting and prayer:** Dr. Crossley points all believers to two examples found in Nehemiah's prayer life. First, "Nehemiah shows where a believer begins a significant work for God—in fasting and persistent prayer (Nehemiah 1:4; cf. Acts 13:3; 14:23)," and second, Nehemiah addresses God "reminding him of his covenant, his character and his promises (Nehemiah 1:5,8-10)." Much of the prayer of believers in the West seems to be shopping lists of supplication—seeking to bend God's will to our own. How does that contrast with the prayers of Nehemiah? How would you describe *your* prayer life? Are you really submitting yourself to God, seeking his will, asking that he would show you how and where you should use your time and energy to bring honour and glory to him?
3. **Strategy for the church:** Nehemiah was equipped and called by God for a crucial leadership role in bringing God's people back to Jerusalem, to re-establish worship, and to fortify and strengthen the people for defence. This role required visionary leadership, an ability to inspire the people to work and an ability to "utilize and arrange the skills and expertise of a whole variety of people (3:1-32)." Dr. Crossley writes, "The task of church leaders...includes instructing, organizing, facilitating and inspiring members of the local church, so that the work of God is strengthened and developed." Have you seen gifted leaders engaged in "the equipping of the saints for the work of ministry, for the edifying of the body of Christ" (Ephesians 4:12)? What are *your* spiritual gifts? How do you, or how would you, function as a church leader, particularly where there may be gaps in your own giftedness?

NEHEMIAH / **REJOICE**

To the Work!
Fanny Crosby (1869)

To the work! To the work! Let the hungry be fed;
    To the fountain of life let the weary be led;

In the cross and its banner our glory shall be,
  While we herald the tidings, "Salvation is free!"

Toiling on, toiling on,
  Toiling on, toiling on;
Let us hope, let us watch,
  And labour till the Master comes.

To the work! To the work! There is labour for all;
  For the kingdom of darkness and error shall fall;
And the love of our Father exalted shall be,
  In the loud swelling chorus, "Salvation is free!"

To the work! To the work! In the strength of the Lord,
  And a robe and a crown shall our labour reward,
When the home of the faithful our dwelling shall be,
  And we shout with the ransomed, "Salvation is free!"

ESTHER / REVIEW

Some key verses from Esther:
1. **Esther 2:16-17**
   So Esther was taken to King Ahasuerus, into his royal palace, in the tenth month, which *is* the month of Tebeth, in the seventh year of his reign. The king loved Esther more than all the *other* women, and she obtained grace and favor in his sight more than all the virgins; so he set the royal crown upon her head and made her queen instead of Vashti.
2. **Esther 4:14**
   "For if you remain completely silent at this time, relief and deliverance will arise for the Jews from another place, but you and your father's house will perish. Yet who knows whether you have come to the kingdom for *such* a time as this?"
3. **Esther 8:4-5**
   And the king held out the golden scepter toward Esther. So Esther arose and stood before the king, and said, "If it pleases the king, and if I have found favor in his sight and the thing *seems* right to the king and I am pleasing in his eyes, let it be written to revoke the letters devised by Haman,

the son of Hammedatha the Agagite, which he wrote to annihilate the Jews who *are* in all the king's provinces.

ESTHER / **REFLECT**

1. **Inner beauty:** Dr. Crossley rightly points out that although Esther was a woman of exceptional beauty, charm is deceitful, and beauty is passing. True beauty is not primarily outward, but inward. True beauty is in a godly character and conduct—a gentle spirit, a loving, kind, tender and forgiving heart (Ephesians 4:32). Ask God to reveal character and conduct flaws within you. Write them down and then pray for God's enabling grace to help you have victory over them, so you may exhibit godly character and kingdom conduct (Matthew 5:1-12).
2. **Submission to the state:** As Dr. Crossley writes, "Mordecai and Esther provide an example of how the godly function under an ungodly government." He quotes William Still, who writes, "God commands 'every God-fearing, believing Christian person to respect the properly constituted government of any nation in which he dwells,'" while at the same time, "When a conflict occurs between obeying God and obeying the state... obedience to the Lord always takes priority."[7] Dr. Crossley also writes, "There is nothing inappropriate about a godly person being elevated to a position of responsibility and trust by an ungodly government or by a pagan king," pointing to the examples of Joseph, Obadiah, Daniel and Nehemiah, as godly men who did not compromise their faithfulness to God. List the many benefits of having strong, mature Christian men and women serving in trusted roles in society, positions such as teachers, professors, police, military and elected officials.
3. **God-given opportunities:** The book of Esther focuses on God's divine providence. Esther's appearance was purposed by God and her strategic placement within the palace was by the sovereign hand of God. Esther was an instrument in God's purpose and plan to deliver God's people from God's enemies (Esther 4:14). As Mordecai said to Esther, "Who knows whether you have come to the kingdom for such a time as this?" (Esther 4:14). Dr. Crossley challenges us: "There may be times when, like Esther, we must be ready to take our life in our hands and risk everything for the cause of God." Have there already been such moments in your own life?

---

[7] Still, *Eight Sermons on the Book of Esther*, 22.

Are you willing now to step out in faith, to surrender all, and to risk your life for the glory of God and the advance of his kingdom?

4. **Sovereign protection:** God is in absolute control over all circumstances and every situation in your life. There is no earthly atom nor cosmic power outside of God's control. Divine providence is the outworking of God's loving, sovereign decrees. Nothing—absolutely nothing—is left to chance. Everything in your life is working for your ultimate good (Romans 8:28). Even your current or future trials are God-ordained opportunities for your Christian growth (James 1:2-4). How does the knowledge of God's sovereignty give you strength and confidence to face the challenges of everyday life, as well as the rare but significant moments when tremendous courage and faith are required?

ESTHER / **REJOICE**

A Sovereign Protector I have
Augustus Toplady (1774)

A sovereign Protector I have,
    Unseen, yet forever at hand,
Unchangeably faithful to save,
    Almighty to rule and command.

He smiles, and my comforts abound;
    His grace as the dew shall descend;
And walls of salvation surround
    The soul He delights to defend.

Kind Author and Ground of my hope,
    Thee, Thee, for my God I avow;
My glad Ebenezer set up,
    And own Thou hast helped me till now.

Application index

all things work together for good, 237
backsliding and apostasy, 333-335
called to service, 338
clouded judgement, 301-302
discipline, 303-304
exposure of sin, 303

faith and obedience, 92
fasting and prayer, 438
father's responsibility, a, 261-262
fleeing persecution, 336-337
friendship, 263-264

genealogies, 408-409
gifts for the work of God, 142-143
God pursues and restores his backslidden people, 216-217

God-given opportunities, 456
God-honouring prayer, 330-332
God's power and provision, 335-336
God's work in God's way, 299-300
grace and gifts, 265-266
grumbling, 143-144

holiness, 121
human plans and divine purposes, 299
inner beauty, 454-455
instructing the young, 167
justification by faith, 67-68

law, 92-96
leadership skills, 385
love for God's people, 238
marriage to the ungodly, 332-333

ministry support, 194–195
models of faith, 192–193
monogamy, 301
Moses and Christ, 166–167

obedience, 168–169, 264, 382
only by grace, 66
orderly worship, 385–386
personal sacrifice, 438
prayer and intercession, 68, 259–261, 382–383
prepared for service, 142
pressing forward, 145–146
providence, 237, 265
pure worship, 366–367

redemption, 91
religious superstition, 266–267
relying on the promises of God, 302
remembering, 167–168
repentance, 407–408
revelation of God, 192
right priorities, 425
rulers and nations, 367–368

seeking God, 406–407
separation, 122, 193–194, 425–426
service, 384
signs of backsliding, 238–240
sovereign free choice, 66
sovereign protection, 456–457
strategy for the church, 438–439
strength and weakness, 220–221
submission to the state, 455–456

true conversion, 237–238
true repentance, 425
unbelief, 144–145
vows to the Lord, 217–220

wandering from God, 216
weakness of the law, 221
wicked youths, 366
women in the Bible, 240–241
worship, 121–122

General index

Aaron, 75, 76, 78, 81, 82, 87-88, 105, 110, 118, 129, 132, 133-135, 137, 210, 221,300, 404, 470-472
Abel, 46, 58, 62, 81
Abraham,
　call, 50-51
　covenant, 50-51, 53, 61, 75, 76, 80, 128, 176, 186, 205, 294, 295, 375, 415, 446
　Hagar, 27, 50, 55, 187, 467
　Sarah, 27, 50-52, 60, 67, 467

Adam and Eve, 24, 26, 27, 31, 33, 45-46, 47, 51, 56, 59, 60, 61, 63, 66, 138, 163, 248, 292, 374, 375, 401
adultery, 12, 105, 272, 280, 296, 303, 333, 430

apostles (disciples), 3-4, 6, 12, 16-22, 43, 162, 166, 263, 338, 455
ark of the covenant, ark of the Testimony, 82, 83, 86, 87, 90, 109, 151, 158, 179, 180, 250-251, 266-267, 278-280, 293, 299, 300, 312, 313, 377, 382, 489, 491, 501
atonement, 82, 87, 95, 103-112, 116-118, 121, 471

backsliding, 197, 201, 216-217, 238-240, 267, 316, 333-335, 484-485, 495

Cain, 27, 46, 58, 62, 499

Christ (Messiah),
  authority, 16, 53, 55, 379
  co-Creator, 54
  glory, 38, 404
  holiness, 86, 90, 105, 112, 326, 380
  incarnation, 25, 27, 38, 55, 61, 64, 79, 86, 91, 95
  King, 38, 208, 231, 249, 257–258, 296–297, 326–329, 378–381, 404
  Lamb of God, 5, 38, 63, 64, 90, 103, 111, 114, 468
  miracles, 2, 4, 19–20, 160, 402
  person, 2, 29, 38
  preparation and coming, 7, 34–35, 37, 65, 92, 153, 159, 160–161, 249, 256, 336, 364, 376, 377, 401, 408, 414, 423, 430, 466, 496, 504
  Priest, 38, 57–58, 87–90, 113–115, 404
  promised Seed, 4, 24, 26, 38, 46, 48, 50, 59–60, 401, 466, 491, 500
  prophecies, 2, 48
  Prophet, 38, 159–161, 247, 249, 255–256, 404
  resurrection, 3–4, 115
  second coming, 24–26, 361–362
  sonship, 2, 37, 401, 404
  suffering, 38, 111–112, 162, 164
  teaching, 21, 160

Christ and his church, 23–26
  in 1 Chronicles, 378–380
  in 2 Chronicles, 400–405
  in Deuteronomy, 159–164
  in Esther, 451–452
  in Exodus, 84–90
  in Ezra, 422–423
  in Genesis, 54–64
  in Joshua, 187–190
  in Judges, 214–215
  in 1 Kings, 326–329
  in 2 Kings, 361–364
  in Leviticus, 110–119
  in Nehemiah, 436
  in Numbers, 136–141
  in Ruth, 231–235
  in 1 Samuel, 255–258
  in 2 Samuel, 288–297

Christophanies, see theophanies
circumcision, 93–96, 101, 180
covenant,
  covenant with Abraham, 50–51, 53, 61, 75, 76, 80, 128, 176, 186, 205, 294, 295, 375, 415, 446
  covenant with Adam, 51, 375
  covenant with David, 276–277, 294, 295, 318, 322, 348, 349, 354, 372, 374, 375, 376–377, 390, 392, 395, 399, 401, 402, 446
  covenant with Moses, 80, 102, 150, 154, 156–157, 164, 168, 180, 186, 193, 205, 212, 221, 247, 264, 308, 365, 405
  covenant with Noah, 48
  New Covenant, 12, 34, 152, 187, 333, 385–386
  Old Covenant, 68, 80, 87, 92–93, 95–96, 111, 113, 121, 247, 333, 404, 405

creation, 12, 14, 24, 33, 36, 42, 44–45, 47–49, 56, 108, 117, 301, 374, 381, 414, 492

divorce, 43, 156, 301, 430

election, see also sovereignty, 66, 91, 100, 155, 466
Esau, 52, 59, 66, 332, 337

Fall, the, 26, 27, 44–47, 49, 55, 59, 67, 292
flood (time of Noah), 29, 44, 46–48, 49, 57, 414
friendship, 61, 72, 206, 263–264, 488

Garden of Eden, 31, 45–47, 138, 163

God,
  authority, 54, 101, 455
  Creator, 54-55, 80
  Father, 2, 16, 37, 54, 112, 150, 161, 164, 286, 288, 293, 332, 364, 380, 469, 495, 499, 504
  holiness, 80, 105-107, 119, 121, 471
  love, 54, 66-67, 81, 89, 169, 217, 231, 234, 236, 304, 334, 466, 476-477, 485
  plurality of his being/Trinity, 2, 54, 163, 286, 379-380
  unique, 150
  wrath, 13, 77, 111, 114, 130, 163, 177, 280, 291, 292, 304, 471, 499

grace, 42, 46, 51, 55, 65, 66-68, 73, 80, 86, 93-96, 111, 118, 168-169, 189, 192, 217, 220, 231, 234, 237, 265-266, 466-467, 469, 476-477, 489, 504, 506, 511

Hagar, 27, 50, 55, 187, 467
holiness, 80, 86, 90, 100, 102, 105-108, 119, 121, 122, 216, 326, 380, 471
Holy of Holies, 82, 87, 106, 109, 114, 118, 278, 396
Holy Spirit,
  coming/sending, 32, 34, 93, 95, 116
  gifts, 266, 384, 489
  help to God's people, 12, 16-22, 25, 34, 43-44, 204, 207, 261, 285, 346, 425, 483, 489, 499
  inspiration of the Scriptures, 9-22, 151, 204
  role to exalt Christ, 17, 22, 122

human nature, see sinful nature

idolatry, 104, 110, 126, 136, 154, 155, 186, 201, 207, 211, 212, 215, 221, 320, 333, 351-352, 353, 358, 374, 397, 415, 435, 482
image of God, 45, 465
Isaac, 27, 36, 44, 49, 51-55, 58, 59, 61, 63, 66, 68, 72, 76, 94, 128, 402, 414, 423, 467
Ishmael, 52, 58, 59, 66, 467

John the Baptist, 2, 160, 361-362, 364, 402, 403, 437
justification by faith, 67-68, 92, 95, 297, 467

law, 1, 3, 8, 14, 22, 34, 42, 73, 78-81, 86-87, 90, 92-96, 101, 103-110, 116, 119, 135-139, 150-169, 187-189, 192, 213, 219, 221, 225, 228, 230-231, 233, 238, 240, 247, 251, 254, 278, 300, 308, 317, 318, 320, 323-325, 332, 346, 349, 353, 358, 362-365, 373, 393, 394, 396, 398-399, 405, 406, 416, 420-423, 430, 432, 445, 448, 450, 469, 475-476, 478, 482-483, 494
leadership, 76, 121-122, 175, 178, 200-201, 205, 221, 240, 250-251, 255, 261-262, 345, 385, 391, 402, 415, 419, 420, 426, 431, 436, 439, 446, 487-488, 493, 502, 509

marriage, 14, 24, 29-30, 43, 42, 108, 156, 194, 200, 225-226, 228-229, 233, 235, 275-276, 301, 312, 332-333, 366, 394, 422, 435, 448, 492, 495
monogamy, 301, 492
Moses,
  authorship of Pentateuch, 3, 42-44, 72, 93, 100-101, 126, 150-152, 363
  birth and adoption, 74
  call, 75
  Exodus from Egypt, 77-78
  family, 75, 78
  giving of the law at Sinai, 79-81, 102-110, 153-159
  miracles, 75, 78
  ten plagues in Egypt, 76-77
  wilderness years, 133-136

Noah,
  ark, 46, 47, 57
  faith, 46
  family, 46, 48, 66
  flood, 29, 44, 46-48, 49, 57, 414

obedience, 30, 51, 64, 67, 77, 80, 92, 95, 103, 107, 110, 135, 138, 150, 154, 157, 167, 168-169, 180, 190, 193, 200, 205, 210, 211, 217, 219, 225, 241, 252, 264, 266, 318, 325, 373, 375, 382, 394, 422, 433, 436, 455, 457, 468-469, 476-477, 481, 484, 488, 489, 501, 511

Pentecost, 6, 19, 21, 32, 57, 60, 109, 110, 115, 116-117
Pentateuch, 42, 100, 101, 127, 144, 150, 151, 152, 159, 174, 219, 394
prayer, 6, 13, 22, 53, 68, 78, 82, 92, 122, 133, 165, 179, 182, 234, 243, 250-251, 253, 256-261, 272, 330-332, 356, 367, 377, 382-383, 391, 395, 405, 406-407, 421, 424, 427, 432-434, 436, 438, 445, 467, 469, 474, 481, 487, 495, 501, 509
prophecy/prophecies, 2, 3-5, 8, 23, 25-26, 32-37, 48, 58-64, 87, 139-141, 156, 159-164, 174, 187, 247, 257, 266, 293-297, 318, 320, 334, 348, 351, 354, 360, 361-364, 373, 375, 378-380, 393, 400-405, 413, 414, 417, 422-423, 426, 436, 446, 451-452, 469

  redemption, 37, 86, 90, 91, 100, 119, 168, 184, 228, 230, 235-236, 404, 468, 476

Sabbath, 56, 82, 101, 108, 109, 117, 430
Sarah, wife of Abraham, 27, 50-52, 60, 67, 467
Satan, the Evil One, the devil, 4, 31, 35, 45-46, 56-57, 60, 138, 151, 188, 290, 327, 400-401, 451-452

Scriptures,
  arrangement, 8
  authority, 10, 13, 14, 21, 37, 101
  authorship, 11-13, 15, 42-43, 65, 72, 100-101, 174-175, 201, 444-446
  division/types, 8, 12
  help of the Holy Spirit, 16-19, 65
  inerrant, 11, 13
  infallible, 10-13, 16, 44, 101
  inspiration, 7, 9-22, 65
  personality, 12
  private reading, 6
  reliability, 22, 43
  revelation of Christ, 37, 43-44
  revelation of God's will, 10, 79, 126, 192
  translation, 22, 42

Septuagint, 42, 126, 150, 246
service, 142, 265-266, 338, 384, 436
Seth, 46, 47
Shekinah glory, 27
Shem, 47, 48, 49, 59, 66
sinful nature, 45-46, 56, 65, 80, 90, 111, 221, 291, 364
sovereignty, 10, 42, 64, 66, 91, 128, 155, 157, 369, 407, 457, 512

tabernacle, 29, 79, 81-91, 102, 105, 106, 108, 110, 111, 115, 127-129, 133, 136-137, 176, 210, 219, 256, 259, 267, 278, 287, 293, 312, 363, 372, 384, 402, 403, 489, 501
tempt, temptation, 14, 93, 154, 200, 208, 272, 495
Ten Commandments, 14, 80, 82, 95, 154, 176, 212
Terah, 49, 50, 59, 186
theocracy, 80, 102, 127, 155, 208, 260
theophanies, 26-27, 34, 55, 180, 187, 205, 208-209, 211, 214, 361, 398
tithes, 104, 143, 156, 194, 430, 479
Torah (law), 8, 42
Tower of Babel, 36, 44, 48-49, 57

General index 519

types,
  definition, 28-32
  Ahithophel, 292
  ark, 47
  bondage in Egypt, 84
  Canaan, 188-190
  desert journey, 128
  Elijah, 361-362
  Esther, 452
  Feast of Pentecost, 116
  flood, 29, 57
  Ishmael and Isaac, 58
  John the Baptist, 361-362
  pillar of cloud and fire, 130
  Queen of Sheba, 328
  Ruth, 231-233
  Sabbath (rest), 56, 108
  song of Moses, 85
  tabernacle, 29
  types of Christ,
    Aaron, 87
    Adam, 56
    altar of sacrifice, 86
    ark, 86
    Boaz, 184, 192-193, 231, 233-235
    cities of refuge, 139
    David, 28, 257-258, 288-291, 297-298, 326-327
    Elijah, 362-363
    Elisha, 362-363
    firstfruits, 117
    high priest's garments, 88
    Isaac, 63, 402
    Israel at the Exodus,
    Jacob's dream of a ladder, 30, 53, 57
    Joseph, 31-32, 58-59
    Joshua, 152, 187-189
    king, 257-258, 380, 404
    Lion of Judah, 64, 277
    manna, 30, 85
    mercy seat, 86-87
    Melchizedek, 29, 57, 404
    Moses, 166-167
    Noah's ark, 57
    Passover lamb, 30, 38, 84, 90, 114
    pillar of cloud and fire, 85
    priest, priesthood, 57-58, 87-90, 113-115, 255, 404
    prophet, 159-161, 255-256, 404
    rest, 188-189
    sacrificial system, 30
    Samuel, 246-247
    serpent in the wilderness, 30, 138
    scarlet cord, 188
    Solomon, 327-329
    son of David, 378-380
    tabernacle, 86-87, 403
    temple, 30, 403-405
    temptations of Eve, 56-57
    water from the rock, 30, 85, 137
    water of purification, 139
  types of Christ and the church,
    Adam and Eve, 56
    Boaz and Ruth,
    crossing the Jordan, 188
    David and Mephibosheth, 288-293
    festivals, 115-119
    marriage, 29
    sacrifices, 111-113
  types of the church,
    David, 381
    entry into Canaan, 188-189
    mixed multitude, 85
    priesthood, 115
    warfare, 190
  waters of Marah and Elim, 85

worship, 6, 62, 76, 81-82, 100, 102-110, 121-122, 127-130, 142, 154-155, 175, 205, 210-211, 216, 240, 278-279, 310-311, 314, 320-324, 330-331, 346-357, 365, 366-367, 376, 378, 381, 385-386, 390-392, 395-398, 406-407, 418, 420, 426, 434-435, 449, 471, 481, 487, 489, 490, 495, 499, 502, 506, 507, 509

www.ingramcontent.com/pod-product-compliance
Lightning Source LLC
Chambersburg PA
CBHW070255240426
43661CB00057B/2562